**DOROTHY KILGALLEN—ACE REPORTER—
HER "HOME" WAS THE STORK CLUB.**

Her beat was New York's glamorous Café Society. Her weekly appearances on *What's My Line?* made her a star.

She hobnobbed with Ernest Hemingway and Judy Garland . . . feuded with Frank Sinatra . . . covered the Lindbergh kidnap trial, the Sam Sheppard murder case, the Grace Kelly wedding . . . and the biggest story of them all —the JFK assassination.

From her public success to her private torments, from her unhappy marriage to her flagrant, torrid affair with a leading pop singer and her liaison with the mysterious Out-of-Towner who may have been the last to see her alive, from her bouts with pills and alcohol to her controversial death in 1965, this intimate, no-holds-barred biography tells it all.

"A PAGE-TURNER IN EVERY SENSE OF THE WORD . . . AS READABLE AND DRAMATIC AS A BEST-SELLING NOVEL."
—*Book-of-the-Month Club Magazine*

"READABLE AND ENJOYABLE . . . COMPETENT AND SENSITIVE . . . LEE ISRAEL HAS PEGGED KILGALLEN RIGHT."
—*The Washington Star*

Lee Israel

KILGALLEN

A DELL BOOK

Published by
Dell Publishing Co., Inc.
1 Dag Hammarskjold Plaza
New York, New York 10017

ISBN: 0-440-14565-1

Reprinted by arrangement with Delacorte Press
Printed in the United States of America
First Dell printing—August 1980

**FOR ARTHUR FIELDS—
EDITOR AND FRIEND**

ACKNOWLEDGMENTS

I am especially grateful to those "collaborators" who signed on for a longer season than we reckoned. Who among them were Dorothy's friends, told me more than they ever said: Bob Bach, Jean Bach, Edgar W. Hatfield, Dr. Donald Hoffman, Kerry Kollmar, Mark Lane, George O'Toole, Johnnie Ray, Elaine Shepard, Liz Smith, and Marlin Swing.

The book was enriched considerably by: Sydney Boehm, H. Huber Boscowitz, Lillian Boscowitz, Mary Brannum Bringle, Harold Carthage, Sylvia Carthage, Harvey Daniels, Emmett Davis, John A. Doyle, Bill Franklin, Martin Garbus, James W. Gardiner, Mark Goodson, Dorothy Gulman, Anne Hamilton, Candy Jones, Irene Corbally Kuhn, George Kuittinen, Billy Livingston, Mary Anita Loos, James McAleer, M. D. Morris, Michael Sean O'Shea, John Parsons, Howard Perry Rothberg III, Gloria Safier, Richard Smith, Herb Spiro, Allen Stokes, Jean Stralem, Joe Tonahill, Kevin Walsh, Midge Willer White, Miles White, Roosevelt Zanders.

And I am grateful to: Bella Abzug, Charles Allen, George Allen, Dr. Michael Baden, Ben Bagley, Patrick Blue Baker, Pearl Bauer, Timothy Bay, Melvin Belli, Paul Benson, Sister Berenice-Rice, Homer Bigart, Earl Blackwell, Mal Braveman, Carol Bruce, Mae Brussell, Thelma Carpenter, Maurice Carroll, Igor Cassini, Evelyn Clement, James Clement, Harriet Conarroe, Millie Considine, Rosemary Cox, Sister Margaret Crowley, Richard Currier, John Daly, Alvin Davis, Sam Day, Anita Diamant Berke, Tony DeFillipps, Dorothy Ducas, Nina Dusenberry, Shirley Eder, George Eells, Catherine T. Engel, Lee Evans, Jack Faragasso, Morton Farber, Gil Fates, Mary Ferrell, Ed Fitzgerald, Pegeen Fitzgerald, Arlene Francis, S. Fuss, Paul Gallico, Eleanor M. Gehres, Michael Gehringer, Carmen Gebbia, Lora Goldman, Will Goldman, Jesse Gourdet, Sheilah Graham, Ruth Greenfield, Nick Gurwitz, Hope

Hampton, William O. Harbach, Larry Hart, Barbara Hayden, William Hellerstein, Beatrice Helpern, Skitch Henderson, Richard Hill, Eric Hirschhorn, The Reverend John Hinkamp, Joy Hodges, James Horan, Betty Lee Hunt, Eddie Jaffe, Penn Jones, Jane Kean, John J. Kilgallen, S.J., Stewart Klonis, June Knight, Albin Krebs, Nick Lapole, Dan Lavezzo, Phil Leff, Betty Griswold Leggett, Jim Lehrer, Ernest H. Linford, Marien Lo Preto, Jack Lotto, Dr. James Luke, Harriet Lyons, Bill McCormick, Marlene C. McGuirl, Bernard Malamud, Irving Mansfield, Charlotte Manson, Sylvia Meagher, David Miller, Jimmy Mitchell, Richard Montague, Carrie Munn, Maggi McNellis Newhouse, Lee Nordness, Mildred Noxon, Jack O'Brian, Tom O'Toole, Harriet Oxman, Seymour Peck, Jim Piazza, Jack Harrison Pollack, Frances Preston, H.D. (Doc) Quigg, Tony Randall, Francesco C. Ribando, Sr., Victor Riesel, Grace Robinson, Marie Rossi, Martha Rountree, Al Rylander, Adelaide Santonastaso, Dr. Leah Schaefer, Frances Shemanski, Gertrude Schimmel, Ralph Schlegle, Eunice Lederman Schwartz, Norman Schwartz, Ed Seay, Edith Selig, Jim Shanahan, Shirley Ann Sheets, Linda Shepard, J. Stephen Sheppard, Bobby Short, P. T. Sinko, Louis Sobol, Anna Sosenko, Irwin M. Taylor, Jack Tirman, Mary Anne Travers, Sandra Turner, Paul D. White, Theo Wilson, Irving Zussman.

And to the peerless staff of the Billy Rose Theatre Collection at Lincoln Center—Paul Myers and Monty Arnold, David Bartholomew, Roderick L. Bladel, Gilbert Bledsoe, Donald W. Fowle, Maxwell Silverman, Dorothy L. Swerdlove, Donald Madison, and Daniel Patri—who endured Dorothy's shedding Leviathan scrapbook for too long—thank you.

Finally, for their dedication, diligence, and taste—my editors: Ruth Pollack and Linda Grey.

CONTENTS

KILGALLEN

There will be no sweet smells of childhood here. The little girl, to a great extent, will have to be deduced from her adult fantasies and actions. Since that little girl lived for a very long time in the late-blooming woman—indeed, may have first emerged then—the loss is unfortunate but not devastating.

The Kilgallens—Dorothy, her parents, her sister, and two of her three children—were always extraordinarily chary of public disclosure about family affairs. The columnist's messy and still unsolved barbiturate death in 1965 turned their vigilance into virtual obsession. Dorothy's father, Jim Kilgallen, does not discuss his daughter even with friends of long standing. He is ninety years old at the time of this writing. He has been married to Mae Kilgallen for sixty-six of those years and to the Hearst Organization for fifty-seven. In the more recent tributes to Jim, Dorothy's name has not even been mentioned.

When I first undertook *Kilgallen* in 1975, I wrote to members of her family requesting interviews. The first rejection came from her only sister, Eleanor, who is a vice-president of the Music Corporation of America.

Eleanor Kilgallen contended in her reply that her sister was treated unkindly during her life and after her death by her colleagues in journalism and that she has therefore "made it a policy never to discuss my sister in regard to any publication." [1]

A second letter was dispatched to Jim Kilgallen at his residential address on New York's Park Avenue. The response came again from Eleanor, at the behest of her mother, Mae, in behalf of Jim, who was recovering from a "serious illness." Mae Kilgallen, it was reported, felt that

it would be unwise to put her husband "through the emotional ordeal" of discussing Dorothy's life.[2]

Presently, back at his desk in the offices of Hearst Newspapers, Jim Kilgallen spoke tersely for himself.

> I have had a firm policy ever since my daughter passed
> away not to grant interviews to anyone concerning her
> career. Sorry. I trust you will understand why I am
> totally disinterested in seeing my lovely daughter's life
> publicized for commercial purposes.[3]

Jill Ellen, Dorothy's only daughter, sent a handwritten
note on small Cartier paper. In script very much like her
mother's, Jill responded as though she had been asked to
tea: "Regretfully, I must decline your thoughtful request
to meet with you. Very truly yours . . ." [4]

Eldest son Dickie ignored several letters requesting his
cooperation.

His younger brother, Kerry, who was eleven at the time
Dorothy died, volunteered to do what he could to enhance
what he hoped would be a tribute to or at least an accurate
rendering of his much maligned and grievously misunder-
stood mother, though it was made clear to him by his
family that his cooperation might mortally imperil both of
his octogenarian grandparents.

Kerry wanted to know more about Dorothy's death, a
matter that remained as unresolved to him as it did to the
general public. His family had told him nothing except the
fact that she had been found in bed. He had been rifling
through her pocketbooks for spare change on the morning
of her death and surmised, from a spray of light under the
closed anteroom door, that she was still up and reading.
He was relieved to learn, after years of feeling "super-
guilty," that she was already dead at the time of his morning raid, and that there was nothing he could have done to
save her.[5]

The family sentinels have effectively entombed the childhood years of Dorothy Kilgallen's life. She was apparently
a meek and unprepossessing youngster, and known consequently only to the Kilgallens. Teachers do not remember
her. School records tell little. More than a score of letters
were dispatched to Dorothy's classmates of the College of

New Rochelle, where she spent a freshman year. No one remembered Dorothy Mae. Dorothy herself was indisposed to reminiscing with adult friends about anything that happened prior to the time that she followed her father to Hearst.

Bits and pieces are all. A dream told. A vagrant recollection. Jim's anecdotal, unrevealing writings. Dorothy's earliest published stories. Bits and pieces.

James Lawrence Kilgallen—Jimmy or Kil to all—was born in Pittston, Pennsylvania, on July 11, 1888. He was taken, shortly thereafter, to Chicago where his father, John, an Irish immigrant, worked as a stock handler in the yards. The family bought a small house on the South Side. Jim's mother, Mary Cavanaugh, was native-born.

In a professional memoir written for the Hearst newspaper chain, *Sixty-Five Years of Deadlines and Headlines*,[6] which consisted of characteristic paeans to colleagues and tales of "the era of wonderful nonsense," Jim claimed he was poor as a boy but "never knew a moment of unhappiness." It would appear, however, that he did not remain close to his parents, both of whom lived to a ripe old age, or to his five brothers and sisters.

The Reverend John J. Kilgallen, a Jesuit, was a first cousin to Dorothy, the son of one of Jim's brothers. The priest was twenty-four years younger than Dorothy. He was raised in Chicago after she had already made a name for herself—a situation which, in most families, would impel proud or ironic reminiscence. Not so in the Kilgallen clan.

> I know nothing about Dorothy Kilgallen's life, most especially about her childhood, and I do not remember meeting Dorothy till the wedding day of her daughter Jill. I must say that no other aunt or uncle ever related stories about Dorothy to me. . . . This may seem strange to you (and to me), but such it was in those early days of mine.[7]

Jim's first and only ambition was to become a newspaper reporter. The dream had been instilled after a neighborhood youth, Charles Cecil Fitzmorris, "hooked on" to the Chicago *American* and was sent around the world as a stunt.

Jim wrote that the trip cinched it: "I thought: 'What a life —that's for me!' " [8]

He went to work, after graduating from the sixth grade, as a telegrapher in the stockyard district. He moved closer to his dream when he affiliated himself, as a telegrapher, with the Chicago *Daily Farmers & Drovers Journal*. At seventeen, he became a reporter for the meaty publication, covering the cattle and hog market and writing a women's column under the name Winnie Winthrop.

When Dorothy eventually chronicled her father's career, she omitted the hogs and jumped directly to Winnie.

Jim moved into the majors. This he claimed to have done after hearing with his trained telegrapher's ear a message tapped out in a Western Union office about the impending failure of a local bank. He hied over to the bank and questioned the president, misrepresenting himself as a reporter for the Chicago *Tribune*. He was ejected from the bank but taken on by the *Trib*'s associate editor, Walter Howey, who was impressed with the young man's flimflam.[9]

He had begun to arrive, moving with such luminaries as Ben Hecht, Charles MacArthur, Ring Lardner, Floyd Gibbons, Walter Noble Burns, and Howey himself (the prototype editor of *The Front Page*) in the Jerusalem of journalism.

The slightly built, dapper, rough-around-the-edges, ambitious, amiable, and quick-like-a-hare James Lawrence Kilgallen married Mae Ahern at her Catholic church in Denver, Colorado, on July 10, 1912.

Less is determinable about Mae. It took Dorothy's dossier from the Central Intelligence Agency to elicit her mother's place and date of birth: St. Louis, July 27, 1888. Mae was one of at least three children. Her father, William, was American-born. Her mother, Delia Conlon, emigrated from Ireland in 1879.

Jim would describe his wife as "a stunning red-head, 5 feet 2 . . . could have married into money if she wasn't brave enough to settle for something else." [10] During a trip to Denver, he would inform a reporter from a Catholic newspaper that Mae had been a "well-known singer and theater figure in this area." In yet another article, Jim claimed that his wife had sung at the Tabor Grand Opera House there.

Despite Mae's purported celebrity, the marriage was not reported by the local Denver papers of July 10, 11, or 12. Programs from the Tabor do not confirm, if in fact she sang under the name Ahern, that she was a performer of prominence.

Whatever the status of Mae's singing career, when she abandoned it, she became totally dedicated to Jim, receiving his accolades as though they were her own.[11] She called him Jim; he called her Mae. No darlings, dears, or sweeties ever passed between them. She was a devout Catholic with a vigorous sense of sin. Indeed, the only room of her own that Mae Kilgallen would inhabit, after taking her marriage vows, was the confessional.

Their first child, Dorothy Mae Kilgallen, was born in Chicago on July 3, 1913, in a thirty-dollar-a-month apartment on Garfield Boulevard and Morgan Street. The name Dorothy was taken because it meant "gift from Heaven." [12]

When Dorothy was still an infant, the Kilgallens moved to Laramie, Wyoming, where Mae had relatives named Gish with whom they lived. Jimmy bought into the Laramie *Boomerang,* which had been founded by humorist Bill Nye.

He is remembered by one of his former newsboys, Harry Small, as fast-stepping, diligent, occasionally hot-tempered. Small's only visual memory of Jim has him rolling up his sleeves and shouting, "Let's go to press." [13]

At fifteen months, Dorothy Kilgallen made her theatrical debut in Laramie in an Elks Club production of a farce, *One Thing After Another.* Mae had one of the singing leads. Dorothy, billed as "Tootsie," burst into impromptu tears during the first act, but resumed her composure in the second.[14]

The Kilgallens stayed two years, Jim struggling to compete with the more popular Laramie *Republican.* A fire in the press room dashed any hopes he had of keeping the paper solvent.

Dorothy Mae was six years old when her sister Eleanor was born in Indiana, where Jim was managing editor of the Indiana *Daily Times.* In Dorothy's first recorded memory, rendered when she was a peerless cosmopolite, she called the area in which they lived "rather suburban." She remembered decorating little pull toys with flowers, and calling them ding-dongs. She saw her first play in Indiana, starring Fred Stone. It made her "momentarily stage-struck." [15] Her shyness was a considerable deterrent, though she did continue, throughout her youth, to write, produce, and star in little plays for her friends.

The family was forced to leave Indiana after Jim wrote an exposé about the timeworn local jails, contending that any prisoner could escape merely by smashing the walls with his fist. Four incarcerated readers tried it. Jim was brought up on charges and sentenced to twenty-eight days for contempt of court. The case was dropped when he moved on to Chicago.

There he joined the Hearst syndicate's feisty International News Service, which was forever doing battle with the Goliaths at Associated Press and United Press. He was presently beckoned to their New York office to work as roving correspondent.

Jim remained with Hearst a lifetime, building a reputation with the organization for accuracy, alacrity, and loyalty. There are many within Hearst whose attitude toward the elder Kil verges on reverence. His editor, Barry Faris, recalled the thirty-three-year-old Jimmy Kilgallen: "When he got hold of a story, he was just like a bulldog—he'd get his teeth in it and never let go." [16]

In his early career with Hearst, Jim was forced off a moving train at the point of a gun as he was on his way to cover a prison massacre in Illinois. He secured an exclusive interview with Al Capone. He stalked Thomas Alva Edison for days. Edison, who was deaf by this time, had once worked as a telegrapher. The persistent reporter won him over by slipping a note into his hand that began, "As one operator to another. . . ." [17] He covered the execution of Ruth Snyder and Judd Gray, at which photographer Tom Howard secreted a camera into the death chamber and snapped a picture of Mrs. Snyder as the volts shot through her body. His first front-page story for INS was about the infamous Hall-Mills trial.

Jim's most bulldoggish exploit involved pursuing fugitive Sam Insull halfway around the world as the utilities magnate attempted to escape extradition. The reporter hired an amphibian plane to set down beside Insull's freighter, suffered a multitude of rebuffs, and finally ingratiated himself into an explosive exclusive as he accompanied the industrialist on his long, peaceable voyage back to the United States.

There was no felicity in Jim's prose. But he was a respected and reliable Hearst craftsman with a talent for friendship. Irene Corbally Kuhn, a newspaperwoman who came up in his time, observed:

> He was just a lovely, simple man, not very well-educated, but with a kind of Irish quality that just enfolded people. Jim Farley had it. Jimmy developed it. Hearst always nurtured people like that when they had qualities that enabled them to get close to big people.[18]

He had, additionally, an understanding of the organization that nurtured him. In his simple, enfolding way, Jim wrote, "If I were permitted to select one newspaperman for my personal 'Hall of Fame,' I would unhesitatingly nominate William Randolph Hearst, Sr." [19]

Dorothy Mae's growing-up years were filled with Jim's newspapering exploits. He was away a good deal of the time. His dispatches were like letters home. Mae learned journalistic lingo, as in "Your father got good play today." Jim brought his little girls two shiny dimes from John D. Rockefeller, and, at the suggestion of a press agent, a piece of wood purportedly taken from Rudolph Valentino's coffin, etched with Dorothy's initials, D.M.K.

In later years, Dorothy would write about her father:

> When I was a little girl his conversation always seemed more interesting to me than that of the man next door who was a lawyer, or the man next door to our right who was a certified public accountant. . . . Other girls in our block had fathers who made more money than mine, but they worked in offices or stores; my father was always tossing things into a suitcase and taking a train or a plane to some place where a story was breaking. . . . I remember Mother wanted me to be an English teacher. She thought it was a nice profession for a girl, with good hours and Saturdays off and three months vacation every summer.

But, Dad, without ever saying a word, won.[20]

When Jim moved to INS in New York, he settled his family in Brooklyn.

They moved to an Irish-Catholic enclave back of Flatbush Avenue. Theirs was one in a row of semidetached houses—huddled, middle class, and unbeautiful. The family had grown. Grandmother Ahern and her nervous daughter, Esther, had come to live with them. Dorothy attended a red-brick school, P.S. 119, a block away from the house. She pulled As and Bs in academics. Her conduct was unfailingly Excellent. She received religious instructions at St. Elizabeth's and attended St. Thomas Aquinas Church every Sunday. She and Eleanor were both dutiful daughters.

Dorothy read early and prolifically and favored the *Elsie Dinsmore* series.

Elsie, a character copyrighted by Martha Farquharson in 1868, was the quintessential Victorian little girl: "Truthful, diligent, respectful, gentle, patient and forgiving to a remarkable degree," though forever castigating herself for feeling or expressing hostility. She read her Bible regularly and yearned "to be more like Jesus."

The Elsie Dinsmore series was a didactic primer on righteous Christian behavior. Just below the surface, however, lurks a clear fantasy that undoubtedly accounted for its marked success among little girls of the nineteenth century whose fathers were, at least, emotionally absent.

Elsie's mother was conveniently dead and her father, a retired naval officer, she had not seen since her birth eight years before. She was raised by relatives. Upon his return, he does not know how to deal with his princess or she with him. He is not a cold man, but he cannot communicate his love.

"How to gain her father's love," the narrator reveals, "was the constant subject of her thoughts, and she tried in many ways to win his affection. . . . She strove to anticipate and fulfill his wishes." But Elsie and her father were at cross-purposes emotionally. She laments that "he seldom noticed her."

There is a story about Dorothy, at eleven, so archetypal as to be almost an embarrassment.

Jim, who made it a practice when chronicling his daughter's life to interject his own fantasies into hers, had one version of the episode. "Dorothy," he wrote, "used to sit on the front stoop and tell her little pals and younger sister,

Eleanor, how some day she would 'amount to something'—
be a big star and go to faraway places she had read
about." [21]

Another version was told by Charlotte Manson, a girlhood friend of Dorothy's. It places the child on the stoop,
but she is provoked. One of her pals had accused her
of being "stuck up" in spite of the fact that she was "not
even good looking." Dorothy replied, "I'll show you.
Someday I'll be very famous and all of you will read
about me."

She was not good-looking. A graduation picture from
P.S. 119, when she was almost thirteen, shows her in a
sea of middy blouses. She is of average height, painfully
skinny, mousy to a ludicrous extent. In her high-school
picture she is standing between a very beautiful girl and
one of the two black students in the class of several hundred. She has become austere. Her dark hair is parted
severely in the center. She wears pearls. Her mouth is
tight and her features immobile. The camera was no
friend to her.

And the world was somehow disappointing. She
dreamed, according to her closest friend in later years,
of tiny, tiny pussycats and minuscule cookies. When she
awakened, the actual size of things dismayed her.[22]

She found a critical voice to address her violated sensibilities. Her first piece of published writing appeared,
when she was twelve, in the Brooklyn *Eagle*. The paper
had printed an article demeaning her screen idol, Ramon
Novarro. She came heatedly to his defense. The *Eagle*
ran her letter, which she signed *Dorothy Laurington*, in
full.[23]

Jim would write that his Dorothy Mae was so bright
that Erasmus Hall High School devoted a month's study
to her high IQ.[24] Her records at Erasmus do not show
that such a test was conducted for the reasons he stated.
If such a battery was run, it was more likely done to
determine the disparity between the height of her 140 IQ
and the depth of her grades. Something was apparently
bugging Dorothy when she first entered Erasmus, probably the little-fish-big-pond syndrome. Though she was a
precocious, facile writer, her English mark was 55. She
failed Latin, French, and Physical Education. Her grade
in mathematics was 30.

Whatever was going on was resolved when she established a beachhead at the school literary magazine, *The Erasmian*. Here she gained a kind of recognition and found an outlet for her early anger.

In one of her first efforts, she wrote about the vendetta of an Italian peasant girl who is spurned by an English flier. The story was summarized in a *New York Post* series about Dorothy:

> When he flies away without her she tortures her dog to appease her bitterness. The flier returns later, tarries a while, then tries to sneak off without her again. This time the plane crashes, the flier is killed, and the girl, an evil glint in her eyes, walks off stroking the file with which she had cut the wires in his plane.[25]

A subsequent *Erasmian* effort, written when she was a junior, showed a less primitive sense of grievance. The heroine is a newspaperwoman named Carol Rhodes and the story is called "Reviewed." It is climaxed when Carol excoriates in print the first literary attempt of a social rake named Jerald Halliday. The heroine experiences pleasure in writing what she pleases, suffers no compunction in "thus denouncing another's work," and derives a schoolmarmish thrill when, as a result of her criticism— "One year later Jerald Halliday wrote a good book."

She was reared, in the Kilgallen tradition, to avoid dealing with emotions, especially with anger. Dorothy would say, during an interview about her early married life, that she *never* argued with her husband and that she considered arguments of any kind "selfish." She learned from Mae, who avoided asking Jim any questions when he arrived home late at night after quaffing with his colleagues. A close friend to Dorothy in later years, Jean Bach, commented on what she perceived to have been Mae's message to her daughter. "It's the thing of suffering in silence," Jean Bach observed, "of not confronting. That made you a superior person." [26]

Dorothy never learned, as we shall see, to deal with her own anger or with any of the nonpious larger emotions. When she was an associate editor of the magazine and in her senior year, a piece of fiction was submitted to her by a sophomore named Bernard Malamud—the very same. It was a story, Malamud recalled, written when he was "just beginning to sense something" about himself. The short work of fiction was seminal but characteristic of Malamud—"a story about a crippled boy or man who managed to win a sort of victory."

Editor Dorothy Mae rejected the story. She returned it to the young aspirant with a handwritten explanation: "This is too depressing for *The Erasmian.*" He was annoyed with her, knowing that she had "described it foolishly."

Malamud retained a clear, visual impression of the sixteen-year-old, though he had no dealings with her after high school and little to do with her then: "Unique, tall, animated, immaculately dressed. A woman without a chin, very careful about her physical appearance. Though visibly adorned with rouge and lipstick, it was well-applied. She had a sense of her own importance."

He perceived then that they were writing for different reasons. Dorothy, he asserted, was doing it "as a means, not an end in itself. Not to be honest, but to be famous." [27]

On the couple of occasions that Malamud saw Dorothy, she was with another editor whom she was dating at the time, John Woods. A handsome WASP who was one term ahead of her, he was Princeton-bound and pronounced *column* as col-yoom. [28]

Woods was the first of Dorothy's handsome WASPs, the kind of man she would refer to consistently in her writing as "collar ads." On his graduation, she needled him gently in a short essay she wrote endowing senior celebrities with appropriate gifts: "To John Woods, collar-ad, a comb, a brush, and a mirror."

In September of 1930 Dorothy went on to the College of New Rochelle, a bucolic school for young Catholic women run by Ursulan nuns. It was a place of old wood and peace, tea dances and compulsory chapel attendance. She lived on campus but returned home for weekends, avoiding all social activities and, as far as can be determined, making no close friends. Most of the students were from small towns and less sophisticated than Dorothy.

While she was attending college, she began to date another young Protestant, George (Kit) Kuittinen. He found her very attractive.[29] Her skin was fine and Irish—flawless porcelain; her eyes very large and blue. Though she was thin, her breasts were well-developed and her legs excellent.

At the school, she sat occasionally with Sister Berenice-Rice in front of a building in which Charles Dickens had once eaten dinner. The nun had something in common with Dorothy, having been drawn to the newspaper field in the twenties before she took her vows.

She recalled that Dorothy spoke a great deal about her father, never about the rest of the family. As the summer of 1931 drew near, Dorothy was considering accepting a job on the New York *Journal*, which had been offered to her by one of Jim's colleagues. There would be a two-week trial period and a stint for the entire summer if she worked out. The nun advised her to take the job.

"Be sure to come back in the fall," she told Dorothy.[30]

Dorothy promised that she would return.

All that the archives hold about this famous alumna is that she resided on third-corridor Brescia Hall and left behind a string of As and Bs.

Ambition is one of the larger nonpious emotions and therefore subject to some mythologizing by Kilgallen *père* and daughter. There were many versions written by each of them about Dorothy's entrance into the profession. She probably came closest to the multilayered truth: "He never suggested that I follow in his footsteps. But the footsteps were there, and what other way could I have gone?" [31]

We can be fairly sure that she was dressed in white organdy, carrying an opera bag "with Alice blue draw strings" as she arrived at the burly, littered offices of the *Evening Journal* for her first day of work that blistering summer of 1931. Marjorie Hall, who was on the staff of the paper, remembered the somewhat bizarre sight of her. Newspaperwomen did not, as a rule, dress as though they were on their way to a school prom.

We can be certain that she was terrified. She would not be eighteen until July. And Jim Kilgallen had laid down some heavy tracks. Dorothy was blessed, however, with the appearance of equanimity: part defense, part feint, and predominantly endowment. Her features were immobile. The mouth spoke only when it talked.

A few years later, she was standing on the steps of Sing Sing with a group of colleagues when a man, incensed at something she had written about his sister, who was in the Death House, pointed a gun at her. She disarmed him by simply standing her ground. The incredulous reporters lauded her coolness. She confessed later to a *Daily News* staffer that she fully expected to die then and there. She had not moved because she was not able to move.

Dorothy reported now to Amster Spiro, who was sitting at the arc of the giant horseshoe comprising all of the paper's editors and rewrite people. As he was one of the legions who adored Jim Kilgallen, we may assume that this tall, street-wise city editor, who had a dimple on the end of his chin and read Yiddish with ease, greeted Dorothy warmly but with dispatch. Amster Spiro, "Spi" to his friends, was that day involved headily in pulling together the lead story that would roll off the *Journal* presses as THE MURDER OF 100 PIECES—give or take a few. A head, two forearms, and the feet of a male about thirty-five years old had been found strewn around Manhattan. Hatchet murders were the house specialty of the *Journal*, whose front page was a virtual abattoir of murder most foul.

Among William Randolph Hearst's first journalistic coups in 1897, soon after he purchased the paper with the proceeds of his mother's sale of her considerable Anaconda Copper holdings, was the solution of a heinous hatchet murder.

"The Chief," which is what his lieutenants really called him, had been a shirt-sleeve editor then. *Journal* writer James Ford noted: "When peace brooded over the city and nobody was being robbed or murdered, he would come down to the office with despondency written on his face . . . but the tidings of some new crime or disaster would rouse him to instant action." [1]

Returning to his MURDER OF 100 PIECES now, Amster Spiro turned his new cub reporter over to Assistant City Editor Garry J. Finley.

"You've got Kil's kid," he informed Finley, "go easy on her. She's just out of the convent."

Even for one who had been exposed to city rooms from infancy, Dorothy obviously had to be taken in hand if she was to survive that summer. But Finley did *not* go easy on her.

It was said about Garry Finley, a runt of a man who drank too much and talked out of the side of his mouth, that, having been jilted by a newspaperwoman, he hated them as a group. He had been engaged for many years to Marjorie Smith. When she left him to marry the picture editor of the *Evening Graphic*, he was consoled in a speakeasy called The Rainhouse by Johnston Kerkhoff, top rewrite man and elaborate practical joker. Kerkhoff, in the tradition of top rewrite men and elaborate practical jokers, plied Finley with booze and convinced him to take some kind of revenge on the picture editor, whose name was Ryan Walker. Kerkhoff and Finley filled their pockets with change, stumbled to the telephone, and apprised the *Graphic* that Walker was dead. They then telephoned the police, the fire department, an undertaker, and several hospitals, summoning each to the residence of Marjorie Smith's intended.

They rushed over to the scene to observe the chaos. Finley grinned as Ryan Walker's block was cordoned off.

"You're a good pal," he told Johnston Kerkhoff.[2]

During Finley's first tutorial session with Dorothy, he discovered that his soft-spoken charge had never seen a dead body.

"What do you do at wakes?" he asked.

"Oh, I never look," she replied.

He explained that she would have to get accustomed to the sight of death if she was going to be of any use to the paper, and assigned her to the morgue. Her job was to describe incoming suicides in detail so that friends or relatives might come and claim them. Dorothy was in no position to complain. Good reporters, many of whom were queuing up on Fridays during those Depression years in front of Amster's desk to receive an envelope and a mournful handshake, never turned down an assignment. Further, she would not have given Finley the satisfaction of manifesting her displeasure.

On her first day at the morgue, as she took notes in her ubiquitous stenographer's pad, one of the attendants noticed that Dorothy's lovely, almost translucent complexion was turning the color of the corpse about which she was writing. He offered her a stick of gum. Dorothy considered chewing vulgar, but she took the wad. It worked. Without having to swallow, she obtained sufficient sugar to keep herself upright and functional.

In later years, she would fall half in love with the sight of death. At the Sam Sheppard trial in 1954, her description of the battered Marilyn Sheppard was more poetic and certainly more authentic than anything she had ever written. But, as a cub reporter, she chewed. She chewed for one entire week until Garry Finley decided that she had had enough.

At least one observer mistook her survivalist device as a sign of insouciance. Hearst sob sister Elsie Robinson caught her act. She would recollect, in a piece about Dorothy written for the *Journal* in 1936:

> It was an extremely messy murder, which left indiscreet scraps of evidence littering a vacant lot. . . . Yet there in the midst of messiness stood the epitome of all

Innocent Young Girls . . . little Miss Kilgallen, meek, mum, Minnie Mousish, chewing the world's record wad of gum and coolly making corking copy of each bloody shred.

Dorothy had no problem learning to write for the *Journal*. She had been nurtured on Jim's spare, compositionlike prose, *viz:*

> It was difficult to interrogate Mr. Peters in view of his embarrassment at being dragged into the Starr Faithful case. He is a good-looking man, almost six feet tall, with a florid face, blue eyes, a round baldish head, and gray hair about the ears. He employed excellent diction in his conversation.

She was offered, of course, nothing so spectacular as an exclusive interview with one of the leading figures in the Starr Faithful case. She did cover, in her first weeks: A CONVENTION OF BEAUTY PARLOR OPERATORS AT A PENNSYLVANIA HOTEL; THE 102ND BIRTHDAY OF JOHN R. VOORHIS ("the grand old man of Tammany Hall"); THE OPENING OF A MODEL HOME IN FLATBUSH; and THE VISIT OF FORTY COLLEGE GIRLS FROM NEW ORLEANS ("They think New York policemen are very cute.") She interviewed THE TOPMOST TENANTS OF THE EMPIRE STATE BUILDING; SOPRANO MARION TALLEY, who admitted she owned a farm in Iowa; and SOPHIE MELVIN ("The slender, emotional girl, darting through the crowd of strikers, is Sophie Melvin, acknowledged leader, despite her twenty-one years, of 1,000 striking Paterson textile workers. Although an organizer since she was seventeen, this blue-eyed woman has lived close to the people: she knows their hardships, their struggles, and their needs. 'These people are not Communists,' she explained passionately in an exclusive interview with the *Evening Journal*. 'But they are starving.')"

When the traditional language of the Hearstian sob sister was appropriate, she spoke it like a native. That first summer, an epidemic of polio ravaged the city; almost two thousand cases were reported to the Board of Health from her home borough alone. When Dorothy telephoned the night city editor to get her day's assignment in mid-July, she was asked to comb the city hospitals, find several typical young victims, and chronicle their agony. A couple of her more seasoned colleagues, fearing contagion, had already turned the assignment down.

She discovered "Sunny Sally," "Angel Face Tommy," and "Smiling Ben." She seemed particularly taken with Tommy, a four-year-old from the Lower East Side: "He's fighting, this mite of a youngster with sun-kissed blond hair and deep brown eyes, against the ogre of childhood, infantile paralysis. Today he turned his brave brown eyes to the nurse and said, 'I can't talk.' " The two-part series concluded, "Rich and poor, they are all battling for life. And they are equal in the face of death."

Her accounts of their travail were given prominent play. Dorothy glowed when Jim wired his congratulations from out of town.

Summer came and summer went. Her quick success and the pride she experienced when she saw her stories in print made a return to tea dances and bed at ten quite impossible. Dorothy broke her promise to Sister Berenice-Rice. She had probably never intended to keep it.

In addition to her growing competence as a writer and reporter, Dorothy had a *style* and an approach that made her a refreshing addition to the newsroom and an asset to her editors. There were other women working for the *Journal*, some of them extraordinarily talented. Margaret Moores Marshall, middle-aged, intelligent, versatile, was among them. She always carried a big fabric portmanteau and reminded James "Red" Horan, who had begun work two years before Dorothy as a copy boy at twelve dollars a week, of "a midwife running to deliver. She was very nice, very formal, and always stopped to ask, 'James, how are you?' " Jeanette Smits was a college graduate, not much older than Dorothy, freckled and good-looking. She was a top rewrite person and had been instrumental in the capture of "Two-Gun" Crowley. But there was a grayness about her. She chain-smoked, bathed infrequently, looked and smelled of tension and long hours.

"Into this circle comes Dorothy," Horan recalled.

She's young. She's fresh-looking. She must have spent a fortune on clothes because she had the appearance of having just stepped out of the traditional band-box. No smell of tobacco. Just perfume.

There were a great many young girls in and about that city room. You'd see them one week and that would be it. But there was something about the way Dorothy handled herself. I had the opinion that she was born for the business. That soft, quiet way of hers hid a steely ambition and a drive and also a very keen intelligence.[3]

Which is not to say that she was invincible.

She covered her first murder case with Syd Boehm, who would leave the paper in 1944 for a more lucrative career as a motion picture writer and producer, and Eddie Mahar, who stayed long enough to make his own assignment, as city editor, when Dorothy overdosed on Seconal and alcohol in 1965. The victim now was an eighteen-year-old girl who had been beaten to death with a stool in a Cushman's bakery in Washington Heights. Dorothy was used, by Spi, with the hope that her combination of innocence and grit might yield a bonus from the cops at the Wadsworth Avenue police station.

The *Journal* published nine and ten editions at the time, paper being as cheap as coverage. While this mini-murder squad was riding uptown with no more knowledge than that the girl had been discovered and that a blunt instrument had been found, newsboys were already bounding off trucks with the Racing Final, yelling, "Extra! Extra! Murdered Girl in Cushman's Bakery."

Dorothy scurried out of the police station as fast as her little bowed pumps could carry her. She wasn't sure what she had, but the gambit had worked to the extent that the sergeant, taken by her apparent needfulness, had told her something that he had withheld from the other reporters. The girl's address book had been found in her purse.

When Eddie Mahar learned of the discovery, he jumped into the nearest telephone booth.

"Mahar! Give me the desk! They just found the kid's love diary. They're putting out a dragnet for everyone in it."[4]

Ishbel Ross, in *Ladies of the Press*, would write that "other reporters were cynically amused by the astonishing ability of the Hearst press to find secret love diaries."

Dorothy may or may not have been amused. But this was not the kind of journalism Jim Kilgallen practiced, nor would his daughter ever resort to such flagrant dissembling. She would not have the need professionally.

The *Journal* trucks fanned out to the five boroughs with this second "exclusive" while Boehm, Dorothy, and a photographer went searching for the body. It had been moved, they discovered, to a neighborhood funeral parlor. Dorothy pretended to be a relative of the girl in order to gain admittance, but she was turned away. The next step, for the trio, was to enter by less conventional means. They found a basement window, jimmied it open, and clambered in one by one. The Cushman victim was found laid out in a temporary coffin. Dorothy, wearing a black felt hat that looked like two crossed bird wings, took out her steno pad and began jotting.

The photographer was snapping pictures around her. As Dorothy and Boehm looked on, their colleague pinned open the eyes of the battered girl, straddled the coffin, and began to snap. "I was horrified and began to shake all over," Boehm recalled. "Dorothy left immediately."

In tandem with Boehm again, in 1933, she helped expose the so-called Marriage Mill that was operating in New Jersey. The paper had received a tip that young women, under the age of legal consent, were being licensed to marry in Mayor Frank Hague's Jersey City bailiwick. Boehm was a natural for the assignment; he specialized in exposing vice and corruption. Spi suggested that Dorothy would make the perfect underage bride. For legal and personal reasons —Boehm was already married and Dorothy was Mae Kilgallen's daughter—they agreed to conspire to secure a license, but they would under no circumstances subject themselves to the ceremony.

With Dorothy "wearing a corsage and what might have been an Easter bonnet," Boehm wrote in a letter of 1976, "we went to New Jersey via the Hudson tube. Oh, yes, that corsage. I had instructed Dorothy not to spend more than a buck if she expected to be reimbursed. Even though a dollar was a dollar in those days, Dorothy—her whole life would be orchids and champagne—bought herself two orchids! Oddly, she was reimbursed without question."

They hung out in front of the County Clerk's office in Newark looking nervous, overdressed, and prenuptial. In a matter of minutes, the couple was accosted by a runner.

"You kids want to get married?"

Boehm said they did but that his fiancée was only seventeen.

"You got thirteen bucks, mister?" the man asked.

"Sure," Boehm replied.

"She's eighteen," the runner said.

He drove them to the City Clerk's office in West New York, New Jersey, where they obtained a license under assumed names with no proof of age required. The clerk offered to perform the ceremony. Dorothy uttered one word into Syd Boehm's ear: No!

"She's a Catholic. Very devout," Boehm explained. "Maybe we'd better go and find a priest."

"No problem," the official said. "For another thirteen dollars, I can have a priest here in five minutes."

Now, with the possible involvement of the Holy Roman See, no matter how corrupt its representative, Dorothy began to tremble. Boehm thanked the man amiably and told him that she preferred to be married by the priest who had baptized her. They left with their license.

Amster Spiro decided that he wanted more and, this time, pictures. Dorothy agreed to participate further in this one only if they circumvented any possible participation of the Catholic Church. The next day, in Weehauken, with Dorothy's orchids beginning to wilt, they called on the minister of a small Baptist church who, Boehm was assured, would marry Shirley Temple to Fatty Arbuckle if they had the thirteen dollars.

"Do you two kids love each other?" the minister asked.

"Very much," Dorothy answered.

"Then I'll perform the ceremony now and we'll do the paperwork later."

Dorothy's eyes widened with panic. Boehm took the Baptist minister to the side and explained that the marriage rite was not really what they had in mind. He simply wanted to take his seventeen-year-old inamorata to Canada for a little fun without running into the Mann Act. The holy man smiled with understanding, went to his desk, pulled out a large marriage certificate, and filled in the bogus names they had given to him. He looked lasciviously at the young bride.

Together Dorothy and Syd Boehm finessed him into the

street, where, from a concealed doorway, photographer Ben Auermuller got a picture of Boehm holding the beribboned marriage certificate while the minister patted Dorothy's ass.[5]

There had been a time when Mae Kilgallen could pack Jim for an out-of-town assignment on a moment's notice. Packing, looking neat, brushing Eleanor's hair, and imparting guilt appear to have been Mae's fortes. As Dolly Mae grew more and more successful, Mae packed for two and sometimes three. The Kilgallens were becoming the King Family of journalism.

Syd Boehm remembered checking into a hotel with Dorothy in Stamford, Connecticut. They were covering the disappearance of a wealthy broker who was snatched off his luxurious cabin cruiser and his wife and five-year-old child set adrift. Dorothy was to stay with the wife, who was ferrying daily from Stamford to be interrogated by the Mineola police.

Dorothy disembarked, having secured an interview with the woman. In the crowd of newsmen gathered on the Mineola side, Dorothy spotted dapper Jim in his traditional bowler, pockets jammed with pencils. She ran off the boat, in her new Empress Eugenia autumn hat, and embraced him.

When she returned to the hotel later that afternoon, Dorothy was pleased to find Mae, who had decided to join her daughter in Stamford. Connecticut was so lovely when the leaves turned! Syd Boehm was not hampered by Mrs. Kilgallen's presence. He was not among the men to whom Dorothy appealed. But he was surprised. He would write, in 1976: "Dorothy, unquestionably, was the only newspaperwoman in New York who remained a virgin until her marriage bed. It definitely was not for lack of guys who tried BUT—within an hour of arriving on an out-of-town assignment, Mama Kilgallen would arrive and stay for the duration." [6]

Mae, who would exclaim to her grandson in later years, "I would rather have seen your mother *dead* than living with a man she wasn't married to," need not have worried. She and the Church had done a nifty job on Dolly Mae; she was not about to jump the gun. The more realistic possibility, given her taste in men, was that she might marry out of the faith.

John Woods, the "collar-ad" whom Dorothy had dated at Erasmus, was by this time out of her life, studying at Princeton. Her main man continued to be Kit Kuittinen. Kit was two years older than Dorothy, prelaw at Duke University, and a member of Sigma Alpha Upsilon. He was of Scandinavian descent, six feet tall, athletically built, with dark brown hair and hazel eyes. He dressed nattily in Chesterfields and bowlers and kept a small sailboat in Huntington. He had met her originally through a buddy who was dating a girl friend of Dorothy's. In these two meshing Brooklyn sets, he was the one and only Protestant.

Kit enjoyed the *gemütlich* Kilgallen household, especially on Sunday, when the family, sometimes joined by Paul Gallico and Jimmy Cannon, sat around the radio. The men talked sports. The women talked small. Little Grandmother Ahern bustled around, fluffing pillows and serving cookies. Jim and his friends drank in two rooms, politely in the parlor, more robustly in the kitchen. Kit enjoyed Jim's company, and Jim delighted always in the fact that Dorothy dated "college boys." Mae was amiable to the young Kit Kuittinen. "But I always had the feeling," recalled Kit, "that Dorothy's mother was more than a little concerned about the fact that I was a Protestant." [7]

Dorothy was working pre–Newspaper Guild hours: six days a week and half a day on most holidays. Kit was home from school only on weekends, and a good deal of that time he spent puttering around his boat. It was a passion they could not share, since Dorothy had no interest in the out-of-doors. They did, however, take ferry-boat trips up the Hudson to dine at the Bear Mountain Inn. They each talked about writing the Great American Novel, neither believing the other would do it: "She seemed to love the action of the newspaper game so much, I just couldn't see her sitting still that long." [8]

She took her collar-ads quite literally. Looking at Kit's perfect profile on one of their moonlit voyages, she talked him into seeing a friend who owned a modeling agency. He was reluctant, but broke. Kit eventually appeared in a pulpy romance magazine as the all-American dream, sitting in an all-American convertible. He lived in constant fear that one of his all-American fraternity brothers would discover the photograph.

Often their dating plans were interrupted by a phone call from the office. "Come along, Kit," she would say to him, grabbing her steno pad, "we'll cover this together."

"We hit many a Western Union office together," Kuittinen recalled. "I was editing my school newspaper at the time and had literary aspirations of my own. Dorothy would type out her story and I would do my version, and then she'd kind of paste them together."

He took her up to The Bronx when the ferryboat *Observation*, crammed with workmen on their way to collect their paychecks, blew up in the East River, killing forty of the passengers and injuring a hundred others. Many of the victims found floating in the river had been boiled alive when the engine exploded and turned the ferry into an erupting geyser.

This was the biggest story of the day, and by the time Dorothy and Kit sped to the scene, many of her *Journal* colleagues were already there. She interviewed several witnesses and walked attentively up and down the wharf counting bodies; she criss-crossed her father, who had started his count from the other direction.

The lead story that appeared the next day was a pastiche of inputs. But a good deal of it was unmistakably Dorothy's. She had a more feminine touch than anyone on the staff and this she coupled with a growing talent for effective particularization: "One body was hurled through a fourth story window of a power plant; three others were carried *like leaves* to the roof of a building in 135th Street. . . . They were found *in the most out of the way places;* one somehow got inside a boathouse that has only a *tiny door;* others landed in small boats tied up to the shore (italics added)." [9]

Kit Kuittinen remembered the scene: "Bodies were floating around like a bunch of dead fish. She had no problem with that. What was important to her was that there was a story to be told and she was going to tell it."

It could not have been so simple. Working for Hearst in the so-called era of wonderful nonsense was fun and Nancy Drewish. But there is no gainsaying that the job was also a combat zone in which Dorothy was, on a daily basis, ex-

posed to the most gruesome displays of death and mutila-
tion. And for this exposure she was singularly ill-equipped.

She had learned her father's trade astonishingly well.
However, there is every indication that she hadn't a conscious clue as to why she had even entered the newspaper
business in the first place.

Sitting in front of Brescia Hall at the College of New
Rochelle with Sister Berenice-Rice, she had spoken of emulating her father, of a burning ambition to be a great
journalist. Fourteen years later, she would emphasize to an
interviewer from a Jesuit publication called *The Queen's
Work:* "I never had the *slightest* ambition to be a writer,
much less a newspaper writer. I wanted to be a teacher of
dramatics. Dad had such odd hours and was always out of
town. I never picked up a newspaper—except to look at
the fashion advertisements."

She was like an alcoholic after a blackout who awakens
in a strange place and confabulates a truth to explain.
Dorothy made up two truths. The one, to please her father,
she had told the sister at college. The second version, told
to the Jesuit, was an introjection of her mother's desire for
Dorothy Mae: to teach English or dramatics. Though she
had settled in actuality upon her father's fantasy, she now
compensated her mother, to whom virtue was denial, by
feigning an ultrafeminine indifference to the brawny business of newspapering.

In fact, the young reporter's eyes were not on those
boiled bodies but on a style of life far from the grime of the
city room and the homely environs of Flatbush Avenue.
Writing a series of stories called "Romances of American
Beauties" in 1933, Dorothy met and was totally taken with
Lillian Emerson Harts, who would, through a second marriage, become Lillian Boscowitz and Dorothy's closest
friend. A young socialite who was born into oodles of
Southern money, she had been presented to the Court of
St. James's after an education at L'Ecole Française and a
youth spent mixing in European society.

Dorothy described her:

> She is blonde without being yellow-haired, and her
> coiffure has little curls around the edges, making a
> frivolous halo for her dimples and wide, sky-blue eyes.
> Now she is the wife of William Harts, Jr., who brings

her flowers every night when he comes home from work and laughs at the same things she does. They are such a nice, happy couple that you are tempted to knock wood when you look at them. She looks as if life were a lot of fun for her.

She and Lillian were not yet friends because they were not yet peers. But Dorothy would come back with a jerry-built personality, the right clothes, the proper credentials, and a collar-ad by her side.

Dorothy was with the *Journal* for less than two years when Amster Spiro ran a little layout about her in which she was called the paper's Baby Star. Spi had an almost Panglossian concept of her capabilities, and he liked her a lot. It was he, however, who began referring to Dorothy as Betty Boop. Not without affection. And never, of course, to her face.

Betty Boop was a cartoon vamp, one of the first animated creatures to move around primitively on the movie screen. In 1932, she emerged genielike out of an ink bottle, undulating in a hubba-hubba pose, one hand splayed on her spit-curled hair, the other wrapped around her sinuous waist. It was those enormous, appealing eyes that made Betty. They danced and darted poignantly, imprisoned in an otherwise motionless face. Betty Boop had no chin whatsoever. Her face stopped at her tiny lifesaver mouth, which emitted small squeegee sounds. Her breasts were well-developed and she wore stiletto pumps. The one black garter with which she had been created was eventually removed by the censors.

Now it was Dorothy's physiological Boopishness, combined with a growing competence, that had a tendency to take people by surprise, to compel them to do for her what they might not have done for another reporter. As Damon Runyon noted:

> She has soft, dark hair, and huge, appealing blue eyes that gaze at you with an expression of infinite innocence buried in their azure depths. She looks so young and helpless that you say to yourself: "My goodness, I must assist this poor little child in her work. I must shield her from the rough edges of life."
>
> That is, you say this to yourself, if you are a man

out on an assignment against Miss Kilgallen and un-
acquainted with her. Maybe you disregard her as an
unlikely opposition in your pursuit of news, and turn
your watchfulness to the hard-eyed members of the
sterner sex, and you are positively shocked when you
pick up the *Journal* the next day and discover that
the little girl with the eyes of a gazelle has scooped
your head off.

Ah yes, that Kilgallen girl! [1]

There were those who, for some reason, did not pick up
the *Journal* the next day. And they came away with an entirely different impression. Will Goldman, of the Long
Island Press, sat beside Dorothy at the trial of stout Alice
Creighton in Mineola. Mrs. Creighton was charged with
lacing the chocolate pudding of her lover's wife with an
arsenic compound called Rough-on-Rats. Dorothy had, by
that time, written reams of by-lined, front-page stuff on
some of the splashier trials of the time. Goldman, however,
remained under the impression that this was her first, that
she hadn't a clue as to what she was about, and he felt compelled to assist the poor young thing in every way he
could. To this day, he will not acknowledge that the lively,
Hearstian running story that appeared under Dorothy's
name could have been written by the inept innocent whom
he met for the first and last time in Mineola.

She wasn't playing at coyness. Indeed, she was more intense than coquettish. Goldman was picking up on her
style and her expectations. As competent as she was, she
had grown accustomed to male assistance. Jim had habituated her.

In the Hearst press of the early and mid-thirties, reporters made their names covering trials and executions. In
other kinds of stories, there was little cohesion. Europe?
Hardly seemed to matter. An occasional flattering picture
of Adolf Hitler or of a militant *frau* raising her arm in a
hefty *heil* appeared under the caption, "Spirit of Modern
German Womanhood." Without a war, there was no running story in Europe, not, at least, of sufficient dramatic
impact to compel a continuum of reader thralldom. The
Great Depression prevailed; it lacked allure. How many
sob sisters in tatty rags could be dispatched by the Chief

over caviar at San Simeon to personalize the perils of poverty by falling in a dead heap on the streets of San Francisco? That trick had been turned with some regularity by his early women stars, some of whom wrote under the *nom de guerre* "Annie Laurie." The first Hearst sob sister, Winifred Sweet, had collapsed on Market Street in the line of duty.[2] In 1931, Adela Rogers St. Johns had "sneaked" a frayed dress from the MGM wardrobe department and played destitute in downtown Los Angeles.[3]

It was an idea whose time had gone.

For the sure-fire elements of nitty-gritty, life-and-death drama, the yellow press relied primarily on the murder trial, and the ghoulish particulars of important executions. Baby Star Dorothy Kilgallen was naturally assigned within these areas. Her ability to place her apparent innocence in the service of her competence paid great dividends. She had no problem asking for help when she needed it. And men, especially, responded.

Warden Lewis E. Lawes of Sing Sing for many years refused to allow women to witness executions. On such awful nights, female reporters were not even permitted to enter the dismal Administration Building, a short bus ride away from the Death House on the Hudson. In August, 1934, Anna Antonio, a pitiful little woman who was found guilty of hiring two men to kill her husband for his $5,300 insurance policy, was scheduled, along with her cohorts, to be electrocuted. The story was big. She was one of a handful of women so sentenced in the state. There had been several dramatic stays. She was a mother. Her little boy, Frankie, had been playing catch with her in the prison yard that very afternoon. Her two small daughters, to whom she would leave a scrawled recipe for making spaghetti, kissed her good-bye just hours before the sentence was carried out.

Amster Spiro dispatched Dorothy to Ossining, hoping that she could somehow talk her way into the death chamber. She failed and stood huddled and concerned on the steps of the prison as a veteran New York reporter emerged from the ritual. It was after midnight.

Dorothy approached him, introduced herself, and explained her predicament.

"I'm in a terrible fix," she said. "I've got a story to file in two hours and I haven't the faintest notion of what went on in there. Can you fill me in?"

The reporter was taken by Dorothy and her guilelessness. There was no time for talk, but he invited her to drive with him to the Western Union office and take whatever she needed from his duplicates.

Using all her background information, the essential data contained in her colleague's dupes, some "poetic" license, and her rare gift for riveting metaphor ("Then the switches disconnected, a sound like a dropping of a sack of wheat in the distance"), she did not disappoint her editor.

"I couldn't refuse her," the older writer, who has requested anonymity, recalled. "She was so young and earnest. It seemed to me that her story was better than mine. What the hell—we came out before they did anyway."

Dorothy, characteristically, never forgot that act of generosity. They remained friends for life. Dorothy was as retentive a friend as she was an enemy. And her talents could be galvanized by pique.

When Sheilah Graham arrived in the United States from England, she went to work for the *Evening Journal*. She was not nearly as talented as Dorothy, but she was young, and pretty, and fiercely ambitious for fame. They were assigned to cover, in tandem, the impending execution of three young men who had killed several people in New England. Graham was supposed to turn the hard news over to Dorothy and concentrate on feature material. Using her own Tootsie-Roll innocence, Graham talked her way into the jail where the boys were being held. "I said to the jailers that I'd never been inside an American jail, and they took me inside," she recalled. "Once inside, I got to talk to one of the defendant's mothers, who gave me just the sort of thing I was supposed to turn over to Dorothy."

The two reporters were sharing a room in a local hotel. Since their arrival, Sheilah Graham had watched Dorothy, each night, painstakingly curl her bounteous eyelashes with a little curling iron. The ritual amused the young Englishwoman and, at the same time, somehow angered her. It was so *Dorothy*, so quintessentially Dorothy. After her good luck at the jail, Graham returned to their hotel. She sat up in the bed they shared, watching Dorothy sleep, staring intently at the curled lashes. Dorothy suddenly woke up.

"Can't you sleep?" Dorothy asked.

"I think I have a very good story," Graham said.

"What is it?" Dorothy asked, sitting up in bed.

"I shan't know until tomorrow," Sheilah Graham replied.

Graham recalled: "It was at that moment that I decided not to tell her. I can't tell you why. The following morning, at nine, I telephoned it in myself. They were terrifically excited at the paper. Big headlines. They advised me to get off the feature staff and stay with Dorothy on the news. She never liked me after that. We were sort of rivals." [4]

When the three young men were scheduled to die at Charlestown Prison, Dorothy turned her attention to getting into the death chamber. No, there was no way that they were going to allow anyone but the three male representatives of the major news services to witness the procedure. A compromise was negotiated. She would be permitted to remain in an adjoining room, where a deputy warden would communicate with her over a prison telephone. While Sheilah Graham bided her time back at the hotel, Dorothy sat alone in the bowels of Charlestown Prison—a dreary little room with a lightbulb, a table, and a telephone. She used the deputy warden as her eyes.

"Who's first? How is he walking? Is he clean-shaven? Tell me about his eyes. What color is the door through which he walked? What is the electrocutioner wearing? How many volts? Is he dead? Who pronounced? Is there an odor in the room? . . ."

The story read convincingly. "To be a Hearst reporter," wrote W. A. Swanberg in *Citizen Hearst*, "required talents unsought by sober journalists—a lively imagination, a fictional sense that could touch up news stories with vivid glints, balanced by a subtle understanding of how far one could go without being accused of fakery."

She had just turned twenty when she was assigned to cover her first big murder trial single-handedly. The defendant was Jessie Costello. The place was Salem, Massachusetts. And the scene was one of the most extraordinary in the long history of juridical comedy.

Jessie, thirty-one, was a dark-eyed, Junoesque housewife from Peabody, accused of poisoning her fireman husband, Bill, with cyanide of potassium. Bill and Jessie had produced four children, but the fireman had apparently been a poor mate. He was sullen and pugnacious at home, disposed to reading, praying, or warming his stockinged feet on a radiator in catatonic silence, communicating with the steam.

Jessie would assert that she had not administered the poison discovered in Bill's disinterred body and that it had been purchased to clean the boiler. The state claimed that she had poisoned him so that she could freely continue her love affair with a policeman named Ed McMahon. The affair with McMahon, Jessie protested, was purely spiritual. McMahon said otherwise. He claimed that she had first rebuffed him in a parked car, exclaiming, "Here! Here!"; but she eventually warmed to him. For three and a half months, McMahon boasted on the stand, their relationship was decidedly carnal: "pretty near every day." His clinical delineation of the carnality was too lurid for the newspapers to print in detail. It was bound in red, however, and distributed by a savvy publishing company.

Because of his prideful revelations, McMahon was tagged The Squealing Policeman and The Kiss-and-Tell-Cop. Jessie was called, in various tabloids, The Smiling Widow, The Poison Widow, The Maid of Salem, and by Grace Robinson of the New York *Daily News*, "the perfect female murder defendant."

The trial was news in the first place because Jessie was facing the chair and the state of Massachusetts had never before burned a woman sitting down. Also, wearing her widow's black even during a record-breaking heat wave that July, she photographed stunningly, waving her properly gloved hand, a jaunty tilt to her head, an innocent, unruffled smile on her face. Her serene self-assurance provoked an astonishing wave of public passion in her behalf.

Mobs packed the streets of Salem to cheer her robustly as she rode, in a limousine, from the jail to the courthouse. Her accommodating guards permitted her to stop regularly on the second-story landing of the courthouse, where a large window faced the street, and acknowledge her admiring minions. She once directed her attention to a group of performing midgets who were passing through town. The manager billed them thereafter as "the troupe of midgets who were waved at by Jessie Costello."

The Kiss-and-Tell-Cop was vociferously booed. At the beginning of the trial, a group of women who had organized to defend Jessie Costello accosted the twelve male jurors as they entered the courthouse. "You're all rats if you believe McMahon," one woman shouted. "You shouldn't go home to your wives if you find her guilty," screamed another.

The judge overruled the motion for mistrial that followed the episode, satisfied that the women's expostulations had not reached the jurors' ears. It was, however, obvious from the start that the panel was firmly in Jessie's camp. During one court recess, the twelve men, good, true, and smitten, rose in the jury box, singing to Jessie, "Let Me Call You Sweetheart," "Sweet Adeline," and "My Wild Irish Rose."

During the five weeks of Jessie Costello's flying circus, Dorothy stayed at a small hotel with the other noncelebrity press and worked a seventeen-hour day. She filed 250,000 words about the trial.

She was feeling like Queen of the May and doing a journeyman job. Her stories appeared daily on the front page of the *Journal* under banner headlines: BY DOROTHY KILGALLEN. Then, as Jessie herself was about to take the stand, Adela Rogers St. Johns arrived in town. She rented an oceanfront house in Swampscott, chose the best typewriter in the press room, took over several telephones— and tried probably to take over Dorothy, too. St. Johns was covering the trial for the afternoon Hearst service; this made their respective stories directly competitive.

The two reporters—a generation apart—had an astounding consanguinity. Like Dorothy, St. Johns was mad for her father, Earl Rogers, a prominent California trial lawyer. It was he who had convinced his daughter to abandon her early desire to become an actress and enter the newspaper profession. She was seventeen when he introduced her to William Randolph Hearst, who took her on because she was Earl Rogers's daughter. She became the reigning female superstar of the Hearst Organization.

Now well into her thirties, she still dressed with her father in mind. What she wore was as important to her self-image and professional status as how she wrote. She noted in her heady and first-rate autobiography, *The Honeycomb:*

> Mr. Hearst *starred* reporters. My clothes for the Hauptmann trial [which she would cover, a year later, with Dorothy in attendance] were on my expense account, Hattie Carnegie had worked them out as a

wardrobe. . . . They had to be things Papa would have approved, still they had to be noticeable.[5]

In fact, Dorothy and St. Johns were too close for each other's comfort. And for Jim Kilgallen's. He had reined Dorothy away from the St. Johns prototype since her early childhood. In a subsequent profile of his daughter, Jim boasted that Dorothy was "feminine to her fingertips." He contrasted her to other newspaperwomen with their "mannish hats and clothes." The reference was clearly to St. Johns, whose ultratailored wardrobe included a collection of soft-brimmed hats by Dobbs.

Dorothy was prepared, before Salem, to recoil from the imperious, hard-drinking luminary who was one of the few reporters in the Hearst organization given the freedom of the first-person *I*. Whenever she covered a story, Hearst trucks carried a huge portrait of her by James Montgomery Flagg: ADELA ROGERS ST. JOHNS SAYS.

Given the Hearst pecking order, Dorothy would ordinarily have been subordinated to St. Johns. But such was not the intention of Amster Spiro with regard to the Costello trial. He made the choices at the *Journal*. It fell to him to decide to use the syndicated material provided by St. Johns or the coverage of his own reporter, or *both*. Spiro was no friend to Adela Rogers St. Johns. In *The Honeycomb*, she whacks at him as "the most terrible of The Terrible Men." [6]

Spiro opted to run Dorothy's story next to Adela Rogers St. Johns's, giving each equal play on the front page of the *Journal*. The subject was the cross-examination of Jessie.

Dorothy's lead paragraph read:

> Crying her innocence of husband murder in the same quick breath that denied any guilty love, Jessie Costello stood today on the dangerous brink of the State's cross-examination abyss, fighting like a beautiful tigress, wary but unafraid.

Adela Rogers St. Johns's lead paragraph read:

> Fighting like a wild cat, every claw and tooth bared, Jessie Costello is still undergoing the deadly ordeal of cross-examination.

Adela Rogers St. Johns's coverage of the Costello case in the *Evening Journal* ended with the cross-examination of the wild cat/tigress. Dorothy had her front page back the next day.

And she determined to stay on top of things.

Ed McMahon, the Kiss-and-Tell-Cop, was seething at the treatment he was receiving from the press. There were many lucrative offers for exclusives in the wings, but he refused to see any reporters. Dorothy decided that he *would* see her. Dressed in a pair of low-heeled shoes and a little white dress, she rang McMahon's doorbell. He mistook her for one of the neighborhood children and opened the door.

Once inside, Dorothy convinced McMahon that he had an obligation to himself and his family to tell his side of the story. Presumably, the price was also right. His side ran in two installments: "By Ed McMahon as told to Dorothy Kilgallen":

> "I can't call it love," the Kiss-and-Tell-Cop revealed exclusively to the *Journal*, "Love is what you feel for women like my wife, Mary. . . . Loving Jessie was like getting drunk and doing something you're sorry for afterwards."
>
> He told how he first met the smoldering widow. She was driving through town. He was directing traffic. "Hey, Cop," Jessie said to McMahon, "How would you like to be in here with me?"

Ah, yes, that Kilgallen girl.

The life she was living was as schismatic as it was episodic, split down a hollow center. She dated fellow *Journal* reporter Herb Spiro, Amster's genial younger brother. They drove, at her request, to the far reaches of The Bronx to catch any of the few Ramon Novarro features still in distribution. She wept at romantic novels, talked about movie stars with her sister Eleanor, shopped with her mother at Abraham & Straus, and slept in a girlish room decorated in mixed Louis's, with French dolls lolling.

At the dinner table, she sat quietly as Jim regaled guests with stories about his career. He encouraged Dorothy to tell some of her own. "She had a very high voice and she spoke much too quickly," her friend Eve Wynn recalled, "but once she warmed up and shook off some of her shyness, she was a good raconteur." [7]

Her personality had not yet begun to fulfill itself. She was self-conscious, callow, and uneasy. Yet when she was unencumbered in the field, she was a consummate actress in the service of a headline. The childhood time she had devoted to acting out her little plays for friends proved to be mighty useful in her work.

In 1935, accompanied by photographer Ray Howard, she walked confidently into a trashy saloon in upstate New York to ply an ex–furnace salesman with booze. His name was Harry Nabinger and he was an important figure in the lurid trial of Eva Coo, who was scheduled this night to be executed at Sing Sing prison.

Harry Nabinger had left his wife and children to become Eva Coo's lover. Dubbed Little Eva by the press because she wasn't, Eva had been a local whore who resided in a small town near the Baseball Hall of Fame. She was blond and puffy and known to be big-hearted because she took in indigents and cared for them. What was not known was that Eva took out insurance policies on her needy charges, one of whom was found dumped in a ditch off a major highway in a simulated hit-and-run accident. After a sensational trial, Eva was convicted of the crime. Nabinger was not successfully implicated, though Dorothy had her doubts. On the night of the execution, she was at the bar not to secure a confession but to chronicle his reactions as the time approached for Eva to die.

She entered Noble's Tavern a little after seven in the evening. Eva's own player piano honky-tonked in the background. Nabinger was seated alone in a booth, smoking cigarettes ("the ten-cent kind"), watching the clock, and drinking beer.

Dorothy and Ray Howard bellied up to George Noble's bar and sent Nabinger several rounds of loosening liquor. He refused to talk at first, but finally beckoned them to his table.

"You stay here," she said to Howard, "he'll be freer if I'm alone with him. Make sure his glass is filled."

She sat with him for almost four hours while he rambled on about Eva.

" 'I was disillusioned and I thought I was hard-boiled,' "

Dorothy quoted him in her *Evening Journal* article of June 28, 1935. " 'I heard Eva was hard-boiled. I wanted to see if she could be as tough as I could. Well, I found out she was toughest. She made me look like a sissy. So I stayed on at the roadhouse. I was drunk most of the time.' "

"Will you go home now, Harry?" Dorothy asked.

"I'll never go back home," he slurred. The bartender brought another round. Nabinger stared at her.

"Say, you know I've got a swell kid. My oldest boy. He's taller than you. He's got red hair and blue eyes and he's captain of his football team. He's a swell kid."

Nabinger began to cry. She sat through it.

"Let's dance," he said. "No, let's not. I don't want to dance. This is getting me. I know you think I was in on it."

Dorothy eyed him equably. "Were you, Harry?"

"Listen, I never knew she meant to do it. She stole and she cheated and she ruined men's lives. What time is it?"

"It's after eleven," Dorothy replied. "I've got to call the office."

"I know she won't go," he shouted after her, "something will happen at the last minute."

She telephoned her night city editor, apprised him that Harry Nabinger was loose and lively, and that she'd have her death-watch story in before deadline.

"Is Eva gone?" Dorothy asked.

Journal reporter Joseph Harrington had just phoned in the details of the execution. The prison barber had shaved her head at 10:20. She'd asked him to "save the front." When he complied, she thanked him and said it looked "real nice." She was pronounced dead at 11:07 P.M.

"What were her last words?" Dorothy asked.

The editor checked his notes and read more of Harrington's stuff to her: "Taking her seat, to the two prison matrons, she said, 'Good-bye, darlin's.' "

"To the matrons?"

"Yeah."

"How did she go?"

"Harrington said she was 'game.' "

Dorothy returned to the bar, where Nabinger had begun talking stuporously to Ray Howard. She signaled Howard with a slight nod of her head to prepare his camera. Nabinger walked toward Dorothy unsteadily, his hands leaning into his pants pockets. She said to him softly, "Eva's gone, Harry. She went at seven past eleven and she was pretty game and her last words, to you, were 'Good-bye, darling.' "

Nabinger freaked. "She's not dead. She's not. You're lying. I'll kill you."

He reared back like a palsied pitcher to throw his fist at her. Ray Howard dropped his camera. George Noble jumped over the bar. They pinioned Nabinger's arms.

"I'm sorry, Harry," she said to the sobbing man and went to the telephone to call her story in.

With all of her triumphs, there seems to have been a realization, by Jim and Dorothy, that this was a time for some kind of quantum leap. In four years, she had gone about as far as she could go. Dorothy Kilgallen could out-write, out-wit and out-ruse anyone in yellow journalism. But none of it was moving her into the preferred place, the magic circle. Local girl was making good locally. That was not good enough for Dorothy, who wanted out of the provinces.

Jim, perceiving that the truth was not good enough for his beloved daughter, began taking liberties with it. He would, for instance, claim and have it bruited about within the Hearst organization that she had ferreted out a confession from a high-school girl who had, together with her boyfriend, hacked her mother to death.

Jim wrote:

> the girl was grilled by the police for hours to no avail. She finally asked to go to the ladies' room. There were no matrons available so the police asked Dorothy to go along. . . . After giving Gladys the sympathetic approach, Dorothy asked her how she felt: "How would you feel if they were pelting you with questions, questions, questions?" Dorothy said, "Why don't you tell the truth, Gladys?" Running a comb through her hair, Gladys replied, "Yes, I did it." The *Journal-American* banner read the next day, GLADYS MAC-KNIGHT CONFESSES.[8]

That version of the event copped, for Dorothy, the famous Pall Mall Big Story Award for Notable Service in the Field of Journalism. The award was a gimmicky by-product of a radio and then television program of the forties and fifties that dramatized heroic episodes in the lives of working reporters.

The episode, as rendered, might have focused upon Dorothy the kind of attention she craved at the time; but it did not happen the way Jim wrote it. Dorothy did have her private time with Gladys MacKnight in a Bayonne police station. The young woman, still dressed in the tennis clothes she had been wearing at the time of her arrest, did not deny to Dorothy that she had done the murder. Neither did she confess to her. After a whole night of grilling, with the police whipsawing the two defendants (separating them and telling each that the other had confessed), Gladys broke down and confessed to a police captain named McGrath. After confessing to McGrath, Gladys said to Dorothy: "What the hell. You can only die once. But I'm not afraid of the chair. We were all liquored up. We were under-age and we were not responsible." [9]

Jim would also claim that his daughter was the first reporter to interview Richard Bruno Hauptmann, the alleged kidnapper of the Lindbergh baby. She was not. It was Jim who conducted the first interview with Hauptmann, in his cell. The closest Dorothy got to the beleaguered German carpenter was when she sat behind him during his trial in Flemington, New Jersey. The small courthouse was jammed to the eaves with hundreds of press people. She and the rest of the Hearst reporters were taking turns sitting behind the defendant. Her turn came on the day when the ladder used in the kidnapping was produced in court. Dorothy leaned over, tapped him on the shoulder, and asked: "Well, Richard, what do you think of that?"

He replied, "The man who made that ladder vas a bum carpenter!"

At Flemington, during "the trial of the century," Dorothy must have felt like a flea. She was one of three hundred reporters and writer-types to converge on the small New Jersey town, whose population had been 2,700. She was competing with Damon Runyon, John O'Hara, Walter Winchell, Fannie Hurst, Alexander Woollcott, Edna Ferber, Arthur Brisbane, Ford Madox Ford, and especially Adela Rogers St. Johns. Two and a half million words were dispatched daily from the scene and published in newspapers all over the world.

She tried, this mite of a youngster, to come up with something—anything—during the five-week trial which began in January of 1935. But the territory was overrun. Every conceivable angle was being worked by the press to shed some new light on the crime or dominate the story of the trial.

William Randolph Hearst paid for Hauptmann's entire defense; in return, he agreed to talk only to the Hearst press, which competed among themselves. Anna Hauptmann, his wife, was paid by the *Journal*. Dorothy, for a time, was one of three reporters who stayed with her night and day, escorting her to and from the courtroom, sitting with her in the court, and forming a protective cordon around her to isolate her from the competition. Dorothy hated the job and the woman and was relieved when William Randolph Hearst learned about the situation, and ordered it discontinued.

Dorothy was then assigned, along with several other *Journal* staffers, to cover the running story of the trial. Her writing appeared and had some prominence. But this was an operation directed by the Chief. Adela Rogers St. Johns, dressed in her expense-account Hattie Carnegies, dominated the courtroom, the press room, and the front page. The judge deferred to her. Bailiffs ran errands for her. She spoke to Hearst every night at his castle in San Simeon. And she carried out, center stage, the mandate she had first received from him: "We cannot endure the kidnapping of our children. In this trial, I am sure we can produce a flame of national indignation that will deter other criminals."

Neither Hauptmann nor Dorothy had a chance:

NATION ITSELF ACTS AS JURY TO TRY HAUPTMANN— Adela Rogers St. Johns is in Flemington to write a spectacular daily article on the trial of Bruno Richard Hauptmann for the kidnap murder of the Lindbergh baby. Read her story every day in the New York *Journal*.

ADELA ROGERS ST. JOHNS SAYS: Somebody kidnapped that baby, somebody killed him and left Lindy and Anne to those nights and days of hell and crucifixion. Who was it?

Today we begin the trial of Bruno Hauptmann for that crime.

ADELA ROGERS ST. JOHNS SAYS:
In this small, drab old courthouse packed with humanity, we are again living every horror, every anguish, every suspense, every dastardly step of the murder of our Little Eagle.

ADELA ROGERS ST. JOHNS SAYS:
Not one person in that courtroom would have been surprised if suddenly Lindy had risen from his seat and grasped Hauptmann by the throat . . . we were waiting for it.

ADELA ROGERS ST. JOHNS SAYS:
KEEP YOUR HANDS OFF OUR CHILDREN

Dorothy was envious. And she took her anger out on Sheilah Graham, among others. Graham was contriving to secure an exclusive interview with Betty Gow, the child's Scottish governess, by pretending to be a correspondent from Glasgow. She was about to pull it off when a nettled Dorothy learned of the ruse and complained to the lawyer who had set it up. She queered it for both of them. "She didn't get it. I didn't get it. So nobody got it," Graham recalled.[10]

According to St. Johns, she and Dorothy clashed at the very beginning of the trial. Dorothy bristled that she knew the truth about how St. Johns had managed all that "Adela Rogers St. Johns Says" jazz and it had nothing to do with her talents as a reporter.

The trial of the century made Dorothy's status painfully clear to her. Adela could be bruised but not touched. She was the Chief's faithful, adoring adjutant. And Dorothy could never compete successfully on the older woman's turf.

On a Sunday night in the late summer of 1936, Dorothy was out on the town with Herb Spiro. They dined at a fancy restaurant called Armando's. Dorothy favored Armando's because pretty people went there and because the management featured a quiz competition on weekends which she and Herb often won. This Sunday was no exception. To celebrate their victory, the couple went to the Stork Club for a nightcap. Here they were reconnoitered by Walter Winchell, who was at his usual table, reconnoitering. Winchell called. Dorothy, unimpressed by journalistic celebrities, groaned. Winchell was sitting alone, and that meant merciless exposure to his habitual monologues.

In the course of his rambling, Winchell mentioned a globe-girdling air race between Herbert Ekins of Scripps-Howard and Leo Kieran of *The New York Times*. Helluva stunt! The dash would begin when Pan American Airlines set a firm date for the inauguration of its passenger service between Manila and San Francisco.

"Gosh, Dorothy," Herb said, "that would be a wonderful thing for you to do." He splayed two canonical fingers to indicate the fantasy headline: "GIRL AROUND THE WORLD!"

"Spi would never let me go, would he?" she queried.

He would when he was reminded of Nellie Bly.

Nellie Bly was born Elizabeth Cochrane in Cochrane Mills, Pennsylvania, a town founded by her father, a judge. Rendered penniless in her teens, she began her reporting career in Pittsburgh. She moved up, in 1887, to Joseph Pulitzer's gamy New York *World*. There she made a quick and splashy success through a series of stupefying adventures. She plumbed the ocean's depths in a diving bell, soared in a balloon, and exposed the abuses inside a mental institution to which she gained admittance by posing as a lunatic.

Nellie was twenty-three years old in November, 1889, when she was dispatched by the *World* on one of the most colorful circulation gimmicks in the history of two-penny journalism. Pulitzer sent her on a trip around the world with orders to beat the fictive record set by Jules Verne's Phileas Fogg, the protagonist of *Around the World in 80 Days*.

She left with no more clothes than could be packed into her tweed portmanteau and carrying purse. She wore a double-peaked, rakish cap. She picked up a monkey along the way, and returned, a day ahead of schedule, a very famous woman. Traveling time—by boat, mule, trains, bullock carts, catamarans, sampans, and, she claimed, "half a dozen other conveyances peculiar to Eastern countries"—seventy-two days, six hours, eleven minutes.

Amster Spiro obviously had Nellie on his mind in late September, 1936, when he summoned twenty-three-year-old Dorothy Kilgallen to pack her own portmanteau and prepare in forty-eight hours (though her *Evening Journal* would assert it had only been twenty-four) to dash around the world in twenty-one days. It was a plum assignment—the plummiest. Dorothy had dreamed since childhood of the romance of foreign ports. And stardom, too. Amster Spiro assured her that her running story would be front page all the way. Dorothy was jittery with excitement, if not entirely surprised.

Whose idea it was finally to dispatch Dorothy is anybody's guess. Dorothy's own rendition changed several times. She would tell one colleague eventually that it had been her idea from the beginning, though the story is belied by the recollection of Herb Spiro. His brother Amster, prodded by the public announcements of both the *Times* and Scripps-Howard's *World-Telegram*, could easily have thought his own thoughts of a modern Nellie Bly; and the paper, at the time, credited him with the notion to include Dorothy. Jim Kilgallen, of course, cannot be discounted, either. He had been inspired to enter the profession in the first place by the fantasy of a globe-girdling adventure, and was now most eager to advance the progress of his little girl's career.

Whatever the genesis, the idea was a timely one indeed. Speed, in the mid-thirties, was a national obsession. Highways were being built to accommodate automobiles that could go as fast as sixty miles an hour. Ocean liners like the brand new *Queen Mary* or the *Normandie* were continually breaking new records. The streamlined look, functional in cars, trains, and automobiles, had insinuated itself even into the design of stationary objects. Frederick Lewis Allen, in *Since Yesterday*, observed that the spiffy new trains made of stainless steel or duralumin, when placed on exhibition, drew crowds that "surged entranced. . . . It was all new and exciting, this world of beautiful speed."

Flight—higher, faster, and first—made international colossi of people like Amelia Earhart, Charles Lindbergh, Howard Hughes, James Mollison, Jean Batten, J. H. Doolittle, and Wiley Post. Yet *commercial* air travel, which epitomized the possibilities of speed made available to the ordinary traveler, was in its infancy in the 1930s. In 1924, when Dorothy was eleven, there was not a single commercial airline operating in the United States. Not until May, 1936, when the dirigible *Hindenberg* inaugurated regular air service between Germany and the United States, was the North Atlantic bridged by a regular airline.[1] The journey was still considered too perilous for passengers traveling in airplanes.

The notion to send a reporter around the world aloft—as a passenger—to essay the experience of globe-girdling originated with Scripps-Howard, several of whose editors were scrupulously attentive to the proposed new service and its implications for months before the actual date was set. When they received word that the *China Clipper* would be licensed to carry passengers from Manila to San Francisco on October 16, 1936, they assigned the story to Bud Ekins.

Ekins was thirty-six at the time, a hard-working, rock-ribbed, real McCoy international newsman: scrappy, shrewd, and competitive. He was a native of Minneapolis, a minister's boy, who had worked for *The New York Times*, the *Graphic*, and even the *Evening Journal*. He had joined United Press International in 1925 and had managed their offices in the Far East for six years. He had recently been expelled from Ethiopia, where he was covering the Italian campaign to conquer the African nation. His anti-Fascist reporting had angered Mussolini.[2]

Utilizing the *China Clipper*, Bud Ekins set out to break the existing round-the-world speed record of John Mears and Captain C.B.D. Collyer, who, in 1928, had circled the globe in twenty-three days and fifteen hours. He would do it, he asserted, "by means of regular transportation services." [3]

The problem, of course, was to get to the *China Clipper* in time for its inaugural departure from Manila. In the nine days that Ekins claimed he had to prepare for the trip, he scrutinized the schedules of every airline in the world, gauged their speed and reliability, considered alternate scenarios in case of missed connections, and covered bases that neither of his prospective competitors knew existed.

In fact, during this period of intense preparation, he was unaware that his two competitors existed at all.

On Saturday, September 26, four days before the first leg of the journey, his newspaper headlined: WORLD-TELEGRAM MAN TO GIRDLE THE GLOBE BY REGULAR AIRLINES.

The seemly gray lady of journalism, *The New York Times*, quietly announced, on the very next day, a similar endeavor. Their Leo Kieran had been contemplating the dash for almost a year. He told young Bob Trout, of CBS radio, that if his scenario succeeded, he would set a new record for circumnavigation. But his primary goal was didactic: to demonstrate the possibilities of globe-girdling as they existed for the ordinary passenger in the new air age.

Like Ekins, Leo Kieran was an experienced reporter in his middle thirties at the time of the trip. His own seasoning had rendered him a lot less tough than Bud Ekins, though he was not lacking in tenacity. He was a slender, blue-eyed, fair-haired man from a literary New York family.[4]

Dorothy was, in every way, the dark horse on this one. At twenty-three, she had never even been out of the United States. Her experience aloft was limited to one short flight just to get the feel of it. Her 7A teacher, back at P.S. 119, had written at the bottom of an otherwise excellent report card, "not proficient in geography." And now, assuredly, she was the only one of the three reporters who was impelled, upon receiving this exhilarating, jazzy international assignment, to secure not only passport, visas, and flight reservations—but also the permission of her *mother*.

She telephoned Mae with trepidation, asserting—and meaning it—that she would turn down the assignment if her mother opposed it. Mae Kilgallen was a nervous, fretful, insular woman whose sensibilities were invariably a generation behind her worldly husband's. They were more consonant with Dorothy's Chicago aunts, Mrs. Margaret Gallagher and Mrs. Clair O'Connor, who would declare, on being apprised of their niece's itinerary by a *Journal* reporter in search of a story, that Germany and France were safe enough, but "China and the heathen Orient is no place for a little girl." It may be surmised safely that Mae was never more regretful that Dorothy did not finish college and go on to teach English composition at Erasmus Hall High, a trolley-ride away.

Though Mae decreed on manners and morals for her two daughters, Dorothy's career and all pertinent decisions were Jim Kilgallen's bailiwick. "It's a hell of an assignment," he told Mae. "I won't stop her." [5]

By the time the *Evening Journal* made their sudden decision to enter their girl reporter in the dash, Bud Ekins and Leo Kieran had already planned itineraries and secured reservations. The centerpiece of the action, as acknowledged by all three newspapers, was the westerly inaugural passenger flight of Pan American's *China Clipper*, leaving

Manila in mid-October. The linchpin was the *Hindenburg*, set to sail from Lakehurst, New Jersey, to Frankfort, Germany, on September 30. Since this was the only way to traverse the Atlantic quickly, and the October trip was the last crossing of the season, the German behemoth was the only game in town.

Between Europe and Asia, three airlines operated scheduled passenger service: Air France, KLM, and Imperial, the British precursor of BOAC. Leo Kiernan, early on, made no secret of his intention to fly Imperial. Bud Ekins was going KLM, the Dutch line that flew American-built planes.[6] But as late as September 29, neither he nor his paper were revealing that fact.

Dorothy hadn't a clue as to how she was going to get to the *China Clipper*. The *Hindenburg* ticket, in fact, was the only leg of the trip that was problem-free for her.

Dorothy's race really started stateside. Darting in and out of Yellow Cabs with loyal Herb Spiro at her side, assigned by his brother, Spi, to do nothing but facilitate her preparations, she had two days to secure sixteen visas, sundry reservations, her first passport, five dresses, a new hat, and a stylish winter coat with fox furs. The fox furs, like the *Hindenburg*, were no problem. Securing her visas was. She had first to obtain a passport. And for the passport, she needed either a birth or baptismal certificate. Both of them had been somehow lost or misplaced in the Kilgallens' home in Flatbush. Mae Kilgallen had, therefore, to swear out an affidavit that Dorothy had been born in the United States.

Jim Kilgallen was doing his part with his political dialing finger, obtaining whatever dispensations he could on his daughter's behalf. Among the many calls he made was one to Irene Kuhn, a journalist who had been stationed all over the globe on various assignments.

"You know, Irene," Jim said. "I think my little girl is trying to emulate you."

"Oh, really," Irene answered. "What's up?"

"Well, you've always been known for your adventure. And Dorothy's about to undertake something. It's confidential, but she's going to try to break a world's record by flying around the globe. I wonder if you'd provide her with a couple of letters of introduction to some of the people who might be able to help her in Manila and Shang-hai. . . ." [7]

Meanwhile, back at the city room, Amster Spiro was muscling her aboard whatever conveyances he could book. The inaugural flight of the *China Clipper*, which could carry no more than a dozen press people on the long last hop of its trans-Pacific journey, had been booked solid for months, long before the final date was even determined. There was simply no room, he was told, for an additional passenger and her luggage.

Spi checked the *Clipper* passenger list, found it to consist entirely of men, and decided to turn a full load into a feminist issue. Unless the airline permitted Dorothy to board, he threatened to run a front-page exposé on the lack of female facilities on the new *Clipper* flights.

Not for nothing was Amster Spiro the highest paid editor in the Hearst organization.[8] Juan Trippe, the young president and founder of Pan American, found a spot for Dorothy on the Manila–San Francisco flight of the *China Clipper*.

What did remain to be handled on behalf of Dorothy, even as she left her South Street office to catch the *Hindenburg*, were the intermediary jumps between Germany and Manila. In their introductory, front-page splash about the trip, the *Evening Journal* implored:

DOROTHY NEEDS HELP!
Any American firm with representatives traveling in Europe is asked to cable their representatives to sell a seat to Dorothy Kilgallen and notify the New York *Evening Journal*. It's a girl against the world—and the girl needs help.

A squally autumn rain pelted New York City on the day of the dashers' departure, grounding the shuttle plane that ordinarily flew from Newark to the naval base at Lakehurst from which the *Hindenburg* was set to sail at 11:17 P.M. Each of the participants was forced to alter his plans and motor to the site of the giant airship.

Their departures were timed officially by the National Aeronautical Society, which had representatives with stopwatches at *The New York Times*, the *World-Telegram*, and the *Evening Journal*.

Leo Kieran, in a soft camel's-hair coat, with one piece of luggage and a copy of the newly published *Gone with the Wind* under his arm—a gift from his publisher, Arthur Sulzberger—left *The New York Times* building in Times Square at 7:43 P.M. The paper had arranged for him to duck into a waiting American Airlines limo that was slated to pick up Bud Ekins, and then proceed to Lakehurst escorted by motorcycle police. Kieran declined the VIP car and the escort on the grounds that an ordinary traveler would not be accorded such privileges. Instead, he walked with his new wife and several colleagues east to Vanderbilt Avenue and waited, in the rain, for the airlines bus.[9]

Bud Ekins, whose departure from the *World-Telegram* building was clocked at 8:17:30 P.M., accepted the perquisites. He wore a dark new suit, carried several more shirts than Kieran, and had with him, for luck, a black glove from a mysterious woman, whom he refused to identify, and the very same pocketflask that Nellie Bly had toted around the world, rather less publicly.[10] A New York police escort convoyed him and his entourage to the Holland Tunnel. On the Jersey side, representatives of the Newark and Jersey City police departments took over. Among the escorted entourage, riding in the car with Bud, were two goons from the circulation department, for protection.[11]

Ekins's bruisers were there because of a rumor that had originated within the Hearst organization, whose editors had a tendency to endow others with their own world view. Sitting around one day discussing the race, the guys in the city room playfully entertained the possiblity that someone in Ekins's camp might make an attempt to eliminate Dorothy from the running by causing her to be snatched en route to the *Hindenburg*.[12] As they were perfectly capable of any kind of foul play themselves, it was reasonable for them to assume that others were. What began as a playful possibility became a serious threat. Like a cat spooked by its own shadow, Hearstlings responded nervously to their own murky mendacity. Dorothy, they decided, had to be heavily guarded. Ekins responded in kind.

According to the *Evening Journal*, their Dorothy had chosen to leave the office at 5:24 P.M., well before her rivals. She had hied over to the Vanderbilt Avenue station of American Airlines and there taken "the bus" to Lakehurst. That it was followed by three newspaper trucks filled with large men from the circulation department armed with wrenches and blackjacks did not necessarily render the car in which she rode any less "regular."

Dorothy was met by her father inside the damp passenger hangar at Lakehurst. He had come in specially from an out-of-town assignment to act as buffer, PR man, and coach to his daughter, who, as she was being interviewed and photographed, was knocking out an overnight about the first leg of her journey. She carried one bag and, for luck, the portable typewriter that Jim had used when he was in hot pursuit of Samuel Insull. Eleanor was home comforting Mae, who had been too overwrought to see Dorothy off.

As Dorothy sat dealing with her sudden celebrity, she wore what even Bud Ekins conceded to be "a really stunning traveling outfit": basic black dress, beautifully detailed; belted black coat trimmed at the neck with fox furs that seemed sanguine in service. Over her intricately curled, luxuriant hair, she donned a small piece of felt, fringed by a veil, which she lifted to type. She sat bolt upright, as she'd been trained to sit, with her thin but well-shaped legs planted firmly on the ground.

"Aboard Dirigible *Hindenburg,*" she typed. "I'm off on a race around the world—a race against time and two men. I know I can beat time. I hope I can beat the men."

In her thin, high voice, she answered other newsmen's questions with an edgy blitheness. It was the first time that questions were being asked of her. And in addition to being girl around the world, she was girl in search of a public *persona.* She ran the gamut from Betty Coed to Buster Brown.

Yes, the preparations had been hectic and she did have to break a date here and there: "But I love calling a young man on the telephone and saying, 'Sorry, I can't go to the Yale-Cornell game, I'm on my way to Hong Kong.' "

Yes, she had taken along a good luck charm, her father's perdurable, no-nonsense portable: "My own is two shades of orchid and far prettier. But it's a sissy's typewriter."

Yes, her mother was quite well, but "she was a bit upset."

Jim stood over her, shaking hands with colleagues and introducing them to his "little girl." His dapper hat, more Bond than Fleet Street, was pushed to the back of his head as though, in spite of the cold, he had been mopping his brow.

Microphones were stuck in both their faces. "Of course, I'm a little worried," Jim said. "But it's a fine assignment." Suffering her usual panic at the sight of a microphone, Dorothy leaned over shyly, bit her lips, and said only: "Gee, I hope I'm around in time." [13]

Telegrams continued to arrive. Dorothy opened each one excitedly and handed it in turn to Jim to take home to Mae. He stuffed them into his already overburdened pockets, out of which note paper and pencils jutted.

Amelia Earhart cheered her on with a personal telegram:

> I know you can make it, Dorothy, but you must follow your normal schedule of eating, drinking, and sleeping, even though on such a trip. Forget you are flying and you won't even get air weary. Imagine you are back in the Evening Journal office and stick to one brand of bottled water throughout.[14]

Women's groups from all over the country wired their good wishes and solidarity. The president of the New York State Federation of Business and Professional Women's Clubs exulted: "It is the sort of achievement which all women in the city can unite in cheering." [15]

She posed for endless pictures, all of them replicating previous reality: calling Mom, opening telegrams, typing a story, speaking into a microphone.

Aware of the camera, she appeared tight and callow and solitary. There was no ease in her.

The *Hindenburg*, two footfall fields long, floated on its moorings at 11:00 P.M. On its 150-foot fin, a sizeable swastika predominated. ("The swastika must not resemble a postage stamp," Adolf Hitler had personally commanded. "It must be big, beautiful, and clearly visible.") Ekins and Kieran and an almost full complement of passengers had boarded.

At 11:05, the cry went out, "Where is Miss Kilgallen?" The *Journal* would print that departure time had been set at 11:17, that Dorothy had almost missed the dirigible while concentrating on the completion of her overnight story in the crude structure that functioned as the passenger terminal, and that she had to thumb a ride across the field to get within boarding distance of the ship.[16] Dorothy was photographed on the steps of the *Hindenburg*, svelte and dry, hardly the look of a mad dasher in the pelting rain.

Bud Ekins's account, told to the *New York Post* in 1960, seems more credible by far:

> It was like a scene from a Mack Sennett comedy. I arrived in a car with two big guys from the circulation department to protect me. When Dotty arrived, she was in a big black limousine, with detectives on both sides of her, and behind her were two or three newspaper trucks filled with bruisers from the circulation department. When she got out of the car they surrounded her and made damn sure she got on the ship —only of course they stopped to pose for pictures first. And while all this was going on, Kieran, as befitting a man from the *Times,* had arrived all by himself carrying his own suitcase.

Before the boarding, Dorothy kissed Jim lovingly on the mouth, told him that her coat was warm enough, bade him to assure her mother that she would attend Sunday mass whenever possible and to remind Herb Spiro that they were to collaborate on a screenplay about the race just as soon as she returned.[17]

The anxiety that Dorothy felt on boarding the *Hindenburg* was presently abated by the isolating, almost preternaturally quiet drift of the giant airship—a dazzling in-flight peacefulness that astonished all its first-time passengers. Lady Drummond-Hay, the journalistic dean of flying female passengers, had been aboard the *Hindenburg* on its inaugural North Atlantic crossing earlier that year. At the pope's insistence, she reported, and much to Hitler's dismay, a mass had been celebrated to sanctify the passenger lounge. The ship was so steady that not a drop of the ceremonial wine had been spilled.

Dorothy stood on one of the several observation decks until the ship headed out to sea, and then proceeded to her stateroom. Actually, the stateroom was somewhat smaller than an ordinary Pullman compartment. There were twenty-five such cubicles on the *Hindenburg*, all of them electrically lit, with toilets, hot and cold water, a berth that converted into a sofa by day, and fresh jonquils for each passenger. The walls were decorated in pearl gray linen, and a cord could be pulled for assistance from the one stewardess or any of the six stewards.[1]

Mrs. Emily Imhoff, who was working that flight, was beckoned by Dorothy to help her with her hair. Mrs. Imhoff, along with the rest of the crew, was most favorably impressed by the young journalist. They all perceived that she was terribly nervous upon boarding but that she relaxed once she had staked out the territory. She was well-mannered, jolly, inquisitive. The German staff was impressed by her industriousness, her cleanliness, and her efficiency.[2]

The first night aboard was festive. Dorothy changed her dress and met her two colleagues in the commodious passenger lounge. Starving after the frantic hurly-burly of preparations, she wolfed down several ham sandwiches and a lot of fine German beer. The three unwound together until almost four in the morning, and they decided to pool some of their notes. But Ekins was still not pooling a word about his plans.

Dorothy was not yet sure what her office had arranged for her once she landed in Frankfort but expressed the hope that Spi had somehow managed to obtain a seat for her on British Imperial Airways, which flew from Brindisi, on the southern heel of the Italian boot, through to the East. It was precisely Kieran's route. Ekins listened smugly.

Though they maintained the facade of friendship, the trio broke gingerly into enemy camps. Kilgallen-Kieran versus Ekins. Ekins thought Dorothy rather silly and no threat at all. He was threatened somewhat by Kieran at first, but his guilelessness and his excessive drinking mollified those fears. Dorothy liked Kieran for his casual charm. She was not threatened by him and he was implacably unthreatened by anyone. Ekins she found arrogant, secretive, and, worst of all, competitive.

The trio's dynamics resounded in their copy, which they were impelled, because of the expense involved, to file in cable-ese, which read like terse, hurried Pig Latin. Kieran's stories were given respectable play every day, usually in the second section of *The New York Times*. There was no mention of a race, except against the clock. Kilgallen and Ekins were mentioned, but only as traveling companions engaged in a similar endeavor. His stories consisted of news about weather, delays, food, comfort or the lack of it, topography, and scheduling.

Bud Ekins's stories were splashed on the front page of the *World-Telegram* daily under headlines like: EKINS DODGING STORM AT SEA. While he performed a journeyman's job of reporting, he also launched, from the beginning, an *ad hominem* attack on both his rivals. "Gallantly ignoring a stomach ache that may have been caused by the egg Miss Kilgallen fried in the ship's kitchen," he wrote on their second day out, "Leo Kieran wanders about trying to get other passengers to write stories for him."

He had started jabbing at Dorothy on the first day out, remarking that she had changed the part in her hair from the side to the middle, "giving rise to the suspicion that she had done so after seeing the *World-Telegram*'s picture of Nellie Bly." [3] A good globe-girdler Nellie Bly had been; a beauty she never was. To add insult to calumny, he wrote: "She certainly knows how to apply lipstick and mascara, but she had better stop biting her lips. It gets lipstick on her teeth."

Dorothy did not yet respond in kind, though she did tally small victories such as having a stateroom in the forepart of the *Hindenburg,* which gave her a racing lead over her two rivals, who were aft of her.[4] But the race had not really begun yet. That was coy frippery.

The thrust of her copy and the success of her running stories were not dependent on brickbats or descriptions of the wondrous sensations of flight or painterly pictures of the luxurious *Hindenburg.* Dorothy's copy was relentlessly about Dorothy—her reactions, her opinions, her activities. It was the first time she was allowed the freedom of the *I,* and it was a heady experience. She loved it. And it was precisely what Amster Spiro had in mind when he sent her.

A successful editor of an early Hearst rag once noted that what the organization pursued in its famous stunt stories was the evocation of the "gee-whiz emotion" in its readers. Blatantly opposing phenomena—Abbotts and Costellos —were the best evokers of the gee-whiz emotion. When, for instance, the *Graf Zeppelin* had made its first flight over the North Pole, William Randolph Hearst himself suggested that a submarine be dispatched to race the lofty craft from beneath the ocean's depths. Their headlines would have undoubtedly played on the high-low theme, as in: THE SKY ABOVE, THE SLUDGE BELOW. When it was suggested to him that sending a submarine under the polar depths was reckless if not impossible, he suggested cutting holes through the ice to permit the ship to pass. When it was suggested to Mr. Hearst that his idea was not, given current technology, feasible, he lost all interest in the *Graf Zeppelin.*

Thus, Dorothy's assignment. A woman competing in a manly task was eminently gee-whiz-worthy; a *girl,* jejune and starry-eyed, was gee-whiz-worthier. Her own innocent, excited, first-time-out-emotions—the gee whiz that resulted from her own gee whiz—were featured. She was encouraged to go with those emotions. It was gimmicky, but authentic. Dorothy's innocence and her professional ebullience were as much a part of her as her competence, her tenacity, and her febrile need to win. She was a very young twenty-three, in spite of the fact that she had seen crime and corpses in abundance.

Receiving a radiogram aboard the *Hindenburg* informing her that the paper had managed to secure reservations for her across Europe and Asia, she led her dispatch off with: "Hooray! Three cheers for Imperial Airways and a tiger for Merry England." When she was given the standard tour and allowed to fool with some surrogate controls on the dirigible, she exulted: "Thrill of thrills. I actually stood at the controls of the giant Hindenburg, actually steering her." There was no poetry in her prose, no lucky phrase about the feeling of making the giant sway. Her communicated exhilaration sufficed.

Despite the *Hindenburg*'s excruciatingly slow passage over the Atlantic—the bad weather had slowed the ship down for some time to less than 40 knots, half its usual cruising speed—and the resulting concern about missed connections, the two days that Dorothy spent on the dirigible were the most pleasurable lap of the journey.

There were parties on each of the two nights aloft. Dorothy did her share of drinking and dancing. She laughed at Leo Kieran's Fred Astaire impression as he glided her around the floor. She managed, despite the weather, to glimpse the exciting coastline of England and a little of Ireland. She would remember, with great fondness, Mrs. Imhoff's inimitable wake-up knocks on her door: "Get up! We have outside Inklunt." [5]

Dorothy continued to get on splendidly with both crew and passengers, though the language barrier made for some misunderstandings. At one point, she wandered into the kitchen, where the cooks were singing a spirited, militaristic song about the glorious future of Germany. Dorothy, seeing such beatified faces, assumed the song to be about love. She clasped her two hands over her heart in pantomimed query. The gesture was construed as a salute. And Dorothy was quite perplexed when the kitchen staff dropped their ladles and snapped to attention. [6]

As the airship sailed smoothly toward Frankfort, she made the acquaintance of General Ritter von Epp, governor-general of Bavaria, one of Hitler's oldest and most trusted friends. A period of mutual seduction followed. The stocky, mustachioed Nazi, who charmed Dorothy with his

Prussian good manners, endeavored to obtain whatever favorable attention he could cull for his nation and his führer through her and her newspaper. He was on his way to lunch with Hitler, and he invited Dorothy to join them. She, on the other hand, wanted whatever favors von Epp could bestow upon her, notably his arm as he de-ballooned. As the highest ranking officer aboard, he would be the first off the *Hindenburg*. She had been vowing to Ekins and Kieran that she would be the first to touch German soil, and she knew that von Epp could arrange that.[7]

Dorothy was the more successful of the two cultivators. An INS representative in Germany cabled the *Evening Journal*:

> DOROTHY ACCORDED ALL COURTESIES DISTINGUISHED VISITOR WHEN LANDED GERMANY STOP THIS DUE FACT SHE MADE FRIENDS WITH GENERAL VON EPP GOVERNOR BAVARIA ONE HITLERS STRONGEST MEN VON EPP FIRST DISEMBARK FOLLOWED EXFIRST REGULAR PASSENGER VON EPP HELPED HER DOWN STAIRS AND LANDING[8]

This was translated into the gargantuan headline: DOROTHY WINS FIRST LEG OF AIR RACE.

She was impelled to refuse von Epp's invitation because of the exigencies of time and scheduling. For years, she referred to that refusal as her greatest journalistic gaffe. "Imagine," she would say, "I actually turned down an opportunity for a private interview with Adolf Hitler." [9]

In fact, it was a blessing for Dorothy and the world that she never availed herself of that opportunity. The Germans, in 1936, were involved in a vigorous campaign to publicize, especially through aviation-related people, the invincibility of German air power. Charles Lindbergh had been gulled by a display of German aviational superiority, and it is believed by some that his credulity was an important factor in Chamberlain's capitulation.[10]

Given Hearst's pro-German sensibilities and Dorothy's political ignorance, it is well that she attended to her itinerary.

The *Hindenburg*, jockeyed into its huge hangar by two hundred fifty uniformed Nazis,[11] arrived in Frankfort six hours late. The Lufthansa plane, which all three reporters had planned to board—Ekins to catch his first KLM connection at Athens, Kilgallen-Kieran to get to Rome—had long since taken off. While Dorothy and Kieran waved to a crowd of German enthusiasts who had come to see the *weltflieger*, Ekins, without a parting word, walked across the field to a waiting KLM Douglas plane and was aloft within minutes. He fudged rather well in his account. But according to one source, it was at this point that Ekins first circumvented the rules. The *Bee-Hive*, house organ of the United Aircraft Corporation, referred to that plane in its November 1936 issue as a "chartered Hornet-powered Douglas of KLM." He used it to catch up with the regular KLM flight in Athens.

Dorothy was convoyed through the crowd of well-wishers by General Ritter von Epp and Hearst's man in Germany, Pierre Huss. With the assistance of each, she booked a regular flight to Munich, after which she now planned to take a series of precariously scheduled trains that might get her to Brindisi just in time to catch the Imperial Airlines flight. It was a risky affair but the only law-abiding scenario to which she would consent.

Tragically, the *Hindenburg* flight from which she departed with so many happy memories was the last safe North Atlantic crossing the dirigible would make. On its return trip to the United States, in the spring of 1937, it exploded at Lakehurst, killing thirty-six people. Mrs. Emily Imhoff was among those who perished.

Dorothy warmed to both Hitler's Germany and Mussolini's Italy, the former for its charming customs and gracious manners, the latter for its colorful and operatic military costume. With time between connections, she hit the October Festival in Munich, rode a red horse on a merry-go-round, and learned to say "tomato soup" in German. Moving through Bologna, she marveled at the theatricality of the young soldiers she saw everywhere:

> The cream of the Italian military, their uniforms looking like stage costumes, was strolling around the stations. What splendid uniforms the Italians wear! And such variety. It looks for all the world like a style show staged for my benefit.[12]

In Florence, she was cheered by a mass of parading Fascisti who presented her with a bouquet of red carnations.

This was all quite wonderful, but her mind was always racing ahead. There was, at the moment, no *now* for Dorothy. She glanced frequently at the two watches she wore: the petite feminine one, on her right hand, which she adjusted to local time; her father's bulkier job, worn on her left hand, running eastern standard. Real time.

She panicked when the train to Rome was delayed forty-five minutes, seriously imperiling her chances of catching the Brindisi-bound train that would take her to the Imperial flight. In the Rome station, she saw two railway policemen coming toward her, probably to check her papers. Across the tracks, the Brindisi train strained, ready to go. There was no time for delay. She grabbed her case, ran around the back of the first train, leaped across the tracks in her open-toed opera pumps, and jumped aboard the already-moving Brindisi express.[13] She was very much her father's daughter, though Jim, if his hagiographers are to be believed, might have chicken-fed the tracks with marbles just in case the police had given chase.

Back at South Street, New Yorkers were queuing up to grab the *Evening Journal* hot off the presses. Dorothy's dispatches, headlined in extrabold, 8-pica streamers, outshouted the Civil War in Spain, the Roosevelt campaign, and even the latest and most lurid hatchet murder. At a press conference of Jim Farley's, the master pol and postmaster general who was managing FDR's presidential campaign, the first question asked was: "Where's Dorothy now?" Hearst photographers covered the Kilgallen home in Flatbush, snapping pictures of Eleanor; Jim; Mae; Cotton, the cat; and Mitzi, the poodle. Mae said that her nervousness had abated but that Jim was impossibly jittery.

An exhausted, sinfully grimy Dorothy Kilgallen arrived at the Italian resort town of Brindisi at 4 A.M., October 5 (October 4 back in Brooklyn). She had not been able even to shower since the *Hindenburg* and she looked forward to a leisurely bath before she boarded the Imperial plane in two hours. Her felt fringe was looking worn.

She taxied to the Hotel Internazionale, where she was dismayed to learn that the tubs were full up with Italian tourists, who were using them as beds. Moreover, the plane had not even arrived yet, and its departure time had been moved up from 6 A.M. to noon. Her feelings were mixed.

At least there would be time for a night's sleep in an immobile bed.

She was fast asleep, wearing one of the several pairs of pajamas her mother had packed for her, when a voice from an adjoining room called, "That you, Dorothy?" [14]

It was Kieran, who had himself just arrived in Brindisi, relieved, since it was after 6 A.M., to find that the flight had been delayed. Dorothy put on her flannel robe and the bunny mules her paper described as a gift from singer Helen Morgan, and invited the weary Kieran in, her curiosity overwhelming her need for sleep.

Leo Kieran told of his frantic dash from Frankfort to Brindisi. The train he was on was not scheduled to get to Brindisi until well after six. He rushed off in Bologna, looking for another connection. The situation was further complicated by the fact that his Italian was limited to the phrase "*Presto! Presto!*" which, though not irrelevant, was not entirely sufficient, either. The connection he sought did not exist on Sunday. And there was no choice then but to rent a car, which for Kieran, who had stood in the rain on Vanderbilt Avenue rather than avail himself of either special or privileged transportation, was a most compromising maneuver. The 450-mile drive to Brindisi, along narrow mountain roads, had been the hairiest experience of his life.[15] He told Dorothy that he was several times tempted to yell, "No. *Presto. Presto.*" They laughed heartily over breakfast about the vicissitudes of their respective dashes, but she was not above reminding him that he was fortunate that the plane had been delayed.

Weighing on her mind, however, was the progress of the adversative man from the *World-Telegram*. Her own paper had learned of Ekins's special flight and cabled the news to Dorothy. He was now referred to by the boys in the city room as "that sonuvabitch from the *World*." Dorothy hadn't realized, back in Frankfort, that Ekins was playing by somewhat different rules. But she was fast catching on.

He and his paper had been wily. The term *regularly scheduled* had been avoided. Instead, the *World-Telegram* had described Bud Ekins's endeavor as "the inception of the first attempt to circumnavigate the world by means of regular commercial airlines . . . *over routes available to anyone.*" They had not averred *planes available to anyone.* Strictly speaking, that did not preclude chartering the plane of a commercial airline or availing oneself of a special plane offered by a commercial airline, providing it flew over a route that was customarily traversed by a scheduled flight.

Dorothy's copy from Brindisi announced her somewhat altered game plan. She boasted that she had so far "stuck religiously to regular service, available to anyone." She claimed that she would continue to do so as long as possible. "But," she added, "I'm not going to miss the *China Clipper* at Manila." She warned that she would charter planes if and when that proved necessary.

This codicil reflected a pattern, a mind set, that prevailed over the years and reached into many areas of her life. She would play by the rules until such time as someone else fractured them. And then she would play by ear. In publicly announcing her intention to charter if necessary, she never mentioned Ekins's behavior as justification. Her "brothers" at Hearst did that for her.

Her competitor, Bud Ekins, was a sonuvabitch, but he was a smart and a knowledgeable sonuvabitch, and the *World-Telegram* must have been delighted that he was *their* sonuvabitch.

The American-made planes of the KLM route that he had chosen flew at a top speed of 220 miles an hour. Imperial's flew at 140 miles an hour. Ekins's route was longer, but there were only four overnight stops on his way toward the *Clipper*, compared with six on the Imperial route. Additionally, he had checked the records of both airlines, and KLM was, by far, the more reliable of the two.[16]

Smug Bud was leaving Athens while Dorothy and Kieran were discussing him at Brindisi. He would write, farther along, in Karachi:

I haven't had any news about either Leo Kieran or Dorothy Kilgallen since Athens (this part of the world being somewhat less accessible than 42nd Street and Broadway), when I heard that both had reached Brindisi after having gone all over Europe by railway and auto in an attempt to make connections. *That's too bad.*

Ekins's lead did not seem to be significant yet. It merely brought him closer to Manila, where they would all have to bunch up and wait for the departure of the signally important *China Clipper* on October 16.

Dorothy was now totally dependent on factors over which she had no control whatsoever. From Brindisi to the China Sea, her fate was wholly in the hands of Imperial Airways to take her to Athens, Alexandria, Gaza, Baghdad, Basia, Bahrein, Sharjah, Karachi, Jodhpur, Delhi, Calcutta, Rangoon, and Bangkok, at which point she would leave Imperial and take the steamship *President Pierce* across the China Sea to Manila. There was no air route from that part of the world into Manila.

Quite incredibly, as in something out of a catechism of myths about women circa 1930, she responded to her predicament by buying a new hat. Actually, she didn't buy a new hat; more precisely, she caused a new hat to be bought for her. She cabled her paper from Brindisi before boarding the six-hour-late Imperial plane:

> TELL MOTHER SEND HAT FRISCO WHERE EYE CAN
> UPPICK IT STOP HAT CUMGRAPES ON IT MADAME AGNES
> SHALL KNOW WHAT DO STOP LIKE THIS HAT BECAUSE
> MAKES ME LOOK LIKE SOMETHING EX DELLA ROBBIA
> STOP ANYWAY THAT'S WHAT SOMEONE TOLD ME ONCE [17]

Also, in Brindisi, she and Kieran were informed that Mayor Rossi of San Francisco was offering a solid gold nugget from the original Mother Lode to the first of the racing reporters who, traversing the site of the prospective Bridge Exposition, dropped a European or an Asian flag of his or her choice into the San Francisco Bay. Kieran was amused, but he demurred, the idea seeming too stuntlike for his taste. Dorothy inquired as to whether Mr. Ekins was playing. He was. She told reporters, as she boarded the steps of Imperial's *City of Stonehaven*, "Tell Mayor Rossi I accept his competition." [18]

While Dorothy tapped out a story on her lap-portable describing Imperial's lateness and Kieran's luck, Kieran sipped a cocktail at his seat across the aisle.

From Brindisi, *The City of Stonehaven* headed for Athens, the European terminus of the route. Dorothy glanced down at the Greek islands from ten thousand feet. "They take the cake for magnificent scenery," she wrote. "They are everything that Byron and Shelley wrote about."

Her discovery of the beauty of the Parthenon ran on the front page of the *Evening Journal* next to another discovery: the burlap-wrapped legs of a young girl floating in Boston Harbor.

As she neared the exotic countries of Africa and Asia, home of the heathen, Dorothy's stories got splashier play. Enormous 12-by-8 inch pictures of her, smiling her original Lakehurst smile, in her original fox furs, were mocked up over maps of the progress of her journey, with arrows indicating fourth day, fifth day, sixth day. Readers were warned about what the plucky girl from Brooklyn might expect: mangrove swamps, crocodiles, king cobras the length of subway cars, scorpions, vaporous forests, jungle fever, arid desert stretches over which previous travelers had disappeared. . . .

In that very first story, blue-skied at Lakehurst, Dorothy wrote: "I wonder, like the girl in Gilbert & Sullivan, what on Earth the World can be."

Certainly this air race was no way in which to find out.

Most of Dorothy's fellow passengers were British, connected either with the military or the foreign service. Many of them were bound for Palestine, where Great Britain, just months before, had declared martial law as a result of the large-scale attacks by Arabs upon Zionist immigrants. The situation was being kept as quiet as possible. All the reporters had experienced some difficulty securing visas into Palestinian territory and were compelled to convince the British consulate that they were interested in speed, not politics.[1] The British passengers were disinclined to be interviewed by Dorothy and deftly turned the tables on her, questioning her about Hauptmann and Hollywood and her life stateside.[2]

With the non-Europeans that Dorothy encountered in her brief time on the ground, a natural xenophobia, exacerbated by barriers of languages, kept her at arms' length. Her observations and interests revolved increasingly around food, shopping, and clothes—all of which she was disposed, by the nature of her assignment and the limits of her sensibilities and her overwhelming provincialism, to compare unfavorably with their American counterparts.

She was like the sailors Joseph Conrad described in *Heart of Darkness*: ". . . in the immutability of their surroundings—the foreign shores, the foreign faces, the changing immensity of life glides past, veiled not by a sense of mystery but by a slightly disdainful ignorance . . ."

The catacombs in Alexandria disappointed and spooked her with their "foreign statues and religious symbols." But, she added, "if anybody at a party ever asks me if I've seen a catacomb, I can say yes. That's about all I got out of the experience."

After meeting her first "sheik," she exclaimed, "Give me a Yale man any time!"

The streets of Baghdad she found "noisy, smelly, and strange in a way that's romantic if you're in the right mood and a nuisance if you're not." In a nightclub there, with Kieran, she listened to a knowledgeable explanation of the differences in musical scaling and rhythms between East and West, and politely asked if the band would play some American swing music.

The costumes of the Arabian men resembled bed sheets to her. She found it difficult not to imagine how they would appear "in our swanky New York bars, togged out like a pajama party at a girl's boarding school." [3]

The more alien her experiences became, the "New York-ier" became her point of view. The farther away she went, the more aggrandized her social references: swank bars, future parties, Yale men. There was even one reference to her old "prep" school. Whether she meant P.S. 119 or Erasmus Hall in Flatbush was not made clear. There was something in the alien that frightened her enormously. And as she became less secure, she created a distancing world that was not yet hers. The change was reflected in her writing as she changed gradually from jejune and gee whiz to worldly wise and amused.

In Karachi, on October 9, Dorothy and Kieran learned that Bud Ekins, thousands of miles in the lead, had not elected to fly from Singapore south to Hong Kong, as they had assumed he would. He was, instead, speeding circuitously southwest, in the direction of the Dutch East Indies.

His route perplexed Kieran and worried Dorothy, who, like all mystery lovers, abhorred befuddlement. Kieran pored over his maps. Dorothy queried her home office. There was nothing remotely resembling a regular air route that connected the East Indies to Manila, in the Philippines. Nor was Bud Ekins giving anything away in his stories. He had written, as he was winging toward Djakarta (then called Batavia):

After Batavia, I shall swing north again, crossing the equator for the second time in two days, and with luck I should be in Manila Saturday. How? I'll let you know in a future dispatch. I can say only what I have said all along, that I expect to fly all the way to Manila.[4]

Ekins knew precisely what he was doing. Months before, he had pondered the one gap in total globe-girdling by air: the China Sea and the necessity of crossing it by boat from Hong Kong. An affiliate of KLM, KNILM, solved his problem. While regular air service went no farther than Tarakan, on the northeast coast of Borneo, the Dutch were eager to extend that route into the Philippines to connect with the new Clipper service. The prospective route involved island-hopping from Borneo, across the Celebes Sea, and then down to the Philippines. Ekins, back in the United States, had discovered that the Philippine government had granted the Dutch permission to conduct a series of survey flights designed to acquaint the crews with the prospective route. He had requested and was accorded permission to join one such flight, from Tarakan to the Philippines.[5] Small wonder that Ekins, aware of what would appear to have been incredible aeronautical arcana, had been so close-mouthed.

The combination of Ekins's inexplicable itinerary, the ponderous pace of Imperial, and the intense desert heat began finally to unnerve Dorothy. She complained of Kieran's brown shirt, which he had worn every day since Brindisi. He washed it regularly, but it was beginning to bore her. His vocalizing nettled her. And the Imperial pilots—whom she had once described as reassuringly "strong and straight" —were beginning to lose her confidence.[6]

She cornered the pilot whenever possible and lectured him on the necessity of punctuality. "After all," she told him, "it's your schedule as well as mine. You're late and just to keep your own record straight, you ought to make up that lost time." She reminded him that it was "not every pilot who has a chance to take part in an air-race."[7] She even suggested that he shorten the layover at Jodhpur, India, in order to make up the six hours he—or at least Imperial—had lost back in Brindisi.

Unswayed, he set down at Jodhpur with no adjustment in scheduling. For Dorothy, however, the stop was not a total loss. The maharaja of Jodhpur, whom she understood to be as wealthy as Rockefeller, met her personally at the airport. Her first instinct was to curtsy—twenty-three years as a devout Catholic had made her obeisance-prone—but she held back, followed the lead of another passenger, and settled upon a deferential, blushing, "Your Majesty." He invited her, on her next and presumably more leisurely visit, to stop in to see him and his wife at the palace. She replied, "And you must come and see the Kilgallens when you happen to be in Brooklyn." [8]

In the Indian desert, she posed with Kieran and four passengers in the sweltering heat. She wore a lightweight linen suit and a newly acquired pith helmet. In an effort to keep traveling as light as possible and because she had not yet been able to find herself a pair of canvas shoes, her ensemble was not completely ensembled. As she leaned against the plane, she held her black leather pocketbook firmly by her side. On her feet, sinking into the sand, were the same open-toed opera pumps on which she had scrambled away from the railroad guards in Italy. She cupped her right hand over her eyes, in an attempt to block out the assaultive desert sun.

It had become a trying trip. And Calcutta, the geographical halfway mark, was a nadir for Dorothy. There was no maharaja here to smooth her ruffled feathers. After a quick stop at the cable office, where she filed her story, she headed to the Great Eastern Hotel for a bath and a night's sleep.

She had grown accustomed to lizards by this time, learning that they had a tendency to know and keep their place. She had even acclimated herself to the frequent and unannounced incursions, in India, of soundless and sundry servants, who stole in and out of hotel rooms throughout the night as if they themselves did not exist. But the unspeakable rogues' gallery of insect life of every color, size, and description swarming in her bed and bath at the Great Eastern was too frightful to live with. She threw up her hands in utter disgust and decided to seek sanctuary in the hotel lobby, where she met Kieran, similarly appalled by his roommates. They sat up in wicker chairs until the dawn, smoking and talking chiefly about bugs.

Thereafter, Calcutta could do nothing right: The taxi to the "so-called airport . . . wheezed and coughed." Her driver had but one eye, which Dorothy viewed, without compassion, as chiefly a danger to her own safety. She would continue to berate by name, in print and on the radio, the hotel in Calcutta that had served her so poorly.

Dorothy was feeling pettish, aggrieved, and frustrated. The news she received at the Mingadalon Airport in Rangoon was the last straw. H. R. Ekins was not only in Manila, five thousand miles ahead; he was preparing, when weather permitted, to board not the *China Clipper*, the capstone of the whole damned race, but the *Hawaii Clipper*, a sister ship.[9] There was not to be a bottleneck at Manila, as Dorothy had all along assumed, prior to a three-way Mickey Mouse race across the United States. Ekins's cheating was not merely cute, it was about to prove efficacious.

With his scenario unfolding like a well-made play, Bud Ekins had set down in Manila six days before the scheduled departure of the *China Clipper* on October 16—time enough for a resourceful, knowledgeable newspaperman, who scrupled about nothing except results, backed by the mighty UPI, bolstered by a publicity-hungry Pan American Airways, to finesse.

He was received enthusiastically in Manila, whose economic future depended upon its strategic location in the commercial air age. Thousands of Manilans cheered him at the airport, from which he was taken by royal escort to visit President Quezon at the palace. He presented Quezon with ceremonial letters from FDR, Mayor La Guardia, and Roy Howard of his newspaper chain.

Foremost on his mind, however, was the erratic and murderous typhoon that was ripping through the Pacific, killing hundreds in the Philippines, destroying villages, and delaying all air traffic in the area. As he had suspected as far back as Karachi, the *Hawaii Clipper* had been unable to take off on schedule—two days before Ekins's arrival—and was still waiting out the storm. This Clipper plane was not yet a regularly scheduled vehicle. It would not be licensed to carry passengers until October 21, after its return run to San Francisco.

Ekins left the palace with jubilation and hurried over to the offices of Pan American. He met with the airline's manager in Manila, and asked for permission to take the *Hawaii Clipper* back to San Francisco. Ekins was signed on as a titular crew member to avoid problems with customs. He had only to wait out the storm and he would have his victory as well as his speed record.[10]

Ekins was clearly violating the spirit as well as the letter of the law by using transportation that would by no means be available to the ordinary traveler. From Dorothy's point of view, the rules were consequently rendered null and void. And she was probably relieved to have the freedom to finagle restored to her professional life.

In Bangkok, she stepped off the Imperial plane and raced to the offices of the Aerial Transport Company of Siam. She pulled out a roll of traveler's checks and asked for the first charter that would take her directly to the Philippines. Money was no object and she preferred an American pilot. Such a flight, it was explained to her, was impossible. The six-hundred-mile-wide China Sea was not within the flying range of any of their planes. Nor was there an American pilot available.

The manager of the company told her that she could charter a plane to take her as far as Hong Kong, where she might make other arrangements. The best available pilot was a chap called Luen Phongsobhon. Siamese. She was skeptical.

She was dismayed to find out that the pilot spoke very little English. It was, however, explained to her that he was the best man for the job, having been trained in France and the United States, and knowing Indochina intimately. They would take off first thing in the morning.[11]

Kieran was puzzled by Dorothy's decision. Her route, because it was more direct than his, might save several hours. But, he argued, Imperial's progress had been reliable enough since Brindisi, and they would both be there in time to board the S.S. *President Pierce*.

Dorothy did not tell Kieran that those couple of hours might enable her to make an air connection to the Philippines, that she would try not to board the *Pierce* at all, and that she had on her mind catching the *Hawaii Clipper*, not the *China Clipper*. Despite his scrupulous fidelity to the rules, she could not risk full disclosure to yet another rival.

"There's no point in half-hearted fighting," she was to write in a subsequent story, "because you don't know whether you have a chance to win. There's too much Irish in me for anything like that."

Dorothy had not been off the front page of the *Evening Journal* since the inception of the trip ten days before. But this decision, to pull out all the stops, was stellar stuff and provoked the boldest streamers of the race. Under the headline SIAM LINDY SPEEDS DOROTHY OVER CHINA, her paper described the territory over which she intended to fly as continuous jungle where fierce primitive tribes hunted heads and helpless white women.

On the morning of October 12, Luen helped Dorothy into the rear seat of his small but sturdy two-seater *Puss Moth*, and they began their day-and-a-half-long adventure over Southeast Asia. They flew northeast, refueled on the Siamese side of the Mekong. Once out of Siam, over French colonial territory, there were no aeronautical aids at all, and Luen was forced to sight-fly. During part of the journey, he followed the coastal railway to Hanoi. It took a tremendous amount of concentration. And Dorothy was no help at all.

With the pilot in earshot, she shouted questions at him which he could not distract himself to answer, had he even understood them. She wrote that he was not much of a conversationalist and answered her queries with "inscrutable Oriental shrugs." [12]

She implored him every hundred miles or so to please try to get more speed out of his plane. To her first requests, he did not respond at all. Finally, he turned around and informed her that he held all the speed records in Siam. "I must have hurt his sense of pride," Dorothy wrote.

They landed smoothly in Hanoi for their first night's layover. She shopped in one of the finer French stores and was finally able to buy herself a pair of sneakers.

On the second day out, Siam Lindy heard a noise in the motor and made a somewhat bumpy emergency landing. For the first time since she had boarded the *Hindenburg*, Dorothy felt genuinely threatened. She was not a physical coward, but she was a distinctly dutiful daughter. She wondered, in those impacted moments before Luen brought the *Puss Moth* to a sudden landing, how Jim and Mae would manage to get her body out of Indochina and safely back to Brooklyn.

Luen analyzed the problem as a disfunctioning spark plug, replaced it, and took off again.[13] Further along the route, he lost his way, landed in a rice field, and had to ask directions to Fort Bayard from some laborers. They were aloft again, but they had lost several hours. She worried now about missing even the *President Pierce*.

To justify the expense of the charter, Dorothy wrote her Hearstling heart out, distilling the two episodes into one:

Dawn found us sailing serenely northward—over French Indo Chinese jungles where tigers and great constrictor snakes lie in wait for little girls . . . Bump! Bump! Splash! We thumped down jarringly in the middle of a rice field. The plane was not damaged—but in a second I thought all my worst fears about Kwangsi Province were realized. Appearing like gnomes from the ground, about 600 chattering natives, nearly naked, surrounded the plane. They spoke no English, of course, and could not understand Siamese.

They landed in the British colony of Hong Kong a little more than an hour before the S.S. *President Pierce* was scheduled to sail on October 13. Her paper had attempted to find a charter for her across the South China Sea, but it was no go. She jumped into a taxi and rushed toward the port. "Jinrickshaws," she wrote, "cleared aside as though our car were preceded by a magic ray."

Ekins was still storm-struck in Manila. But to risk remaining in Hong Kong would be to risk missing even the *China Clipper*. Dorothy decided to board the steamer, knowing that her chances of catching up to him were considerably diminished by the 37-hour crossing.

Leo Kieran was already aboard. He had beaten Dorothy by several hours. He was shaved, showered, and dressed in a sporty new outfit he had purchased in Hong Kong. He laid a consoling hand on Dorothy's shoulder and suggested they repair to the cocktail lounge.

After being stuck in Manila for three full and anxious days, Bud Ekins took off on the *Hawaii Clipper* on the morning of October 14, local time. Dorothy and Kieran were having a late breakfast on the leisurely cruise when they received cablegrams from Ekins informing them that he was off and running. He congratulated Dorothy on her grittiness in chartering the *Puss Moth* and invited both of them to dinner when they finally arrived in New York.[1]

Only a miracle or an accident could now alter the inevitable. She expressed much more than she ever could have consciously come to grips with when she wrote, aboard the S.S. *President Pierce:*

> I think I deserve a break. Maybe the *China Clipper* will overtake the *Hawaii Clipper* in mid-ocean. Maybe [italics mine] *something will happen*. I really would like to win this round-the-world jaunt.

To all realistic intents and purposes, however, it was over. Ekins had won.

When the race ceased being a competition for Dorothy, she shifted into a more pleasure-oriented gear. She treated herself, just before dinner, to a shampoo, wave, and manicure—the better to face her first full-length mirror in weeks. She was surprised to see that her petal-soft white gardenia skin, so relished by beaux and family, had turned a rosy hue, stigmata of the lower class. Well, it had been unavoidable. It was reversible. And she was fortunate not to have come down with a case of sun poisoning.

They dined at the captain's table. She ate her first "civilized meal, from hors d'oeuvre to brandy and coffee." In spite of her sun-spoilt complexion, Dorothy found herself the center of attraction throughout the meal, as she had never before been. She fielded countless questions from the handsome ship's officers. They listened long. And she regaled them with anecdotes and witticisms that brought hearty laughter. "I can even tell funny stories now," she would tell a reporter from her paper.[2]

In Manila, she and Kieran were feted by the royal family. There were tea dances, lobster dinners, and other state occasions. They would be four days in Manila. Ekins had, in a rush of luck, gotten out *entr'acte* on the *Hawaii Clipper*. The *China Clipper* was delayed now by the backside of the same typhoon.

When she and Leo Kieran were asked to speak on the Manila radio in a program slated to be relayed to the United States for broadcast coast-to-coast, Dorothy must have winced. She agreed finally, on condition that she could prepare the script. Ad-libbing was out of the question, since she became tongue-tied so easily.

She wrote an exchange between her colleague, herself, and an interviewer, and they spoke it into a microphone. In her shy, helium-high, still-stilted voice, she told about her Siamese adventure.

> DOROTHY: We were in a little plane, with absolutely no elbow room, and I landed in a field of coolies to ask directions and, of course, the pilot was Siamese and didn't speak a *word* of English and we had a terrible time. You beat me though, Leo.

The Kilgallens and several neighbors gathered 'round their living room radio to listen to Dorothy's broadcast. Jim's eyes misted when his daughter, asked if she had any messages for the people back home, called out, "Hello, Mom! Hello, Pop!"

Jim went directly to the telegraph office to dash off congratulations to her. The message was characteristically comparative, bestowing value in terms of others: "Your broadcast splendid. You have done a knockout job and have stolen the story all around."[3]

On Monday morning, October 19, Dorothy left Manila aboard the *China Clipper*, with a complement of fourteen colleagues, all of them men. Six of them had taken the San

Francisco–Manila inaugural flight and were returning. The others had hopped on at Honolulu and were slated to return there. The *Clipper* made four stops—Guam, Wake, Midway, and Honolulu—in its trans-Pacific run back to San Francisco. The trip covered 8,200 miles and consumed five days.

There were parties continuously, in the air and on the ground—a five-day stag party to which Dorothy considered herself invited. As she recalled it, without guile, "For once," Dorothy laughed, "I was Queen of the May."

Leaving Guam for Wake, she was apprised of the inevitable. Bud Ekins was back in New York, breaking the record he had in mind for circumnavigation. His time: eighteen days, fourteen hours, fifty-six minutes. He was the first man to circle the globe, entirely by air, over established passenger routes—though some of them had not been quite established yet. He had planned to drop the flags of both the Netherlands and the Philippines over the site of the Bridge Exposition—both of those countries had been mighty good to him—but the Department of Commerce wisely forbade the hurtling of artifacts out of aircraft. Mayor Rossi gave him his gold nugget anyway. And Ekins returned to crowds, headlines, congratulations, and a hefty raise from his grateful newspaper.[4]

But Dorothy was not ready to deal with Ekins yet. She was having far too good a time.

At Midway, Dorothy had a couple of drinks, accompanied the guys on a moonlight stroll, and set out to "scamper" on a coral reef. Her wiser but no more sober colleagues suggested with firmness that that was not a good idea. "And I," she wrote, "a pioneering woman globetrotter, bowed meekly to male advice."

She enjoyed being dominated by men. Always had and always would. It made her feel very Dolly Mae-ish and intensely feminine.

As the plane, sounding of song and typewriters, smelling of gin and gardenias, headed for the terminus in Alameda, California, on October 24, all kinds of wheels had been set in motion on behalf of Dorothy.

Jim Kilgallen had been dispatched to California to meet her.

Standing by, too, was Elsie Robinson, a kind of Hearstian heartline who wrote in a style that combined the colloquialisms of Ring Lardner with the sensibilities of a nicotine-poisoned Orphan Annie. Waiting for Dorothy to land, she wrote:

> Didya hear it? . . . Was it . . . ? Aw. No.—can it be . . . Not yet.
>   We clump back, grin at each other over upturned collars . . . light another cigarette . . . wish we'd waited for that other cup of coffee . . . What's a cup of coffee on a morning like this when the kid's comin' in.[5]

Dorothy flew off the plane tearfully, right into the arms of her father. Her first words were: "How did Spi like my work? Does he think I did all right?"

"He asked me to give you a pat on the back," Jim replied.

They submitted to a quick ceremony. Mayor Rossi presented her with what he called a Dorothy Kilgallen Clipper Hat. It was a rather smart, broad-brimmed affair, entirely fruit-less, more Adela Rogers St. Johns than Dorothy Kilgallen and just the kind of style Dorothy took pains to avoid in order to maintain her femininity in a man's profession. She wore it until she left California. The hat was never seen again.

Jim and Dorothy were convoyed through the crowd to a single-engine, one-thousand-horsepower Vultee, W. R. Hearst's own private plane.[6] The fact was not divulged by the Hearst press, which was still maintaining the ruse of nonelitist transportation. There was no time to take her luggage or his typewriter. Kieran, after all, was still in the race, though he boarded the regularly scheduled flight out of Alameda.

The Kilgallens' cross-country trip was made in thirteen hours, twenty-four minutes. At 5:45 A.M., Dorothy arrived at Newark, where she kissed a waiting Mae and Eleanor. They'd come out to meet her wearing fox furs identical to the one that Dorothy wore as she deplaned.

A big crowd awaited Dorothy, many of them celebrities. It was an unholy hour, but Amster Spiro had made the rounds of some of New York's chicer spots and, according to Syd Boehm, "ordered and I *mean* ordered" some of the most famous habitués out to Newark to greet his returning star.[7]

Dorothy, alone in a chauffeured car, was driven back to

her office on South Street, where she clocked in and ate a gargantuan American breakfast. Her traveling time, South Street to South Street: twenty-four days, twelve hours, fifty-one minutes. Breakfast: huge glass of orange juice, toasted butter cakes, two eggs, strawberry jam, coffee.

She placed second, having reached Newark only an hour before Leo Kieran. They were both six days behind Bud Ekins.

None of the globe-girdlers had lost.

Leo Kieran had stuck stubbornly to his original plan. In a *New York Times* story of October 16, he pointed out that he was the only one of the trio who had not resorted to extraordinary transportation. Ekins, he revealed, had been taken on the *Hawaii Clipper* as a member of the crew; Dorothy had flown from Bangkok to Hong Kong "direct by special plane." Thus, he concluded, "your correspondent remains the only one of three globe-girdling reporters to make the trip using no forms of transportation than those open to the ordinary traveler."

Dorothy had set some kind of niggling record, sitting in the Vultee coast-to-coast. No woman before her had done it any faster. She claimed that she was the first woman to fly the Pacific in a passenger plane. In fact, Lady Drummond-Hay had done it aboard the *Graf Zeppelin* in its twenty-one-day around-the-world trip of 1929.

The significance of the trip, for Dorothy, transcended the establishment of an aeronautical record. It launched her as a celebrity. As a result of her adventure and the publicity it engendered, Dorothy Kilgallen became, like Nellie Bly (who, incidentally, had done her share of cheating), a *very famous lady.*

Every house on her block was decked out with American flags and pictures of Dorothy. On her return, there was dancing, crying, hats and horns and New Year's rattles. She was mobbed after mass at St. Thomas Aquinas Church. Children asked her for autographs and told of class projects that had related to her race. Jim Mollison, the famous curly-haired aviator, came to call at her house. She found him very attractive.

She received hundreds of congratulatory letters. Novelist Faith Baldwin asked to call on her and penned prettily on stationery from the St. Regis Hotel: "You're a better heroine than any of mine." [8]

From the White House, Eleanor Roosevelt wrote:

> Dear Miss Kilgallen,
>
> I have been so interested in your flight around the world with the men, and even though I am sure you are disappointed in not being the first to arrive I wanted to tell you I was rather pleased to have a woman go! It took a good deal of pluck and it must have held a good many thrills! [9]

For her and Kieran, there was an official ceremony at City Hall. She leaned over and kissed, for the benefit of photographers, a beaming, blushing, and astonishingly rotund Fiorello F. La Guardia. La Guardia took them both impulsively into a meeting in progress of the Board of Estimate. "Gentlemen," he said, with Dorothy in hand, "I want you to meet the 1936 Nellie Bly." The city controller, noting Dorothy's redness and Kieran's deep desert tan, teased, in the style of the day, "You look like a couple of foreigners to me." [10]

Her dispatches were pulled together by Herb Spiro and published as a not-very-successful book, *Girl Around the World.* A song was written about her called "Hats Off to Dorothy." She lectured at the Columbia School of Journalism. She appeared on Kate Smith's coast-to-coast radio show. She posed for a widely distributed full-page advertisement for Camel cigarettes, in which she was pictured wrapped in furs in front of the Vultee, being photographed and interviewed, and, up in the left-hand corner, in a Peter Pan collar, holding a cigarette. The testimonial read: "I snatched meals anywhere, ate all kinds of food. But Camels helped me keep my digestion tuned up."

Hollywood beckoned.

In early November, Dorothy was off to the West Coast, with Mae Kilgallen by her side. She had several opportunities in California. She was to file, for the *Evening Journal,* an anecdotal column about movies and movie stars. She was to test for the role of "A Reporter" in a film with Bruce Cabot called *Sinner Take All.* And she was to deliver to Warner Brothers an autobiographical screenplay about her experiences as a globe-girdler: *Fly Away Baby*, it was called. Herb Spiro, with whom she had originally discussed the idea, was eased out. She would have several collaborators, but the thrust of the scenario was hers. The three main characters in the screenplay were based on the three main characters in the real-life air race: Dorothy (Torchy Blane), Kieran (Hughie Sprague), and Ekins (Lucien "Sonny" Croy).

Dorothy had not yet settled Herbert Roslyn "Bud" Ekins's hash. All the exposure of his wily ways throughout the race had been done for her by her colleagues at Hearst. She had never once confronted Ekins personally or in her journalism. The stateside dinner to which he had so arrogantly invited Dorothy and Kieran had not come off. By the time they returned, he was on a publicity jaunt for his paper. It is doubtful, in any case, that either Dorothy or Kieran would have accepted his invitation. Once, to a newspaperman in Hawaii, she censured Bud Ekins. And then it was only to say that he had turned a sportive dash into a roughhouse race. Beyond that, she was gracious and magnanimous. Very much the lady. Very much Mae Kilgallen's nonconfrontational daughter. She described both her rivals as fine fellows and splendid reporters.

Dorothy's unconscious grievance committee had temporarily tabled the motion to censure. Though she could never deal directly with her anger, Dorothy did not favor losing, and she was not one to leave a score unsettled.

In the movie script that she had tucked under her arm, the three reporters were described:

> *Torchy Blane*—the "smart blond" of the *Morning Herald*, a girl reporter with plenty of self-reliance.

> *Hughie Sprague*—a "trained seal" of the *Express*, a carefree soul who always manages to keep his sense of humor and himself well-oiled.

> *Lucien "Sonny" Croy*—the handsome son of a wealthy publisher with the pleasant personality of a snake.

The fictional race is concocted by Sonny as a pretext to make a connection, aboard the dirigible *Hindenburg*, with an international "fence." Sonny, it is revealed, has murdered, in cold blood, the owner of a Tiffany-like jewelry store. To pay his gambling and tootsie-keeping debts, he has stolen $250,000 worth of gems.

Torchy, a supersleuth, is on to Sonny from the beginning, but she is unable to convince her handsome Irish fiancé, a police lieutenant, of his guilt. She endeavors, therefore, to follow Sonny around the world, involving herself only incidentally in a three-way race.

"Take care of yourself, you little idiot," her fiancé cautions.

"You, too, you big roughneck," she remonstrates.

In the course of the race, Sonny cheats outrageously. He puts a handful of dirt in the gas tank of her Imperial plane. He buys up all the seats on a Hanoi-bound transport. He is, in addition, very nasty to Hughie, portrayed as an ineffectual, uxorious fop.

Against all odds, Torchy emerges totally victorious. She solves the murder, recovers the jewels, gets off a pride of thirties-style wisecracks, wins the heart of her police lieutenant fiancé, only to jilt him at the altar for a better story —and finishes *first* in the race.

Glenda Farrell played Torchy Blane in the movie, which opened at the Palace Theatre in New York in July, 1937. A reviewer for the *New York Post* rated it "Fair-Good." He commented on two interesting phenomena: the absence of the usual disclaimer about all events and persons in the film being fictitious, and the delineation of Sonny Croy. "In umpty-ump years of screen-viewing," he remarked, "we've never before come upon a fourth-estater who was such a bad man."

Dorothy had taken no time off for good behavior when she left for California, accompanied by Mae, on November 13. Mae explained her presence to the curious press. "After all, Dorothy Mae is only twenty-three. She needs me to look after her." Mother and daughter put down safely in Burbank during an unusually chilly, sunless spell. The ranchers in the valley were nursing their oranges around the clock.

On the lots, Selznick was shooting *A Star Is Born* with Janet Gaynor. Twentieth Century-Fox's new release list included *Love Is News*, with Tyrone Power, and *One in a Million*, starring Sonja Henie. Sylvia Sidney and Henry Fonda were doing *You Only Live Once* at United. And MGM had just begun *Captains Courageous*, for which Spencer Tracy took a permanent wave, and *Maytime*, in which Nelson Eddy took Jeanette MacDonald. *Sinner Take All*, the movie in which Dorothy was to be "discovered," would go into production presently.

After being greeted at the airport by Ann Sheridan and Carol Hughes, the two women checked into comfortable quarters at the Hollywood Knickerbocker.

Dorothy was to begin filing, almost immediately, a daily column for the *Evening Journal: Hollywood Scene as Seen by Dorothy Kilgallen*. About this column, the paper maintained the lowest possible profile. If Dorothy took to Hollywood and succeeded in her work, her copy could elevate the second-rate, scanty movie coverage offered by the *Journal*. Under optimum conditions, the column might be picked up and syndicated by King Features. There was, in the interim, however, as little fanfare as possible about the nature of DK's assignment. Amster Spiro commented: "We want fresh and breezy changes in the news dispatches from the West Coast. She has been ordered to discover Hollywood—the *real* Hollywood." [1]

Spi had a magical faith in the efficacy of surprise. As in the air race, the enemy was to be caught off-guard. Now, however, the adversary was not Scripps-Howard or *The New York Times.* It was Hearst's own Louella Parsons.

By the early 1930s, Louella had already been syndicated in 372 newspapers throughout the world. Her West Coast outlet was the influential *Hollywood Examiner.* In New York, she appeared daily in old man Hearst's pet paper, the *American.*

Her biographer, George Eells, wrote:

> The year 1936 brought forth the announcement that "cold figures" proved Louella was "far and away" the United States' most popular "motion picture columnist, critic, and feature writer." The survey, commissioned by Hearst's New York *American,* was conducted by the McCann-Erickson advertising agency and limited to 149,704 persons in the New York area who had bought a new automobile in the preceding nine months. The results claimed Louella had no close rivals in her field.[2]

However fatuous the *American*'s hype—and surveying automobile purchasers in a depression year was like taking a head count of cake-eaters in pre-Revolutionary France—Louella had nothing approaching a close rival in her field. To be a rival in her field meant eventually not to be in her field at all.

Louella's career with William Randolph Hearst began in 1922, when she took him to task in the New York *Telegraph* for not sufficiently publicizing the role of Marion Davies in the motion picture *When Knighthood Was in Flower.* Davies was William Randolph Hearst's mistress and obsession. Every reviewer in the organization wrote orgasmically about her artistic endeavors. After *Knighthood* was released, the *American* headlined, MARION DAVIES IN GREATEST ROLE IN CAREER. A *Journal* reviewer raved: "Bewildering in its magnificence . . . best of all, fortunate in its lovely star, Marion Davies."

When W. R. Hearst happened upon Louella's printed suggestion to bring still more coals to Newcastle, he is reported to have said: "We must hire that woman!"

By hard work, predation, paranoia, monopolizing news

sources inventively, idolatrizing her boss and his lady, routing or subjugating all possible rivals, Louella Parsons, in 1937, was a fearsome force. She was to the Hollywood Hills what the wildebeest are to East Africa: On the choicest grass, she grazed.

Louella made a public display of welcoming the young grunion, Kilgallen, to the Pacific Coast. She noted, in her column of November 18, with reference to Dorothy's work on the screenplay for *Fly Away Baby:*

> Who better than Dorothy Kilgallen could write a movie account of her own Nellie Bly exploits—Miss Kilgallen, here with her mother, is dividing her time between writing for the *Evening Journal* and her assignment.

Had Louella designated the paper properly as the *Evening Journal* of New York, she would not have endued Dorothy with any muscle. A New York outlet meant very little to the sources of news in Hollywood: the studio flacks or the stars themselves. A writer for the lowliest trade paper there had far more clout than a representative of even the more prestigious New York papers.

Dorothy's first column:

HOLLYWOOD SCENE
as seen by
DOROTHY KILGALLEN

appeared in the *Evening Journal* on November 17. Under the lead, "Here is everything you ought to know about Hollywood and a few things you shouldn't," was a series of lackluster items, the most revelatory of which had to do with Harpo Marx, who, she asserted, could really talk and, furthermore, was getting "a little bald under his fright-wig." Her most insightful item bade her readers to "watch for" a new tune called "Too Marvelous for Words"; it was a suggestion that had nothing to do with Hollywood and everything to do with her fine taste and intense feeling for popular music. She ended three columns of type with the less than startling observation that a musical number in a new Busby Berkeley movie would take "five days to film and five minutes to show on the screen."

She knew that her first shot was nothing to write home

about, much less put in the newspaper, but making contacts in a new town meant time, cultivation, education. There was also the mouth factor. Getting people to talk *about* you is often tantamount to getting them to talk to you. Nobody, to be sure, was taking much notice of Dorothy yet, except perhaps Louella.

But Dorothy had faced mangrove swamps, desert heat, and the grit of Bud Ekins. Louella could not have seemed so formidable an obstacle.

There were, in the meantime, other irons in the fire. The day on which her first column appeared, she was due to report to MGM to be made up and tested for that film debut in *Sinner Take All*. She was up at six A.M.; by seven, huddled in her Kolinsky fur, she stood in front of the Knickerbocker and waited for the studio car. She hoped it would be a Rolls and was somewhat disappointed when an ordinary Cadillac appeared.

At the studio, she was bunned, coffee-ed, and escorted by her producer to the sunlit makeup room. There she was introduced to her makeup man, Jack Dawn, and his assistant, Dolly. She changed into a smock. Her hair was shampooed and tucked under a towel, isolating her face.

Dawn scrutinized her prized complexion. Unlike a multitude of beaux, he did not bother to compliment her.

"Give her a number twenty-six and spread it light," he ordered his assistant.

The pancake turned her gardenia skin a burnished, orange hue. She sat passively—intensely aware of having "an experience," more so than on the hectic world race that had brought her here in the first place—to be modulated into screen-test perfect.

"What kind of mouth shall we give her?" Dolly asked Dawn.

"What's the matter with the one God gave me?" Dorothy peeped. She rolled her eyes with embarrassment as she always did after telling a joke.

The technicians, Dawn and his Dolly, referred to the picture of Margaret Lindsay that sat on the makeup table. In Dorothy's role, as it was originally conceived, her resemblance to the B-movie star was an integral part of the scenario. Margaret Lindsay would play the scion of a rich family whose members were being picked off one by one.

The reporter—Dorothy—would be used by co-star Bruce Cabot as a decoy to protect the heiress. The flacks at MGM, with the cooperation of Hearst, had released the story that Dorothy's resemblance to Lindsay was so startling that she was plucked right out of the studio commissary by a talent agent who was totally unaware that she was the Amelia Earhart of the *Evening Journal.*

Back in makeup, Jack Dawn frosted Dorothy when he called for false eyelashes. She was aghast. "Even my worst enemies have to give me my eyelashes!" she wrote.

He penciled her eyebrows almost to the ears and took a final look at the picture of Margaret Lindsay.

"Wouldn't it be funny," he said, "if it turned out you looked like Bruce Cabot instead."

Dorothy was done. The artists praised their burnished Galatea.

"Great," said Dawn.

"Terrific," said Dolly.

"Colossal," said the producer.[3]

For the test, she was asked to sit on a high stool, turn her head to the left, turn her head to the right. Smile!

Dorothy had trouble with the last.

"You are having a great time!" the director shouted.

"That's what you think," she said.

On the following day, she returned to the set, was chided for forgetting her false eyelashes, and spoke one of the five lines she was intended:

REPORTER TO COP: Have a heart, Murphy. I've got to get inside.

There were several takes. She found the pace of movie-making maddeningly slow and wrote: "Oh, give me a police card and let me cover a nice, soft sixteen-hour-a-day murder story!"

Yet the utterly thrilling possibility that she could be importantly discovered existed for Dorothy.

Hollywood Scene as Seen by Dorothy Kilgallen was changed presently to *As Seen in Hollywood by Dorothy Kilgallen,* which was good thinking. The new column head emphasized her trump cards: the personal, the attitudinal, the Eye. It placed her in less direct competition with chronicler Parsons, whose own column was called *Louella Parsons' Hollywood—News of West Coast Studios.*

Dorothy got no closer to the hub as the weeks went on. Sets were closed to her. Telephone calls were unreturned. She was roundly ignored by most of the community.

But the new, more personal approach gave her leverage. She used her Hearstian head to conceive novelty features. In the cleverest of her gimmick columns, she endeavored to find out whether it was possible for a plain, unconnected girl from Peoria—Mary Warren, she called her—to crash the redoubtable studio gates.

Dressing up in her best "day clothes"—she figured that Mary Warren would have probably invested a couple of bucks in a small but good wardrobe—Dorothy left her hotel at eight in the morning. She breakfasted on toast and coffee at the corner drugstore, figuring further that Mary Warren would not squander her little nest egg on scrambled egg. (Dorothy, a hearty eater, did not mention what she had consumed back at the hotel.) Thereupon, she presented herself at the front gates of every major motion picture studio. To each studio guard, she repeated, "I'm Mary Warren from Peoria and I'm looking for a job as an extra." Invariably, the guards told her that they did not do any hiring at the studios and suggested Central Casting. At one studio, she even asked for a specific executive with whom she had lunched the day before. The gesture was in part a fillip for the piece; she was naturally refused an audience. But it related her obliquely with the real Dorothy Kilgallen, gave her a story to look forward to telling, and probably assuaged whatever fear she was feeling while connecting with the reality of actually being a nobody again.

In the Mary Warren column she recapitulated her experiences, revealed that even Central Casting required some referral, and advised all the Mary Warrens from Peoria to stay home, work locally, and hope to be discovered there. "What was possible ten years ago in this town is no longer possible," she concluded.

Increasingly, she insinuated into the column her own responses to Hollywood. And her responses grew more acerbic as her frustrations increased. She constantly compared Hollywood to New York, and invariably found it wanting in style, manners, and mores.

She chastened Joan Crawford for combing her hair at a ringside table. When, at her first premiere, she noticed that none of the women wore orchids, she took the men to task for their lack of courtliness. The informality of dress shocked her. The language appalled her. The endemic athleticism bored her. She wasn't even too impressed with the prevailing pulchritude.

In a published piece, written as a letter to her sister Eleanor about the premiere of *Lloyds of London*, Dorothy admitted that Loretta Young looked "really stunning swathed in mink." She added, however, that the star was accompanied by "a little man who wore a gray fedora with his dinner jacket, if you can *picture* that." She approved, also, of Myrna Loy "because she's not good at sports. It's so comforting to find another woman in the world who isn't always leaping around with a tennis racket or a golf club." She noted, with delight, the arm-in-arm arrival of Mr. and Mrs. Henry Fonda. "But," she wrote, "she's a New Yorker and she looks like New York."

Louella would have been made livid by the upstart's pronouncements. The veteran columnist was a scold and a tattletale. But she was the quintessential Hollywood patriot. What she did was for the good of the community and the glory of the motion picture business. She had to have been appalled by Dorothy's heretical and systematic destruction of the myths that she had spent her career creating and nurturing.

Louella was very close to Marion Davies, consequently to Hearst, and a frequent visitor to their resplendent residence, San Simeon. Some say she had merely to say the word to rout Dorothy. Perhaps. More likely, she would have been too proud or too smart to make so blatant a move. It would have exposed her as frightened and vulnerable. Better to wait it out, accumulate, and inform.

There is, incidentally, no evidence that Dorothy was ever invited to San Simeon, or that she ever actually met William Randolph Hearst. Jim Kilgallen himself had spent decades in the organization and hadn't once shook his hand. Had Dorothy been invited, she would have gone. But it would have been a professionally survivalist gesture. It is not

likely that the young Dorothy Kilgallen would have con-
doned the adulterous relationship between her boss and his
mistress, Marion.

A recurring technique in *As Seen in Hollywood by
Dorothy Kilgallen* was the continuing frontal attack on
personalities who were somehow nettlesome to Dorothy.
She poked away at two of the most palpable symbols of the
town's arrogance: Simone Simon, a new French import
who had become an overnight sensation the year before
and now closed her sets to the press; and Constance Bennett, who in the early thirties had been the highest paid
performer in motion pictures, but who was currently experiencing a temporary decline in popular appeal.

Dorothy commenced nattering away at the two of them
shortly after her arrival: "Simone Simon is causing so
much trouble on *Seventh Heaven* they're considering replacing her . . ." "Simone Simon should save a little pep
for the camera. Even then she would be the most difficult
star in the business." One entire column was devoted to
countervailing what she considered to be the unjustified
boosting of the young star by her studio's publicity department. Dorothy called her "a stocky little girl with small
eyes and a square chin and freckles. She doesn't powder
her nose. She can't act, and she has never played in a
stand-out picture, or even a very good one."

About Constance Bennett, she wrote: "Connie Bennett
is afraid of crowds . . . and a lot of people are afraid of
Connie Bennett," and then, somewhat obliquely, nevertheless killing two birds with one stone, "Simone Simon is fast
taking Connie Bennett's place as the most heartily disliked
actress in Hollywood." There would, unfortunately, be more
to come.

She managed some kind words for certain members of
the film community. Characteristically, those were the ones
she got to know and meet, or the ones on whom she developed distant crushes. No one was more favorably regarded by her than Tyrone Power, the Byronically beautiful
young actor whose career zoomed after *Lloyds of London*.
"Now there is a dream man!" she wrote in a column about
the premiere.

Stage-trained, intelligent, literate, and Roman Catholic,
he was an ideal prospect for Dorothy. He even had a

"background," being third generation of a distinguished line of actors. His great-grandfather, the first Tyrone Power, had been the leading Irish comedian at London's Drury Lane in the early nineteenth century. He was a sweet and tender man, not at all "Hollywood," a term Dorothy used increasingly as an opprobrious adjective.

They were the same age. They met, probably in a publicity-related arrangement, just prior to his sensational appearance in *Lloyds of London*. They continued to see each other, lunching, nightclubbing, laughing a good deal. She bought a cherry-red hat for their day at Santa Anita. He wore a pork-pie hat and camel's-hair coat. Dorothy taught him a bit about picking horses, a skill she had learned from Jim. He tried to teach her to drive a car. They were neither of them successful. Tyrone lost more than he could afford during their day at the races. Dorothy shook like a leaf behind the wheel and finally had to give it up as a lost cause.

They had a nice friendship, which Dorothy took too seriously. Over the Christmas holidays, he went to Chicago to visit Sonja Henie. Dorothy invited Herb Spiro and Eleanor to come out. Herb recalled that Dorothy appeared "overwhelmed" by the movie star's attention.

He became a kind of symbol to Dorothy of Mr. Right. A year later, *Cosmopolitan* would publish one of her short stories, this one called "Holiday from Hollywood." Tyrone was all over "Holiday from Hollywood."

The milieu of the story was again the city room. The heroine was, once again, a peppy, pretty, Irish girl reporter, Judy McClain, who is coerced by her editor into showing visiting superstar Anthony Barrett the sights of New York. Judy takes on the assignment with crackling prejudices. She is a crime reporter and this is sissy stuff. Besides, she is already attached to colleague Mike O'Hara, a tough, laconic, hard-drinking newsman. Relenting, she meets Barrett at the train station:

> Anthony Barrett stood framed in the doorway of one of the cars.
>
> Judy's heart took an unrehearsed spin.
>
> "Hold it a minute," said the photographers.
>
> Anthony Barrett blinked and smiled. He was a spectacularly handsome young man with wide shoulders and wavy hair and bright black eyes. He wore a polo

coat and a brown porkpie hat. He looked a little sleepy, but agreeable.

"He's certainly beautiful. I'll give him that," Judy said to herself. "His IQ may be low, but he's quite a sight to see."

During their first night on the town—the Stork, "21," El Morocco—Judy falls hard.

The night went quickly, for the dream boy proved to be amusing (which surprised Judy) and literate (which seemed incredible) and protective (which was touching).

His protectiveness, as a matter of fact, rather stopped her. It had been a long time since anyone had felt an urge to protect Judy McClain. She thought instinctively of Mike. Mike admired her, worked with her, scooped her, and occasionally said he loved her. But never did Mike express any desire to shelter her from the perils of a wicked world—a desire electrically evident in the glance Anthony Barrett gave her as he pulled out a chair, in the touch of his hand as he helped her into the car.[4]

Judy realizes that it is Anthony Barrett and not Mike O'Hara whom she loves, under most dramatic circumstances. With Mike's encouragement, Judy is about to rush off on another adventure. A balloonist plans a flight into the stratosphere.

Mike wants to go, but realizes that Judy's participation would make a better story. Impersonating a man—replacing Mike at Mike's behest—she is about to step into the balloon's gondola. Barrett arrives on the scene, fights Mike off, and stops her forcibly from entering the gondola. The story is ruined, but not the relationship. Anthony Barrett sweeps her off her feet into the sunset as simply his wife. Music swells. Credits roll.

Dorothy wrote trashy pulp with her fingertips, so bad that, had *Cosmopolitan* not been the Hearst house organ, it might never have been published. But it was revealing trash.

In her primal search for safety through the approval of

her father, she had been chivied into this least safe of professions. To please her Mike-like father, she had counted boiled bodies on a Manhattan pier, worked trials around the clock, circled the globe, competed with barracuda Louella, and was well on her way to becoming a barracuda herself. She grieved over the loss of safety in the search for it, and never quite outgrew the resentment she felt. That part of her which was perceived and would continue to be perceived as "intensely feminine" yearned to be stopped, protected, indeed dominated by a man of style who would pluck her out of the gondola.

By the time Herb and Eleanor arrived, Dorothy had abandoned any plan to stay in Hollywood. Louella had made it just too rough for her to function with significant success as a columnist. And Dorothy never would have settled for satellite status.

As well, Dorothy had picked a dangerous enemy in Constance Bennett, who was in and out of litigation throughout her career. She was once sued by a taxi driver over a four-dollar fare that she refused to pay, claiming he had taken the long way around. She was displeased by a portrait painted of her and again summarily withheld payment. When a judge ruled that she was obliged to pay for services rendered, she put her foot through the offending painting. She brought suit, too, against Ben Hecht and Charles MacArthur for breach of contract. When Jimmie Fidler, a Hollywood columnist, uttered remarks that she took to be "malicious and with intent to injure her in her career," she rocked him with a lawsuit for a quarter of a million dollars.

In a column in January, 1937, Dorothy went after Constance Bennett again, this time making substantive, injurious charges that must have been based on what she considered to be solid information. Setting up a bogus question-and-answer column, Dorothy posed this query to herself: "Why was *Ladies in Love* made?" She answered: "To use Constance Bennett. She was under contract to make two pictures for Twentieth Century-Fox. The first picture chased people out of theaters. The Company offered her $100,000 not to make another picture. Connie refused. So what she got was *Ladies in Love*. And it served her right."

Bennett seethed. And sued. On January 23, 1937, a formal, full-column apology was made, under Dorothy's by-line. It read, in part:

> Miss Bennett's pictures have been successful and there was no intention on the part of Twentieth Century-Fox to induce cancellation of the contract at any time. The writer regrets her erroneous reference to the matter, and desires to withdraw the statements completely, with her apologies to Miss Bennett thereof.

In the Bennett-Kilgallen debacle, there are several elements to be considered.

Dorothy was a new girl in town, looking for mean and juicy stuff. But she was neither a fool nor an amateur. She was doubtless passed the information by someone whom she considered to be reliable.

William Randolph Hearst and his empire were in big trouble. The old man's insane extravagances had finally cost. His debts amounted to $126 million. He had either to save his mind-boggling possessions or his newspapers. Though he chose to keep the papers, there was restructuring to do: merging, firing, whittling down. In the vast austerity program that followed, the *American* would combine with the *Evening Journal* to become the New York *Journal-American*.

A legal judgment such as the one that Dorothy had almost precipitated could not be tolerated at this time by Hearst. Nor could Dorothy any longer be tolerated by Louella. Louella lived in constant fear of being canned. With merger imminent, the threat loomed large—no less so because it was chimerical. This was clearly the time for Louella to make a move.

Hollywood savants concluded with amusement that the Constance Bennett item was Louella's *coup de grâce:* an intentional, litigable plant. Dorothy's sauciest story was a diabolical goose from the older columnist.

Shortly before Dorothy left Hollywood, she wrote plaintively to Herb Spiro: "Get me out of this town." [5]

Sinner Take All had been completed on December 19, 1936, and given an immediate preview. Dorothy's five lines were cut to one. Whatever connection she was supposed to have had to Margaret Lindsay was extirpated during the shooting or in the cutting room. When the movie opened in New York that February, it was totally ignored by Rose Pelswick, the reviewer for the *Evening Journal*. Dorothy had doubtless requested the omission. Non-Hearst reviewers noted Dorothy's brief appearance without malice.

She made several minor attempts at acting in the forties. But what she had discerned as failure in *Sinner Take All* evidently cut deep. Twenty-five years later, she was asked by the producer of her radio program, "Breakfast with Dorothy and Dick": "Hey, Dorothy, didn't you once appear in a movie?"

"What on *earth* ever gave you that idea?" she replied.

Dorothy returned home to a prewar New York as innocent and ignorant as herself, as frivolous as she would like to have been.

It was a time when the fact that the rich had finally come out to play was widely publicized. The phenomenon was called Café Society. Café Society was a *shiddoch* between the rich and the restaurants, a commingling therein, right out in public, of old wealth and new money, and of both of them with the talented, the exceptionally amusing, the extraordinarily attractive. Edith Wharton mourned the passing of the old ways in a *Harper's* essay in which she described the style of life "as divides my contemporaries from the era of the New Deal." She wrote:

> Though my parents were much invited and extremely hospitable, the tempo of New York society was so moderate that not infrequently they remained home in the evening. . . . The New York of those days was a place in which external events were few and unexciting, and little girls were mostly to "be happy and building at home."

Fortune traced the beginnings of Café Society to a third generation of wealth finally bored with Newport, and to the rise of "the high-grade speakeasy in the middle-twenties," notably the Bath Club (which became El Morocco), Jack and Charlie's (which became "21"), and the Stork Club (which moved east).

The Depression, too, was blamed. *Fortune* claimed that the days of "hunger marches and bread lines" made elaborate dinner dances in the great houses "vulgar if not dangerous ostentation." The rich decided, therefore, to entertain on their Long Island estates, far from the madding crowd, or less elaborately, in public hotels and restaurants. The magazine concluded:

> And thus slowly, compounded of many different elements, at the outset unconscious of its own development in the obtrusive presence of noisier events, Café Society was born.[1]

Whatever its roots, Dorothy was widely attracted to this glamorous bazaar. She wanted *in*. But she could never have made a statement so lean and hungry as the one society photographer Jerome Zerbe made in which he described his El Morocco subjects as "the top, top social."

> These are the people whose houses, one knew, were filled with treasures. These were the women who dressed the best. These were the dream people that we all looked up to and hoped that we or our friends could sometimes know and be like.[2]

Dorothy knew the rich were different. She liked the difference. And she genuinely liked the rich. Never so crudely in touch with her drives as Zerbe, she would have found his explication vulgar and offensive. Had she the consciousness, she would have been too proud to express so boldly the urge to move up and among.

Perhaps, too, her indirection bespoke a qualitative difference. She never seized, she accreted. She did not fashion herself so much as she felt herself being fashioned by events. She felt herself not so much choosing as being somehow "elected."

There was a gauzy, ethereal quality about her. One of Dorothy's debutante friends, Rosemary Cox, evoked in her mind an essence of the young journalist, "swirling around the dance floor, all white and gossamer." That is probably how Dorothy saw herself, and it is not quite the same as sizing up treasure. It is rather the ripening of the little girl who dreamed of tiny pussycats.

After her trip around the world, Dorothy somehow met Hope Hampton, the sequined, boaed "Duchess of Park Avenue," who had left show business to marry millionaire Jules Brulatour. Dorothy was then lugging Eleanor around to New York functions. Hope Hampton recalled the many opening nights when she would leave the theater and find the two sisters nestled inside her impressive limousine:

> You could hardly see them it was so dark inside the car. They'd be waiting for me to come out. Then we would all go to El Morocco. Dorothy just simply loved me. And she used to go crazy about beautiful jewelry. Her whole face lit up.
> When she became successful in her own right, she would cross the room at El Morocco. Just like a child, she'd say, "Hopie, look! I have real jewels. Just like yours." Can you imagine it? Right in the middle of El Morocco. Your mind's not on things like that.[3]

Dorothy was refashioned in her new professional bailiwick. After the Hollywood fiasco, she spurned the grime of the police beat and the ordeal of the running trial story. She began to specialize in the social and the upper-crusty. She covered the wedding of Franklin Delano Roosevelt, Jr., to Ethel du Pont. She wrote a feature about debutantes and their diets. She talked herself, with triumphant temerity, into the suite of tennis champion Helen Wills. Sounding like Celia Johnson out of Noel Coward, she criticized Wills: "I'm sorry she was so smart and cool and ruthless at Wimbledon. I think sometimes it is more important to be gracious than to win." [4]

Single-handedly, she covered the coronation of George VI for the *Journal*, filling the entire front page of the paper for days with background stories, profiles, hard news of the coronation and all related social functions. On the *Queen Mary* and in London, she learned about keno, plover's eggs, curtsies, the proper response to royalty, and the significance of royal ribbons. The last bit of information she picked up from a viscount whom she described to Eleanor as "terribly cute." Mae was along for the ride and took to calling movies the cinema.[5]

Among the many social events she covered as a working reporter at the coronation was a reception for parliamentary delegates. There she curtsied to the Duke and Duchess of Kent and referred to the occasion as "my debut in London society." [6]

It is well within the realm of possibility that in Dorothy's perplexing psyche, dusty with moonbeams and communion wafers, she was actually seeing these professional events as a kind of social baptism. Ignoring P.S. 119 and Erasmus Hall—and she ignored them as often as possible—she was, after all, convent-bred. Eliminating her six years of crime reporting, one could say that she had traveled abroad after the convent, a ritual observed by every predeb before her formal introduction to society and marriageable males. Casting aside, just for the moment, the fact that she was covering for Hearst and doing the job of six reporters, she had even made a "debut in London society."

In her "official" coronation portrait, which was hung alongside those of the Duke and Duchess of Kent on page two of the *Evening Journal*, she sat demurely in simple evening attire with square bodice and short, puffed sleeves. Her hands, like those of the duchess, are folded serenely on her lap. Like the duke, she looked bemused and benevolent. Her eyes fronted for a sweeping fantasy.

She would live wilder fantasies in her lifetime.

The announcement ran as a full-page in the Hearst newspapers:

THE FIRST AND ONLY WOMAN BROADWAY COLUMNIST
DOROTHY KILGALLEN'S
VOICE OF BROADWAY COLUMN
STARTS MONDAY
A MAN'S JOB
BEGINNING MONDAY IN THE NEW YORK
JOURNAL-AMERICAN, DOROTHY KILGALLEN
WILL REPORT DAILY ON THE DEEDS AND MISDEEDS
OF BROADWAY . . . ALWAYS A MAN'S JOB . . . BUT
DOROTHY HAS BEEN DOING A MAN'S WORK . . .
AND DOING IT BETTER!

One of the fantasies that Dorothy promulgated was that *The Voice of Broadway*, the column that she took over on November 14, 1938, was somehow foisted upon her. In 1944, she would tell *The Queen's Work*, a magazine for and about Catholic women, that she had been a kind of reluctant bride. The interviewer for *The Queen's Work*, Leo P. Wobido, S.J., wrote:

One of her pet peeves was chatter columns and she positively resented her boss's proposal that she take over the *Journal*'s Broadway column on the death of the famous O. O. McIntyre. . . . She thought to herself as she turned in her sample stint, *"Well*, here's the column that will end all Broadway columns."

O. O. McIntyre, who died in February of 1938, had been writing for many years a column called *OO McIntyre's New York Letter*. His was a highly successful endeavor. He wrote as a small-town boy in love with the big city. *The New York Times*'s obituary observed: "To him, the towers of Manhattan were studded with minarets and neon lights of Broadway flickered like jewels. . . . Accuracy was his enemy and glamor was his god."

Despite his constant references to the town in which he grew up, Gallipolis, Ohio, McIntyre had ceased, long before his death, to be the rapturous rustic he proclaimed. When he moved from the Ritz Towers, where he had long lived, it took twenty-six moving vans to carry his furnishings, his mammoth wardrobe, and his two hundred walking sticks. At the time of his death, he had an estimated seven million readers and an income of $200,000 a year.

Louis Sobol, a small man with big ears and a sweet disposition, had created *The Voice of Broadway* at the New York *Graphic* and brought it with him when he moved to the *Journal* in the 1920s. The column consisted primarily of gossip and table talk and was widely syndicated by King Features. Sobol had never developed a strongly idiosyncratic personality as a gossip columnist. After McIntyre's death, William Curley, editor-in-chief of the *Journal*, moved Sobol into O. O.'s spot in the lead, second-section space of the Hearst papers, and instructed him to generalize his approach. *The Voice of Broadway* was dropped altogether for several months.

It was resumed in November of 1938 because of the tremendous pressure placed on the *Journal-American* by advertisers—primarily nightclubs and restaurants—the activities of whose denizens the column reported. The pressure was understandable.

The New York World's Fair was about to open, and many millions of tourists were expected to flock to the city. Billy Rose's spectacular Diamond Horseshoe was scheduled to open at Christmas. Felix Ferry was putting the finishing touches on Fefe's Monte Carlo, the poshest of rooms from whose blue-glass bar one watched twinkling murals of Monte Carlo Bay at night. The Pago-Pago Room was putting in a pool.

There was activity galore at the fifty "top crystal and chromium clubs" in the city, whose gross, by 1942, exceeded $85 million a year. Each of these places had a press agent, and each of the press agents beat the drum for his unique attraction. The Stork Club had special dollar debutante lunches. Zorita was charming snakes at the Onyx Room. Brenda Frazier, the most celebrated debutante of the time, whose fan mail exceeded in quantity that of most Hollywood stars, was in the snakelike conga line at La Conga. The Arthur Murray Dancers were demonstrating the Lambeth Walk at the Savoy. Helen Wainwright was plunging nightly into five feet of water at the Pago-Pago. The curtain rose intermittently at Fefe's Monte Carlo, where Anita Colby and other top models paraded around the big stage showing the latest in haute couture. There were acrobats flying from tabletops, balloon nights, performing seals, society singers, rumba bands, swing music, and a profusion of celebrities who helped pull in the paying customers.

The celebrities of the day included actors, of course, politicians, models, debutantes, and the newly visible rich. While some of them might have moved their feast initially to avoid the limelight, they had grown accustomed to it. Jerome Zerbe, who took pictures at El Morocco and the Rainbow Room, and who attributed the success of El Morocco to his widely publicized photographs, claimed that there were only three members of Café Society who genuinely disliked being photographed. He named Mrs. Vincent Astor and Allan Ryan, Jr.; the third, presumably, was so private that his or her name was unutterable.[7]

Sherman Billingsley, of the Stork Club, boasted that he was able to afford lavishing gifts upon his celebrity diners because he had never spent one penny on publicity. What he meant, of course, was that he had never spent one penny on advertising. The gifts—champagne, brandy, cocker spaniels, cigarette cases, expensive perfume, free dinners for ten, hundred-dollar bills curled inside the balloons for which his customers jumped—generated their own publicity, as did the jumpers. Had he been compelled to pay for the column space his peculiar genius for generating items and courting the press engendered, he might have found himself back where he started: bootlegging in Enid, Oklahoma.

Without the Broadway column, the town would have been all dressed up with no place to go.

Dorothy was a natural choice for the new *Voice of Broadway*. She was already a name big enough to make the columns herself. Her dating relationship with top-flight sportswriter Paul Gallico, whom she apparently met through Jim, was mentioned in several Broadway columns. Danton Walker of the *Daily News* caught them dancing at the Stork. Winchell had them on the verge of matrimony: "Paul Gallico, in England, confides to intimates there that if Dorothy Kilgallen would have him—she's the one he'd like to Love, Honor & O, Boy! . . ."

She was already leading the life of a Broadway columnist, out almost every night with a stable of escorts. She was meeting the "right" people, befriending a group of wastrels, debutantes, and lounge lizards whom she eventually ordained "the East Side Crowd" and "the Lunch Bunch," an inane group of frolickers who grew wiser with age. Two of them, debutante Rosemary Cox and playboy Billy Livingston, looking back at their behavior, uttered almost identical judgments. Rosemary Cox recalled, "Mike Todd threw us out of his Aquacade for making noise and throwing peanuts. Billy was always carrying on. We acted like a bunch of shits." [8] Billy Livingston did not disagree: "There was a *terrible* depression going on . . . I look back and I realize what a little shit I must have been." [9]

So natural did Dorothy's ascension to Broadway columnist seem to her new friends that none of them is able to recall her transition from feature writer to *The Voice of Broadway*. There was, in fact, a small party for her at the Stork. But to that she invited her newspaper colleagues who did not necessarily mix with her frolicking acquisitions.

Most important, from the standpoint of the Hearst hierarchy, Dorothy could write with enough personality to become—they hoped—a kind of female Walter Winchell. She had emerged in all the stories she had filed, from a multitude of courtrooms, at Lakehurst, aboard the *Hindenburg*, from Munich to the Philippines, from Hyde Park,

Hollywood, London, and the Stork, as herself a star, alternately fizzy, opinionated, reverential, overweening, overwhelmed, imperious, zealous, vain, foolish, and shrewd. She was as ebulliently small-town as O. O. McIntyre and as provincially snobbish as the boutonniered society dandy who became the first "Cholly Knickerbocker," Maury Paul. She shared an additional characteristic with Maury Paul—he, too, lived with his mother.

Editor William A. Curley, a stocky and bombastic little man who was married to Marion Davies's ward, met with Louis Sobol to discuss Sobol's successor.

Ed Sullivan was mentioned, but they agreed that Dorothy was a more exciting choice. These were austere times and, as a woman, she would be cheap. As a woman, too, Curley suggested, she would be a novelty, a first. In truth, Virginia Vale, a shy woman who lived quietly at the Beaux Arts, wrote a column about Broadway that had an incredible syndication. Since she had no New York outlet, however, the Hearst publicity people could safely claim, at least to their readership in New York, that Dorothy was THE FIRST AND ONLY WOMAN BROADWAY COLUMNIST.

It was the old gee-whiz factor again, though the froufrou, coo-coo bailiwick of Café Society and the traditional language of the Broadway column, largely invented by Winchell, was a basically feminine phenomenon.

But could she get around? Sobol suggested that they call her in and find out. Curley buzzed. Dorothy appeared. She assured them eagerly that she knew her way around, had enough beaux to function as escorts, and, if the necessity arose, would be more than willing to make her nocturnal rounds alone.

Did she want it?

Louis Sobol grinned knowledgeably, many years later: "She wanted it." [10]

Dorothy had never been ashamed of her family or her household. Brooklyn was another matter. When she became *The Voice of Broadway*, she persuaded the family to move into Manhattan. It seemed a far more convenient and appropriate habitat for a Broadway columnist. They took a large apartment on East Seventy-second Street. Dorothy explained the change to the amiable crime reporter Grace Robinson: "We're moving nearer to the Stork Club." [1]

If Mae Kilgallen had any misgivings at all, she would have been loath to reveal them to Dorothy. At this point, it was very likely that what she feared most in the world was the idea of one of her daughters leaving home to lead the vulnerable life of a bachelor girl in New York City. It was inevitable, of course, that Dorothy Mae would marry. But before such time, Mae did everything in her power to see that her eldest daughter was, if not "happy and building at home," at least sleeping there.

Their apartment in New York was as warm and homely as an Easter ham. There were cabbage roses on the flocked wallpaper, shirred silk around the reading lamps, and fresh fruit wherever one turned.

This was a cocoon for Dorothy, the only fixed star in her changing universe. They were a very close family, huddling rather than confiding. And she, their dutiful, achieving daughter, was the point around which they all orbited. Mae doted on her. Jim adored her and never ceased talking about her accomplishments. And Eleanor, who was now thinking about going into the theater, and had already played some summer stock, was a bosom buddy.

A secretary at the *Journal-American*, who will be called Shirley here, met Dorothy in the washroom one afternoon.

Dorothy, rummaging through her handbag, said to Shirley, "I hope Mommy put in an extra handkerchief for me."

"Don't you prepare your own handbag?" Shirley asked.

"Oh, no. When I'm getting dressed Mommy always goes through my bag and cleans it out and prepares it for the day," Dorothy answered.[2]

The secretary was startled. Not only did the intrepid, self-reliant *Journal* star have a hovering mother, she apparently had nothing to hide from her.

Dorothy had dates and escorts. But there were no serious entanglements. Whom she loved did not love her back, and who loved her was not necessarily suitable.

Tyrone Power, who became a national heartthrob just after Dorothy left Hollywood, took her out once when the family was still living in Brooklyn. Eleanor was sworn to secrecy, but she did tell one friend, Charlotte Manson. The two teenagers crouched around the outside of the house and peered through the windows, giggling and gasping, as the movie star shook hands with Mr. and Mrs. Kilgallen. Dorothy entered, dressed like a fairy princess. They left in his limousine for their night on the town.[3] He married his first wife, actress Annabella, soon after.

Paul Gallico, who would leave the newspaper business to begin an extraordinary career as a fiction writer, was the only one about whom Dorothy hinted that there was something tantalizingly reciprocal. With Gallico, however, there were many problems. He was sixteen years older than Dorothy, already twice divorced (one of his ex-wives was the daughter of Adela Rogers St. Johns). Walter Winchell's item notwithstanding, Gallico did not consider the relationship a serious one.

He would write, several months before his death in 1976:

> I do remember Dorothy as a gay, enchanting person, bright and witty and fun to be with, and we dated for a year or so. We used to like to dance, which means that we were seen from time to time in night clubs and of course attracted the notice of columnists of the time. One thing is certain. Dorothy and I were never engaged. I was very fond of her. She seemed to enjoy my company and that is as far as it went.[4]

Several of her escorts, just bread-and-butter newspaper-men, would not or could not mix it up in Café Society, and fell by the wayside. Herb Spiro began to discern changes and did not approve of what he saw. Her debutante friends he considered childish and boring:

> We walked out of the Stork with one of them one night. She and Dorothy were acting like schoolgirls, giggling and skipping and being awfully gay. I felt like kicking them both in the ass.[5]

Her new friends included a trio of not-very-prominent debutantes, all younger than Dorothy, whom she had met just prior to her ascension, on that story about debs and their diets. The friendships continued. A pardigm of Café Society, they suited each other's needs. The group gave Dorothy a feeling of belonging to a "social set." She shared with them the perks of power and mentioned them frequently in *The Voice of Broadway*.

Rosemary Cox, the tall, bubbling daughter of P. T. Cox, one of the contractors who built New York's West Side Highway, was one of the debs. She had been educated at Sacred Heart in Connecticut, made her debut in New York, and considered "21" and the Stork Club "home."

There was Mary Anne Travers, six years younger than Dorothy, the granddaughter of James Butler, an Irish immigrant who started a hugely successful chain of grocery stores. His daughter married Walter Travers, who was in stables and stock. Mary Anne went to Palm Beach in the winter, to the family farm in the summer, and to Sally Victor for hats.

Martha Stephenson, the third member of these lunching ladies, was the prettiest and the most prominent. She attended Spence School and was graduated from Miss Porter's. She was a debutante of the 1938 season and once worked a week singing in a nightclub. When Martha's stepfather, a stockbroker who lost a great deal of money in the Depression, became entangled in an alimony battle with her mother, he described, in court, the values with which Martha had been reared:

> Why, when Martha was only sixteen they used to call her not at home but in night clubs. I thought it was

terribly cheap and morally destructive. A girl has no right to live in night clubs. I sent her to the best schools in the country but her thoughts were always on clothes and on going to the movies. . . . When I remonstrated with my wife, I was told that I was older than she. And when my children grew up, they called me "an old-fogey with mid-Victorian ideas." [6]

"I never understood what Dorothy saw in us," Mary Anne Travers recalled. "She was so much more intelligent. She never would have been included, but she was very good to us." [7]

The Lunch Bunch and their beaux were out for fun, and Dorothy was an open-sesame playmate. She might call one or all of them of an afternoon to come along and watch Billy Rose audition new girls for his Diamond Horseshoe or Mae West carry on during the rehearsal of *Catherine Was Great*. (Once, when Dorothy was present, Miss West, displeased with the progress of a rehearsal, undulated down the aisle, complaining: "This is a $200,000 show; and I'm not going to see $200,000 go down the tur-let!") She was implored to attend all of the important openings and to bring as many friends as she chose. "There were new shows at the St. Regis and the Iridian Room all the time," Rosemary Cox said. "Dorothy would call and say, 'Won't you come?' We would all have a beautiful dinner, a marvelous table. And there'd be no bill. We were free-loading. But we all liked her." [8]

It was easy to like Dorothy socially. She was a generous friend and a pleasant companion. Her manners were impeccable. She never gossiped or bad-mouthed anyone. She liked her new life. She loved her job. She was proud of the columns she was turning out, though never boastful. She had an innocence that the worldly found amusing, a flighty, gesticulating insecurity that the more sensitive of her friends found poignant.

All her hostility and psychological quirkiness emerged in the column, but that was a separate room and not yet over-burdened. The side that she showed to the people whom she meant to please and have love her was amiable and sweet. Billy Livingston, one of her young, rich, and quite clever new friends, who looked like Douglas Fairbanks and was said to have been one of the best ballroom

dancers in New York, observed: "There were two Doro-
thys. One was in her fingers at the typewriter and the other
was the person." [9]

In her way, she was climbing and being climbed all over.
It was a tasteful act, however, and everyone seemed to
benefit.

Mary Anita Loos befriended Dorothy in the late thirties. She was the niece of the Anita Loos who wrote
Gentlemen Prefer Blondes, a much taller version of her
aunt, with the same driving energy and the same bobbed,
banged haircut. She had studied archeology and anthro-
pology at Stanford University. After graduating, she traveled through Greece and Egypt, excavating with the School
of American Research.

She came to New York "just to see what was going on"
and landed an unexpected job as a press agent for Fefe's
Monte Carlo because she was smart-looking and college-
educated. She had not made a debut ("We don't go in for
that sort of thing in California"). She knew none of the
people about whom she was supposed to write ("Maury
Paul captioned the pictures for me"). Though she wore
red shoes, her feet were planted firmly on the ground. Unlike most of Café Society, she even knew there was going
to be a war.

Press-agentry was like summer camp to her, and she
was distanced enough from the whole scene in New York
to regard it with an amused acuity. Dorothy's place in the
ranks was also clear to her:

> It was one of those heedless, luxury-glutted times that
> usually happens before a disaster. We were rushing
> headlong into war. Everything was excessive. Glamour
> was the word. Everyone was competing to be glamour-
> ous. And newspaper people especially were treated
> like royalty.
>
> What Dorothy did, which was unique, was to fash-
> ion herself into a glamour girl. She was the first news-
> paperwoman to put on her dancing shoes and get
> around with various escorts and *make* a personality
> out of herself. If she had been a little younger, she
> undoubtedly would have had facial work done and
> corrected her weak chin. She had a very good figure,

marvelous black curly-Irish hair, beautiful eyes, and a startling complexion.

She became, in a sense, the pulse of Café Society. Most of the society editors were older and most of them were gay. She was young and she was fresh and she'd accrued a certain amount of prestige and publicity on account of her trip around the world. When she got into writing her column, she ran with and reported on the younger people. To some extent, she was accepted by them. And she mixed café society, society, and show business—which was the first time that was done.[10]

Mary Anita was one of the few people in whom Dorothy confided. One afternoon, after they had been to a museum, she asked the twenty-six-year-old columnist if she intended to marry. Dorothy said that she was "dying to find someone." She had seen the ravages that solitude had taken on her live-in Aunt Esther. And she was tired of scrounging up escorts to take her places.

A few months later, Mary Anita had a small party for Dorothy. She asked her if there was anyone special she wanted to have there. Dorothy smiled coyly. She had recently met a young actor with brown eyes and a streak of red in his hair whom she rather fancied. "You might ask Richard Kollmar," she said. "He's sort of cute."

She had been aware of Kollmar from the first time she saw him perform in *Knickerbocker Holiday*, the musical in which Walter Huston introduced "September Song." Kollmar was making his Broadway debut in the show, playing an important featured role as Brom Broeck, the young rebel who was almost hanged for challenging the tyrannical rule of Peter Stuyvesant in New Amsterdam. She had mentioned him in her very first column, in this piece of historical revisionism:

> Most of the papers editorialized that Governor Lehman was the first fourth-term Governor in the history of New York. They forgot Daniel D. Tompkins, who was Governor for five terms—1807–1817. His great-great grandson, Richard Kollmar, is the baritone of *Knickerbocker Holiday*.[11]

And then she wrote:

> Richard Kollmar, *Knickerbocker Holiday* baritone,
> gave a combination New Year's Eve and birthday
> party Saturday night, to which guests were asked to
> come in kiddie costumes.[12]

An obvious press-agent feed. But Dorothy would never
have used it if the man and his kiddie costumes had not
appealed to her.

Just two days later, she devoted almost a third of her
column to him. She elaborated on his distinguished ances-
try, mentioned four women he was taking out:

> Mary ("My Heart Belongs to Daddy") Martin, Jean
> Rodney (the young producer), Ann Wisner, a society
> girl, and Brenda Frazier, who needs no introduction.
> . . . He is 28, tall and dark, with hair worn long for
> his role and a quiet manner.[13]

Presently, Dorothy received a telephone call from Kollmar's press agent. Mr. Kollmar wanted to meet the woman
who was rewarding him with such sumptuous validation.
Would she have lunch with him at the Algonquin?

Richard Kollmar arrived punctually at 12:30 in a Cadillac driven by a black chauffeur. The car was Richard's,
purchased second-hand and cheap. The chauffeur he hired
for special occasions. On this special occasion, Richard had
the chauffeur accompany him into the lobby of the legendary hotel so that Dorothy would be sure to notice. The
two self-made cosmopolites fell into easeful conversation,
both having a tendency to drop important names, a love of
popular music, and a newly acquired appreciation of *haute
cuisine*.

He did a good deal of the talking in his radio-rich baritone. Dorothy was impressed by the fact that he planned
to do Shakespeare someday and claimed to spend much of
his free time editing the military papers of his famous
forebear, after whom he said the Tompkinsville Ferry out
of Staten Island was named. She suggested that Tompkinsville in Staten Island was probably named for him as well.
He paused, considered it, and laughed. Richard was one of

those rare laughers who inclined his head and actually emitted the sound *ha ha*.

Having loosened up some more, he made a joke about the fruit-heavy Sally Victor hat she was wearing. "Do you grow your own?" he asked. She, in turn, kidded him about his bright orange socks. "Do you knit them yourself?" [14]

That same night she and this handsome stranger went to hear Artie Shaw and ended the evening at the Stork, where he must have been impressed with the effulgent greeting she undoubtedly received from Sherman Billingsley. By the time Mary Anita's party for Dorothy arrived, they were comfortable with each other and openly affectionate in word and gesture. They had established, too, an actively attentive, sparky, and rhythmic way of talking to each other, aggressively *engagé*. It was apparent to all of Dorothy's friends that this was the man.

He proposed on their sixth date, the courtship having been interrupted while he left town with the show. Dorothy told him that she wanted very much to be his wife, but that the problem of religion had first to be solved. Richard was an Episcopalian, and she would not consider marrying outside the Church. He would have to convert.

Thereupon, he spoke to his mother, Christine, who traced her roots back to Plymouth Rock and had little use for Catholics, less for Irish Catholics. He had brought Mary Martin home a couple of times. And Christine had hoped for something there. She cried and forbade. Richard would not relent. Finally his more equable father, John Kollmar, convinced Christine that she would have to consent or lose her only son. "Well, I suppose all the churches will someday be one," she sighed.[15]

He had then to ask formally for Dorothy's hand. Jim consented readily. Mae had not been fond of Richard from the beginning. She, too, was brought around by her husband, having lost her strongest case when the young actor agreed to convert. They planned a large wedding at the Kilgallens' new church, St. Vincent Ferrer, during the fashionable month of April.

Richard Tompkins Kollmar was born in Brooklyn on New Year's Eve in 1910. His family moved shortly thereafter to Ridgewood, New Jersey, one of Manhattan's commuting suburbs, to which many former Brooklynites had fled, like the Kollmars, to escape the polio epidemics of the early part of the century. "The Hill," that part of Ridgewood where the family lived, was a pristinely WASP community of about five thousand people. Income there was less important than church membership, community service, American bloodline, and dedication to the Protestant work ethic.

John Kollmar, Richard's hardworking and unprepossessing father, functioned as secretary-treasurer of the Triangle Film Corporation, when the hub of the film industry was located in Fort Lee, New Jersey. On the advice of his wife, Christine, John elected to stay put when movies moved West.

John went into business as a local contractor and built many of the houses in Ridgewood, his own modest single-story dwelling among them. He was a spectacularly bad businessman, however, losing money on many of his contracts. When he had finally to dissolve his business, he accepted a job with the Ridgewood Board of Education as a county clerk in charge of purchasing. He stayed with the board until his retirement many years later.

Christine was a conventionally pretty, prematurely gray-haired woman of middle height who took preposterous pride in her family tree. She was a member of several old-American "Daughters" groups. A large portrait of her most distinguished forebear, Daniel D. Tompkins, was displayed prominently over the living-room fireplace. Richard, an only child, was said to resemble him: They both had high, prominent foreheads, deep-set brown eyes, and red highlights in their hair.

Mother and son had a close and loving relationship, though from infancy, Richard's behavior had puzzled and intrigued her. He was an intensely interior child. Placed on a rug, surrounded by his toys, he sat mute and undiverted. She rattled and rolled for him to no avail. Growing up for Richard was a process of laboriously learned and not entirely successful accommodations to external demands. He was neither autistic nor stupid. But he was strange.

"He learned to speak and to reply to people, to come to," a cousin, Betty Leggett, remembered. "But his mind was always elsewhere. If you were *really* looking when you talked to Dick, you could see that he wasn't listening." [1]

Richard's inability to concentrate on the business at hand made schoolwork a monumental chore for him. He required constant tutoring, especially in math, to get him through the Ridgewood public school system.

In spite of his handicap, he was a stylish youth who managed to tantalize his playmates: George Allen, George's brother Charles (called Pete), Edward (Chinky) Wohl, and Edgar Hatfield. He could not attend, but he would be attended to. He was an esthete, sensitive to the point of fragility. On those infrequent occasions when his parents argued, he became literally ill. While the other boys favored dogs with which they could romp, Richard preferred cats because they were softer and nicer. On the Fourth of July, the other boys set off firecrackers; Richard produced and orchestrated displays of fireworks.

Theater was always his passion, and he mesmerized his friends with entertainments and energetic companionship. He was fun to be around though removed enough so that Charles Allen would refer to his friendship as "a show of camaraderie."

He loved to dress up. At one of the many costume parties given by the Kollmars for their son, Richard wore an authentic little pilgrim's outfit rented from a theatrical costumer. That was another surprise for the neighborhood youngsters, most of whom came in sheets or cowboy clothes. His family could least afford such an extravagance.

Richard Tompkins Kollmar was marching to some distant

drummer. And he went, not infrequently, in search of the source. Before he was twelve, he had run away from home more than a dozen times. Those were usually short junkets, involving truancy and a thumbed ride. On each of those occasions, he would forewarn George, "I want to get away from it all for a while." When he was twelve, however, he took off on a more ambitious search.

When his absence was discovered, the police were called in. The Kollmars waited frantically for word. It was almost a week later when they received a telephone call from Richard. He was in St. Louis and wanted additional money to get to California, where he hoped to make his way as a motion picture actor.

John went after him and brought him back. The Allens heard the commotion as the prodigal returned. A screen door was slammed. Christine shrieked.

Richard informed his friends the next day that he had left home to make his fortune in order to help his family through their financial difficulties. His actions in later life belie the explanation. Richard was lavish but never generous. He was more likely looking for fame than fortune, more likely escaping from the financial crisis than attempting to allay it.

"It bothered me that he could have done that and I wouldn't have known," recalled George Allen, who is now a retired Singer sewing-machine-company executive living in Cape Cod. "He must have lived within himself a great deal." [2]

On his return, young Kollmar was sent to a work school for problem boys. It was affiliated with the Episcopal Church and located in New Jersey. There were cows to milk and hay to tend. He seemed to enjoy the experience and never again attempted flight.

Despite his fragile sensibilities and his theatricality, Richard was never considered unmanly by his Ridgewood coterie because he evinced from early childhood a strong, almost obsessive interest in beautiful women. A neighborhood family, the Dunnings, had invented the rear-screen projection process that makes automobiles appear to move. Richard played tennis on their court, once met Mary Pickford there, and talked about it forever.

One of his first local girl friends was Jean Fullertan, a

tall, lovely blonde who left Ridgewood, changed her name to Jean Muir, and starred on stage and screen until the 1950s, when she was driven out of the profession during the political witch hunts.

He advanced successfully through puberty, growing to five feet ten inches. He had a deep, mellifluous voice enhanced by singing lessons, and a well-shaped, muscular body. With pennies saved, he purchased, from De Pinna's of Fifth Avenue, the first cream-color plus-fours among the Ridgewood set. He cut a dashing Fitzgeraldian figure.

When it came time for college, Edgar Hatfield, the scion of a wealthy family whose father had brought him to live in Ridgewood after the untimely death of his mother, helped Richard gain admission to St. Stephen's College, which became Bard. Richard had trouble maintaining passing grades despite the tutorial assistance he received from Edgar and all of his fraternity brothers. After a year, he flunked out and followed his friend George to a less demanding school in Tennessee, Tusculum College.

There he led a small group of theatrical types who were impressed with his amusing dialects, his knowledge of *New Yorker* writers, and his sartorial flair. He dated the minister's daughter and was, in his fashion, extremely devoted to her. He had several other campus knockouts on the side, more liberated types with whom he was able to indulge his prodigious sexual appetite.

He went on to Yale dramatic school, stayed for a year, and decided to venture forth professionally. He arrived in New York and rented an apartment in the West Sixties, over a French restaurant called Chez Gaby. Edgar Hatfield, just out of Harvard Law, shared the place with him for a time.

Because of his splendid speaking voice, Richard broke readily into radio, though the living he made was an unstable one. Early on, he invited his buddy George to come into Manhattan and watch him perform. George went enthusiastically to a theater where Richard appeared among a large group of actors engaged in the production of a gasoline commercial. By and by, he broke stiffly from the ensemble and approached the microphone. George recalled, "Dick said something like, 'Does it start regularly?' Another guy said, 'Yes, it does,' and Dick went home with fifty dollars." [3]

Even at that early and unspectacular stage of his career, Richard was tooling about in his Cadillac with his *per diem* chauffeur. Once he auditioned for a small part in a radio drama. He appeared with a Barrymore-ish coat slung over his shoulders, trailed by the chauffeur, whom he called "my man." To the utter astonishment of the other actors, he instructed his man to circle in red the four or five lines that he had been assigned to read.

A trained baritone, he sang on the radio for the first time on a Sunday morning program that featured Southern mountain songs. A Mrs. Ethel Parks Richardson, who was connected with the show, was so pleased with his performance that she arranged to have him meet Dorothy Vernon, who became his first agent. Through Vernon and yet another woman smitten with Richard's boyish charms, he auditioned for Kurt Weill and Joshua Logan. This one was big. They cast him as the juvenile lead—the male analogue of an *ingenue*—in the Playwrights' Company production of *Knickerbocker Holiday*, a *succès d'estime* of the 1938 Broadway season.

With the help of a press agent named Anne Ayers and a predisposition to be so publicized, the Kollmar image was forged. He was labeled the debutantes' delight, presented as a forebeared, preppy young man-about-town whose family would have preferred his entering the more seemly diplomatic service. He was dallying in musical comedy, on his way to acting in Shakespeare or perhaps writing a play about his illustrious great-great-grandfather, Daniel D.

"Definitely there were no theatrical forebears," he explained to one interviewer from the Brooklyn *Daily Eagle.* "Mother used to entertain me as a child with dialect impersonations—sometimes it kept me out of mischief for hours. She could imitate any maid, gardener, or window washer that came on the place." [4]

There was always a smidgeon of truth in the presentation. A young Dutch woman had, in fact, come in once a week to help Mrs. Kollmar with the heavy housework. The gardener who worked on a lot of the Ridgewood homes did have an Italian accent.

He described his father either as an architect or a member of the board of education; their relationship was "very pally." The work farm on which he had slung dung became a prep school. Tusculum was "rated high socially." He didn't often graduate himself from Yale—though he did a great deal of talking about the school—probably because there were just too many Yale men in and around the theater who would know better.

He got extraordinary mileage out of Daniel D. Tompkins. An interviewer caught him after a performance of *Knickerbocker Holiday*. In the profile, he is visited by a pair of "young ladies," one of whom exclaims, "Your hair. It's exactly the color of your great-great-grandfather's in the Stuart portrait that hangs in the Capitol!"

"Yes, Mother says it runs in the family," Kollmar acknowledged with a grin.

"That's what I call a tribute," said Kollmar after they left. "You see, they were talking about my very favorite ancestor, Daniel D. Tomkins. He was New York State's youngest governor—served five consecutive terms. He was Vice President for two terms under Monroe and almost made the Presidency. He's a sort of ideal of mine. When I was a small boy and visited my grandfather in Brooklyn, we used to walk through Prospect Park and he would regale me with anecdotes of Governor Tompkins. Even as far back as that, my ambition was to write a book about him. It still is, only now I'm concentrating on the idea of a play. . . . From what I hear old D.D. was quite a boy." [5]

Dorothy wanted "Cholly Knickerbocker" to break the news of her engagement on the Society page. He did, stressing Richard's generational high marks and discovering another gray eminence in the family crypt. He reported in his announcement that the young actor's great-great-great grandfather, Jonathan Griffin Tompkins (Daniel's pappy), had served in the New York State Convention that adopted the Declaration of Independence.

Herb Spiro was among the first to hear the news directly from Dorothy. He was sitting in the city room when Dorothy approached him and suggested that they have a drink at a local hangout called the Little Ritz.

"You'll be getting an invitation in the mail soon to my engagement party," Dorothy told him.

"Who's the lucky man?" Herb asked.

"I'm sure you've heard of him," Dorothy replied. "Richard Kollmar. He's a direct descendant of Daniel D. Tompkins, who served five consecutive terms as Governor and was Vice President for two terms under Monroe. His father, Richard's great-great-great grandfather, Jonathan Griffin Tompkins . . ." 6

The simplest conclusion about the relationship between Dorothy and Richard is drawn often and harshly by many who knew both of them. Richard, a striving actor, saw Dorothy, a powerful columnist, and thought, "That will get me where I want to go," and pursued her. It is a view that appears to redound most negatively upon him, but, in fact, makes a pitiable, foolish, and desperately vulnerable woman of Dorothy. It is a view held by many who loved her, but nonetheless perceived her as an extraordinarily unattractive woman for whom a noticeably attractive man could not conceivably have had genuine feeling.

To hold that view of their relationship is to fail to recognize that power can be as vitally aphrodisiacal when it is held by a woman as when it is held by a man. Even if Richard did perceive Dorothy as a kind of powerhouse, it is quite likely that he was aroused by that power.

Actually, she was not such a powerhouse in those days, and he was not such a mite. They were each at the beginnings of burgeoning careers. Richard had done quite well on his own, or at least without Dorothy's help. He had obtained his part in *Knickerbocker Holiday* by auditioning first for director Joshua Logan and then for writer Maxwell Anderson. There are those who claim he got to them through an important woman connected with the production. Withal, he had not married what he may have exploited (or what may have exploited him); nor would he have obtained the part finally without his boyish good looks and his excellent baritone, both of which made him an excellent candidate for regular employment in the theater and probable, if rather tepid, stardom.

Dorothy was in a position to help Richard. But there were advantages in this merger that would accrue to Dorothy. She sought and caught an "old American," a man whose pedigree would fulfill a dream of hers; would dower her issue with blue-book eligibility. But because Dorothy was a woman and not considered beautiful, because she was an exceedingly romantic woman as well, her own predation is frequently dismissed as benign and unserious. She is invariably, compassionately, regarded as victim.

As far as love is measurable from the outside, Dorothy did seem to be the more "in love" of the two. There is no denying, however, that they had, in the beginning, an extremely sexual relationship. The odds are great that it was not consummated before marriage, but they were intensely physical during their courtship, noticeably *aware* of each other.

Finally, Richard Kollmar was too much the esthete and too weak a man for the supreme sacrifice that is attributed to him by those who would dismiss him as a simple schemer. He was undoubtedly far less aware of the configuration of her face than were those to whom it became a sexist *idée fixe*. Dorothy had the vital and authentic components of beauty that obtain from health, style, and attention. Her hair was lush. Her body was spare but soft, her eyes lustrous, and her skin remarkable. She was said to move, in the arms of a man, with a serene and yielding grace.

According to yet another secretary who does not wish to be named (she did part-time work for Richard early on, and will be pseudonymously called Bea): "He was in love with her, and I think he was impressed, too." [7]

Richard had a tremendous awareness of Dorothy, a need to please that sometimes ended in total calamity. During their courtship, for instance, he was appearing in a campus musical called *Too Many Girls*. He had one of the leads in a cast that included Hal LeRoy, Eddie Bracken, Desi Arnaz, and Marcy Wescott.

Richard did well enough in the show. Brooks Atkinson, of *The New York Times*, called him, "An exuberant comedian unspoiled by cleverness." His only problems occurred when Dorothy stopped by, usually before one of their dates. Whenever she was in the audience, Richard either drew a total blank somewhere or made some monumental blunder. The cast even began placing bets on when and how Richard would blow it.

In his autobiography, *A Book*, Desi Arnaz recalls one of the more memorable episodes that took place because of Dorothy's disconcerting presence in the audience. In *Too Many Girls*, Richard and Marcy Wescott introduced the lovely standard "I Didn't Know What Time It Was." As presented in the show, the song was sung with two verses: his and hers. Richard would sing about his empty life before meeting Marcy Wescott. She, in turn, would recount her arid old life.

On the night in question, Richard drew in his stomach, crossed the stage, and in his big, solemn baritone, sang:

> *"Once when I was young*
> *Yesterday perhaps*
> *Danced with Jim and Paul*
> *And kissed some other chaps. . . ."*

Oblivious to the audience's hysteria, he went through it, never knowing until Marcy Wescott sang the same words back to him that he had gotten his verses confused.

He and Dorothy were out every night. For a while, their favorite haunt was La Conga, one of the only West Side clubs frequented by a group of chic young things whom Dorothy ordained "The East Siders." With the help of several spreads in the *Daily News* and with constant plugs in *The Voice of Broadway*, La Conga became one of the "in" spots. Richard and Dorothy joined the curvaceous conga line with Errol Flynn, Peter Arno, Brenda Frazier, Tony De Marco, and Peggy Hopkins Joyce. La Conga's press agent, Irving Zussman, enjoyed watching Dorothy: "With her handsome fiance, she had sparkle and good humor. She loved to dance. She was having a great time with her life. And she was obviously nuts about Dick." [8]

Dorothy's season lasted from the fall of 1939, when the engagement was officially announced at the Kilgallens' home, until April, 1940, when the couple took their vows before the high altar at St. Vincent's.

At the first affair, Dorothy received a flock of guests who queued up to view Richard and the ring. A toast was made mistily by Jim. Richard sang some of the highlights from his new musical until he was asked to stop by Jimmy Cannon, who was once sweet on Dorothy and had arrived drunk and obstreperous directly from Reuben's, where he had smashed a dozen plates against the wall. Dorothy asked him to leave and the gaiety resumed.

Rosemary Cox was in the kitchen with Jim Kilgallen,

where he retreated to hoist a few away from Mae's censorious glance, when Dorothy called her into her bedroom and asked her to be a bridesmaid at the wedding. Having been brought up with the notion that such honors were reserved for the people with whom one grew up, Rosemary was stunned but compliant. It would not have occurred to Rosemary, fond as she was of Dorothy, to ask her to serve in that capacity. When she was married the following year in the rectory at St. Patrick's, Martha Stephenson and Mary Anne attended her. Dorothy, who was invited as a mere guest, did not even deign to respond to the invitation.

After Rosemary Cox emerged from Dorothy's bedroom, she told Billy Livingston and Mary Anne what had happened. Mary Anne surmised correctly that she would be called in next. "You're gonna have a pretty tough time pretending to be busy in April," Billy whispered.[9]

Predictably, every important club in New York vied for the privilege of helping Dorothy celebrate her engagement. Leon & Eddie's, Fefe's Monte Carlo, "21," the Rainbow Room, the Stork Club—all gave lavish parties for the couple.

According to "Bea," Richard had an eleventh-hour attack of second thoughts, which kept him from sleeping for two weeks before the marriage. In spite of his extravagant ways, he was basically tight with his money. Dorothy's lavish spending on an apartment and furnishings, and specifically on a rug that cost $700, worried him ragged. When Bea came to work for him late one afternoon, he was sitting in a chair, moaning, "I don't think I can go through with this. She's spending all my money. How can I get out of it?"

Bea asked, "Are you sure you want to?"

He hesitated.

"If you're going to call it off you'd better get on with it," she said. "If you're going to go through with it, you'd better reconcile yourself to the kind of life she wants. Do you love her enough to put up with her extravagances?"

Richard lapsed into a long silence. And finally replied, "Yes, I guess I do."[10]

The rehearsal dinner was held at the Pierre. Dorothy arrived, having batted out her last column as a single woman. It was an untypically pensive and soft piece in which she mentioned loving milk, dachshunds, rabbits, (except those in Russell Swann's club act, who had apparently nibbled her orchids), Beethoven, Bach, and Benny Goodman. She admitted to hating alarm clocks and being unable to stay in a room where a clock was ticking. She looked forward with wild impatience to the opening of *Romeo and Juliet* with Laurence Olivier and Vivien Leigh.

Eight hundred guests gathered in the church on the clear spring morning of Saturday, April 6, 1940. Besides the couple's families, the former neighbors from Brooklyn and Ridgewood, there were Jim's legion of friends and Dorothy's more recent acquisitions.

The notables included: Mr. and Mrs. Thomas E. Dewey, Tyrone Power and his wife Annabella, Mr. and Mrs. James A. Farley, Mr. and Mrs. Jimmy Walker, Peggy Hopkins Joyce, Ethel Merman, Helen Mencken, Eddy Duchin, Walter Huston, Milton Berle, Gertrude Lawrence and Louella Parsons.

Toward the impressive altar decorated with white lilies, the participants marched. Eleanor had naturally been picked as her sister's maid of honor. Dorothy's Aunt Esther was among the bridesmaids, as was Bernadette Dolan, the only other nubile whom the bride had known for more than two years. The group was completed by Mary Anita Loos, Mary Anne Travers, Rosemary Cox, and Mrs. Keith Topping. They all wore madonna-blue net gowns and matching hats and carried bouquets of cardinal red tulips.

Richard's old Ridgewood mates attended him. They wore the conventional cutaways with striped pants.

An audible sigh emerged even from the Ridgewood contingent as Dorothy appeared alongside Jim. She was radiant in white chantilly lace. She held orchids and lilies of the valley.

The high nuptial mass lasted well over an hour, a cultural shock to the Protestants and memorably hard on their kneecaps. Billy Livingston compared the ceremony to a "four-day Guatemalan street festival." [11]

After a reception at the Viennese Room of the Saint Regis Hotel, at which champagne, chicken on ham with cheese sauce, and wedding cake were fed to the two family camps, the bride and groom left to honeymoon in Varadero, Cuba. The entire honeymoon package was a diplomatically wrapped gift presented to Dorothy from the North American gambling syndicate that supported General Fulgencio Batista.

Dorothy continued, for a short time, to work out of a glass-enclosed cubicle at the *Journal-American*. She was assisted by Hearst factotum Danny Brooks, ne Panzarella. Danny was a cigar-chewing, dwarfish man who wore pinky rings on several fingers, fooled canonically with his omnipresent rosary beads, called Dorothy "The Boss," and was given to muttering, under duress, "I got connections. I got connections."

He was loyal to a fault, communicating all office gossip to Dorothy, informing The Boss who liked her and who did not.[1] With skin as thin as the rustling outer layer of an onion, she could be inexplicably cool to those whom she was led to believe were in the enemy camp.

Her growing minions of press agents customarily delivered their column contributions directly to Dorothy. They bunched up in a small anteroom outside her office. The *Journal* building, cluttered with paper and notoriously squalid, was a kind of roach-Acapulco. When a waiting press agent one day spotted a large specimen heading under Dorothy's door, he stood up and objected, "Hey, get in line!"

Along the Great White Way, Reuben's, a favorite theatrical hangout, named a sandwich after her. She was the fifth Broadway columnist to be accorded that high honor. At $1.10, the Dorothy Kilgallen was the most expensive fare on their sandwich menu, followed by the Walter Winchell (90¢), the Ed Sullivan (85¢), the Danton Walker (85¢), and the Louis Sobol (60¢).

She and Richard lived in a small, way-station apartment on West Fifty-Fourth Street, overlooking the Museum of Modern Art. Their sunken living room had an imitation fireplace, a sofa, two chairs, and Dorothy's decorative dark-walnut desk, from which she could look out and see the museum garden through ruffled organdy curtains. Bea recalled that the room looked "like a set in Sloane's." The dining area—actually a breakfast nook—was raised off the living room and divided from it by a wrought-iron railing. In their bedroom was a long, commodious vanity table for two.

Dorothy kept a calendar in her desk, on which she carefully chronicled her ovarian cycle, separating the safe days from the risky. She and Richard were following the Roman-sanctioned rhythm method. When she conceived presently but not hastily, it was obviously a choice she had made. She invited Mary Anne and Rosemary to a girlish luncheon in the breakfast nook. Rosemary was amused by the pink pigtail bows Dorothy had tied around the wrought-iron legs of her dining chairs.[2] Mary Anne was astonished by the effulgent, joyous tears that her hostess shed while describing the prospect of motherhood to them.[3]

She functioned with amazing facility. On a particular Sunday, when Bea came to the apartment to work for Richard, Dorothy was at her desk knocking out a story for *Cosmopolitan*, "Peter Sees Pink." She began the story at one in the afternoon. By five, she had finished it *and* her column. Bea joined Richard in the kitchen, where he dictated to her a fictional attempt of his own.[4] It was staggeringly amateurish. But what he admired—and he admired his wife's assiduity—he attempted to emulate.

In June, 1941, to meet the needs of their expanding family, the Kollmars moved to a seven-room apartment on Park Avenue. Richard's taste was more in evidence here. The stark blue-and-white living room was paneled in mirrors. Dorothy's dressing room was done like a circular bandbox: pink-and-white candy-striped walls, and an intentionally garish plaid ceiling. He had a decorator's card and a flair for thematic, sparky, early camp. He designed with company in mind. Hope Hampton contributed a honey-maple crib to the nursery, a room of music boxes and carousels.

A fat baby boy, Richard Tompkins Kollmar II, was born in the fashionable LeRoy Hospital on July 11, 1941, Jim Kilgallen's birthday. Dorothy had asked Maury Paul to announce the child's birth in his "Cholly Knickerbocker" column. Maury Paul, who looked like a dandified Paul Douglas and smelled of My Sin, flushed with anger at the *arriviste*, who frequently scooped him on the activities of the *sooo* social. "You are *not* society, my dear," he hissed, "and I see no reason why your child should be mentioned in anything but a Broadway column." [5]

The arrival of Dorothy's "Broadway" baby worried Richard Berlin, a top Hearst executive, who was afraid of losing his young star. Her paper reported the birth carefully, taking special pains to explain the presence of *The Voice of Broadway* in that day's edition: "Miss Kilgallen," the story explained, "entered the hospital a few hours after she had written the column for today, in the tradition of working right up to the deadline."

In her postpartum column of July 12, which should have been written on the very day Richard, Jr., arrived, she fudged admirably. It was a typical Kilgallen column. There was no mention of labor pains or twilight sleep.

A nanny was hired for little Dickie. And eventually a Jamaican couple, the Applethwaites, for Dorothy and Richard. The woman cooked, which was a very good thing. Dorothy was a total bust in the kitchen, unable to follow simple package directions.

"Sweetie," Richard said over his porridge, "I just don't understand it. When other people add hot water to cereal, they get cereal. When you do it, all I get is lumps." [6]

Dorothy continued to spend lavishly. Richard was growing accustomed to it. Just as she refused to see herself as a cooking person, she abjured dealing with the business of business. She became coy and Dolly Mae-ish with regard to their finances. When an insurance man called at the apartment, she fluttered, "You'll have to talk to my husband about that. I don't know *anything* about money." [7] Against the repeated implorations of Edgar Hatfield, who now functioned as their attorney, they never saved or invested anything. "We don't like to discuss money," Richard told a newspaper writer. "We just like to feel that there's enough in the bank somehow." [8]

Cash flow they had. Not surprisingly—she was, after all, a woman *and* working for Hearst—*The Voice of Broadway* itself yielded Dorothy only $150 a week, though by April, 1941, the column was appearing in twenty-four newspapers and growing in syndication. But it was the hub from which more remunerative enterprises radiated. She made four times as much doing a weekly, scripted radio show for

Johnson & Johnson Band-Aids. The coast-to-coast program was also called "The Voice of Broadway."

With Warren Hull as her co-anchor, the show opened with the click of a telephone being lifted from its cradle. Dorothy's voice was heard next saying: "Hello. This is Dorothy Kilgallen. Yes, I know the latest news about [name of celebrity]. And so will you if you keep listening."

On "The Voice of Broadway" of March 24, 1942, the celebrity guest was Jane Cowl.

WARREN: You mean . . .

DOROTHY: I mean, Miss Jane Cowl, and here she is. How are you?

MISS COWL: (Cheerfully) Just splendid.

DOROTHY: You look, terrific. For the efforts you put into the Stage Door Canteen, I expected you to have, well . . .

MISS COWL: (Kiddingly) Circles under my eyes and a soldier on each arm?

Dorothy had been convoyed into the lucrative Johnson & Johnson deal by her new manager, Mark Hanna. Impeccable in his attire, and terribly social, Hanna would list among his clients Mrs. Franklin Delano Roosevelt, John O'Hara, Helen Hayes, Quentin Reynolds, S. J. Perelman, Faye Emerson, A. J. Liebling, Wolcott Gibbs, and tennis star turned newspaperman Bob Considine. Hanna had a talent for coining phrases—"the greatest thing since sliced bread" was his—and a knack for turning the gifted into the celebrated. When Bob Considine was asked, at Hanna's funeral in 1958, "What did he ever do for you?" Considine began at the beginning. "Mark," he replied, "taught me not to wear white shoes in New York." [9]

Richard, too, was moving along. His last appearance as simply a boy baritone was in *Crazy with the Heat*, a review produced by Kurt Kaznar. He was featured, shorn close in a crew cut and wearing a tight-fitting French sailor's suit, in an elaborate fantasy number, "Some Day Let Paris Be the Same." Casper Reardon played a celestial harp. The Empire State Building rotated. The good ship

Normandie bellowed nostalgically. Fog and several stage-hands crept in on cat's feet. *Voilà!* The skyline of Gotham dissolved to a Paris street scene with flower stalls, strolling lovers, and sidewalk cafés.

Richard was perfect for that time in those parts. Once again, he was tepidly acclaimed as "one of the most attractive of our singing juveniles." But the crew cut embarrassed him and so, finally, did the designation.

He continued to work effortlessly as a radio performer. He played Michael West, Small Town Attorney, on a soap called "Bright Horizons" and David in "Claudia and David." However, he bored easily and wanted much more. Dorothy wanted much more for him, too. He decided to combine all his talents—visual taste, theatrical savvy, pleasant personality, and, most important, an ability to extract money from the rich. He set up an office on Madison Avenue and became a producer. Richard Kollmar Productions was incorporated, capitalized at $100,000.

A prospective partner, James W. (Jimmy) Gardiner, would say of him, "Dick could take someone to a fifteen-dollar lunch at Sardi's. And when it was over the guy would feel that he owed Dick fifteen thousand dollars." [10]

Among those closest to Dorothy, only Jim Kilgallen was radically affected by the war. He signed up as a correspondent for INS and was shipped out to cover the Pacific the day after Pearl Harbor. Thereafter, he saw action in the Mediterranean, reporting the battles of Anzio and Cassino. As a result Mae was left more or less in Dorothy's hands. (By that time, the Kilgallens had an apartment in the same building as the Kollmars.) On Thursdays, nurse's day off, Dorothy took her to lunch, bought her hats, and kept her generally occupied and feeling useful.

Richard, according to Edgar Hatfield, who would grow eventually to despise his schoolmate of old, "played every trick to stay out of the service and he did so successfully." [11] It is likely that Dorothy made an important contribution to keeping her husband at home.

Leaning over her dressing table one evening to prepare her face for the nightly rounds, she was discussing the imminence of war with Bea. "If it happens," Dorothy said, "I'll do anything in my power to keep him out." [12]

He would, however, continue to be embarrassed by his civilian status, having a tendency to explain. He told a female friend that he had a duodenal ulcer. To a male buddy, he confided that the problem was scrotum-related. For appearances' sake, he was named radio advisor to the chief adjutant general.

They put their car up on account of the war. Dorothy used that supreme sacrifice to justify moving her office from the roach-infested *Journal* building to her pleasant new apartment. Subways depressed her inordinately, and the four-dollar roundtrip cab fare, she claimed, was a needless extravagance. She had five telephones installed in the apartment, one private exchange for Richard, one for her mother. "Otherwise, they'd never get me because I'm talking to my 'spies,'" she told a writer for *Editor & Publisher*.[13]

Dorothy's contribution to the war effort, beyond keeping Richard out of it, consisted mainly of her affiliation with the Father Duffy Canteen, named for the Reverend Francis P. Duffy of St. Malachy's Church, the Sardi's of the Holy See. A group of female show-biz types comprised the canteen. They picked up sandwiches and coffee from Jack Dempsey's, the Latin Quarter, Versailles, and Lindy's, to deliver them to soldiers on lonely night patrol in and around the New York metropolitan area.

Dorothy claimed that she was inspired to join by observing the work of Colonel Gertrude Lawrence, who asked her to come along one night. The activity began as a small unit of women, dressed to kill in tailored navy blues, snappy little caps, and gold eagles on their shoulders, saluted the granite statue of Father Duffy in Duffy Square. Thereupon, they piled into a truck and dispensed their fabulous fare. Dorothy wrote:

> By 1 A.M. I was itching to help hand out the coffee and carry trays to the guards. By 3:30 A.M., I knew this was the most satisfying form of war work I'd seen yet. On my way home, I said to Gertrude, "Do you think I could do this, too?" [14]

Dorothy's unit, which went out two or three times a week, included Captain Dorothy Gulman, press agent and close friend; Lieutenant Gertrude Bayne, press agent and friend; Private Eleanor Kilgallen, sister and friend; and, of course, Colonel Dorothy Kilgallen.

They went exultantly to a costumer on Seventh Avenue for their stylish uniforms. Gulman said, "We all want size tens." She was taken aside diplomatically by Dorothy who whispered, "Dear, not everybody is a ten!" She had put on a little weight, most flatteringly in the bust, since the birth of her first child.

The canteen was fun while it lasted. At the end of their rounds, Dorothy Gulman, a young woman with dark, lush, upswept hair and a full, angelic face, took the unit to one of her accounts, Dempsey's or the Barberry Room, where they drank champagne and gossiped. But the end was in sight when the unit began drawing too much newspaper publicity to itself. "The head of it, Pauline-something, got jealous, started giving us orders, and threatened to split the four of us up," Dorothy Gulman recalled. "I said, 'In that case, I quit.' Dorothy said, 'Well, if you quit, I quit.' We all quit." [15]

The young columnist's patriotic fervor was spent in other ways. She began to send to the FBI all subversive communications that came her way, the first of which was a lunatic scrawling from an anti-Semite who accused her of following in the footsteps of "Jew Sobol" and "Jew Winchell" by her "daily hate of Hitler, which proves that you, too, play to the Soviet Marxist Jews!"

She sent the missive to J. Edgar Hoover, along with a note: "I don't quite know what to make of it, or quite what the inference is, but it seems to indicate strange goings-on. I thought I would send you the translation and let you decide whether or not it is worth investigating." [16] Hoover thanked her for her courtesy and asked her to be eternally vigilant.

The Federal Bureau of Investigation maintained a dossier about Dorothy, as it did about all prominent and/or subversive citizens. Some of the documents would be released eventually under the Freedom of Information Act; others were withheld. The earlier comments about Dorothy, made by the bureau in the 1930s and 1940s, characterize her as "cooperative." She did volunteer, for instance, to testify before the Dies Committee on subversive activity in the entertainment field. Whether or not her offer was accepted is not revealed.

As she was surveilling, so was she surveilled. Dorothy was running a feature in *The Voice of Broadway* at the time called "The $64 Question." Between "Did you know that major colleges—NYU, for instance—will feature their girls' basketball teams this winter because of a scarcity of male players?" and "Will the Erroll Flynn scandal result in a revision of all 'morality' clauses in film contracts?" she asked, "What well-known society figure employs a maid who was a spy for Germany in the last war?"

Hoover received an anonymous tip about Dorothy's anonymous tip:

> A 64 dollar question! I think Kilgallen has a hell of a nerve to print that—Why the hell she don't give this to you instead of the newspaper is more than I can understand. If the maid was a spy then, she must be one now—You are doing a swell job. From one who admires you.[17]

Was Dorothy ever questioned about the identity of the Mata Hari maid? Did the maid do windows? Was her identity known to Dorothy in the first place? Would she have revealed a sacred source even to J. Edgar, whom she admired? All 64-dollar questions, unanswered by the dossier.

In fact, Dorothy could *not* have been much help then to the FBI. She had an absurd sense of political reality, credulous and meretricious. New York became a veritable Casablanca for Dorothy during the war years, with Marshall Tito's agents terrorizing Yugoslavs in the United States, vitamin pills being smuggled to Russian children, and an abundance of Mickey Finns slipped to spies of all political persuasions in the most chic spots.

Dorothy would have liked to have established with Hoover the relationship that Walter Winchell enjoyed. In exchange for canonization within Winchell's column and on his radio show, Hoover worked as a kind of super press agent for him, drawing on his vast resources to feed the powerful columnist personal items about his (Hoover's) political enemies.

Inundated by her credulous and indiscriminating leads,

unable to verify many of the explosive political items she ran, the FBI dismissed Dorothy presently as "flighty and irresponsible," [18] which was, in its time, a proper designation. What the bureau *chose* to release years later was a well-edited testament only to her flightiness and her irresponsibility.

Though neither porridge nor politics appeared to be her forte, she enjoyed a full and satisfying life with Richard. She was out with him almost every night until three or four in the morning. She managed, nevertheless, to be at her desk by eleven, alert and mostly merry, and productive.

She enjoyed good health, replenished herself by taking catnaps, which she could induce at the placement of a sleep mask, and was hobbled only once a month by excruciating menstrual cramps, remedied, in the old-fashioned way, by a jigger of warm gin and a lie-down.

Professional recognition, marriage, motherhood, stylish living, and sex took some of the weight off her spine. She was younger at thirty than she had ever been in her life.

Absurd as she could be, she had humor and a sense of the absurd. When she needed a new secretary during the early forties, she went over in her mind all the proper and pertinent questions to ask an applicant. She put on a new pink satin hat, taxied to Richard's office, and asked that Miss Willer be shown in. Midge Willer was twentyish, blond, good-looking, stylishly dressed; her long, malocclusioned vowels betrayed an early education at the Nightingale School. She had been to Katharine Gibbs and worked for a while at William Estey Advertising. Dorothy, however, never got around to eliciting any of that.

"Can you type?" she asked Midge.

"Yes," Midge replied, settling back for the prolonged scrutiny that she had been taught to expect at Katharine Gibbs.

"Would you like to start Monday?" Dorothy asked.[19]

The formal interview ended, the astonished secretary and her relieved employer settled into a half-hour of chitchat-I-like-your-hat.

On Monday, Dorothy attempted, for the first time in her career, to dictate a letter. Midge poised her pencil and waited. Dorothy tried several times to transmit suitable sentences to Midge. To no avail. Accustomed to another process altogether—gestation, during which she leaned back, raised her arms, and nested her linked hands in her imperturbable and abundant hair; hesitation, a stiffening period of adjustment; action, a rush of rhythmic prose played on her Smith-Corona standard—she was now like an instrumentless musician who was simply unable to carry a tune.

After several false starts, she and Midge began to giggle. Midge, from that episode on, composed her own letters from Dorothy's notes.

It was a happy home in which Midge Willer worked— zany, unpredictable, full of love and life. During one Easter season, magician Russell Swann sent Dorothy, who was generous to him in her columns, a pair of domesticated rabbits that he had dyed lavender. They arrived on Easter Sunday; Midge arrived on Monday, hung over after a celebratory weekend with her fiancé. She was sorting the mail before Dorothy's arrival when one of the lavender bunnies hopped through the office and then out again. The secretary made a silent, solemn pledge to herself to extend the Lenten season and lay off the sauce for a time.

The rabbits were returned to Russell Swann when the butler, Julius Applethwaite, a Jamaican with a dignified mien and long white sideburns, objected to cleaning up after them. The Kollmars bought a canary then and named it Dickie. Julius had no problems with Dickie until the bird became ill. He was dispatched, with the canary, to the neighborhood pet store for proper diagnosis and medication. He returned, looking less than delighted. Midge Willer asked him what the matter was.

"Well, I'll tell you, Miss Willer," he said. "I don't mind taking the bird to the store. I don't like seeing any living creature in poor health. But I don't think that I wish to give it an enema with an eyedropper every day for a week." [20]

Richard and Dorothy appeared to have a good and satisfying relationship. "They were very affectionate," Midge recalled. "Golly, I remember having to duck around corners because they were saying good-bye to each other. It was really very sweet. He was always rushing off to do a soap or produce one of his shows. But he'd say, sort of suggestively, 'I'll see you around eight, sweetie.' "

Dorothy worked at keeping herself as attractive as possible for her new husband. The weight that she had put on after Dickie's birth she took and kept off with a variety of idiosyncratic diets. Her goal was to maintain the weight she had been on her wedding day: 119 pounds.

Customarily, Julius entered the office in the afternoon to determine what Dorothy and Midge wanted for lunch. One day, after a lavish party, he knocked softly to say, "Mrs. Kollmar, I have half a pound of caviar left over from last night. Would you and Miss Willer care for some?"

"No, thank you," Dorothy answered. "I'm on one of my things. Miss Willer may have it all. I'm going to have the heel of the rye bread and half a glass of beer with a lot of ice in it."

She had decided, before the marriage, that her husband would never see her except at her best. That was the point of her separate dressing room. They were like two co-stars sharing bed and billing. When they came together to play their scenes, they emerged from separate areas, primed and pretty. Before going to bed, she applied a fresh light foundation and powder. She creamed the makeup off in the morning and applied her daytime face. The household staff was amazed that the foundation never came off on the colored satin sheets upon which she and Richard slept.[21]

Midge never heard any unpleasantness between the couple. "We don't fight," Dorothy told a reporter,[22] "but we do have quiet periods. Most people I know that fight are purely selfish. If they'd only hold their tongues about small issues, twenty-four hours later they'd forget about them and everything would be all right." This was a lesson she had learned from Mae, that somehow confrontation was a sign of weakness. The strong ignore. There were mornings when Midge was able to discern from Dorothy's quiet demeanor that *something* had transpired between her and Richard. But it would pass, usually because of Richard's ability to cajole his wife into appeasing laughter.

Dorothy was faster, brighter, more incisive and logical than Richard, but she maintained a dutifully deferential profile with him in company. She listened with rapt attention to his stories, giggled at his anecdotes, and was avid in the service of his ego. She lavished praise upon him and did everything she could to focus company's attention on his talents and accomplishments.

H. Huber Boscowitz—"Hubie" to his friends—remembered Dorothy's early attitude toward Richard. "She would listen with great respect to Kollmar. It was as though she was sitting at the feet of a master. She was a great audience for him." [23]

Hubie and Lillian Boscowitz became the Kollmars' closest friends. They wined and dined and "gagged it up" together three or four times a week. Lillian and Dorothy spoke on the phone every day, though Dorothy knew better than to call before noon, which was Lillian's rising time. The two women even developed the same mannerisms, their hands fluttering delicately in conversation like two impeccably manicured mutes. It was not clear who was emulating who.

Lillian Emerson Boscowitz was the merry, marcelled socialite whom Dorothy had met when she was preparing her series about "Romances of American Beauties" back in 1933. Hubie was her second husband. Five years older than Dorothy, she had been introduced into European society at age six. Known as the dancing sprite, her luxuriant honey hair done in bouncy and multitudinous ringlets, she performed before royalty to raise money for the widowed women and starving children in war-torn Europe.

Lillian had a short but successful Broadway stage career and was called by critic Robert Coleman "the pride of Fayetteville and Park Avenue." Coleman commented that she was one of the few "society girls" to have made a success onstage. She was rehearsing in a play called *The Sap Runs Dry* when she divorced her first husband.

Typically, Dorothy courted Lillian's friendship, mentioning her often in the late thirties and taking a special interest in her new flame, Herbert Huber Boscowitz. "Hubie Boscowitz, the bridge expert," Dorothy wrote in one of her first columns, "is carrying a small torch for Lillian Emerson, the stage-smitten socialite who's Europe bound."

Hubie was a baldish man with a mustache; he was fun-loving, epicurean, anecdotal, and arch-conservative in his politics. When he wasn't playing tournament bridge with distinction, he worked for the F. M. Burte paper company, where he handled big accounts and made an enormous salary.

He and Lillian were married two years before the Koll-mars, at which point she gave up her career. The couple had no children. They traveled a great deal, lived in a grand style surrounded by good glass and uniformed help, and took immediately to Dorothy and Richard for their flair and their sense of fun.

Lillian had said it to Dorothy way back in 1933: "Unless you can laugh at the same things, you're sort of up a tree, don't you think?" [24]

Richard went to great lengths to amuse. His taste ran to practical jokes: usually expensive and invariably byzantine. Dorothy was a supportive, always appreciative, second banana, giggling in the wings.

The foursome laughed when Richard, whom Hubie had asked to redecorate his bedroom in pony skins, hired a real pony for the room-warming celebration and filipped the animal up the Boscowitzes' stairs.

They laughed when the Kollmars had a party for a shy man from Richard's office who was about to marry. Richard hired a tall, voluptuous Choo Choo Johnson-type to show up during the course of the party, claim she was engaged to the man, and raise a ruckus with his fiancée. Midge Willer hied into the bedroom, where Dorothy was ensconced for fear of spoiling the joke. "My God, Dorothy, this is *terribly* embarrassing for poor Albert," Midge said frantically. "Don't you get it," Dorothy said. "Albert doesn't even know that woman. She's an actress of sorts. Richard just wanted to see Albert under pressure. He made me promise to leave the room if I felt the giggles coming on." [25]

At yet another of the Kollmar parties, a man inadvertently came to their gathering instead of another in the same building. When he realized he was in the wrong apartment, he apologized to Dorothy and left so embarrassed that he forgot his monogrammed hat. The next day, he sent a note, apologizing again. "I left in such a hurry," he wrote, "I seem to have forgotten my hat. You'll recognize it by the initials: E.D.G."

At Richard's instigation, they went out and purchased a police inspector's hat, had it suitably initialed, and sent it to the man with a card: "No need to be embarrassed. We enjoyed having you and here's your hat." [26]

The man remitted the hat, acknowledged the incredible coincidence, and asked them to look further. They sent him subsequently hats from the fire department, the sanitation department, and the United States Marines.

The project kept them entertained, made a fine story for their friends, and possibly made a hat collector out of the errant E.D.G., who caught on before the Kollmars stopped.

Richard and Hubie lunched often at "21," where Hubie had a table of his own and a reputation for ordering bay scallops every day. Their conversation, according to Hubie, "ranged from cabbages to kings." Doubtless, too, their talk concerned Richard's various business ventures, in which Hubie invested.

Dorothy and Lillian, one evening, heard their husbands plan luncheon together—this one at the Colony. They decided to be there on the same day. To "gag it up," they planned to be impressively escorted.

The columnist called Frank Sinatra's agent and arranged to have the young singer—on whom she was decidedly "gone"—accompany her to the restaurant. "Whom can you get?" she asked Lillian. Walter Pidgeon, a friend, was in town, and agreed to escort the pride of Fayetteville and Park Avenue.

When the two women entered the Colony with their attractive and eminently desirable dates—not even acknowledging their spouses, who were seated in a corner booth—Richard was ready for them. He had made up menus, by hand, in fractured French, which he bade the waiter offer them. When they ignored the menus and ordered familiarly from memory, the two women received only tripe. Telegrams and flowers in abundance arrived for Sinatra, at the behest of Kollmar. Richard and Hubie wrote their wives mash notes, like, "What are you doing tonight, baby?" and "Hubba-hubba," a term that Earl Wilson claimed Richard had actually coined.

Even Maury Paul was sufficiently amused to recount the episode in his column, though he bitched it up a bit with his modifying phrases. Lillian was "society's Lillian Emerson Boscowitz;" Dorothy was *journalism's* Dorothy Kilgallen." Their husbands—whom he did not bother to modify at all—he recounted, "chuckled and chortled every time another mass of flowers and batch of telegrams were brought in for Sinatra. It all made for some very unusual diversion at the usually ultra-dignified Colony Restaurant." [27]

Unless you can laugh at the same things, you're sort of up the creek, don't you think?

12/DREAM
WITH MUSIC

The Kollmars and their choice of life-style were assessed by a brilliant associate of Richard's, theatrical costumer Miles White, as he sat in his Manhattan apartment in April of 1977. An elfin man with a warm, half-moon smile, he sat cross-legged on his sofa, chain-smoking through a cigarette holder. His speckled cockateel popped around in its cage, while Miles mused on Dorothy and Dick.

> I liked her. She was always very warm and pleasant to me. She was good to me in the column and eventually on their radio show. But I didn't want to get too close. I tried, for instance, not to drink around her, because I was drinking heavily in those days. She was so *powerful*. I was afraid that she would reveal that I went to Fire Island.
>
> I liked him because he was friendly, a nice guy, easy to be with, and enthusiastic. A little like a college kid and not terribly bright.
>
> Was it your impression that they were *playing* at roles? It was always my impression that they were never real people. Nothing they *touched* was real. There was no reason to pretend you were Ivy League when you weren't, to pretend that you were a fairy princess when you weren't. One time they'd be society types, another time—later on—nightclub impresario types, another time producer types. And Dorothy seemed to go along with everything he did. They were both strangely impressionable.[1]

When Miles White associated himself with Richard Kollmar in the mid-1940s, White was in his early twenties, a red-hot new talent with a string of recent credits, including *The Pirate* with the Lunts, Rodgers and Hammerstein's

Oklahoma, and John Ringling North's *Circus*. He would eventually design the costumes for *Carousel, High Button Shoes, Gentlemen Prefer Blondes*, and *Jamaica*.

Richard Kollmar was in his producing period when he employed Miles's estimable talent. *By Jupiter*, the Rodgers and Hart musical, based on *The Warrior's Husband*, was the first enterprise with which his company had been associated. Richard had had no creative participation in that musical. Dorothy had heard and adored the score. When the show ran into financial trouble on its way to Broadway, Richard raised the capital necessary to keep it going.

The first production in which Richard had any significant creative autonomy was a musical comedy called *Early to Bed*, which opened in New York in June, 1943.

With music by Fats Waller, *Early to Bed* made a kind of theatrical history. Never before had a Broadway production, peopled by whites, been composed by a black artist.

The book, written by George Marion, Jr., was subtitled "a fairy tale for adults." Richard co-produced with his partner, Alfred Bloomingdale. Bloomingdale, the twenty-eight-year-old grandson of the founder of the famous department store, had left the family business for his first love—the theater. The credits read: "Entire Production Under the Supervision of Alfred Bloomingdale." But, in fact, it was Richard who raised a good deal of the money for the production. It was Richard who directed the show. And it was he who stepped into the leading role when Carl Brisson (the father of Fred Brisson) had trouble retaining his lines.

The book, such as it was, concerned the return of a broken-down, middle-aged bullfighter (Kollmar) to a Caribbean island, accompanied by his son. There he mistakes a bordello called The Angry Pigeon for a girl's boarding school. It was a one-joke affair with lines like: "We aren't shaping their minds. We're shaping their shapes." The lyrics most often quoted by the mind-boggled critics, from the song "A Girl Who Doesn't Ripple When She Bends," rhymed "abdomen" with "roamin' in the gloamin'" and "a cobra" with "no bra."

Richard was a glitter boy, lauded most often for his ability to amass and effectively orchestrate the visual elements of a show. His talent consisted primarily in his ability to choose other artists with visual taste. If they were strong enough to resist Richard's corrupting excesses, then his productions worked at least as eye-filling extravaganzas. Critics of *Early to Bed* excepted Miles White's costumes and Jo Mielziner's sets from their excoriating broadsides. A Philadelphia critic, reflecting the general consensus, called the *Early to Bed* book "downright dull and deliberately dirty."

Richard's taste was reflected perfectly in a publicity stunt he conceived during the run of the play. He took three of his chorines—Angela Greene, Choo Choo Johnson, and Olga Roberts—to Coney Island. Photographers snapped their pictures as their skirts blew up over the breeze gates outside the fun house.

But *Early to Bed* worked commercially. *Variety* was right on target when it pointed to the "counter-irritants" in the show, "lush production, champ lookers, tuneful score." It called the production "appropriately escapist for the wartime audience."

Early to Bed ran for almost four hundred performances.

George Freedley, of the New York *World-Telegram*, returned for a second look at *Early to Bed* and made an extraordinarily astute observation. He noticed, in the boys' chorus, an exceptional performer. He wrote:

> I haven't any idea who he is or what his name is or whether I have seen him before, but there is one youngster in the chorus who is having such a good time that his enjoyment is infectious. He is very young, blond, and shaggy-haired and he reminds you of a friendly and rowdy puppy.

The infectious puppy was, in all probability, twenty-one-year-old James W. (Jimmy) Gardiner, the sweet, needy, overweight, and flagrantly homosexual scion of an oil-rich Texas family. Jimmy had been stage-struck since childhood. At five, he ate dried rice for fourteen blocks in a rice-float parade and was chosen Louisiana's Health Boy of the Year. For his birthday party the year before *Early to Bed*, his family brought the entire Jimmy Dorsey band from New York to Houston to entertain.

He met Richard, who was "Mr. Kollmar" to him then,

when he accompanied a friend to a music audition for the show. There was, at the time, a discussion of who would play the role of Wilbur, a fat decathlon thrower, who was originally to have a line or two to speak. Richard, who must have been apprised of the young man's considerable wealth, chimed in, "Jimmy can do it." [2] Without experience or audition, he was signed.

Jimmy worked as hard as anyone in the show to prove his professionalism and counter the innuendoes of the rest of the chorus. He was punctual, humble, eager to learn, and eventually, according to the Freedley review, an asset to the production. In the beginning, however, he had such stage fright that he began to lose weight and imperil the comedic basis of his tiny role. To keep him fat under pressure, Richard spoon-fed him pints of chocolate ice cream.

Jimmy's family, who had always supported his interest in the theater, showed their appreciation to Richard by investing $10,000 in the property.[3]

Other investors in *Early to Bed* were a cohort of nightclub owners, including Leon Enken and Eddie Davis of Leon & Eddie's, Lou Walters of the Latin Quarter, Sherman Billingsley of the Stork Club, Ben Marden of the Riviera, and John Boggiano, the power behind Versailles. Richard was very aggressive in courting these men. Dorothy's name was, of course, never mentioned. But Richard's angels were clearly in a no-lose situation. The fact that *Early to Bed* happened to make money was icing on the cake.

Soon after the New York opening of the musical, when Dickie was two, Dorothy gave birth to a girl. She telephoned Dorothy Gulman exultantly. "She has navy-blue eyes," Dorothy said. "And I'm going to call her either Deirdre or Jill."

Gulman thought that Deirdre was an exquisite choice She guessed, however, that her friend would go with Jill. "At that time," Dorothy Gulman remembered, "everybody was naming their daughters little names, like Meg or Jill." [4] The baby was christened Jill Ellen Elizabeth Kollmar at St. Vincent Ferrer.

She spent what little time she could with the children. The nurse brought them to her when she awakened in the morning. At their bedtime, when she could be there, she held them both close to her breast, and in her high, riskily thin but accurate soprano, sang lullabies to them. Hope Hampton, dressed for a night on the town, lurked recessive and tearful in the darkened nursery once while Dorothy, also in evening clothes, with Dickie pulling at her diamond earrings, sang "On the Good Ship Lollipop" to her babies.[5]

She planned for them lives of ease and grace. The Good Ship, properly navigated, would carry them into charmed ports.

Al Rylander, who was handling column publicity for Columbia Pictures, sat with her at "21" three years after Jill's birth. She confided in him that she wanted her family to have a tree, that she was determined that her children were going to be social register.[6]

Dorothy refused to baby-talk them. If a child was to learn to speak properly, then the child must be exposed to proper speech. In Dickie's case especially, her philosophy worked splendidly. The year after Jill's birth, he was talking rather too well. When a Jesuit journalist from *The Queen's Work* came to call, the dark-eyed little boy said: "I'm Richard Kollmar, Jr. I'm three. My sister's only one. Grandpa's a soldier, but he doesn't have to fight anybody. He talked to the Pope and got some rosary beads for Gramma. The Pope is a big man in the Catholic Church. I was baptized by a bishop. So was my sister."

Dorothy laughed and blushed. The Pope, she told him, was more properly called Holy Father; his position was not a "Big Man" but "The Vicar of Christ." Emendations notwithstanding, she was thrilled that her eldest was clearly a child of exceptional, albeit somewhat frightening, intelligence.[7]

Dorothy, like all successful diversifiers, was blessed with supple energy. No creative *idée fixe* bogged her down, no crisis crippled her. She set a phenomenon into motion—household, column, social habits, family—hired overseers, laid down some rules. And the machinery ran smoothly. When it did not, she responded equably. She had a life now, as opposed to an obsession. If she missed the *China Clipper*, there would be other flights.

She was able, therefore, to assume a tremendous work

load. One of the projects she took on after Jill's birth was the creation of a lavish musical comedy called *Dream with Music*.

Richard had it in mind to produce a classy musical fantasy that would knock the socks off all his detractors. He excused *Early to Bed* as an exigency, a means to an end. He told Elinor Hughes, during the long run of that play:

> I'm not ready for my artistic flop yet because I need a lot of money to back it. But when I have had a few good shows on Broadway and made enough money to play around with, I am ready to put on a fantasy, a kind of *Blue Bird*. No matter if I've lost my shirt. I shall be happy. Because it's what I've always wanted to do ever since I went to the Dramatic School at Yale.[8]

The property that would come to be called *Dream with Music* was not the story he had intended to produce. He and Bloomingdale, according to a column item in the New York *Daily News*, had some kind of "rift" and separated. Richard had optioned a story by George Marion, Jr., called "Allah Be Praised." That musical was to take place four years in the future—1948—set in the harem of an Iranian emir. But the draft board intruded. For a time, it appeared that Richard would eventually be inducted into combat duty. Marion, consequently, took the property to Bloomingdale, who ran with it.[9] Richard avoided induction. By the time he knew he would not have to go, however, it was too late to retrieve the emir idea. Richard decided that he would not abandon entirely the fantasy of the Middle East, and girls, girls, girls. He would contrive another, similar, musical comedy.

One night, over cocktails with Lillian and Hubie, Dorothy conceived *Dream with Music*. They didn't have to go into the future or the past, but into a *dream*. A dream of a glamorous, gorgeous woman who makes her living writing soap operas for radio. She's fed up with the demands of having to knock out a new yarn every night simply to survive. She has personal problems to boot. She's engaged to her boss, an account executive, but she's really gone on a footloose war correspondent who's always running off to China. Her name would be Dinah, in modern, waking life.

On the verge of a nervous breakdown, she falls asleep and dreams that she is Scheherazade, right out of *The Arabian Nights*. Wasn't Scheherazade, after all, the progenitor of the modern-day writer of soaps, impelled to tell a new story of romance and adventure—one thousand and one stories, to be exact—to survive? With this story, she suggested in a rush, they'd have the freedom of a dream, the glamour and sex appeal of the Arabian nights, the contemporary comedy of radio and advertising.

She was urged to write it herself. She agreed, somewhat coyly, but only on the condition that she could have a collaborator, since the medium was new to her. Wolcott Gibbs, a highly regarded critic and essayist who contributed regularly to *The New Yorker*, was suggested. He would imbue the book with a sophistication that would outclass anything George Marion wrote for Al Bloomingdale.

The Boscowitzes made a financial pledge. The rest of the money, with Richard's track-record, Dorothy's clout, and the cooperation of their other rich friends, should not prove to be a problem. They toasted the idea with a subtle sherry. If Dorothy realized that Scheherazade was also the mother of the modern gossip column, she never let on.

The writing team of Gibbs and Kilgallen died aborning. Soon after the breach, Miles White ran into Gibbs at the Algonquin bar. How was the book progressing? Gibbs explained that he had had to give it up. What happened?

"I'll tell you," Wolcott Gibbs answered. "I can sum up the whole show in one phrase. It's the phrase that Miss Kilgallen opened every one of our story conferences with: 'Wouldn't it be cute if . . .'"[10] He was replaced by Sidney Sheldon and Ben Roberts, who, apparently, were less averse to cute.

In his grandiose pastiche, Richard didn't miss a high art. He was perhaps the first popularizer to dip into public domain. The score of *Dream with Music* included themes from Beethoven, Weber, Wagner, Chopin, Gluck, Dvořák, Haydn, Tchaikovsky, Schubert, and, of course, Rimsky-Korsakov's *Scheherazade*.

With the help of an arranger and a lyricist, the classical melodies were metamorphosed into songs called "Baby, Don't Count On Me," "Give, Sinbad, Give," "Love at Second Sight," "Woman Against the World," "Mouse Meets Girl," and "Relax, and Enjoy It!"

From the ballet, he signed Vera Zorina to take the lead as Dinah/Scheherazade; George Balanchine would choreograph. Alfred Kreymborg's lovely poem "Earth Wisdom" was incorporated into the book.

Two hundred thousand dollars, an astronomical amount then, was raised and spent, far less on actors than on challenges for them. There were treadmills, magic carpets, countless cables to help simulate falls, trap doors, mammoth couches, mobile beds, genies appearing out of exploding puffs of smoke, and costumes that weighed more than some of the midgets in the cast. The treadmills overturned chorus girls. Zorina fell and bruised her ankle when a cable snapped.

There were also several plastic moons involved, all of them designed by the Czecho-Peasant Art Company. During a performance in Boston, one of the moons caused a problem. The problematic scene opened as Zorina lay on a couch, waiting for her lover, Aladdin, played by Ronnie Graham. As planned, Graham was to fly onto the stage, look longingly at Zorina, and recite Kreymborg's "Earth Wisdom" to the moon as an invocation, thereby causing the moon to descend and make itself available for Zorina to actually touch. Graham would alight then from the carpet and speak a couple of Kilgallen-Sheldon-Roberts phrases to her, the point being that he was smitten enough and sufficiently powerful to do anything for his beloved.

Unfortunately, set designer Stuart Chaney, during this one performance, was unable to lower the moon so that the audience could see it and comprehend the intent of the action. They saw only Graham as he approached the supine Zorina. His boastful line: "Let me show you where I'm going to put it, darling."

Despite the production problems, Richard and Dorothy were certain that it was just a matter of time and coordination before *Dream* unfolded smoothly. They had a month in Boston to get it together. Scripts could be rewritten. Actors could be replaced. Flaws would be eliminated.

That the fault was not in their plastic moons but in themselves was never acknowledged by the couple. Joy Hodges, who journeyed to Boston to replace one of the principals who found it difficult to be funny on a treadmill, remembered:

It seemed to me that there were excuses. I think he always felt that it wasn't his fault. It wasn't Dorothy's fault. Somewhere along the line, it was always somebody else's fault. I don't think it reached them.[11]

A *Blue Bird* this show would never be. Dorothy lacked a light, deft touch. Her humor was either arch or acerbic. Richard, quite simply, lacked taste. He found out, for instance, that he could emplace women on the stage, nude from the waist up, so long as they didn't move about. So he decided to use actresses as integral parts of the set his inspiration and prototype the ancient Greek caryatids. Like those sculptured female forms used in architecture as columns, his girls would stand stock-still, draped scantily from the waist down, nude from there up, with their arms raised as if holding up the scenery.

"Dick was strangely excited about naked women," Miles White chuckled. "When he found out what he could *get away with*, he asked Stuart Chaney and me to work out something after the fashion of the caryatids. He scouted around meanwhile and found this black girl with the biggest tits you've ever seen. When she was on stage, it was impossible to look at anything else. This was his big, private joke. Dick was being such a big, naughty little boy. Dorothy thought it was funny, too. They were like two kids almost."

Dorothy continued to file her *Voice of Broadway* six days
a week, regardless of the travail associated with putting
Dream with Music into shape for its New York opening.
She was more press-agent dependent during this period—
it is, after all, a bit difficult to survey the Cub Room from
the Ritz in Boston—but the column remained Dorothy's
in style, focus, and sensibility. She patched it together for
two hours in the afternoon. The *Journal-American* had her
copy no later than five.

The Voice of Broadway, in the middle to late 1940s, had
settled into a groove. Like its executor, the column was no
longer callow and overwhelmed. Gone were the school-
girlishly jejune letters to her sister, which had become a
joke among Dorothy's friends. She was bolder about giving
flat-out plugs. Her single-paragraph "Tops in Town," comparable to Winchell's "Bouquets," contained swift, pristine
plugs or payoffs to friends, favorites, and the clients of
useful press agents:

> *Tops in Town:* The charming ice show (Miles White
> —costumed) at the St. Regis . . . Russell Swann's suave
> hokum at the Wedgewood Room . . . Joey Adams . . .
> Leon & Eddie's . . . The Revuers at Spivvy's. . . .

The remainder of her columns typically consisted of
quick items, separated by the customary three dots. "Miss
Midnight's Notebook" was a visual series of rather harm-
less takes on the swank city scene. "Lou Can't Print That"
and "The $64 Question" consisted of blind items or inter-
rogatory sentences, used as much to avoid litigation as to
tantalize and mystify the reader. (Dorothy had begun using
these blind items tentatively, assuming that only the show-

biz hip in New Fork would have sufficient knowledge and interest to know or care which stand-up comedian had been warned by doctors to get on the water wagon or prepare to ride in a hearse. But the mail response was healthy. Her out-of-town readers enjoyed the game as avidly as the cognoscenti.) At least half of *The Voice of Broadway*, sometimes called "Jottings in Pencil," sometimes "Gossip in Gotham," was declarative, name-naming, hard-core gossip about marriage, divorce, nose bobs, public drunkenness, pregnancy, brouhahas, comebacks, broken kneecaps, hairline fractures, lost dogs, nervous breakdowns, gambling losses, political shenanigans, hiring, firing, trysting, fisting, overnight success, and terminal self-destruction among the famous and the notorious.

Her language was clever but column-arch. She described the romance between a Mexican politico and a socialite as "most *caliente*." At least twice every week, a blossoming romance was called "a heart toddy." One did not marry, one "waltzed down the aisle." Married people who were contemplating divorce had "Reno on the bean-o." "Ententes . . . reached fever pitch." Expectant parents were "knitting tiny garments."

Except for legal reasons, when Hearst lawyer Carl Helms excised something from the column for fear of libel, Dorothy's column was seldom touched by her editors. She had a tendency to remonstrate by sending a subsequent column in late or failing to send one at all. In 1944 she took a quantum leap with cute. "There are rumors," she wrote, "that Roy Rogers's horse Trigger is knitting tiny garments." [1]

Dorothy was no innovator. The language, form, and content of the gossip column had largely been pioneered by Walter Winchell. Even her letters to Eleanor, purporting to reveal the inside track on a gossip columnist confiding to her sister, had their genesis in Winchell's "Mr. and Mrs. Columnist at Home," a feature containing revelations of a far more authentic and searching nature than the Eleanor-Dorothy duologues. The Winchell conversations with his wife, June, were discontinued, with the veteran columnist recording the reason for their discontinuation through the device itself, using June's voice:

Don't put me in the paper—don't make me say things
I didn't say. People will think I'm silly or something.
Walda, come here. Be careful what you say in front
of Daddy—he'll put it in the paper.[2]

Until Winchell's power began to ebb, Dorothy was only
second-best. Presidents never confided in her. Criminals
did not surrender to her. Indeed, most of the New York
press agents sent their strongest material to WW first and
Dorothy second. She could not make or break a star or a
show. She would not reach the height of her power until
the fifties, when television would do for her what radio had
done for him.

More than any other tattler of the time, she was fasci-
nated by illness and accident. The *New York Post* would
report in a series it ran about Dorothy in the 1960s that
"some press agents have been inclined to afflict their clients
with sudden viruses, heart seizures, or bone fractures as
the surest way to crash the column." [3]

In this regard, the *Post* was accurate. She chronicled
weird poisonings, everything from "ultra-violet" (Gene
Tierney), to "penicillin" (Dick Haymes and Fanny Brice).
In a column of October 17, 1944, she had Frank Case, of
the Algonquin Hotel, and Ted Weems, the bandleader, re-
spectively "very ill" and "critically ill." Mussolini that same
day was reported "a ghost of his former self—at least 30
pounds lighter than usual with several specialists constantly
in attendance." She was apparently keeping charts on Il
Duce. Four months earlier, she had led off a series of $64
questions with the hedging teaser: "Have you heard the
interesting rumor (probably premature) that Mussolini has
been dead and buried for several months?"

On February 7, 1949, Margaret Truman was due for an
operation, Barry Fitzgerald fell off a motorcycle, Mary
Pickford ran a fever, and Dorothy Lamour had a date at
Johns Hopkins.

The quintessential Kilgallen paragraph would not appear
until several years later. It contained not only feud leading
to fracas leading to injury, compounded by a preexisting
medical condition of a third party, but related additionally
to gambling losses, which also carried considerable weight
with Dorothy. She wrote about Mrs. Horace Dodge, the
former Gregg Sherwood, whose bet a croupier had refused

to take "because of a technicality. Then her number came up on the roulette wheel. Mrs. Dodge became so incensed she tossed an ashtray at the wheel and another at the croupier's head. While the wild scene was played, Dodge had to sit in a wheel chair, watching helplessly." [4]

It is difficult now to evaluate the consequences of those several hundred human *pointilles* that she witnessed each week or accepted as truth from her spies. Some subjects were probably delighted with the attention. The former Gregg Sherwood, it is safe to assume, did not send Dorothy a Christmas card that year. Dorothy was not, however, yet as peevish or reckless as she would become. She could be dangerous, but not often. The public Dorothy Kilgallen—about whom Cole Porter would say, with reference to a missed appearance on "What's My Line?" "I'm sorry. I shall miss hating her this week"—had not yet fully formed.[5]

The lone exception, ferreted out of a necessarily selective reading of *The Voice of Broadway* of the forties, produced this singularly splenetic attack, which smacked of a style to come.

The subject was Peter Lind Hayes. And his offense was obvious. She called him

> a snide young comedian with a patronizing attitude toward the people who go to nightclubs. He was the most heartily overrated nightclub performer of the year when he appeared at the Copacabana and has since gone on to more gruesomely unentertaining perpetuations via the airways.[6]

To the actors and theater people who surrounded her during the production of *Dream with Music*, Dorothy was accurately perceived as a powerhouse. She did not yet have the millions of readers that she would later attract. But she had the ones who counted: producers, peers, club owners, and New York theatergoers. She could, by repeated mentions, manufacture a celebrity. She could, by omission, perpetuate anonymity. With a sentence or two, she might validate an actor's existence; with another kind of sentence, she might imperil a career.

When the decision was made to replace June Knight, who played the wise-cracking secretary to Vera Zorina, twenty-year-old Jane Kean, whom Dorothy had heard entertain at a private party, traveled to Boston to look over the production and consider the role. She sensed disaster. Turning down the offer, however, presented a formidable problem to her. An ambitious actress, she feared incurring Dorothy's disfavor. "I didn't want to be bad friends with her," she recollected. "I turned down the role. But that was not an easy decision for me to make." [7]

Joy Hodges followed Jane Kean. She accepted the part. But she remained chary, aware of Dorothy. And she paid special attention to her eyes: "I think she liked me. And I liked her. But I was very conscious of the fact that she was a powerhouse and that however one acted, whatever one said, was liable to be printed." [8]

They could not have known it then, but Dorothy had rules of sorts that separated her private life from her public life. With rare exception, she did not use, in *The Voice of Broadway*, information that came to her in the course of living her life. Since she lived her life so close to the office, this was another case of splitting hairs whose pH factor only Dorothy knew.

It was probably wise of Miles and Jane and Joy to follow their instincts, though their instincts had a tendency to isolate Dorothy. Had she been another kind of creature, a feet-up, eased-up human being, they might have forgotten about her power and risked exposure. Though she had relaxed considerably, she was still not an easeful person. Though she could be charming and loving, she was erratic. She could grow cool and distant at a lapse in style or a discerned betrayal.

Once, when she and Dorothy Gulman were lunching, Gulman misbehaved. "We were sitting and talking and I got excited—which I do once in a while—and I raised my voice," the press agent recollected. Dorothy's entire demeanor changed. She became quiet and haughty. There was a cooling-off period between the two friends. Gulman went to California at Christmas to visit her client, Dorothy Lamour, and stayed for several months. She returned in the spring. A messenger arrived, bearing Kilgallen's belated Christmas gift to Gulman. It was a heavy gold bracelet, inscribed: "Dear—I love you in May as I did in December." [9]

Even Midge Willer got the treatment. She went to the Stork Club one night, received a job offer from Sherman

Billingsley, and made the mistake of casually telling her boss. The money was very good. But she loved working for Dorothy and had no intention of taking the job. The columnist was ominously silent. Over the weekend, Midge received a pettish telegram from Dorothy, who was obviously seething and hurt.

The telegram read: "If Mr. Billingsley's offer is so appealing to you, please feel perfectly free to accept it— Signed Dorothy Kilgallen." [10]

When Midge went to work on Monday, Dorothy was breaking in a new assistant. Midge had to reassure her. It was not a matter of humble pie; Dorothy abhorred sycophancy. But there were times when Dorothy required either time or explanation to salve her blistering and quirky sensitivities.

Those who depended on her or loved her learned that it was wisest to exercise control around Dorothy, to emulate her own manner. Style was control with grace. The meretricious was one thing, the bawdy another. One did not swear or tell off-color jokes around her. The short white gloves that she wore with every outfit had a significance beyond habit.

"She was like a well-tuned instrument," observed Joy Hodges. "Tight, taut, ready to be played. But I got the feeling that just one turn of the string could break her." [11]

Allah Be Praised opened in New York in April, 1944, and ran for twenty performances. Bloomingdale had finally put $70,000 of his own money into the venture. There was no way to keep it going. The most memorable contribution this musical fantasy made to the theater turned out to be a piece of Broadway apocrypha originally attributed to George Kaufman, but actually said by play doctor Cy Howard, who suggested that Bloomingdale "close the show and keep the store open nights." [12]

Dream with Music was slated to move into Broadway's Majestic Theatre in mid-May. In Boston still, Dorothy was encouraged by the respectful review of Eliot Norton, who predicted that the show could work if it was pruned and lightened in tone.

Richard, in his red rehearsal suspenders, maintained a sanguine demeanor. After a day of grueling run-throughs, he normally relaxed with his cast in one of the neighboring bars. He was well-liked by the people who worked for him, if not universally respected. Dorothy seldom accompanied them. Her work schedule was too consuming. And she was commuting between Boston and New York much of the time.

Despite her hectic schedule, she took time to file several front-page stories on the first trial of Wayne Lonergan, accused of bludgeoning to death his socially prominent wife, Patricia, with a pair of green brass-and-onyx candelabra. Dorothy, surrounded by the largest delegation of reporters in a New York courtroom since the lurid trial of Ruth Snyder in 1927, crammed into the press section promptly at 10:30 each morning. Midge accompanied her reluctantly.

Photographs of the victim, sprawled across her bed in a four-story townhouse on East Fifty-first Street, were passed among the reporters. Dorothy eyed them coolly, noting the painted toenails and the well-manicured fingers. She gave them to a shuddering Midge, who was relieved to see that Patricia Lonergan's face was peaceful and uncontorted.

Dorothy returned to the courtroom now—as she would in the future—because she derived enormous gratification from front-page play. She had seen Wayne and Patricia frequently on her rounds of El Morocco and the Stork. They were an attractive, well-dressed couple. She had heard many inside stories about them, including the ones that concerned Lonergan's alleged homosexual relationship with Patricia's father, William Burton, a brewery mogul.

So she had knowledge and interest. She divulged certain bits of that knowledge cryptically to her readers. But, once again, she tried to find the line between what she had acquired socially and what she had learned professionally in the pursuit of her story.

She wrote in her column, just before the trial began, that Wayne Lonergan's attorney "intends to unfold the whole unsavory past of Bill Burton, the slain girl's father." [13] That was a bit of information that came to her through normal, if somewhat privileged, channels, a lawyer being more inclined to divulge to a star than to a less powerful journalist.

Thyra Samter Winslow of the *Mirror*, who had socialized extensively with the couple, went much further than Dorothy, quoting Patricia at a party: "If he was good enough for my father, he's good enough for me." [14] This was typical of Winslow's coverage, which drew heavily on socially acquired, flat-out revelation.

Dorothy filled with righteous anger at her competitor's tastelessness, never considering that a teasy semidisclosure might be more insidious than forthrightness. She wrote to Billy Livingston, who was serving in New Guinea: "Thyra sold everybody down the river . . . turned in everyone who fed her." [15]

The Lonergan trial interested Dorothy because it involved wealth, beauty, and power. She described the defendant:

> Roman even profile, big shoulders, long white beautiful hands. He looks like a college boy, probably a football player. . . . He looks as little like a murderer as anyone in the courtroom.[16]

She treated the unfortunate spectators less benignly. "They are anything but representatives of society," she observed. She singled out

> a gaunt faced young woman in a shockingly pink wool dress . . . a man who looks like a taxi driver . . . a girl in a thick knitted snood and pearl earrings, rather gross looking, and avid as she listens to the medical evidence . . . an elderly woman with lavender-gray hair and too much pancake makeup.[17]

Throughout Dorothy's reporting, there ran a kind of incredulity. How is it possible, she seemed to be asking, that the appurtenances of wealth and style could not buttress against murder? How could a man with long, white, beautiful hands bludgeon his wife to death? How could such ugliness crash the Stork?

The energy and passion she brought to these stories—and Lonergan was not among her best—derived from a fulcrum of innocence, fear, fascination, and jolting cultural shock.

Miles White put these ominous sequential jottings in his date book for mid-April of 1944:

> Dress parade for *Dream*. Ghastly day.
> Boston rehearsal. 2:00
> Dress rehearsal to 7 A.M. Amateurish.
> *Dream* Boston opening. Party at the Ritz. Drunk!

The Majestic Theatre was packed with celebrities on the evening of May 19, including Al Jolson, Ethel Merman, Ed Wynn, Jack Warner, Milton Berle, and Maggi McNellis. Ten minutes into the show, the groaning began in response to lines like: "He's so important, he can get a room for Errol Flynn at the YWCA," and "I'd hate to lose my head. I'm attached to it."

There was hardly a moment during which the panicky tumult backstage was not perceivable in the audience, often drowning out the actors' voices. The rear ends of the frantic stagehands bulged through the curtain. Sets swayed precariously. At one point, while Zorina was dancing, the house was pitched into total blackness. There was murmuring and laughter. A little ring of light appeared at the back of the theater. It progressed toward the stage, followed by the stage manager. "Ladies and gentlemen," he said, holding a flashlight, his clothes drenched with perspiration. "Ladies and gentlemen. I'm sorry. We seem to have blown a main fuse." He aimed the flashlight at the rattled Zorina, who finished her number while the electrician did his. The production ran well past midnight.[18]

The reviews were predictably disastrous. *Dream with Music* had turned to nightmare. The *News* headlined its philippic: DREAM WITH MUSIC: AN IMMENSE BEAUTIFUL ULTRA-EXPENSIVE BORE. Another review questioned the probity and authenticity of the conspicuously labeled boxes of Lux soap flakes flaunted on the stage by a group of scantily clad women out of The Arabian Nights.

Wolcott Gibbs had some fun with the production in *The New Yorker*. He observed that even the usually tasteful Miles White "seems obsessed with the idea of getting chorus girls up in a curiously sexless arrangement of fishnet and fur." The show, he wrote, "appears to be the work of a group of people who sincerely admire nice things but have no standard of judgment except the prices and name of shops." He paid an ostensible compliment to one aspect of the production: "the magic carpets in flight . . . a very cute effect." [19]

*   *   *

Exhausted by the ordeal of *Dream with Music*, Dorothy sought rest and recuperation at a milk farm owned by the mother of Bob Taplinger. Dorothy Gulman accompanied her. They took massages, dieted, walked in the country, and played a good deal of gin rummy.

Neither broached the subject of Richard, though Gulman had been hearing about the trouble from all their mutual friends since the Boston run of *Dream*. The rumor was rife enough to have reached Mae Kilgallen, who telephoned Gulman and asked her outright about Richard's philandering. The press agent, of course, revealed nothing.

"If I ever find out that he's cheating on Dolly Mae, he'll be in serious trouble," Mae said furiously.[20]

The turbulent episode about which Mae inquired happened while Dorothy was traveling back and forth between New York and Boston. Arriving unexpectedly in Boston, Dorothy, according to at least two sources who were close to the couple at the time, went to their hotel suite and discovered that the bed had not been slept in. She waited there until rehearsals were scheduled at the theater, ripped past her stammering husband wordlessly, and headed for the chorus girls' dressing room. Disheveled and gloveless, she pushed open the door and screamed, "Which one of you goddamn tramps kept my husband out all night?"

Dorothy reported her father's return from the war in her column of August 21, 1945.

> James L. Kilgallen, war correspondent, arrives back from Europe on the Queen Mary today. There is great rejoicing in the vicinity of the city room and also in Ridgewood, New Jersey, where his two favorite juveniles, Dickie and Jill Kollmar, are visiting their paternal grandparents . . . Welcome home, Pop!

Jim had seen a good deal of action overseas, filing numerous stories for INS in his graceless journeyman's prose. At the end, he had walked through Dachau, visited Hitler's blood-stained bunker, and smelled the stench of Berlin. The memories were still with him as he disembarked at Pier 90 among more than fourteen thousand demobilized men. In his correspondent's khaki, he embraced Dorothy, in her summer print.

On this last tour of duty, Jim had been away for seven months. Dorothy wrote to him frequently. "Wish I were there," she almost cabled him once. "I used to be a newspaperman myself." [1]

She also devoted one whole column to this man, her father. She cited his favorite axiom—a person can only wear one suit at a time and eat only three squares a day, no matter how much money he has. She asserted proudly that he was neither awed nor impressed by

> multimillionaires or crowned heads or society queens. For that reason probably he has always completely charmed duchesses, presidents, and kings. . . . When my sister and I would hold youthful debates about where our first million was coming from and how to

get a chinchilla coat, or would we save face socially if Mother didn't get an Aubusson for the living room floor, Dad's attitude was always one of tolerant but complete incomprehension . . . he is a simple person and he scales everything down to fundamentals, both physical and spiritual.[2]

They were a strange family, the Kilgallens. Dorothy totally idolizing her father, yet falling so far from the tree; her competitive fervor matching his, her social hunger not in the least consanguine. Jim, for his part, revered his daughter. He talked about her accomplishments incessantly and functioned, in print, as her Hearstian hagiographer. "The best newspaperwoman I know—and please pardon the fatherly pride—is Dorothy Kilgallen," he wrote in his memoir, *It's a Great Life.*[3] And he never left it at that. He felt compelled, obviously, to balance and justify. He stressed her religious commitment to home and family. His stories were invariably replete with quotes from her, such as: "I guess what I'm proving is that it's possible to rock a cradle and pound a typewriter, too." [4]

Jim brooked no criticism of Dorothy and seemed to perceive no gray areas. He covered a trial that involved Mickey Jelke, accused of running a vice ring in New York, and Pat Ward, purported to be one of his call-girls. Dorothy was watching the story closely and peppering her columns with items about the participants. In one item, she accused Pat Ward's flamboyant, dandified attorney of "setting the Homburg back twenty years." In another, she placed Miss Ward at the Copacabana, dancing with an executive from the garment district. The lawyer disclaimed the last disclosure as inaccurate and cited it as a flagrant example of press abuse. Jim confronted him in the court corridor, raging, "Dorothy never told a lie in her life. Only ham lawyers lie!" [5]

Like a huddling family in a cancer ward, they seemed to have fronted with bravado and to have told each other little or nothing of what everyone silently knew.

Mae Kilgallen, Dresden doll and ruling matriarch, wielded a strange power over them all. Outside of his home, Jim was a bibulous, companionable fellow, universally adored and respected. In his wife's company, he was cautiously deferential. Few people visited the elder Kilgallens in their own home. They socialized primarily at Dorothy's house with Dorothy's friends: once a week for gin rummy and on all the important holidays. "Come to think of it," a close friend of both the Kilgallen daughters recalled, "I can't remember Jim speaking at all."

Mae, who had a profound influence on Dorothy's life, had no fashion sense, though she constantly fussed and primped. When the Kollmars threw a "bad taste party" to which the guests were invited to bring the most horrific gifts they could find, Dorothy giggled with delight as she unwrapped obscene clocks and bellied Buddhas. Mae, standing behind her, clearly loved the stuff.[6]

Nevertheless, Dorothy dutifully accepted her mother's dicta. Even after she had become a television star and was well into her thirties and deeply involved with high fashion, Dolly Mae obeyed when her mother admonished that young ladies did not wear certain kinds of gloves or particular dress lengths on Sunday nights.

Television producer Bob Bach, who would become a good friend to Dorothy in the fifties, recalled: "There were some areas you *never* discussed with Dorothy—health, religion, or personal family matters." [7]

Mae Kilgallen did seem to have an exceptional ability to engender guilt. At a party for Hearstling Frank Conniff, the Kilgallens stood and chatted with Syd Boehm, who had left the *Journal* years before to produce and write for motion pictures. He did well. In the course of their conversation, Mae beamed at Boehm: "Do you know that Dorothy made more than $100,000 last year?"

Jim was embarrassed. He muttered something like, "Oh, come on, Mae! Syd probably makes more than that."

Syd Boehm replied, with an innocent spontaneity, "A lot more."

He watched as Mae Kilgallen's ego shattered. "I could have pulled my tongue out," he recollected. "Her reaction was so sad." [8]

Boehm has not forgotten her crestfallen face, nor the enormity of the guilt he experienced for being even more successful than Mae Kilgallen's daughter.

Eleanor had gone from music to acting, whirled around in Dorothy's orbit for a while as a sort of aide-de-camp, and eventually struck out on her own. After the war, with a woman named Monique James, she opened a small but prestigious agency for actors, Casting Consultants. She was good at her work and well-liked by her clients because she treated them with dignity.

Except for the thick, heavy-rimmed glasses she wore, Eleanor bore a striking resemblance to Dorothy (which scotches the rumor that swam around in the secretarial pools at the bizarre Hearst organization that made Dorothy a doorstep foundling of William Randolph Hearst and Marion Davies, thereby explaining the enormous success of Jim and especially Dorothy, and abating the resentment felt by underlings toward her). Eleanor's taste in clothes —"to the buttons on her little white gloves," according to a friend—was also like Dorothy's, although perforce less expensive.

In keeping with the family disposition, she was a very private, exceedingly controlled woman. An actress who socialized with her in the forties and fifties recalled:

> She put up a wall. There was a certain barrier. And, if you tried to infringe, you were stepping where angels fear to tread. You would get a freeze. There were times when I wondered about the humanity of both those girls.

She spoke in an amusing, pseudohip argot. In a profile of Eleanor Kilgallen that appeared in a 1965 issue of *Esquire*, she is quoted confirming a lunch date: "How's for Tues at Sardi's East? Marvy. I'll make the rez and we'll nip a few touches."

There was an additional trait that the sisters shared. Eleanor abjured vulgarity without avoiding the salacious. "You don't have to be one of those tough dames to succeed," she told *Esquire*. "I've never felt I had to tell dirty stories or use dirty words to function." She went on to explain one of her duties vis-à-vis the actors she handled: "You have to be a lay analyst, you should pardon the expression."

In 1946, when she was twenty-seven—the age at which Dorothy married Richard—Eleanor became engaged to Wilbur Snaper, an affable, direct man who also wore heavy-rimmed glasses. He was in his family's film-distribution business. While he was still in uniform, he met Eleanor at a party given by Shirley Eder, who is now a syndicated columnist based in Detroit.

Mae Kilgallen opposed the union violently. Wilbur Snaper was not only a Jew, he was a *divorced* Jew! But Eleanor would not be moved.

Dorothy really liked Wilbur, though, as a Catholic, she could not wholly support the marriage. Uppermost in her mind, however, was Mae and the startling notion of Eleanor's radical disobedience. Dorothy tried everything short of direct confrontation to dissuade her sister. She was big on dispatching emissaries to lunch. They were usually the husbands of mutual friends. But the younger Kilgallen girl was set on marrying Wilbur. A date was arranged for the civil ceremony.

With reluctant love, Dorothy asked the couple to be married in her apartment. Judge Ferdinand Pecora presided while Eleanor promised to forsake all others, including, unfortunately, Mae. The Kilgallens were conspicuously absent. Jim had wanted to attend. Mae forbade.

It was a joyless affair with champagne and cake.

Several months before Jim Kilgallen's return from the war,
Dorothy had found yet another forum over which to air
her perverse and multitudinous opinions—a morning radio
show called "Breakfast With Dorothy and Dick." The format was rather new, having originated with Ed and Pegeen
Fitzgerald in 1942. The idea was simply to run a cable into
a home and broadcast *live*, the predominantly extempora-
neous exchanges of a married couple as they exchanged
small talk over breakfast.

Pegeen Fitzgerald, a Junoesque woman with a lilting
voice, had been doing her own radio show, called "Pegeen
Prefers." Convalescing from an illness, she was compelled
to broadcast the program from her New York apartment.
Husband Ed, a mustachioed ex-newspaperman, was involved with a separate show, "Almanac de Gotham." He
was free during the time that Pegeen aired her morning
chitchat and, quite naturally, sat down and joined her on
several occasions. What emerged was brisk, off-the-cup
matutinal banter about their household, the people they
knew, their house in the country, the books they had read.
The idea worked. It was a time during which many husbands were overseas, and energetic breakfast conversation
had nostalgic appeal. Ed dropped his own program, and
they became "The Fitzgeralds." They broadcast over the
facilities of WOR, a New York City radio station whose
50,000 watts reached New York, New Jersey, and Connecticut, with a potential audience of almost twenty million
people.

The content of this kind of show mattered less than the
personalities of the couple. Ed was an opinionated, acerbic
Irishman who read widely and mixed well. Pegeen was a
chatty vegetarian with a galaxy of social and domestic interests. She tolerated his outbursts and called him Eddie. He

said "Just like a woman!" occasionally and called her anything that came to mind, including Lambie Puss. One heard them and conjured up visions of wedding pictures on lace. They were best known for their mutual love of animals and their on-the-air endeavors to find homes for stray cats.

There was a great deal of money to be made in radio, and the Fitzgeralds made it. But they never lost the common touch. Ed read their standard opening every morning: "We are the Fitzgeralds at their white-collar tenement on East Thirty-sixth Street." He once commented that their appeal was largely the result of his "complete incivility." Pegeen added that there were times when she tried to put on "company manners, but Ed won't let me get away with it." [1]

In 1944, they asked their listeners to write to them, answering the question, "What do you think this program is about?" They received 3,794 pieces of mail, almost all of it loving, a large majority of it from women. The consensus was that the program was about identification—the Fitzgeralds' marriage seemed so much like their own.

Pegeen and WOR haggled over cable costs. When the couple moved to WJZ, a replacement for them was sought. The Kollmars—Dorothy, Richard, Dickie, Jill, Julius, their butler, and Yasha, a canary—auditioned at home. Though the competition was heavy, they got the job. Mark Hanna negotiated a potentially lucrative deal for them, contingent upon the advertising they drew. "Breakfast With Dorothy and Dick" premiered on April 15, 1945. It was scheduled seven days a week: live, Monday through Saturday, 8:15 to 8:55 A.M., prerecorded only on Sunday, when the broadcast aired from 11:30 until noon.

They were instructed to retain the Fitzgeralds' basic format of extemporized, life-style chatter. But the station apparently realized that Dorothy and Dick lacked some of their predecessors' easy identifiability. The sales staff stressed the Kollmars' "in spite of" qualities. A trade-magazine promotional solicited sponsors for them: "Because they know BIG names, do BIG things, yet reflect the usual assortment of family interests and problems." A *Variety* advertisement called "Breakfast With Dorothy and Dick": "HOMEY AS A FRONT PORCH ROCKER, SMART AS A NEW SPRING BONNET."

At the inception, Richard was considered a stronger commercial drawing card than Dorothy. He still functioned as a producer and was involved with a show about Chicago, which never blew into New York, called *Windy City*. Theatrical production being an exceedingly risky affair, especially for Richard, he had returned earlier to radio and was well known within the WOR listening areas as the voice of "Boston Blackie." In this weekly, half-hour mystery, he portrayed an urbane, courageous chap with no visible means of support who dallied in the solution of murders and the creation of puns such as: "I'm going to find the killer that came into this riding academy and started horsing around."

Since he was comfortable facing a microphone, he worried primarily about the prospect of rising daily at 7 A.M. to get himself in shape for the show. Though it emanated from their dining room, there were newspapers to scan, interesting items to circle, and presently, commercials to prepare. He had none of Dorothy's demanding nocturnal responsibility, but he, too, was a creature of the night. He suffered dreadful insomnia, drank and smoked excessively, and had nothing approaching Dorothy's natural vitality. To solve his personal energy crisis, he had an oxygen tank installed in his dressing room. Each morning, after donning his initialed Sulka robe and ascot, he drew from the tank. He extolled its virtues to Jimmy Gardiner: "Breathes new life into you," he said.[2]

Dorothy needed no artificial stimulants. She began taking speech lessons to lower her voice and professionalize her delivery. But the prospect of extemporizing terrified her. To get over the hump, she scripted the first couple of shows in their entirety, his lines and hers, everything from "Good morning, darling," to the response to the musical question, "Did you sleep well?" Nonetheless, her knees knocked together and her hands shook so violently that she could hardly draw her coffee cup to her mouth.[3]

Dorothy soon disposed of the scripts. The show began to attract a considerable audience. And soon she was comfortable enough to invite the press to come up and watch. A writer for *The New Yorker* visited one August morning.

"Naturally," he wrote, referring to the homey-front-porch-rocker material prepared by the station,

> I was impatient to see the little vine-covered cottage in which Dick had installed Dorothy. . . . I was dis-

appointed to find that they live in a sixteen-room apartment at Park Avenue and Sixty-sixth street. The door was opened by an elderly Negro butler wearing a white jacket. I entered a long, marble hallway, at the end of which I could dimly see Mrs. Kollmar waiting to greet me in a floor-length hostess gown. By the time I had walked the length of the hall, Mr. Kollmar, having left his rocker and come in off the front porch, was at her side. Mrs. Kollmar is a slim young brunette with immobile features. Mr. Kollmar is a stocky, boyish-looking man.

While Dorothy and Dick repaired to their dining-room microphones, the *New Yorker* writer was ushered to another part of the house, where he listened to their broadcast over a console radio.

At 8:15, he heard their standard opening:

"*Good* morning, sweetie," Dorothy said to Dick.

"Good morning, darling," he replied. "It's time for Dorothy and Dick. My, my, this is good orange juice."

"It's Juicy Gem," Dorothy said. "Would you like some toast?"

They discussed the theater, the weather, Dick's very imminent flight to Chicago. Jill entered the breakfast room.

"Are you going to play in your tent today?" Dorothy asked the child.

According to the *New Yorker* man, Jill replied, " 'Wes,' in a high voice, and Mr. and Mrs. Kollmar laughed heartily."

When the program ended, they joined him in the living room: " 'I'm off to Chicago,' Dick said to me. He sounded like a man in a musical comedy who was off to Chicago.

" 'Goodbye, dear,' said Mrs. Kollmar. They kissed. He exited." [4]

While the magazine had good fun with the inanity of the breakfast show, it did not attempt to deal with the special appeal of the Kollmars. Citing the grand surroundings of the apartment, the butler, Dorothy's floor-length hostess gown, it implied that a kind of benign ruse was being perpetrated. Quite the contrary. Despite the promotional campaign, Dorothy and Dick never pretended to live in a vine-covered cottage with vine-covered concerns. Indeed, it was this very absence of ruse that accounted, in part, for the phenomenal success of "Breakfast with Dorothy and Dick."

They were *not* the couple next door. They reminded few people of their own marriage. The point was that they differed. They were rich, mobile, quintessentially cosmopolitan. If Dorothy endorsed a food product—and she endorsed more and more as the show blossomed—she did not pretend to have cooked it. It had doubtless been served to her. As the months went by, their loyal listeners knew the names of their staff, the dimensions of their table, the quality of their glassware, a good deal about the extremely social permutations of the couple, and the names of most of their close, equally privileged friends.

By 1947, for instance, Dorothy did not have to back up and introduce the Boscowitzes. They were old acquaintances, as familiar to the audience as Midge, Julius, Yasha, or Dickie.

> DOROTHY: You know, I never did get to tell you where I went before I met you and Lillian and Hubie. A cocktail party of Pat Smart for Babs Martin, who had just been ill. It was very gay. And I ran into guess who?
>
> DICK: Tony Martin.
>
> DOROTHY: No. Unfortunately, I had to leave before he arrived.
>
> DICK: Of course, I knew Babs when her name was Beckwith.
>
> DOROTHY: No. This is a different one.
>
> DICK: It is.
>
> DOROTHY: I don't know what Babs Beckwith's name is now. But I'm pretty sure that it's not Martin.
>
> DICK: Well, who is Babs Martin? This I don't know at all.
>
> DOROTHY: I'd have to go into some long genealogy for that. You'd know her if you saw her. No, who I ran into was Richard Ney. It was right after his bout with the bobby soxers. Some of them are really little juve-

nile delinquents. I saw Eddy Duchin there, too. I wish he'd go into a spot. He won't. He's such a lazy boy. This town needs a Duchin, an orchestra leader with a real personality.[5]

Dick played tired tuba to Dorothy's frivolous flute. They spoke more than two million words every year, bagatelles to the glamour and glory of their New Yorky lives.

Barry Gray, a prominent local radio personality who was working as a disc jockey at WOR then, heard their program every morning while he was selecting records in the station's music library. In his book, *My Night People*, he wrote, "My God, when Dorothy and Dick said it—you were there!" [6]

On a typical broadcast, they described an exceptional evening at the Stork Club. (Normally, they slept in shifts, catching a few hours before the program, returning to bed, if there was no pressing business, until early afternoon. This morning, they had gone sleepless to their microphones.) The night had begun, as they recounted it for their listeners, after a party at the St. Regis. From there, they repaired to their favorite watering hole, the Stork Club. They were ushered into the Cub Room at three A.M., where sat, among others: Harvey Firestone, Jean Dalrymple, José Iturbi, Bert and Mildred Lahr, Howard Barlow, Mr. and Mrs. LaFayette (DICK: "The lady and gentleman that own the Irish wolfhounds."), and a young woman whom neither of them recognized. Dorothy was introduced, but dismissed her perfunctorily as an unknown of "the Harvey Firestone party."

Dorothy, on the air now, explained a little about the social stratification of the Stork Club:

> I think we should say, for the benefit of our listeners
> —after all, not *all* of our listeners have been to the
> Stork Club, some of them will never be in the Stork
> —that the Cub Room is where *we* sit most of the time.
> It's a sort of a club and that is where you see the most
> celebrities. I think when people come in from out of
> town they frequently make the mistake of going into
> the main room, where the dancing is going on. It's
> sort of logical. That's where all the gaiety *should* be.

But most of the fun is always in the Cub Room because that's where most of the interesting people go.

The interesting people began to talk among themselves, waving and chatting from table to table. A cupcake was brought out for Mildred Lahr, whose birthday was being celebrated that night. Everybody sang "Happy Birthday" to Mildred Lahr. The singing engendered, among all the interesting people, a clubby, musical feeling. As Dick told it: "A movement started to get José Iturbi to the piano. The question was—where do we get a piano?"

Dorothy added: "I think I was the moving spirit behind that because I said to Jean Dalrymple, 'I keep thinking I'm in an MGM movie and any minute he ought to sit down at the piano and some girl should sing.' "

Dick recounted that he had personally spoken to Sherman Billingsley about moving the celebrities from the Cub Room into the main room, where they had a fine piano, "but it seemed that there were still a few couples in the big room and he felt that we would be sort of *bothered* by them."

Some of Billingsley's staff was dispatched upstairs to the Blessed Event Room to fetch a small piano. It was not the best piano, but Maestro Iturbi was gracious enough to consent to play. He began with some Chopin sonatas. They gathered around him.

Several of the interesting people began to hum along, Dorothy and Dick among them. Lo and behold, one voice seemed quite accomplished. The interesting people looked over the top of the piano and began focusing on her.

DOROTHY: The name I hadn't caught. I knew she was in Harvey Firestone's group . . . I thought, "This girl knows something!" She certainly knew more Italian than I do. She *knows* this aria. I listened to the voice for a minute. But I dismissed her as probably some girl from out of town who has a lovely voice but probably hasn't done anything about it. And . . .

DICK: This girl had escaped me, too. But here was this glorious, glorious soprano just echoing around the Cub Room. I turned to Jean Dalrymple and said,

"Look, this kid has got a future. Please tell me who she is. I've got to see her tomorrow."

Dorothy turned to Jean Dalrymple and asked, "That is not by any chance Eleanor *Steber* of the Metropolitan Opera?"

It was indeed Eleanor Steber of the Metropolitan Opera.

Dorothy declared that she had never been so thrilled by music as she had been by Iturbi and Eleanor Steber of the Metropolitan Opera, as they concertized until six in the morning. Dick agreed.

"And then in the middle of this thing," she reminded Dick, "in came Sherry Britton, the stripper, and Barney Ross."

They liked the music, too. It was almost seven when the interesting people spilled into the morning light, José Iturbi and Barney Ross, according to Dick, "exchanging very palsy goodnights."

"It only proves your theory," Dorothy concluded, before segueing to a commercial, "that these things can only happen in New York."

By the late 1940s, breakfast shows were springing up all over the country. A couple in Red Hook, New Jersey, by the name of Klose, sat down every morning with their hired hand to discuss crop rotation and animal feed. Tex McCrary, a journalist, and his wife, Jinx Falkenburg, an actress and glamour girl who turned reporter under McCrary's tutelage, exchanged morning thoughts with political and international ramifications. Faye Emerson, who was then married to Elliott Roosevelt, broadcast "At Home with Faye Emerson"—home being the presidential estate at Hyde Park. "The McCanns" dispensed tips on food and nutrition. And "The Fitzgeralds" continued jauntily at WJZ.

Several rating services showed that "Breakfast with Dorothy and Dick" was the most popular program of its type in the New York area. The popularity of the show, however, was in no way contingent upon the popularity of the couple. On the contrary. With Dorothy in the ascendance as a personality after overcoming her initial terror, the Kollmars were compelling irritants to whom a large part of their audience was drawn in spite of itself, as a tongue to a septic tooth.

Ed and Pegeen Fitzgerald, who made no secret of their negative feelings about Dorothy and Dick, regularly received mail about Dorothy's latest affront. Ed recalled, "We used to pick up these tidbits from our listeners who thought they were funny. She said once that she dined at a home where they had a bottle of catsup on the table and she nearly got up and left." Pegeen added, "She said at their home they *never* used catsup." Ed expanded, "She thought catsup was vulgar." [7]

The station's switchboard lit up with calls from the aggrieved one morning after Dorothy read a letter in which a listener corrected a grammatical error she had made. She accepted the emendation sportingly, looked at the postmark of the letter, and exclaimed, "Fort Lee, New Jersey! If he's so smart, what's he doing in Fort Lee, New Jersey?" [8]

Word of Dorothy's latest offense outreached WOR's broadcasting radius. The residents of Laramie, Wyoming, the town in which she had spent the first year of her life, were incensed when they heard about a discussion the Kollmars had one morning about the greater risk of nuclear attack incurred by living in a big city. Dorothy blurted out that she would rather die happy in a New York holocaust than live to a ripe old age in Laramie.

As Dorothy's public *persona* become more controversial, there arose certain myths about her, none more pernicious than the one that concerned her purported anti-Semitism.

Telephone calls began pouring into her office one Friday afternoon about a story that had just hit the streets. *P.M.*, a liberal New York newspaper, was running a story by Seymour Peck about the breakfast show, which read, in part:

> There is also a child, the son of the Kollmars, and he, like most youngsters, occasionally says something that embarrasses his parents. Once there was an unpleasant remark about Jews. [9]

Dorothy was dumbfounded.

"Is it true?" Midge asked her.

"Of course it's not true," Dorothy replied. "My children have no prejudices at all. My own brother-in-law is Jewish!" [10]

She telephoned Edgar Hatfield immediately. He was to demand retraction or initiate suit. To Edgar, she cited her work on behalf of B'nai B'rith and the Anti-Defamation League.

At *P.M.*, Peck was summoned to the office of his managing editor. "Your ass is in a sling if you can't substantiate these charges," he thundered. "Kilgallen claims she's a good friend to the Jews and she'll sue us into the ground." [11]

Peck tried in vain to contact his sources and rally their support. They were all connected with WOR. Some were "oddly unavailable," others could not state with certainty that they had heard the remark made on the air.

The original story, on which Peck staked his claim, concerned Dickie and The Bronx Zoo. The boy was alleged to have said that his grandmother would no longer take him there because she objected to the proliferation of Jews.

Peck obtained records of the "Breakfast" show from a transcription service that monitored radio twenty-four hours a day. They listened to weeks of the broadcast. They were unable to find Dickie's purported remark. On the following Monday, Seymour Peck was compelled to retract. He wrote:

> Before I printed the story I checked it with several people around the studio whom I considered reliable. However, since the Kollmar denial, I find that none of these people actually heard the alleged remark made on the air. This leads me to believe that the story is without foundation and may have gained credence through the efforts of some malicious force. I am sorry if the incident caused any embarrassment to the Kollmars.[12]

It is possible, however, that the rumor itself was not fashioned out of whole cloth. She could have lied to Midge. She was a painstakingly honest woman when she knew the truth, but on questions that involved professional survival, she sometimes saved for the confessional what she could not tell a judge. Barry Gray contended, in his book, that the best part of "Breakfast with Dorothy and Dick" was their pre-broadcast comments—"the stuff the audience never heard as the engineer fooled with the microphone." [13] That segment of the show was audible to him and to other personnel at the station. If Dickie's mindless repetition was made at all, it was probably during that prebroadcast period that it was overheard by Peck's station sources. Their reluctance to involve themselves in litigation opposing an important WOR personality is easily understood.

Despite the retraction, the original story of grandma's counsel to Dickie lingered on in the public's memory, vague but perdurable. There is hardly a Jew in the East over thirty years old on whose cultural engrams there is not imprinted an association between Dorothy and anti-Semitism. The stubbornness of the association has less to do with fact than with perceived possibility.

Dorothy was extremely vulnerable to the charge. She was associated with the Hearst organization, whose newspapers extolled the virtues of Hitler long after his psychopathic prejudices were public policy. She consorted, somewhat ostentatiously, with many known anti-Semites, the most virulent of whom was Sherman Billingsley. Her politics, though maverick, were right-leaning. Most significantly, she was, in the public mind, a snobbish provincial whose reckless insularity *could* have provided a hospitable environment for the sensibilities of the anti-Semite.

Dorothy ran at the mouth with statements apt to be misconstrued and unlikely to be forgotten. In March of 1945, she told a columnist, Dell Chandler, that she was apprehensive about her children's "air manners" now that they were old enough to play in the public park and mix with children whose parents were not quite as "careful" as she in their rearing habits.[14]

Dorothy was hoist on her own petard. She would have done well to have been more select about who took her children to the park.

Dorothy lived a Gotham gothic.

Even Richard, flaccid with city ways, enjoyed working up a sweat on a country tennis court, buggying over the dunes in Southampton, or tumbling into an ocean wave.

She knew no such pleasures. Visiting the North Shore estate of Donald and Jean Stralem, an enormously wealthy couple whom the Kollmars knew all through their married life, Dorothy sat in a shaded, poolside arbor underneath a parasol.

Of course, the sun literally poisoned her. But there appeared to be more to it than the fragility of her blue-white Irish skin. Mrs. Stralem, sipping sherry in her Park Avenue apartment, remembered that Dorothy never got into a bathing suit: "She took *no* exercise at all. I don't know that I even remember her walking down a New York street." [1]

The children were packed off, with their buxom German governess, whom they called Nu Nu, to Ridgewood or to Eleanor's cottage on Fire Island. But such was not Dorothy's cup of tea.

She and Richard sojourned yearly to the playgrounds of Latin America, the Greek Islands, Rome, and Paris. These trips, however, were merely extensions of her city life. She explored no sylvan paths.

Dorothy assured herself that her life-style was not only satisfactory but that it was superior.

Sherman Billingsley, in the late forties, instituted a Sunday morning ritual at the Stork Club called the Rumba Breakfast. He encouraged his following to come and bring their kids. Eggnogs were served upon entering by a gray-haired majordomo named Jimmy. Everybody danced.

One Easter morning the Kollmars dropped by after their

traditional walk along Fifth Avenue, the one "parade" of which Dorothy heartily approved. She and Jill wore matching Easter bonnets created for them by Mr. John and the little white gloves that had begun to symbolize Dorothy's couture. The children were ogled and petted. The Rumba Breakfast was a warm beginning to a signally enjoyable Easter, after which they were joined, at the apartment, for family dinner.

Dorothy and Richard returned to the Stork on a subsequent Sunday, after services at St. Vincent Ferrer. She wrote presently in her column:

> Dropped in on the Stork Club the other Sabbath morning to catch up with cafe society's latest matutinal diversion, the "rumba breakfast," a pleasant institution and likely to succeed. . . . The main room of the cafe wore a positively 'family' look, with mothers and fathers and debutante daughters occupying ringside tables . . . and even a trio of little boys of nursery school age quietly eating scrambled eggs in a corner.[2]

The column ran in her Minneapolis outlet, where it was seen by a local writer named George Grim. Grim was appalled. Under the headline PARDON ME, I'M HOPPING MAD, he attacked the Rumba Breakfast, addressing his column, with righteous fury, to "The Three Little Boys, c/o Stork Club."

He claimed to understand why those three little boys were eating their scrambled eggs so quietly.

> Maybe you were thinking of the fun you might have had going on a bird walk with your dad, or taking a hike through Central Park in the freshness of a January Sunday morning. Asking your dad how thick did the ice get on the lake, where did all the birds go, why did the sparrows live in New York all winter, when will spring come, where does the little curved path lead. All sorts of questions a boy likes to ask his dad on a Sunday hike. But your dad was doing the rumba. And he did look a little foolish, wriggling and squirming.

On behalf of the three little boys c/o the Stork, Grim went on to attack their dancing moms. He wondered whether the youngsters missed

> the smell of Sunday dinner cooking. The roast in the oven, the home-made rolls getting brown, the good smell of apples baking in a pie. . . . Maybe you wanted to ask your mother what made rolls rise, or where did gravy come from. . . . And when you tried to ask her something she danced by and said, "Don't bother me, kid."

He surmised, in conclusion, that the three little boys wished that they were in "Sunday school or Church." Alas, they sat mute and inglorious, stuck at the Stork, because "a lady columnist named Dorothy Kilgallen thought the Sabbath rumba breakfast was 'a pleasant institution most likely to succeed.' " [3]

Dorothy received dozens of copies of George Grim's scoutmasterly jeremiad in her morning mail and immediately cleared her desk for action. She took the Grim column, with justification, as a frontal attack aimed at the very foundation of her life-style. She must have telephoned an editor at the Minneapolis *Tribune* and demanded equal time in the same spot that Grim had leveled his sanctimonious reproach, the better to reach the readers for whom a totally erroneous picture of New York values had been painted. "Believe it or not," she would write in her hot asseveration, "it is possible to go to church and to the Stork Club on the same day." [4]

On the nitty-gritty issues of her children's education and well-being, she took on Grim point by point. She assured him that she also had a kitchen, but that she could not imagine her son Dickie asking "anything quite as silly as 'Where does gravy come from?' He does know all about the planet Saturn and the law of gravity and the Wizard of Oz, and he can hum strains of Prokofieff and Tschaikowsky as well as sing 'Adeste Fidelis' in Latin."

Jill, she conceded, had never seen her mother "whipping up a batch of rolls (mother is trying to keep her figure and doesn't eat rolls). That doesn't seem to have detracted from her happiness."

She sent George Grim a family picture of the smiling Kollmars. She concluded with:

> I hope that this will show you that the lines of decadence are not yet too deeply etched in our faces, and that our children are neither starved for lack of homemade apple pie (goodness, Mr. Grim had old-fashioned ideas of nutrition!) nor reduced to bitterness because their parents know how to dance.

Dorothy closed the column "with kindest regards," adding, "P.S. How many children has Mr. Grim and are they happy?"

Grim, it turned out, was a bachelor.

The success of their broadcasts—which were yielding them, according to various estimates, anywhere from $75,000 to $100,000 a year by the late 1940s—permitted Dorothy and Richard to enhance their style of life considerably. They turned their sixteen-room Park Avenue apartment into a showcase, fulfilling most of Dorothy's fantasies about herself and the good life.

The Victorian drawing room, where she did most of her formal entertaining, was painted in shades of lavender and mauve, with rosewood chairs, crystal candelabra, porcelain cherubim in various stages of flight, impressionist paintings of pink-cheeked girls in boaters, and an enormous, round velvet pouf that would have comfortably accommodated the tightest rump in an Oscar Wilde comedy.

This was her favorite room. After a hectic day of dealing with press agents and verifying rumors, she would often come here alone to take tea and transport herself into a more innocent century. She explained to a writer, "I guess I've got a little of the Berkeley Square in me." [5]

Her dressing room was a poem of feminine fragility, all white wicker with pale pink trimmings. She had a matching bird there, a pink-and-white canary named Robin, who warbled in the morning light as Dorothy prepared herself for the broadcast. Midge Willer remembers a prie-dieu in Dorothy's dressing room. But it was more for show than for tell. When the secretary's fiancé, Paul White, suggested that they kneel on one of its frosty Bavarian cushions, Dorothy giggled.

She was as profoundly devout as ever. Her home, however, was no place for the gaudy piety of bleeding Jesuses. A small, tasteful crucifix hung over the large bed in the master bedroom. And in her night-table drawer, she kept a delicate box filled with objects out of her Catholic girlhood, including a St. Christopher's medal that she had taken with her on her round-the-world dash.

The Kollmars' living room was forgotten by none who entered, which was more or less the point of it. When they planned the new apartment, they decided to have one fun room in which they would allow their own notions of the bizarre to prevail. To Mae Kilgallen's complete horror, four walls and the ceiling were painted an uncompromising, stygian *black*. The Black Room, as it came to be called by the family, featured authentic examples of Americana. Daniel D. Tompkins hung there, alongside numerous variations on the American eagle. Guests were bidden to close their eyes and play Count the Eagles, a game in which their powers of observation were tested. Dick fashioned a large antique snare drum into a coffee table. Around it sat two tiny red chairs, one for each of the children. The *pièce de résistance* was a nineteenth-century carousel they used as a sofa: it was delicately carved, iridescent blue, and pulled by a large golden swan that appeared to be noshing on the bright green carpet.

Jimmy Gardiner remembered a mammoth picture there of a Civil War scene: "General Custer was chasing some goddamned Indians all over the wall." Dorothy was delighted to discover that one of the military officers depicted in the painting was a forebear of songwriter Johnny Mercer.

The Black Room was more Richard's fantasy than Dorothy's. Richard was an inveterate hobbyist who flitted from collection to collection. Before marrying Dorothy, he had assembled a wide variety of miniature whiskey bottles. Scattered through the Black Room now were his newest passions—cigar-store Indians, music boxes, and toy banks that did everything but tap dance when a coin was fed to them.

He was most dedicated to his collection of hands. Among his two hundred pairs were two wooden artifacts with spikes jutting from each finger and burning candles impaled on each spike. He occasionally served friends from a blue porcelain whiskey bottle shaped like a hand. Then there was the tiny, fragile ring-holder—a hand with splayed fingers—said to have belonged to Anne Boleyn, and a clay casting of Walt Whitman's writing hand.

Dorothy worked in a spare, rather ambassadorial room, using an old mahogany dining table as her desk. The unattractive detritus of work, such as her metal filing cabinets, were kept in a small, recessed office. There were several other undistinguished spaces that Dorothy never bothered to fix up. One was filled, like a warehouse, with the hundreds of gifts she received every year in her capacity as Broadway columnist.

The children rode their bicycles up and down the thirty-five-foot hallway. Marble and mirrored, it was an impressive introduction to an impressive domicile.

Here, at 630 Park Avenue, Dorothy and Richard created some of the best parties in New York City. They threw several big ones a year, the most elaborate on their anniversary and on New Year's Eve, which was also Richard's birthday. They worked excitedly for weeks on these galas, as though they were mounting a show. All the elements were there: theme, costumes, book, sets, cast of characters, costs and ways to cut them, talent, publicity, and awards.

Dorothy and Richard toiled in the Black Room, conceiving their first big anniversary bash. She held the pencil and made lists; Dick held a glass and paced. They decided that the theme of the bash would be Saints and Sinners, more sonorous than accurate—guests were requested to come as their favorite sinners out of mythology, literature, history, or the other media.

Richard envisioned the apartment transformed into a simulated inferno, with their favorite beautiful people cavorting among fire and brimstone. Dorothy opted for something prettier, the site of the Fall, the Garden of Eden. Other diversions would include a gambling room and an arcade with pinball machines and movieolas. Music, they knew, would be no problem. Performers vied for the privilege of working Dorothy's room.

To whose sins would Dorothy aspire? Her sinner had beauty, grace, raven hair, a delectable body, a certain coy girlishness, grit under pressure, and one hell of a wardrobe. She had been portrayed by Vivien Leigh, whose consummate loveliness devastated Dorothy.

The big question was settled. On their ninth wedding

anniversary, they would be Scarlett O'Hara and Rhett Butler in a Garden of Eden, with options to gamble and watch campy silent flicks, dance to a full orchestra in one room, and listen to boogie-woogie piano in another.

Under Richard's supervision, old sets were struck and new ones erected. All remnants of Victoria's repressed England were sequestered, including the pink pouf. He labored long on production sketches and oversaw the work of two men who worked three days transforming their drawing room from Cecil Beaton to Let There Be Light. More than seven hundred hanging vines were purchased at a hefty discount and festooned around the room. Trees were rented. Stuffed tropical birds replaced the porcelain cherubim.

Dorothy broke away intermittently from her frantic working day to survey the transformation, clambering perilously over planks in her ubiquitous bowed pumps. She made sure, too, that coffee and sandwiches were available to the workmen, with whom she chatted amiably and called by name. She was the flip side of the traditional liberal who loved the masses and disdained the individual. Richard, on the other hand, was quite capable of spending months with one of the engineers who rode audio on the morning show without bothering with small talk or appellations.

Like all of his production capers, this one was visually astounding, though somewhat out of whack. Maggi McNellis Newhouse, a good friend to Dorothy and a radio-television personality of the late 1940s and early 1950s who came to epitomize the sophisticated New York woman in the media, would eventually rave on the air about the production values of the Kollmars' party. But she placed their garden somewhat east of Eden. She took the metamorphosed drawing room to be a lush and terrific Tropical Night Club.

Dorothy spent hours writing more than one hundred scorched invitations by hand, as she had been taught was proper. (Her script was chic and distinctive. A graphologist who worked the Stork concluded, on the basis of Dorothy's circled i-dots and calculated capitals, that she was "reserved, cultured, wished to be different, as a result of which she is puzzling at times. She is not an easy person to know.") She insisted that her prospective guests register their costumes by calling Miss Willer at REgent 7-0960. The embarrassment of duplication was scrupulously to be avoided. "We will keep your choice a dead secret and we hope you will, too," she wrote. "If you can't think of a suitable sinner, consult us. We're experts." [6]

The handwritten invitations were no chore to Dorothy, nor was any other element of her punctiliously creative party-planning. Anything personalized and surprising, which she imagined might amuse and tantalize those people about whom she cared, afforded her enormous satisfaction. She was like a child in that regard—a very sweet child—proffering a painstaking, beribboned gift, impatient for the unwrapping and the exhalations of approval. She shopped half a year for Christmas, finding just the right gifts for the hundreds of people on her list. For Earl Blackwell, who founded Celebrity Service and kept enormous clippings files on the famous, she bought little gold scissors from Tiffany's. For Arlene Francis, who habitually sucked on Life Savers, she had surprise packages of penny candies in endlessly multitudinous varieties. When Richard was going through his wooden Indian stage, she was forever finding, wrapping, and hiding the bulky artifacts in some recess of the apartment. And it is no mean feat to either wrap or hide a wooden Indian.

As the anniversary party approached, the radio audience was kept informed of the day-by-day progress of their preparations. One morning Dorothy said to Dick, on the air, "If only we could have something done about those two monstrous mirrors in the *fwa-yay*!"

Dick replied, "Maybe we could paint pictures on them like they used to do in the old-time saloons?" [7]

They talked about the difficulties of getting someone who could work on glass. At WOR, the phones began ringing immediately with artists willing and eager to serve the influential Kollmars *gratis*. Dorothy was not above such usage, because the coin of her realm was *quid pro quo*. Dick's rationale was simpler—he was cheap. They finally chose a muralist named Arthur Nilsen, who was associated with the brokers Merrill, Lynch, Pierce, Fenner and Beane. The artist worked a full day on the mirror mural. He was not invited to the party, but he was served well on the morning broadcast. Several minutes were dedicated to the firm of Merrill, Lynch, Pierce, Fenner and Beane.[8]

* * *

The children were sent to grandma's on the night of the party. At ten o'clock, when the guests began to arrive, Dorothy, flushed and buoyant in her $650 Scarlett O'Hara dress, with her bouncy girls bedecked with gardenias, stood beside Richard, in his dashing Rhett Butler cutaway.

As the bell chimed, Julius ushered in the guests and announced their intentions in his best stentorian:

Ladies and gentlemen—Admiral Nelson and Lady
Hamilton!
Ladies and gentlemen—Adam and Eve!
Ladies and gentlemen—Frankie and Johnnie!
Ladies and gentlemen—Leda and the Swan!
Ladies and gentlemen—The Centaur!

The revelers, all of whom complimented Dorothy and Richard on the splendor of their Eden, were as creative and extravagant as their hosts. Lillian and Hubie came as Salome and Herod. Their butler accompanied them, either with or *as* the head of John the Baptist. His was, in either case, an encumbered role. Hubie recalled the butler's plight with amusement: "He couldn't smoke. He couldn't eat. The poor fellow couldn't do anything." [9]

In the main room, a full orchestra played. Musician Lanny Ross, dressed as François Villon, danced with *Look* editor Pat Coffin/George Sand. The magazine's photographer was popping flashbulbs at stockbroker Paul Zuckerman, who, as the Swan, presented a surreal vision as he moved Leda around the dance floor, his beaked costume-head towering high above his own. Richard walked to the bandstand and whispered something to Lanny Ross as Dorothy stood chatting with David O. Selznick, the producer of *Gone With the Wind*, and his wife, Jennifer Jones. They had arrived directly from an evening at the theater and were the only guests permitted to attend in ordinary evening dress.

Earlier in the evening, showgirl and actress Joyce Matthews, who had not bothered to register her costume, had arrived as Lady Hamilton. Maggi McNellis, who had registered as the flamboyant courtesan, was dancing with her husband, art dealer Clyde Newhouse, when the second Hamilton woman appeared. She picked up her satin skirts, fled from the dance floor, and locked herself in the bathroom. Dorothy was compelled, with polite firmness, to ask Joyce Matthews to leave.

At Richard's instigation, the waltz from *Gone With the Wind* was played. Dorothy and Richard danced. She was a trained and beautiful ballroom dancer. Under yards of antebellum silk, her head tilted slightly to the right, she smiled rapturously. As the tempo increased, she moved with poise and fluidity. She was Scarlett O'Hara in the Garden of Eden, a realistic woman who had confected a fantasy world. With the proper shading, it might always be joyful.

At midnight exactly, Dorothy supervised the sumptuous buffet in "Scarlett's dining room." Several dozen lobsters, two roast beefs, three roast turkeys, and several magnums of champagne were attacked by Madame DuBarry (Ethel Merman, Don Juan (Igor Cassini), Mad King Ludwig and Lola Montez (Bert and Mildred Lahr), Cardinal Richelieu (Bill Hawkins of the *World-Telegram*), Frankie and Johnnie (Eleanor Holm and Billy Rose), Salome and Herod (with their silent butler), Diamond Jim Brady (Quentin Reynolds), and the Centaur (Miles White).

Shy Miles, terrified of big parties, had fashioned his mythic beast out of pony skin, which clung to his body, and plywood. He did not enjoy himself at Dorothy's party. "I went through hell that night," he recalled. "I stood in a corner and got loaded with Eleanor Holm, who was the only real person I could find." [10]

Following the buffet, the sinners spilled throughout the house, some of them playing roulette in "Rhett's gambling hall" with their thousand dollars in toy money, others diverting themselves with the gimmicks that Richard had installed in the arcade. Jennifer Jones tried a "sex appeal machine" and got a reading of Fair. Paul White, who was on the swim team at Princeton and was breaking training that weekend to be with Midge, reached into his fig leaf to retrieve his glasses and peer into the movieola. Richard had personally designed the costumes for Paul's Adam and Midge's Eve, dressing them in leaves and sandals and vines like bandoliers. [11]

It was after two when Richard mounted the bandstand and directed all the diners to line up for the Grand March into the Garden of Eden. Dorothy awarded prizes to Lillian Boscowitz as The Most Sensational Woman Sinner and to Miles White for Best Man's Costume.

The party dispersed into little groups. Dick mingled. Dorothy drank champagne and sang Harold Arlen songs softly.

At 7:20 A.M., the last of the guests were asked to leave so that the Kollmars could bathe and get ready to tell their listeners about the party that *Playbill* later called "the most brilliant gathering of any season." [12]

Dorothy, Richard, Midge, and Paul laughed again as they passed the mural that the man from Merrill, Lynch, Pierce, Fenner and Beane had drawn with a little direction from Richard. Primitive, comic-book art, the mural depicted the Kollmars at the Pearly Gates. St. Peter is yelling "Out!" Dick, who lolls on a nearby cloud, looks bored and resigned. Dorothy, with her skinny legs flailing about, hangs onto the admitting cloud by the fingertips of one hand, gesticulating vehemently with the other. She is angrily disputing the gatekeeper's decision.

By 1950, certain aspects of Dorothy's lapidary scenario were playing spendidly.

Jill Ellen, eight, was enrolled at the Marymount School on Fifth Avenue. She was ladylike and loving, and she curtsied when she was introduced to an adult. She was progressing remarkably well with her piano lessons, taught by Mother Leo.

Ten-year-old Dickie was at Allen-Stevenson, whose illustrious founders' express aim for their students was "the development of straight-forward and manly character." Although he was a bit of a discipline problem, which was ascribed to his being "too bright" for conventional education, Dickie was multitalented and amusing. When he was requested to sing a song at a family gathering in Ridgewood, he cracked, "O.K. But where's the mike?" [1]

Dorothy's *Voice of Broadway* was among the most widely read columns in the country. It is impossible to determine how widely read the column eventually became. Igor Cassini, who took over the "Cholly Knickerbocker" column after the death of Maury Paul, estimated that he had twenty million readers, a figure based on the optimistic assumption that a newspaper is read by three to four people. "Dorothy was probably in that vicinity, too," he maintained. "She certainly was syndicated very widely." [2]

Midge Willer had, by this time, married Paul White and left her job to await their first child. She was replaced by Myrtle Verne, an unattractive New Englander who lived with her invalid mother. Myrtle was efficient, discreet, and totally dedicated to her boss. She would marry no one.

Dorothy attended the opera on alternate Mondays, a chic time, when one could see Mrs. Vanderbilt and her party. She functioned on behalf of a number of social charities, including Mrs. William Randolph Hearst's Milk Fund.

Her picture was taken by Jerome Zerbe as she stood looking earnestly elegant on a long, winding staircase, with
eleven other climbers. She and Richard laid a wreath at the
vault of Daniel D. Tompkins and made the cover of a magazine called *The Masonic Family*. Dorothy was invited to
join the board at Bard, the college out of which Richard
had flunked.

She was in and out of limousines in Cecil Chapman
originals and mink. There is one picture of her perusing a
nightclub menu through a lorgnette. When the occasion
warranted it, Myrtle would be dispatched to Harry Winston's with a diversionary shopping bag, to pick up a
diamond tiara on loan. Dorothy might never own jewels
as resplendent as Hope Hampton's, but she could readily
avail herself of them.

Dorothy and Richard appeared to be a perfectly com-
patible couple. He could still make her laugh. They were
forever dressing up to catch some new or favorite club act.
They both loved good food, nightlife, parlor games, the
company of talented and/or attractive people. They worked
hard keeping their life together sparky, glamorous, and
diverting.

Richard's whoring was common knowledge among the
cognoscenti in New York—as commonly known as Dorothy's fidelity. He brought his women to some parties given
by Charlotte Manson, who was now a successful radio
actress. "He would call me to tell me about his newest,"
Charlotte Manson recalled. "He would all of a sudden appear at my apartment with them. It was unforgivable." [3]

The press agents all knew about Richard. Al Rylander,
a public relations person, was telephoned once by a colleague who had heard from a New York madam that Richard had left a script on her premises. Rylander advised his
cohort: "Have nothing to do with it, if you ever want to
make Kilgallen's column again." [4]

Edgar Hatfield arranged the financial settlements for his
old school chum when pregnancies resulted. A famous strip-
teaser was one of the several women whom Richard incon-
venienced. Hatfield thundered, "The *least* you can do is
take some kind of precautions!"

"I can't be bothered," Richard replied. He was enjoying
his "Catholicism." [5]

Dorothy could not afford a repetition of the incident

in Boston. After Eleanor's marriage, devastating to Mae, Dorothy carried a double burden. It fell upon her to protect her mother from another painful blow and to somehow conform to the myth of marital bliss in which Jim at least pretended to believe. Besides, she had no choice. She was a Catholic, the mother of two children, and there is no reason to suspect that she did not still adore her wayward husband.

When she did occasionally cry out, she chose someone out of her past, someone who was socially distanced. She telephoned Herb Spiro once in 1950, when he was editing a newspaper in Santa Barbara, California. She wept and said her life was over. He assumed she meant Richard, and asked her to come out for a few weeks' rest. She terminated the brief and rather cryptic call abruptly as though suddenly aware of her emotional extravagance. That was the last time Dorothy communicated with Herb.

With a kind of survivalist logic, the couple began a process of partial separation.

After two additional theatrical mishaps, Richard endeavored to find a new outlet for his creative and entrepreneurial energies at the Art Students League. The league, housed behind an impressive French Renaissance facade on West Fifty-seventh Street, was celebrating its Diamond Jubilee in 1950. Its founding had been part of a liberating American movement that emphasized the study of perspective and composition from nude and partially draped models. For that reason, the premises had been raided by Anthony Comstock in 1906. The school maintained an open-door policy, accepting anyone who purported seriousness.

He enrolled as a student in February, 1950, with the avowed intention of improving his theatrical sketching. Richard liked the atelier ambience of the school. He was interested, too, in the Art Students League Ball, an annual extravaganza modeled after the Beaux Arts Ball in Paris.

Just two weeks before Richard enrolled in his sketch class, Dorothy appeared on the premiere telecast of an occupational guessing game called "What's My Line?" The show was produced by the team of Mark Goodson and Bill Todman and had its creative roots in an unsuccessful television pilot project, "Stop the Camera," developed in part by Bob Bach. The show, which never got on the air, featured a group of people on display whose occupations had to be guessed by viewers over the telephone. Those callers who could distinguish the pickle packer from the mortician won prizes.

When young Bob Bach went to Goodson-Todman two years later, he mentioned the aborted concept of "Stop the Camera." Mark Goodson zeroed in on it, expanding the idea during a brainstorming session at which the group was attempting to conceive a new game show for television. When the conference ended, they had the nucleus of the game. A permanent panel of notables would attempt to determine the occupation of a guest, and each of the notables would ask questions until he or she received a *no* answer from the moderator.

In a small studio at CBS, working with friends Gilbert Seldes, Kathleen Windsor, Jan Struther, and John Daly, they played the game until they got it right. Miss Struther, a writer, conceived the notion of using a blackboard on which contestants would be required to "Sign in, please." To sweeten the pot, it was decided to regularly use a mystery celebrity whom the panel would recognize on sight. To preclude such recognition, the mystery guests appeared covered by a bed sheet. After a series of such sessions, the decision was made to take the bed sheets off the guests and put masks on the panel.

No one at the Goodson-Todman organization remembers precisely how Dorothy was chosen to appear on the initial broadcast. It is most likely that she was seen on "Leave It to the Girls," a program on which she had made her television debut in 1949. "Leave It to the Girls," produced by Martha Rountree, featured a group of chic, successful New York career women dispensing advice about life, love, and the so-called battle of the sexes.

"Leave It to the Girls" made mini-media stars out of Robin Chandler, Florence Pritchett, Maggi McNellis, Harriet Van Horne, and especially Eloise McElhone, a plump and peppery young socialite who talked more than three hundred words a minute and said things like: "A wolf whistle is like a train whistle. You like to hear one even though you're not going any place."

The show was gaining wide syndication and selling a lot of oval-shaped Regent cigarettes for its sponsor when one day Dorothy asked to meet with Martha Rountree. She arrived, obviously upset and close to tears. "I'm going to have to leave the show," Dorothy said. "My mother told me that I photograph badly."

Martha Rountree took Dorothy into the projection room and ran some kinescopes of the broadcast. "Maybe television isn't at its best yet," she told Dorothy. "But honey you look the best of anyone I know because your personality and your brains come through."

Had the producer, a petite and lovely Southern blonde, stopped there, Dorothy might have quit then. But Martha added, "I don't like my pictures either. And besides you're prettier than I am."

"She needed reassurance," Martha Rountree recalled. "She was very sensitive about the way she looked." [6]

Dorothy came to "What's My Line?" with a year's experience as a television personality. Far more relevant, in terms of the game itself, was the untoward passion that she brought to any competitive situation, simulated or real. The projected Goodson-Todman show, unlike "Leave It to the Girls," would pit panel against contestant and, to some degree, panelist against panelist. Here Dorothy was on the firmest ground. As a competitive game player, her experience was vast.

Several times a year the Kollmars threw gala game parties to which people such as Faye Emerson and her husband Elliott Roosevelt, Maggi and Clyde Newhouse, and Lillian and Hubie Boscowitz were invited. They played charades until four or five in the morning. Faye Emerson, who was of the theater and accustomed to playing with trained mimes, considered Dorothy the finest, quickest participant she had ever seen. There was also a game called Search Me, in which one had to spot, with the naked eye, a small object camouflaged on another's person. Dorothy lit up victoriously when she stalked a minuscule piece of adhesive tape stashed in the interstices of Maggi McNellis's pink taffeta accordion bustle.

"Dorothy has a tremendous will to win," Maggie once told a reporter. "As a matter of fact, she'd kill you to win. She'll try desperately to beat us at the alphabet game, even though it doesn't mean anything." [7]

The alphabet game, which she could play for hours sitting with friends at a corner table in the Cub Room, involved filling up a card with the names of famous people, whose initials ranged from *A* to *Z*. Dorothy was invariably equipped with the *recherché* initials—the *Q*s, the *X*s, and the *Z*s. And she ruled with an iron hand. Once, she employed the name *Leane Zugsmith*. Hubie Boscowitz objected that he had never heard of Leane Zugsmith, and the fame of the proffered individual had to be mutually accepted. After Dorothy informed Hubie that Leane Zugsmith was "a great American writer," the matter was closed. (She is not, in fact, included in many standard reference works on American writers.) On the other hand, she refused to allow Hubie to submit the name of Ben Hogan, even though he had just won the U.S. Open Golf Championship, because she had never heard of him.[8]

She was aghast when she played one night with a group of Protestants who looked at her card and questioned one of her entries. "Who the heck is Eugene Pacelli?" one of the heretics inquired. Dorothy gasped. "His Holiness the Pope!" [9]

"What's My Line?" premiered on the CBS television network on February 2, 1950.

The show opened cold, with an announcer enunciating a solemn statement about human nature. There followed a full shot of the panel seated behind a long wooden table, looking like four edgy schoolchildren waiting for a homework assignment. Dorothy sat erect and prim, her arms resting bowlike on the table. She shifted her eyes radically right for a quick peep at the monitor as she was introduced by the pixielike poet Louis Untermeyer, who called her "my favorite Broadway columnist and girl-about-town." She, in turn, introduced "that wonderful toastmaster, raconteur, and former governor of New Jersey, Harold Hoffman." A Park Avenue neurosurgeon and psychiatrist, Richard Hoffman, not related to the governor, completed the quartet.

Their schoolmaster, John Daly, a serious newsman who had been seduced out of the ranks by the promise that this was a game show whose difference was dignity, presided to the right of the panel at a table of his own. He sported a bow tie and pompadour. After stumping out a cigarette on the studio floor, he recited, in his crisp diction, the introductory words that would remain standard, more or less, for twenty-five years:

> Good evening, ladies and gentlemen, and welcome to "What's My Line?" In fact, welcome to the premiere telecast of "What's My Line?" And I certainly hope our distinguished panelists are going to do a fine job of human analysis; in other words, to be able to answer the question "What's My Line?" And now to start things rolling, I'd like you to meet our first challenger, whose occupation it is their job to ferret out. Will you sign in please—

There were approving wolf whistles from the studio audience as an attractive young woman in a tailored suit, with a long, tapered new-look skirt, toting a leather shoulder bag, picked up a piece of chalk and signed "Pat Finch" on the blackboard.

Daly rose gallantly, smiled his crinkly smile, and pulled out her chair, making small talk about the appropriateness of the audience response. The panel nodded. Dorothy fussed with her pearls.

Pat Finch was asked to walk in front of the panel and "accede to any reasonable demand" an individual panelist made upon her in an attempt to elicit psychological information. The neurosurgeon requested that she kick. Untermeyer sniffed her perfume and punned on My Sin. The ex-governor instructed her to balance a book on her head. Dorothy studied the statuesque young woman and asked if she might look at the label in her suit jacket. The columnist grinned approvingly and emitted a satisfied "M-mmmm." Daly snapped patronizingly, "M-mmm. Yes, I'm sure that's a very *nice* label. But we won't mention any names."

The studio audience and the audience at home was apprised of Miss Finch's occupation. *Hat Check Girl* flashed on the television screen.

Dorothy posed the very first question on "What's My Line?", her vowels elongated like long stealthy steps: "Are you engaged in selling *ser*-vices as opposed to a *pro*-duct?" What seems child's play now was, of course, quite ingenious then. The standard questions had yet to be devised, and Dorothy was in the process of helping devise them.

According to the rules, the panelists asked questions in turn until they received a *no* answer, at which point, Daly flipped a $5 card. Ten *no*s and the round was lost. Miss Finch's occupation—hat check girl at the Stork Club—was discovered at the $25 mark. She was followed by a *Diaper Service Executive*, the first of many contestants chosen to evoke positive hysteria in the studio audience on account of the scatological ramifications of almost any question; a *Veterinarian;* and finally, by the first mystery guest, for whom the panel donned primitive blindfolds, *Phil Rizzuto*.

The half-hour broadcast, as yet unsponsored, came to a close with a shot of John Daly looking callow and bewildered.

There was a great deal wrong with the "premiere telecast," in spite of the fact that the panel succeeded in nailing everyone but the diaper man. It was poorly directed and, most significantly, badly cast. The neurosurgeon, obsessed with equilibrium and heavy in his own demeanor, was presently replaced. The ex-governor would go to jail for political misfeasance. Louis Untermeyer, who might have developed into a viable personality, was forced out by CBS when his liberal political past was investigated.

Dorothy presented the most formidable problem to the producers, in view, especially, of the network's critique. CBS had liked the show, but Goodson and Todman were advised to lighten it up, go for more laughs. Would Kilgallen wash? Could she ever relax and have fun with it? Failing that, was the American public ready for a lean and hungry woman?

As the broadcast was run and rerun, by the producers, it became clear that Dorothy had made the most significant contribution to every round of play. As John Daly sat with the veterinarian, for instance, the panel was clearly deadlocked. They had established that the man dealt with living things of both sexes. However, they all seemed to be thinking *humanoid*. Governor Hoffman was up, and he was obviously without a clue. He called for a conference, after which, according to the rules, the questioning was to revert back to him. During the consultation, however, Dorothy, with bold usurpation, looked straight into the camera and emitted two repressed but unmistakable barks. Hoffman picked it up immediately. "I bet he's a veterinarian," said the ex-governor.

When the diaper executive faced the panel, it was Dorothy who broke through to the concept of rental. The round was lost only because John Daly insisted that Dorothy's question—"Would you consider this product a necessity?"—be answered with a modified no. When the schoolmasterly moderator flipped the $50 card and identified the man's occupation, Dorothy objected, "We were misled!"

Daly, trying to ignore her, responded, "You can take it out on my hide later."

Dorothy was undeterred. Phil Rizzuto had already replaced the diaper man. The panel had donned their masks. But she was not through yet. Looking like an aggrieved Lone Ranger, she bitched, "If *diapers* aren't a necessity I don't know what is!"

"Joe DiMaggio!" one of the other blindfolded panelists ejaculated as Dorothy stewed over the loss of the last round.

"He's not in town," she instructed her ignorant colleague.

Dorothy's performance was watched and weighed. She was combative, competitive, and tactless. Her mirthless need to win would have constituted an unattractive quality "even in a man." But she was just too good to discard.

The show returned two weeks later with the leavening, lighthearted presence of Arlene Francis. The daughter of a distinguished Armenian portrait painter, Arlene had enjoyed a modest success as an actress, eventually finding a more substantial niche in radio and television, where her ebullient personality and easy wit were put to better use on "The Hour of Charm" and "Blind Date." She had a robust voice pregnant with laughter, and an unflappable adorableness.

Arlene, as the perfect ballast, solved the problem of Dorothy.

Mark Goodson, a craggy, gray-haired man who built a television empire on the success of "What's My Line?" drew on his pipe and recalled the difficulties of perfecting the panel.

I saw the thing happening—people dropping into roles. I could have stopped it very quickly, but I didn't. We didn't change Arlene or Dorothy because they played good roles. The complaints from the audience were far and away greater for Dorothy. She created a furor when she asked to look at people's labels. They accused her of being a snob. If Arlene had asked the same question, I don't think there would have been any complaints. It was a matter of personality. Yet I wouldn't have changed Dorothy for the world. Even the tension between her and John was part of the reality quotient. It turned out that she was exactly right for the show.[10]

Goodson and Todman signed the two women within a month, with Dorothy tacitly assigned the role of unwitting villain. She came finally to realize that her *persona* was very different from Arlene's, and, on several occasions, she said to her co-panelist, while they were being made up, "Why can't I be the adorable one?" [11]

Her desire to be someone else notwithstanding, the show paid handsome dividends to Dorothy. She loved the game and she basked in the fame. "What's My Line?" made Dorothy the most visible and celebrated journalist of her time.

Dorothy's contemporaries, the columnists of the 1950s, were an odd, scrappy lot. They had disparate beginnings as hoofer, bit actress, lawyer, disc jockey, press agent, gag writer. One had even done time as a grave digger. Igor Cassini, Hearst's "Cholly Knickerbocker," was a deposed Russian aristocrat who spent part of his youth as the mascot of the Florentine Fascisti. With their names now above the tattle, they behaved like cocks-of-the-walk, flaunting their power over the weak and pecking savagely even at each other.

A writer for *Theatre Arts*, Junior Spelvin, covered the intramural scene in 1953. He tabulated:

> Walter Winchell is still mad at Sullivan and Barry Gray [who was writing for the *New York Post*] but finds time to engage his old pal Leonard Lyons in mortal combat. Jack O'Brian is mad at Barry Gray and at anybody else Walter Winchell is against at the moment. . . . The only columnist not in an active feud at the moment is Louis Sobol, who's too little and Hy Gardner, who's too insecure. The oldest of the running feuds is between Winchell and Sullivan. Happily, for the reading public, neither can think of anything new to say about the other.[1]

At that time, the most bitter feud prevailed between Barry Gray and Walter Winchell, whom Gray accused of having some thugs work him over. Winchell had been packing a pistol for years and careering around town rushing to the scenes of crimes in an automobile equipped with a police radio and a siren ("Hello, Officer. Winchell!") Gray took out his own pistol permit. When he walked into a famous Broadway hangout where Winchell was already seated, a press agent dodged under a table, shouting, "Hide! Hide! It's High Noon at Lindy's."

Walter Winchell was essentially a mad vulgarian with regard to the power he yielded. As he polished the script for his Sunday-night radio broadcast, he was heard muttering, "Oh, boy, this'll make 'em mad," or "That'll teach the son of a bitch!" After an unfavorable profile of him by St. Clair McKelway appeared in *The New Yorker*, the magazine's editor, Harold Ross, arrived at the Stork Club, expecting the usual VIP treatment. Instead, Sherman Billingsley, beholden to Walter Winchell for the success of his room, asked Ross and his party to leave and never return.

The restaurateur could not so easily comply with another megalomaniacal order from the columnist. Winchell once pointed to a patron and said to Billingsley, in his staccato soprano, "You see that man over there. I want him barred." Billingsley blanched. The patron was William O'Dwyer, who had provoked Winchell's anger when he demoted a detective-friend of his.

"My God, Walter," Billingsley sputtered. "I'll do anything but that! How can I bar the mayor of New York?"

Winchell took his hat off and left the Stork, issuing an ultimatum to Billingsley. He stayed away and did not mention the club in his column. Somehow Billingsley convinced the mayor to return the detective to his previous status. Winchell returned.[2]

Another of the columnists—one who was notoriously envious of Dorothy's position—admonished Winchell, during the old man's waning years: "The trouble with you, Walter, is that you've forgotten how to hate."

Dorothy was not a heavyweight hater. She did not demand supplication. She never talked power or revenge. Nor did she use her column as a brash, masculine, can-do manifesto. There were two wellsprings for the damage she was notoriously capable of doing in the fifties: recklessness, through increasing dependence on "reliable sources," and repressed but increasingly querulous sexuality. When she did specific damage, her crime was usually negligent homicide, as opposed to murder one or two, a juridical distinction of little consequence in understanding the lady.

She was no more capable of confronting the wellsprings than she was of dealing with their consequences. Winchell used to shrug off reproach with his standard, "I'm a shit-heel." Dorothy was less gross and more complex.

Jean Bach, a press agent who was to become one of Dorothy's closest women friends in the early mid-fifties, once read the riot act to her as a result of an item she ran about jazz musician Ray Nance. The item, fed to her by a flack courting favor and accepted recklessly by Dorothy, asserted that Nance was fired, during a State Department tour with the Ellington band, because he fell off the bandstand while under the influence of drugs.

Nance, a highly regarded trumpeter, telephoned Jean, a friend and jazz buff, to complain that the *VOB* paragraph had ruined him professionally. He had been planning to start his own society band. "They're not even answering my calls," he told Jean. Yes, he admitted, he had taken a fall, but he was drunk because of a personal crisis and not on drugs as the item indicated—a very salient distinction in the fifties.

On the telephone with Dorothy, Jean fumed: "Instead of thinking of the six million readers you're titillating, why don't you think of the one poor wretch whose livelihood you're endangering!"

Jean recalled, "It was as though she didn't hear me, or only partly heard me. Her response was, 'I wish someone would think about my life once in a while.' " [3]

Jean contacted a friend at *Jet*, a black publication quite influential in the music business, and an emendation was run. She then began to fret about her own relationship with Dorothy becoming "sticky" and asked Myrtle Verne for advice. Did Myrtle think she ought to write Dorothy a note of some kind? Myrtle said, "Jean, she's got *such* control that she's probably just blocked the whole incident out. I wouldn't even worry about it."

The column, which had almost muted Ray Nance's horn permanently, doubled in syndication as a result of Dorothy's solid celebrity on "What's My Line?" The show, in 1952, had a viewing audience of almost ten million. Contributing, too, was Winchell's decline. In the thirties, he had novelty and language; in the forties, pipelines up to the President. Then there were several nervous breakdowns, the natural attrition of age, and his inability to carry his buttressing success on radio to the new television medium.

The Voice of Broadway became the most influential and widely read of the New York gossip columns.

Dorothy gathered what original, firsthand material appeared during her nocturnal rounds, scribbling notes on matchbooks from El Morocco, Ruban Bleu, Birdland, the Stork, and Gogi's La Rue, a new plush room that Richard had helped design and the always-generous Boscowitzes had designed to help. The matchbooks were tossed into her lucite bag, a faddish transparency created by her friend Carrie Munn.

Dorothy told Will Jones, a reporter from Ohio assigned to squire about some of New York's more glamorous women, "Strange as it may seem, I get most of my stuff during the day. People seem to know the days I'm writing a news column and call me with items. I try to get my secretary to take most of the stuff, but some people won't tell it to anybody but me, and I have to be there to take those calls." [4]

There was a modicum of truth to the implication that she was fed news by nonprofessional suppliers who, for one reason or another, wanted play in the column. Ernest Lehman, who profiled her for *Cosmopolitan*, recounted such an episode. Dorothy had run a lead item about Tallulah Bankhead, who, she predicted, would not prosecute a maid who had stolen thousands of dollars from her because the woman threatened to expose some of the more lurid details of Tallulah's sex life. The paragraph, Lehman wrote, "smoked the story." As a result of the item, Tallulah's lawyer telephoned Dorothy and, in the interest of accuracy, gave her the true and full account. [5]

Some of the daily column consisted of information either personally observed or received in traditional ways. To imply, as Dorothy did, that she was fed by a congerie of tipsters who just *seemed* to know when she was writing was like maintaining that General MacArthur just happened to be pleasure boating by Corregidor one day.

Had she the inclination or the time, Dorothy could not have filled six columns a week with information either personally observed or fed handily to her by an involved party. She relied increasingly for content *and* copy on a Coxey's army of professional press agents whose job it was to place their clients' names, as frequently as possible, in print. As she got bigger and busier, she seldom verified the information that she printed.

By the time Dorothy came along, the peculiar institution of press agentry and its relationship to the Broadway column had long been established. It was a rather simple setup, though more involved than was commonly known and never acknowledged outside the "family" by either columnist or publicist.

Publicists worked as "field agents" (Winchell's vainglorious phrase) or "spies" (Dorothy's cute word) for the columnists, providing a good deal of the information that appeared under the columnists' by-lines. But the main job of the press agent was not to feed the columnist client information; the acceptance of those "plugs" was a bonus for a job well done. The prime function of the publicist was to provide usable news about people *other* than his clients; to write, in effect, a mini-gossip column from which was winnowed the best and the brightest. This other stuff was called free items. Pages submitted to a columnist by a press agent were usually marked "for you" (free items), and "for me" (clients).

Winchell's scale was five to one. In return for five tidbits of information unrelated to a client, he plugged once, usually in that part of the column called "Bouquets." Dorothy was less precise, though her ratio was more like three to one, and she demanded more quality than Winchell in the client-related information.

She profited from a peculiar institution, indeed. In no other profession that comes to mind do so many suppliers clamor so subserviently to do the work of another. The only press agent smart enough to beat the system was Bill Doll, who could not be bothered ferreting out dirt about non-clients. He and another publicist designed to play switch. Doll sent the columnists so-called free items about the clients of the second press agent; the second press agent sent free items about Doll's people.

Because Dorothy did not scale with a great deal of precision, she was called, by some who did not fare well in her column, a no pay-off dame. In fact, those who "serviced" Dorothy well were handsomely rewarded. Their clients were featured in *VOB* with bountiful regularity, and the agents were well paid for this very tangible evidence of their success. Maurice Zolotov wrote, in 1968:

There was a time, not too long ago, when an item in Winchell, Lyons, Sobol, or Kilgallen was so intensely desired around New York that certain persons were paid retainers of $25,000 a year because they had good connections with such outlets.[6]

Certainly many of the people who had access to Dorothy's column made more money from their access than Dorothy made from Hearst for *The Voice of Broadway*.

The sexuality of the press agents' lingo—*servicing, planting, scoring,*—was not without justification. Dorothy was a quirky number, easily tantalized and just as easily turned off. To succeed, a press agent had to apprehend her vagaries, her tastes, her sense and sensibilities, what she liked, what alienated her, how to handle a spat, when to lay back, how to cajole, when to telephone directly and when, more wisely, to work through intermediaries.

Emmett Davis was one of the many publicists who "serviced" Dorothy regularly in the fifties. He is trim, soigné, upper-crusty. Obviously knows his forks. His diction is a series of sudden surprises, characterized by bombastic, regionally hybrid vowels that will never go home again. He worked for society publicist Count Lanfranco Rasponi before striking out on his own. Emmett has publicized opera singers, racehorses, the Colony, Salvador Dali, Elizabeth Arden, and the ex-King and Queen of Yugoslavia, Peter and Alexandra.

He spoke, in the summer of 1977, about a recent score.

"I had something in Liz today," he said, referring to Liz Smith, the New York *Daily News* syndicated columnist who had herself serviced Dorothy as a press agent.

I know the sort of thing she likes. Dorothy Rodgers and Ilka Chase were at L'Aiglon Tuesday for lunch. [L'Aiglon, a swank French restaurant on New York's East Side, was one of Emmett's current clients.] They were doing a new sidewalk outside. Now the girls had to go over planks to enter the restaurant. And the owner said, "Wouldn't it be fun if we could do your footprints." Being the ladies they are, they declined. They are two good names. They each have a book out.

And going over a *plank* to get into lunch! Do you see what I mean? This, for me, was a *Liz* eye-*tem*. If Aileen [Suzy Knickerbocker] reads it, she'll understand that that, for me, was a *Liz* eye-tem.

Liz is wonderful. *Much* easier to work with. But they're all spoiled. I guess psychologically they hate to admit that they couldn't exist without us. You can't write a column *six* days a week without a lot of *peephole* feeding you information. If all the press agents died tomorrow, the columnists would have a hell of a time. It's *phiz*-ically impossible to be everywhere and check everything.

In Dorothy's day, Emmett made *VOB* three to four times a week. "Between Rasponi and me," he claimed, "we knew everything that was going on in the *see-tee*. And she was impressed with him, of course, because he was *Count* Rasponi."

Emmett Davis, like his successful cohort, came to understand the rules of the game. If columnist *A* (and Dorothy was *A* to most by the early-fifties) did not use an item within three to four days, he or she felt free to rework the tattle and send it to *B*. You were screwed if *A* dallied and used it on the day that *B* ran with it, because of the keen competitiveness among the Broadway columnists and because the simultaneous publication of two similar or identical items made apparent the dependency of the columnists on some outside force. "But," Emmett Davis declared, "you didn't *dare* call Dorothy or any other columnist to ask, 'Are you going to use it?' She got angry if you called."

After Davis left Rasponi, he had a clever idea. Columnists, he knew, got a hundred releases a day on the same dull white paper. He had his own stationery done in his favorite color, pumpkin. Emmett sent the first of his pumpkin papers off. He recalled:

The first time I used it, I sent some stuff to Wind-shell. He sent it back with his own rye-ting scrawled across the top: "I've had enough of yellow journalism. USE WHITE PAPER!" So anything I sent to him in the future was on plain white paper. Dorothy *loved* the pumpkin.[7]

Since she seldom checked a story, Dorothy relied heavily on the reliability of her sources. If a press agent sent her a bum tip, he or she was barred from the column for a period of time, depending on the agent, Dorothy's mood, and the seriousness of the infraction. Emmett had given Dorothy a scoop about Ali Kahn, who was enormously important in her column at the time because of his own celebrity and because he was courting superstar Rita Hayworth. Emmett was told that Ali Kahn had booked passage on a particular ship and was due to arrive in the United States on some Rita-related business. He informed Dorothy immediately. Emmett learned subsequently that the prince was not taking the boat after all. He telephoned Dorothy to correct himself. Though she had not yet printed the item, she had obviously planned to give it good play. She was furious with Emmett. "Don't bother to send me anything in the future," she shouted at him. And slammed down the telephone.

Emmett waited until he had something that he knew she would love. He called Myrtle and insisted upon talking personally to the columnist.

"What is it?" Dorothy snapped.

"I have a very, very exciting eye-tem," Emmett teased.

"Well . . . ?"

"Well, I have no in-tention of telling you since you said you didn't want to hear anything from me. But *should* you want to hear from me again with other eye-tems, I'll be happy to tell you." [8]

Dorothy giggled at Emmett's creative play and benevolently accepted the item that he fed her. He was off the black list and entitled, once again, to service *The Voice of Broadway*.

Copy poured on Dorothy—over the telephone, in the mail, under the door, through the transom, whispered into her avid ear; hand delivered by messenger, cab driver, or by press agents themselves. When she and Richard bought a town house, special locked boxes were installed on a gate beside the house, one for press-agent drops, the other for the final column copy picked up by a *Journal* messenger.

One of Dorothy's favorite publicists (who, for fear of incurring the wrath of a veteran Broadway columnist, prefers not to be named and will be called Mitch) sent one to five pages of gossip to her every day. He, in turn, had his own coterie of informers: restaurant owners, hatcheck girls, friends who derived pleasure simply from seeing their own datum in print, grudge-bearers, tit-for-tatters, and compulsive *yentas*. Like all of his peculiarly skilled colleagues, Mitch was thrilled to pick up the *Journal-American* and find his items run *exactly as he had written them*. That was the mark of the true craftsman. That was proof that he had Dorothy down to a fine art. "I learned to write the way she thought," he said donnishly at his favorite Broadway restaurant. "It was a kind of a game. You pondered her style, her sensibilities. You studied her work as one would study the works of a great writer." [9]

Eddie Jaffe, a short, burrowing, kindly man who put pearls in the mouths of vaudevillians back in the thirties and forties and was largely responsible for the myth of the literate stripper ("I once made up an item about Margie Hart. You know Eleanor Roosevelt wrote a column called *My Day*. Margie was supposed to have said, "I'm writing a column called *My Night*."), took his stuff personally to the house, giving it to the butler or sliding it under the door. "She would rewrite the items sometimes, sometimes not, depending on her mood, how she used them, and what else she had. You had to understand each of the columnists and what their interests were. Dorothy had a more feminine view than the other columnists, which was natural, since she was the only woman."

"More feminine?"

"Bitchier," Eddie Jaffe grinned.[10]

Of the many survivalist truths in which Dorothy had to believe, her own responsibility as a newsperson was of primary importance. She was, after all, Jim Kilgallen's daughter, and particularly proud of her training as a reporter, which distinguished her from the grave digger, the bit actress, and the deposed aristocrat. Since it was a fact that she could not possibly gather all of her own news or even take the time to verify the news that was bestowed upon her, she had to believe in the responsibility and accuracy of her delegates, the press agents. She was substituting for empirical knowledge an exiguous faith; her behavior with regard to that faith became characteristically religious rather than appropriately rational. When a particular publicist had proven himself over a period of time, he was invested with a kind of infallibility; challenging his revelations was taken, by Dorothy, as an act of apostasy.

During the revival of *Pal Joey*, Dorothy received a tip that the show's stars, Vivienne Segal and Harold Lang, were not getting along. *Item:* October 27, 1952—"The Vivienne Segal–Harold Lang feud is the talk of Shubert Alley." Jimmy Gardiner dropped backstage to see the stars on the day that she ran the item. Harold Lang and Vivienne Segal, who had adjoining dressing rooms, were talking, laughing, and kissing. Jimmy broached the subject to Segal, who said that Dorothy was completely mistaken. Jimmy surmised that the source of the story was a press agent who had been spurned by Harold Lang.

Jimmy left the theater to meet Dorothy, Richard, Maggi and Clyde Newhouse, and Julia Meade at El Morocco. He informed Dorothy that what she had printed was clearly untrue. Dorothy replied that she knew it was true.

"Dorothy, I saw them with my own eyes!"

"They're not even speaking."

"They touched. They hugged. They spoke."

"I know they're not speaking," Dorothy said, before turning pettishly away from Jimmy.

"Vivienne said you were full of shit."

"They're not speaking," Dorothy bristled. *"I got it from a very reliable source."* [11]

Item: October 30, 1952—"Vivienne Segal denies—and vehemently—the report that she and Harold Lang are feuding."

With all the skilled assistance she received—and there were days when *VOB* was just a paste-up of press agent feeds, though it is generally estimated that about half of it was hers—the column remained a creation of Dorothy's. Her anima pervaded.

Illnesses, especially those whose degree of seriousness was known only to "a few intimate friends," continued to fascinate her. She was still not over the wonder of wonder drugs. Almost any celebrity on penicillin was shooed into the column. Illness clouded by mystery was terrific. Her readers were told that Mrs. Morey Amsterdam was in the hospital with a mysterious ailment for which doctors had no name. Her readers learned, within days, that the doctors had finally found a name for Mrs. Amsterdam's condition: pregnancy.

A product of her own snobbishness, she adored gossip about menials who behaved like aristocrats and rich people who worked anyhow: Three of the waiters at Chambord "drove to work in Jaguars" . . . Lili St. Cyr's maid "turned on the gas jets," and not to make dinner . . . "Grace Kelly, the pert video actress, doesn't really have to work that hard. Her dad's a millionaire Philadelphia builder."

Items about booze and drugs were usually blinded. But she ran them obsessively: "The family of a young society girl is going through the tragic motions of having her put in a sanitarium. They just discovered she was a reefer addict. . . . A tobacco heir recently underwent the cure for alcoholism at a local hospital, but apparently the treatment was a failure. He's on those binges again. . . . Insomniacs took 3½ billion sleeping pills last week. . . ."

Garbo was sneaking in to see Cecil Beaton at his Sherry-Netherland suite. Edith Piaf had her nose bobbed. The wives of Mario Lanza (neurosis) and Robert Mitchum (reefers) were both upset. And the *Call Me Madam* troupe was "still shivering over the recent attempt on Harry Truman's life. If the assassin had succeeded, it would have closed the topical musical for good."

There would come a time when a gay press agent who summered on Fire Island provided her with all the inside dope on the boys in the next bungalow—strapping matinee idols by day, "Fire Islanders" by night. Now she used such revelations sparingly, as in: "The newspapers will never print the real story behind a recent show business marriage crash. It was a *Well of Loneliness* theme."

Dorothy was at her best, which is to say her worst, when certain repressed passions infused her work. More so than any other columnist of the day, she was tantalized by the black community. That was great for Billy Eckstine, who could do no wrong, and dreadful for Billie Holiday, who "just can't seem to stay out of trouble." Dorothy reported every arrest, drug bust, fracas, and romantic tribulation in the singer's tortured life.

Dorothy got to the blacks ahead of most because of her involvement with popular music and jazz. She lived her life to music. It was an opiate, an aphrodisiac, a bonding between herself and kindred souls. Allusions to lyrics permeated her prose. Cole Porter's tidy, consummate cleverness thrilled her. She knew every word, each alternate verse of "Down in the Depths," the song her good friend Ethel Merman had introduced back in the thirties. Lines from that song—

> *Here I sit above the town*
> *In my pet pailletted gown*

and

> *While the crowds at El Morocco punish the parquet*

and

> *I'm deserted and depressed*
> *In my regal eagle nest*

—pleasured Dorothy. In her own regal eagle nest, she tapped out her daily column to music constant in the background.

Nothing she wrote was more characteristically "Dorothy" than her coverage of the purveyors of romantic pop. They fared precariously in *The Voice of Broadway*. She transformed what were essentially sexual feelings into spiky belligerence or needling surveillance. The more appealing the singer was to her, the more dogged her pursuit.

She hounded Frank Sinatra in the fifties, when he was not yet in a position to hit back, delineating him as the despairing victim of his unsuccessful marrage to Ava Gardner. On October 16, 1952, her column head read: LANA, AVA HAVING GAY TIME IN MEXICO. The lead item:

> Lana Turner and Ava Gardner, who dashed off to Mexico together, ostensibly to forget their man-troubles, are the talk of Bill O'Dwyer's bailiwick. The girls are really living it up North of the Rio Grande. Fernando [Lamas] seems to be taking his loss cheerfully, but Frank is giving pals the torch talk.

Eight days later, Dorothy continued the saga:

Frank Sinatra is frightening his friends by telephoning in a gloomy voice, "Please see that the children are taken care of" and then hanging up. He called the next day to apologize, blaming it on The Glass.

The following April, she reported:

Frank Sinatra, who tossed Lana Turner out of his Palm Springs house when he found her visiting his wife a few months ago, may make more blow-up headlines before long. Lana and Ava had plans to do some vacation chumming in Europe.

Accorded the proper kind of personal attention, Dorothy could be turned around. She began needling handsome Vic Damone after the singer went off to Korea. Damone's life was apparently not so pregnant with possibilities as Frankie's, but on his return from the service, she began using items to imply that he was in grave financial straits, an accusation which, in show business, can become a self-fulfilling prophecy.

Damone's manager implored Bob Bach to intervene. Bob coaxed her into attending the singer's Copacabana opening. Between shows, Damone hovered hesitantly.

"Ask Vic to come over," Bob said. "You know how shy he is." [12]

She looked up and waved. Damone approached. They chatted over several drinks. Her column the next day contained a glowing tribute to his talent and personal appeal.

Sinatra and Damone were typical types for Dorothy. In 1952, however, there emerged, at the dawning of the corseted Eisenhower years, a twenty-five-year-old farm boy named Johnnie Ray. Johnnie had been singing professionally for seven years when his record "Cry," flip side "The Little White Cloud That Cried," jumped onto the charts and sold two million copies for Columbia, making it the second biggest hit in the company's history. With a hearing aid protruding from one ear, the deafness resulting from an accident at a Boy Scout jamboree back in Oregon, he looked like a pale, anguished El Greco saint. There was a Kol Nidre choke in his voice, and a demented, revivalist abandon in his performance. He jumped, wept, thumped, whispered, knelt, and contorted in a way that no white performer had done before.

He was a joke to Dorothy and her friends in the beginning, a teen-age idol, a hoot. Then she began to listen. In early 1952, she wrote an arch *apologia pro Dorothy Kilgallen* in *VOB*:

> I have a terrible confession to make. A simply awful thing has happened to me.
>
> How am I going to say it?
>
> Goodness, it's too frightful really. (Steel yourself, girl. Get it off your bodice for once and all.)
>
> All right. Here it is.
>
> I've come to just love Johnnie Ray's record of "Please, Mr. Sun."
>
> Now will anybody ever speak to me again? [13]

She reported his opening at the Copacabana, one of the most tumultuously successful appearances in New York nightlife, as "endsville . . . He held the town's toughest audience spellbound (or maybe it was paralyzed with astonishment)." [14]

It was Dorothy, in fact, who was astonished by her own response to the young singer as she witnessed his performance for the first time. Marlin Swing, a television producer who would become a friend to both Johnnie and Dorothy, gathered from her subsequent reminiscences of that evening that she was "smitten, overwhelmed by the electricity of his new style." [15] Her makeup man on "What's My Line?" Carmen Gebbia, listened patiently as she raved about Johnnie and reached his own conclusions. She had never mentioned Richard to him, yet she yammered on about a pop star whom she had not yet met. [16]

Her reportorial surveillance began. As news of Johnnie's behavior on the road reached her desk, her tone changed. Johnnie and his opening act, comic Gary Morton, were arrested in Minneapolis and charged with disorderly conduct. Disorderly it indeed had been. Johnnie was booked for roller-skating through the lobby of a posh hotel, squirting guests with a water pistol. Dorothy wrote: "Show business insiders weren't surprised at the news of Johnnie Ray's arrest in Minneapolis. His drinking bouts here were on the spectacular side. Ask the staff at the Warwick Hotel." [17]

She reported subsequently that he was "laying omelettes in Boston." [18] In Europe, she revealed, he was "causing Britons to lift their eyebrows in amazement. The same sort of thing got him into trouble in the United States." [19]

Johnnie played Scotland in April, 1953, and committed a monumental sin of omission. Whoever was handling his press neglected to accord Dorothy the special attention to which she had grown accustomed. She japed, in the column, "The boy ought to be his own press agent. In Scotland, he's frittering away the dull hours by writing to every columnist and disc jockey whose name he can recall. Despite the fact that the letter is the same for everybody and might as well have been mimeographed, it's amazing how many of the typewriter and microphone boys reported its contents to their followings as solemnly (or in some cases breathlessly) as if it had been a holograph from Albert Schweitzer." [20]

It was their first quarrel.

As "What's My Line?" became a national television institution, a litany evolved. Standard responses were given to common queries from the press. Many of those questions concerned the relationship among the permanent cast of the show: John Daly, Bennett Cerf, Arlene Francis, and Dorothy—especially Arlene Francis and Dorothy. The group learned to waffle. But, in truth, Dorothy was rather an outsider.

Mark Goodson theorized about the distance. "There were a lot of things in back of it," he said. "She did run a gossip column. She did print things about friends of theirs. And, also, she was not a part of the liberal establishment in New York—the chic, inside group of people in theater and communications. People are not religious anymore. But they've substituted for it patterns of words and beliefs that are similar to religion. Dorothy was a Catholic. She worked for Hearst. Her children did not go to Dalton. If she were alive today, she would probably not be boycotting lettuce. The rest of the panel was keenly aware that she did not fit the pattern." [1]

She was guilty on several counts. Dorothy was not only a Catholic, she was a practicing, devout Catholic. When Bishop Fulton Sheen, the flamboyant, wild-eyed prelate who was the only member of his profession to make the cover of *TV Guide*, guested on "What's My Line?" she genuflected and kissed the ring on his extended hand. She had worked her whole professional life for Hearst. Jill had gone from the Convent of the Sacred Heart to Miss Hewitt's, where she was being prepared for her formal debut. She had been taught by Dorothy that a lady was fully dressed only when she donned her white gloves. Troublesome, too-bright Dickie, who explained Buxtehude to Dorothy when he was twelve, was dashed off to a series of schools.

Despite all these symptoms of "otherness," Dorothy was not, by a long shot, the political philistine that her more liberal colleagues presumed her to be. In the fifties, careless political labeling was rampant in the country.

On June 27, 1950, President Truman ordered armed intervention into the Korean conflict. During that same month, a booklet called "Red Channels" was distributed to every radio and television station in the country and to all advertising agencies that handled broadcasting accounts. Within was a listing of every prominent liberal in the industry and a dossier of his or her political history, be it communistic, progressive, prematurely anti-Fascist, or suspiciously pro-Negro. When the book was issued, Dorothy had been saying, "And on my left, Louis Untermeyer" for almost five months. She had hit the nail on the head. Poet and anthologist Untermeyer was among the listees.

Within months of its publication, "Red Channels" became the most effective blacklist in the history of the entertainment business. A well-organized consortium of individuals, veterans' groups, columnists, and congressional committees, using "Red Channels" as a scouting manual, set out to force the politically tainted to recant, renounce, name names—or be systematically driven from the media.

Among the activists was a greengrocer from Syracuse, New York, Lawrence Johnson, and his daughter, Eleanor Buchanan, a widow of the Korean conflict, who conjoined to galvanize their fellow patriots to action. Buchanan's standard philippic called for the routing of the likes of Untermeyer. "It sickens me," she railed,

> to know of those banquets engineered by Red sympathizers on radio and television to raise funds for their henchmen, and those do-nothing patriotic citizens who discuss the wrongs of the world over a dinner table while my quiet unassuming Jack ate his lunch surrounded by dead Chinese.[2]

Johnson organized a campaign against Stoppette, the Poof-There-Goes-Perspiration deodorant, that was one of the program's major sponsors. Stores that stocked Stoppette were picketed by the American Legion. The Chicago advertising agency handling the account was warned to get Untermeyer off the air or the pressure would increase. Baldish Jules Montinier, the Swiss chemist who created and owned Stoppette, agonized. He considered himself a liberal, but he felt compelled to placate the reactionary activists.[3]

In May, 1951, the owlish, avuncular anthologist was replaced by Bennett Cerf, an owlish, avuncular publisher.

Obviously, from the choice of his successor, Untermeyer had been a perfectly acceptable panelist. He was well-liked by everyone, including Dorothy. But what could she do? What could anyone do?

Louis Untermeyer commented on the situation in a letter of October, 1977:

> Besides murmurs of personal regret, no one connected with *What's My Line?* attempted to do anything on my behalf. Intimidated as they all undoubtedly were by McCarthyism (or sympathetic to it), the feeling must have been: the less said the better. I can't say Dorothy Kilgallen behaved worse than anyone else. There was little behavior.[4]

In politics, as in every area of her life, she was first and foremost an unserious style-junkie. It is safe to assume that she considered the Rosenbergs only somewhat more unattractive than the junior senator from Wisconsin—and neither one a credit to his race. She was not equipped for excess of any kind.

Bob Bach recalled Dorothy's timidity vis-à-vis Untermeyer. It was no different from that of her more liberal colleagues:

> There was no discussion of Louis Untermeyer. Martin Gabel was blacklisted too, and I know that she thought that was laughable. But she was right in the middle and she didn't want to take a stand. She couldn't afford to become too involved or to speak out. When it eased up in the late fifties, she was more ready to say, "Thank God it's over." But she was more likely to laugh or change the subject or talk about who was playing the Paladium.[5]

On their radio program, the Kollmars discussed the Russian movies, sympathetic to the Soviet Union, that were featured at a theater in New York.

DOROTHY: I have another theory about the Stanley and the Russians. This is strictly my own theory and unofficial. But it certainly wouldn't surprise me to hear that this has been permitted to go on, that this little advertisement for the Soviet Union has been allowed to continue all these years, simply through courtesy of the FBI; who might have a little operation going themselves—might be taking little snaps of the people going in and out.

DICK: You mean they're taking movies while the Stanley is showing them?

DOROTHY: I wouldn't be a bit surprised, you know. Those boys don't miss much I don't think. And, of course, well, I think we went there once to see a Russian musical, didn't we, years ago? Because we'd heard it was so hysterical and it was. The whole love story was based on the fact that this boy was terribly attracted to the girl because she'd managed to . . .

DICK: Oh, she won a prize at the state fair because she grew the biggest pigs.

DOROTHY: Yes, and he'd ploughed more acres of something so he was pretty alluring to her. And they wore fur hats all the way through and we almost died laughing.

Later on in the broadcast, Dick theorized that most communist-front organizations were permitted to operate so that the FBI could more effectively finger subversives. After a meeting of such an organization, Richard speculated that, "in about an hour, when the place is empty, the FBI comes back in and they pick up every little scrap of paper, cigarette butts, anything that could ever be used as evidence."

Dorothy concluded: "They probably take little candid snaps. Now they have cameras the size of cigarette lighters. They can take pictures under all circumstances."

The Kollmars had been parsing the *modus operandi* of

counterespionage for less than ten minutes when an FBI informer telephoned the bureau's New York office to report on the nature of the conversation. She characterized Dorothy and Richard as "idiot-type people" whose program consisted of "chatter and comments." Hoover was, nonetheless, sent a complete transcript of the discussion, printed under the description: *Kollmars Tell How F.B.I. Operates at Radical Meetings.*[6]

Dorothy's dossier does not indicate which tale told by what idiot signified anything, or whether or not the FBI came in, after the broadcasting room was empty, to collect Richard's cigarette butts. But the very fact that they were surveilled while surveilling the subject of surveillance indicates that she was not, *ipso facto*, the political basketcase that the bureau thought her to be.

She did run occasional items during the McCarthy era that smacked of the trendy philistinism of the right, as in:

> Friends of the late John Garfield are desperately trying to halt the plans of a leftist group to stage a memorial to him and Canada Lee. The pinkos would take the opportunity to extol Garfield and Lee as "martyrs" to the current "witch hunt" against Communists.[7]

Dorothy had never been a friend or fan of Josephine Baker, the black singer whose charges against the Stork Club in October, 1951, split the city into two warring factions. Miss Baker and a group of friends arrived one night at the chic Cub Room, ordered drinks, and waited inordinately long for the arrival of their supper. The group left the Stork angrily, alleging racial discrimination. Liberals honored the picket lines that were subsequently formed. Conservatives maintained that the service accorded Josephine Baker was no slower than usual and that the incident had been ignited and fanned by subversives.

Billingsley implored Dorothy to ignore the episode. She acceded, in spirit, to his request. But she buried in her *VOB* this seemingly innocuous, insidiously clever line: "The Stork Club has a new fall dress—dark red and black velvet."[8]

With the exception of one column that she wrote in 1951, Dorothy never used *The Voice of Broadway* to separate anyone from gainful employment in show business because of his or her political persuasion. In this regard, she towered above the pygmies at the *Journal-American* who were engaged in a concerted campaign to cleanse the State Department, the Executive, the teaching profession, and the Morosco Theatre of the scourge of the Phantom.

According to Adela Rogers St. Johns, a confidante of and emissary for the old man, William Randolph Hearst was a prime political mover. She told Joseph G. Goulden, author of *The Best Years*, that her boss had spurred the congressional pillaging of Hollywood by Parnell Thomas and his committee in 1947:

> Hearst had spent millions of dollars of his own money before Congress moved in with that committee. Everybody in Congress, in those early days, got all their material from us [the Hearst organization]. We had two floors of the Hearst magazine building on Eighth Avenue in New York devoted entirely to the testimony and investigative answers we had gotten. The Hearst crew put all the material together—chiefly through a man named Jack Clements, who knew more about communism than anybody else, and J. B. Matthews— and then the committee got into it. Hearst forced that. . . . Out of this, of course, came the Hiss case and the breakup of the group in the State Department. We made one fatal mistake—and how could anybody have known it? We were looking for a senator to carry the ball. I went down and tried to get Millard Tydings. . . . He said, "Nooooo, noooooo, they'd beat you to death before you were through."
>
> The only guy who would go was [Joseph] McCarthy. We didn't know he was a drunk. If McCarthy hadn't been an alcoholic, the whole story would have been different, because he had the material, but he kept blowing it.[9]

The *Journal-American* columnists carried on intrepidly what their employer had initiated. Igor Cassini and Westbrook Pegler, in 1948, allied themselves with a Connecticut housewife, Mrs. Hester McCullough, who endeavored to deny any and all gainful employment to Larry Adler and Paul Draper. When the entertainers sued Mrs. McCullough for libel, Pegler called their legal redress "a new communist

bully tactic" and suggested the institution of a legal slush
fund for the likes of Mrs. McCullough and Senator Mc-
Carthy. After Adler and Draper were compelled to seek
work in Toronto, Cassini expressed regrets that his column
was not syndicated there so that he might fully inform
Canadians of their dangerous political leanings.

Paul Draper was booked finally on Ed Sullivan's "Toast
of the Town." The *Journal American* consequently ran a
story about an American Legion commander in Jackson
Heights, quoting him: "We will be very careful in the
future about watching CBS shows." E. J. Kahn wrote, in
The New Yorker, that the paper carried on "as if Draper
had been caught practicing vivisection on Louella O. Parsons." [10]

Television columnist Jack O'Brian lambasted that network for permitting Lena Horne to appear. "Amazing, isn't
it," he wrote, "that so many of these pink teas seem to
'just happen' to the Columbia Broadcasting System?" [11]

The *Journal*'s entertainment editor joined the rout. Gene
Knight did a body count in 1950, swaggering:

> On October 7, I announced in this column that a band-
> leader in a midtown restaurant is listed in "Red Chan-
> nels" as being associated with more than a dozen or-
> ganizations listed as Communist front by the Attorney
> General. The band leader is no longer there.
>
> On October 14, I reported that a singing act in a
> swank East Side spot loves to perform at pink rallies.
> The act is no longer there.
>
> On October 19, I stated that a singer in a down-
> town nightclub is listed in "Red Channels" as being
> associated with five organizations labeled Communist
> fronts by the US Attorney General. The singer is no
> longer there. [12]

When Judy Holliday was listed in "Red Channels," she
sat petrified for almost an hour outside the office of *Journal* columnist George Sokolsky, who was in conference
with Westbrook Pegler. Sokolsky acted as an unofficial
"clearance expert" for various congressional committees.
She did not recant satisfactorily and was called before
Senator Pat McCarran's Sub-Committee on Subversive In-

filtration in the Entertainment Media. Victor Riesel, another *Journal* columnist, found her performance wanting there, so he composed "An Open Letter to Judy Holliday," reminding her that she still owed "the world of decency a debt." [13]

Dorothy avoided the red baiters at the *Journal-American*. Riesel doesn't remember that she came to their parties.[14] Cassini, mellowed with age and travail, reflected:

> She did not express too many political opinions in her column. I went much more after the Drapers and the Adlers. I think that Dorothy Kilgallen, being a woman, was not as impregnated with politics as I was.[15]

Dorothy, however, was no Lillian Hellman. She wrote one full column, just after the release of "Red Channels," on the subject of blacklisting, communism, Korea, and the state of her own offended intelligence. She reaffirmed her love for show people, declaimed "the unthinking boycott and the casual blacklist." She maintained that the inclusion of a performer's name in "Red Channels" or any publication like it was insufficient "to create the general inference that he is guilty of anything, including beating his wife or liking garlic." [16]

But Dorothy would not permit the inference that *she* could be hoodwinked by anyone. In a kind of come-on-now! spirit, she blinded several paragraphs about performers who were sanctimoniously pretending that they were not now nor had they ever been. Dorothy knew better.

There was a "Miss A," currently professing innocence, whose political history Dorothy knew intimately. Way back when it was fashionable and fun, Dorothy had been present in Miss A's

> glamorous drawing room one evening when she [Miss A] told about going to a Communist school. I tell you she had us all in stitches as she described the 'cell' to which she belonged.

Then there was an actor in *South Pacific*, a director, and a prominent radio actress. Dorothy implied that they had

all come to their senses since Korea, but that she knew
there was a time when each had flirted with the party line.
She concluded:

> "Red Channels" may have made some mistakes in
> linking innocent persons with communism. And this,
> if so, is deplorable. But never let anyone tell you that
> it didn't hit a great many nails on the head.[17]

Something about Dorothy's priorities was revealed in the
first important encounter with the Central Intelligence
Agency. The agency was interested in an item that appeared in *VOB* on March 7, 1951:

> Radio Free Europe, which operates along lines simi-
> lar to the Voice of America, but is privately con-
> trolled, has suffered the disappearance of important
> documents. Some believe a subversive has infiltrated
> the organization despite painstaking loyalty checks.

The CIA left a telephone message with Myrtle Verne.
Dorothy did not return the call. On March 12, an agent
appeared at the house. Dorothy was unavailable. Myrtle
warned him that her boss would never reveal the source
of a story. He tried intermediaries.

His delection-riddled report follows. Released under the
Freedom of Information Act, the blanks indicate omissions
of names withheld under subsection (b6) of the law, which
relates to "unwarranted invasion of the personal privacy
of other individuals." If one has in hand a copy of the
original report, it is possible, by counting missing letters
and inferring from context, to fill in the blanks. The first
two references are undoubtedly to Myrtle Verne. The next,
up the ladder, is probably Paul Schoenstein, her editor-in-
chief, and the last probably Richard Berlin, by this time
president of the Hearst Corporation and chairman of the
board of Hearst Magazines.

The report reveals that Dorothy was less than free with
her information and more than an ardent protector of
sources than a patriot.

> We tried diligently to get Miss Kilgallen's _____
> to arrange a meeting for us with Miss Kilgallen, but

_____ procrastinated until we lost all patience with her. We called _____ who is attached to the Hearst Publications _____ and he informed us that he knew Miss Kilgallen very well indeed, and would see her just as soon as she came in the office, to arrange the necessary interview with her for us. When we did not hear from _____, we called his office and found that he was not present. We left our name and number, and later in the morning _____ called us from the hospital, where he had been sent by reason of a sudden heart attack. Despite his condition, he called _____ for Hearst Magazines, and asked him to arrange the meeting with Miss Kilgallen which _____ had promised for us.

A very short time after our conversation with _____, _____ called, and said that he had immediately talked with Miss Kilgallen in her office, and that, while she was entirely willing to have me come over and call, she wanted to warn in advance that if we still were endeavoring to find out the source of her information on which her item of March 8th was based, she would not, under any circumstances, make a further disclosure. She was polite about it, but very firm. _____ told us that Miss Kilgallen and _____ are two persons who absolutely refuse to disclose the sources of their information. He said that Miss Kilgallen would be willing to publish a retraction in her column, if someone in authority at the National Committee for a Free Europe would write her a letter, saying that there was no truth in the item that appeared in her column of March 8th insofar as it pertained to the affairs of N.C.F.E.

We explained to _____ that we respected Miss Kilgallen's desire to keep her sources of confidential information undisclosed, but we thought that in view of the fact that the security of an important organization was involved, she might be persuaded to tell us —off the record and in confidence—what we wanted to know, if we gave our assurance that there would be no repercussion. _____ said he would do everything in his power to get Miss Kilgallen to change her mind, but he despaired of any success.

Dorothy had her old-time religion to fall back on in the CIA matter. No appeal to patriotism, no promise of confidentiality, would extract from her the name of a source. She would have had no such orthodox out in the matter of "Miss A" and the Communist school, though. *There was no source to protect here.* Dorothy had made it very clear, in her column, that she herself was there: "She was a Communist at one time, all right—and I don't mean just a party-liner. I have it on the most splendid and unimpeachable authority: the lady herself."

Dorothy's FBI dossier indicates that the FBI considered questioning her about the "Miss A" column, but, despairing of success, let the matter drop. However, another cohort of patriots took up the cudgel. The McCarran Committee began holding hearings in Executive Session on April 27, 1951. Senator Pat McCarran, in an attempt to strengthen his pending bill that would limit the emigration of eastern Europeans, was looking to establish a connection between susceptibility to communism among entertainers and a background that was foreign, preferably Jewish. Among those he interrogated were Judy Holliday, Philip Loeb of "The Goldbergs," Sam Levenson, and, to preclude any ugly conjectures, the all-American Burl Ives.

Dorothy was, at some point, slated to appear before McCarran in Executive Session as a "friendly witness," meaning that she was not charged with anything except a patriotic duty to reveal the identity of "Miss A" and other subversive types to the committee. An FBI memo of April 27, 1951, explained:

> [Blank] advised me that they started holding hearings in Executive Session before the McCarran Committee today. They are being furnished a lot of information collected by writers regarding Communist influence in the radio and television field. He handed me the attached memorandum which lists as friendly witnesses the following individuals . . .

Dorothy's name was listed.

Dorothy might have actually gone to Washington, D.C. Martha Rountree, who was based there, remembered that Dorothy was in town and telephoned her. It was mid-June, 1951.[18]

A great deal had happened in the year between the "Miss A" column, which whetted McCarran's appetite, and Dorothy's scheduled appearance before the committee. She knew of and eventually reported on the "quiet depression" of actress Mady Christians, following her listing in "Red Channels." [19] Miss Christians, who had originated the role of Mama in *I Remember Mama*, had been rendered unemployable. She suffered a massive attack of hypertension and died in October, 1951, after writing to a friend, "I cannot bear to think of the things which led to my breakdown. One day I shall put them down as a record of something unbelievable." [20] Lena Horne, a close friend of Dorothy's, had also been listed, and was compelled to explain her opposition to Jim Crow to the publisher of the crimson pamphlet. Before she was somehow cleared, her career was jeopardized. Only a month before Dorothy's slated appearance, Louis Untermeyer was dismissed from "What's My Line?" And her own newspaper was daily demanding the cashiering from their profession of talents whom Dorothy knew and respected.

If, indeed, she got as far as Washington, she might have met or lunched with Pat McCarran. She had agreed even to talk to the CIA. That did not mean that she was about to tell anything. With the CIA, it was a matter of principle. With McCarran, there was a change of heart.

The Boscowitzes do not remember that she appeared before the committee. A close associate of the late senator, Jay Sourwine, does not remember any connection between the committee and Dorothy.[21] The Office of the General Counsel, which has a declassified Master List of everyone who ever appeared before a Senate Judiciary Committee in Executive Session, has no record of an appearance by Dorothy.

It was one thing to tap out a pettish reminder to certain entertainers that they weren't fooling her. It was quite another, a year later, to depose and name names. Dorothy was not made for such stern stuff.

She was at her best with half a bottle of champagne under her belt, surrounded by attractive people, feeling attractive herself, listening to something tasteful and rhythmic.

There was a party once, during the early fifties, at the Greenwich Village apartment of Bob and Jean Bach. Adlai

Stevenson was running for president. Lena Horne was standing in front of the piano. To the tune of "I Love to Love," Lena sang:

> *I love the Guv*
> *The Guv-naw of Illinois.*

As she was singing, she looked at Dorothy and said, "Hope I'm not offending you."

Dorothy raised her glass and replied in a shy, slightly inebriated voice, "That's all right. It's a better song than 'I Like Ike.'" [22]

At the age of forty, Dorothy had still not expelled the superannuated little princess who resided within. "She always wore those little white gloves," Arlene Francis remembered with a fond, quiet smile that made her face appear uncharacteristically reposeful. "I never remember her without those little white gloves." [1]

After Mark Goodson had purchased his first burgundy Rolls-Royce, he took Dorothy to a play opening, instructing the driver to let them off a block from the theater, out of sight of other celebrities and the gathering crowd. "Why are we stopping here?" Dorothy asked. He explained that he just wasn't comfortable being seen in so grand a car. That was a sensibility completely alien to Dorothy. "Mark," she said laughingly, "if this were my car, I'd have the chauffeur drive me right to my aisle seat." [2]

She continued to identify in some goofy way with England's royal family, which gave her related reporting a distinguished zest. In the spring of 1953, Dorothy prepared to cover the coronation of Elizabeth II. She wrote, before she left for London, "Breathes there a girl with soul so dead that she wouldn't play princess for a few hours if she got the chance." [3]

She stayed at the Savoy. At four o'clock, on the morning of the coronation, she rang up Earl Blackwell, who was also at the hotel. "I need some help getting into this dress," she said. He zipped her into her spectacular Ceil Chapman original, a voluminous silver gown with more than fourteen thousand embroidered jewels and pearls that were encrusted at the scalloped neckline. She placed a tiara on her head, put on her white mink cape lined in silver lamé, grabbed some pencils, and she was off to Westminister Abbey. [4]

Dorothy's apparent fragility continued to bring out the

chivalric in the male animal. A brigadier general, veteran of sundry campaigns in India and Africa, caught her act as she attempted to hazard the narrow steps of the church. "You want a train bearer with that gown," he said. The old duffer assumed the role, guiding her into the abbey through the still-deserted passageway that led to the triforium, where the press was to be seated. "We must have made quite a sight," she wrote, "wending our way through, he with mustache bristling and sword clanking, me with tiara on head but Western Union copy paper under my arm." [5]

The ceremony began. Dorothy wrote in continuous longhand, finishing several pages and giving them, sealed in an envelope marked International News Service Telephonist, to a royal usher in red knee breeches. He dropped the copy down a chute leading from the triforium, whereupon it was taken by a page, hurried to the INS telephone hut, read to a typist at the news-service office on Fleet Street, carried to Western Union, and cabled directly to the *Journal-American*, which hit the street directly with the banner headline: DOROTHY KILGALLEN'S STORY: ELIZA-. BETH ENTHRONED IN ANCIENT SPLENDOR. [6]

Her story was skilled, rapturous, and, at times, appropriately fanciful, a considerable feat at an altitude of fourteen thousand embroidered jewels:

London, June 2—Elizabeth II, a slender young woman with a beauty that brightens the heart, today was crowned Queen of England in a ceremony of surpassing splendor.

Silver trumpets heralded her coronation with notes of joy. Bells tolled, cannon boomed in thundering salute, and the great Gothic shell of Westminster Abbey rang with shouts of "God save Queen Elizabeth."

As she sat upon her throne, clad in cloth of gold and wearing her jeweled crown, the handsome Prince who is her liege and her beloved knelt at her feet and pledged her his life.

Putting his strong hands in her fragile hands, he spoke these words of homage.

"I, Philip, Duke of Edinburgh, do become your liege man of life and limb, and of earthly worship, and faith and truth I will bear unto you, to live and die, against all manner of folks. So help me God."

And so saying, he rose tall in his ruby red shoes and touched her crown lightly and kissed her cheek.

She indulged in a bit of fantasy as she focused on the prince bathed "in the mystic light of the nave." She wondered

> if he had any impulse to turn and look at his young wife, and smile as her long ordeal was beginning and whisper, "Courage, darling—you'll be wonderful." But perhaps that had been done in the privacy of the Palace.[7]

She indulged in a bit of identification as she described Elizabeth after the crowning:

> The young Sovereign stood straight as a ramrod, her head held high, her hands at her sides, her lovely eyes looked directly ahead of her. It gave the effect of composure and fearlessness. Yet there was something infinitely touching about her aloneness at the moment of recognition.[8]

Dorothy told her favorite story, which was fed to her from someone "in the inner-circle at the Palace," royalist lingo for "a very good source." The inner-circle member had, it seemed, walked into Elizabeth's room several days before the coronation. She was sitting at her desk writing letters, dressed in a simple daytime frock, wearing King Edward's crown. "The crown is very heavy and tiresome to wear," Dorothy wrote. "Elizabeth—like any sensible woman with a new pair of shoes—was breaking it in." [9]

For her exhaustive front-page coverage of the coronation, Dorothy was nominated for a Pulitzer prize. Also, she was cited for excellence in reporting by a group of old-time newspapermen, the Silurians. She was the first woman to be accorded that honor. After twenty-two years functioning as a journalist, it was her first serious award.

Her own consort, Richard Tompkins Kollmar, was involved now in the business of art. He had been inspired by his course work at the Art Students League to rent a loft at 74 West Forty-seventh Street and install there six staff artists to turn out original work with commercial themes, each to sell for less than one hundred dollars.

The artists worked under the supervision of Bob Lynch, a rudderless fellow, himself a skilled portraitist. He met Richard at the league and promptly became a boon companion and right-hand man.

In addition to the work turned out by his staff people, Richard acquired paintings during "open calls," a theatrical institution he introduced into the art world. Once a week, hundreds of scuttling free-lancers queued up at the loft hoping to make a sale. The hundred-foot loft space had been bisected: The unfinished front half was for the workers with their paint pots; the rear, richly carpeted, lushly draped, with copies of Old Masters on the wall and Richard's initials everywhere else, was the domain of RTK. Jack Faragasso, one of his staff people, described him: "sitting there, like a Medici prince, making these judgments."

"They weren't bad paintings," Faragasso, now a successful commercial artist, recalled. "Whatever was popular— that's what we'd do. French street scenes and clowns were in demand, so we did them. I once painted a clown and called it 'Poor Richard.' If you look carefully, you'll recognize the model." [10]

When Faragasso went to work there, he signed his paintings Jack, which is what he liked to be called. Richard asked him what his real name was. It was John. "Then that's how you'll sign your paintings," Richard insisted. "You can't use Jack. It has no dignity." Richard's father was commonly called Jack.

Richard's venture, eventually called "the little studio," was quite sound commercially. He rented gallery space at the Carlton House and at Gimbels. With a little help from their friends and an enormous amount of publicity—much of it generated on the Kollmars' radio show—the little studio was burgeoning, according to Hubie Boscowitz, into a little gold mine.

Dorothy involved herself to some extent. She showed up at all the important parties at which the function was basically the encouragement of patronage. She received at the official opening of the loft. All their wealthy friends were invited and entertained roundly. They were given sketch pads and allowed to draw from models who were actually naked, and served canapés by tall, beautiful women dressed in little aprons designed so that their bare asses showed when they turned around. Miles White had once again been recruited: "It was embarrassing. There were all these straight business types. None of them could draw. I made a point of just sketching those poor girls' faces." [11]

Richard remained affiliated with the Art Students League, chairing their annual ball, which was organized for the benefit of the scholarship fund. Under his aegis, the lavishly costumed affairs became major, if somewhat controversial, New York events. It was necessary eventually to hire Pinkertons to prevent the unticketed from crashing.

They were staged in the grand ballrooms of some of the best hotels in town, but hardly ever in the same place twice. The Waldorf-Astoria asked them not to return because of the degree of nudity among the revelers. The Plaza Hotel took unbrage at Leda, a magnificent blonde carried on a palanquin high above the throngs of dragons, Kubla Khans, slave girls, Roman emperors, a two-legged stovepipe hat with eggy Barney Google eyes, and sundry witty visual jokes with mammary or priapic themes.

In addition to music, good eats, and splendid pageantry, a famous "Dream Girl" appeared at each one of the balls. Paulette Goddard was the first, followed by Dagmar, Arlene Dahl, and Deborah Kerr.

The functions cost about $30,000 and brought only about $5,000 to the school. But the publicity they generated encouraged other contributions and endowed the league with some jazzy cachet. Stewart Klonis, director of the league, was grateful to Richard, although he argued with him over the extent of the nudity. To no avail. Richard was the worst offender, hand-picking some of the more attractive women students, taking them to Brooks Costumes, and overseeing the creation of their tantalizing plumage. He favored ostrich feathers.[12]

The base for all of Richard's operations—artistic and otherwise—remained the loft on West Forty-seventh. It served as a convenient pied-à-terre for him. Dorothy saw her husband less and less. After the broadcast, she went back to sleep until noon and he until four or five in the afternoon, at which time she was writing her column. Given their nocturnal habits, staying out all night was customary rather than cause for suspicion. But they lived an early version of an open marriage. There was no candor about the openness and a distinct difference in their practices. Dorothy had dates. Richard had affairs.

Bob Lynch once told Jack Faragasso that he was certain Dorothy knew nothing about Richard's extramarital activities. Since Lynch was so close to the situation—he lived at the loft and socialized with the Kollmars on those rare occasions when they were a couple—that could mean one of two things. Either they had it out "in the privacy of the palace," or they never had it out. Lynch was close enough to Richard that he probably would have known about any confrontation. More likely, Dorothy chose the path of peace and least resistance, permitting Richard to believe cozily that what she didn't know wasn't hurting her.

In the two best profiles written about Dorothy in the fifties—Ernest Lehman's *Cosmopolitan* article, a distillation of a week spent following her about, compressed into "24 Glittering Hours with Dorothy Kilgallen"; and a piece by Will Jones, the newspaperman from Ohio—Richard remained a spectral, offstage figure, a kind of flighty Godot.

Lehman reported this encounter, reminiscent of the *New Yorker* profile of the forties:

> Richard Kollmar came hurrying out of the bedroom, fully dressed, and put his arms around Dorothy.
> "Good-bye, honey," he said. "I'm off and running."
> They kissed. "Good-bye, lambie," she said. "Have a good day. I hope the show goes well tonight." [Richard was making a very rare television appearance.]
> "Yours, too."
> "Will I see you?"
> "You can never tell," he called back.[13]

Exit Richard Kollmar from Dorothy Kilgallen's glittering hours. She did the town that night with Hubie Boscowitz.

In the beginning of the Will Jones piece, the reporter meets Dorothy for a night on the town: "Dick is Miss Kilgallen's husband, actor Richard Kollmar. I asked her where he was. 'He's working,' she said. 'We may see him at the party if he can get away.'" They did see him fleetingly at the party, a birthday celebration for Mrs. Donald

Stralem. He gave his wife the traditional press peck and, according to Jones, "disappeared into the crowd." [14]

Will Jones and Dorothy went to the theater that night to catch the opening of *The Four Poster*, a play with Hume Cronin and Jessica Tandy about a long, successful, rather traditional marriage. It was one of the more realistic comedies of its time. There were references to underarm shaving and ablutions overheard. Jones liked the play so much it made him homesick. Dorothy decided straightaway that she didn't like it at all. She said to the interviewer, as they dashed across the street for a drink between the first and second acts: "It makes marriage seem too tawdry. Maybe that's not the exact word, but I hope you know what I mean." [15]

Richard's separate activities compelled Dorothy to look elsewhere for male escorts. She never went out alone, and if a date kept her waiting, she hid out in the powder room for fear of being seen unescorted and judged undesirable. Sunday nights were especially important to her. When she did well on "What's My Line?" she felt ebullient and completely *en rapport* with the spirit and excitement of her city. When she hadn't done so well, she needed a drink or two and a sympathetic ear as she scrupulously evaluated where and how she had failed or been misled. In any case, it was no time to go back to an empty house.

Bob Bach was a particularly attractive and companionable squire. The son of a prosperous German-Jewish couple, he was raised in an affluent Westchester community. He prepped at Riverdale with the Kennedy boys—Joseph, Jr., a classmate, and John Fitzgerald, who was two years behind Bob. When his father lost his Fifth Avenue jewelry business during the Depression, Bob was forced to abandon his college plans. He took a number of odd jobs and worked his way into the nascent Goodson-Todman organization after several years of music-related activities, on *Down Beat* magazine and then with disc jockey Martin Block. He had always liked Dorothy's column because of her obvious interest in the big-band scene. They met as colleagues through "What's My Line?" where he lined up contestants and mystery guests ("My father knew I had *really* made it when I could tell him on Thursday who the mystery guest was going to be on Sunday." [16]) and became chums quickly. They did her rounds together every Sunday, Dorothy's hired limo waiting at the stage door.

Almost a full year had passed before Dorothy met Bob's wife, Jean, a strikingly attractive, gray-eyed blonde with fragile features, a Jane Wyman hairdo, and first-rate mind. She was the daughter of a Fitzgeraldian couple from the Midwest who never had much money but were nonetheless courted by the very social. Her father, an advertising man, left her mother to become Irene Castle's fourth husband. Jean went off to Vassar, where she remained for a year. When the money ran out, she went to work, as Dorothy had, for a Hearst newspaper: "Daddy was intrigued with newspaper work. I guess I was living out his dream." She wrote a social column called *By Jean*.

Jean had been married to Bob for two years when he began squiring Dorothy around town. She did not like or approve of the columnist. She found the morning chatter show of the Kollmars insipid and offensive: "I remember once when they spent the entire broadcast sneering at people who had affection for trees. I was ill for half a day." [17]

The Bachs were similar, in their respective consciousnesses, to John Hammond, a white man from a very prominent New York family who fell in love with the big-band sound early in life, became a titan in music management, and through his friendships with black people, expanded his universe and his awareness. Hammond would write in his autobiography, published in 1978, "The strongest motive for my dissent was jazz." [18] Jean spent her youth following big bands around, learning their arrangements, and associating with black musicians. She never set foot inside the Stork after the Josephine Baker affair.

There had been an early episode that had unfavorably disposed Jean to Dorothy. Jean had been personally zapped by *The Voice of Broadway*. When she met Bob, she was still married to jazz musician Shorty Sherock. Shorty was on the road and their marriage was on the rocks but not yet over when she picked up the *Journal-American* to discover that her marriage was indeed over and Bob was "looming in the background." She was horrified and had immediately telephoned her husband to soften the careless blow.

To make matters worse yet, in 1950 and 1951 the Kilgallen dame was not only stealing her new husband but taking him to some of the best jazz joints in town.

Jean finally met the enemy when the Bachs were invited, along with a couple of hundred other New Yorkers, to ring in 1952 with Dorothy and Dick. The party was one of their more memorable productions. Barbara Carroll played soft piano in one room, Lester Lanin and his full orchestra entertained in another, a Dixieland group caterwauled in a third. Couples danced in the Black Room, which was bathed only in ultraviolet light. A dramatic, innovative touch, the limited spectrum had the unforeseen and unfortunate tendency to turn false teeth or cultured pearls a fluorescent, ghastly green.

Jean and Dorothy had exchanged only cordial hellos. Then it was almost dawn. Judy Garland had just finished an impromptu set. Richard had passed out with several shades of lipstick on his collar. The Bachs were preparing to leave, but Jean was unable to find her evening purse. Dorothy approached the situation with humor and avidity. To her astonishment, Jean discovered that she liked Dorothy.

Presently, the twosome became a foursome. While Dorothy and Bob were toiling in the CBS vineyards, Richard, who found Jean quite attractive, would often call her for dinner. They caught up with their respective spouses later in the evening. They all loved music and laughed a good deal when they were together. Jean knew the score on the Kollmar marriage, though even when she and Dorothy became the closest of friends, it was never discussed. Richard had propositioned a couple of Jean's girl friends, one of whom, a prominent person in the fashion industry, found his impatient approach rather amusing and told her all about it.

Fortunately, it was possible to know all about Richard, to love Dorothy, and to be comfortable in their company. "I knew what was going down in that relationship," [19] Jean recalled. "But preserving illusions was Dorothy's whole act. I never saw them being unpleasant to each other. They were courtly and decent and loyal and they showed up for each other's birthdays. They did all the *pro forma* things. I had respect for that. It's dishonest, but in my opinion attractive."

Through her friendship with the Bachs, of whom the Boscowitzes wholly disapproved, Dorothy was convoyed out of the restrictive environs of the Stork Club and encouraged to experiment with a kind of experiential funk. Their favorite haunt became a Saroyanesque piano bar in a seedy West Side hotel, the Carnival. Richard had discovered it while doing a little prowling on his own and had designed the room. The main attraction was a pianist named Nicky De Frances, who played like Erroll Garner and freshened his full makeup as the evening progressed. The regular customers included a world famous astronomer who was jailed for writing obscene letters to little girls, and one of the first transsexuals, about whom the Bachs and the Kollmars were unwholesomely curious. They bribed a friend of Dorothy's to take her out and report back with full, clinical details. One night, they brought along Walter Winchell, who demonstrated an old soft-shoe routine and tried to convince them to accompany him on his crime alert. Primarily, they sang along and dug the music and laughed uproariously at almost anything.

The two couples were parting one night on Park Avenue, doing post mortems on the fun they managed to have together. Dorothy and Richard were about to leave for Paris on their annual summer sojourn. Jean mentioned that she had never been to Europe.

"Come with us," Dorothy said.

Bob hesitated. They were in no position financially to keep up with the high-living Kollmars abroad. Dorothy assured them that there was nothing to worry about: "We get everything free. All you kids have to worry about is the plane fare."

"Robert," Richard said, in his most commanding baritone, "it's settled. We won't take no for an answer." [20]

Dorothy and Richard left a day before the Bachs. After a leisurely Saturday lunch at the Stork, they were driven to the airport; they read the evening papers on the plane, tucked in for the night, and arrived in Paris in time to attend mass at the Madeleine. On Monday evening, their driver, Heeber, who was provided along with a staid and stately Humber by Rootes Motors, took them to the airport to meet Bob and Jean. "Have we got a surprise for you!' they shouted at the disembarking Bachs. They would not divulge. After a sumptuous dinner, Heeber headed for

James L. Kilgallen (*front center*) in the composing room of his newspaper, 1914. (*Western History Research Center, University of Wyoming*)

Dorothy's graduation from Brooklyn's P.S. 119. She is twelve years old. (*She is second from right, second row from top.*) (*Billy Rose Theatre Collection at Lincoln Center*)

At home with Cotton, a
souvenir of the Hauptmann
trial, in 1936.
*(Billy Rose Theatre Collection
at Lincoln Center)*

Dorothy and her competitors, Leo Kieran (*left*) and
Bud Ekins (*right*), boarding the airship *Hindenburg*, 1936.
(*United Press International*)

A triumphant Dorothy being greeted by her mother, Mae,
and sister, Eleanor, after her round-the-world race. Jim
Kilgallen had flown with her from California to Newark.
(*United Press International*)

This ad appeared later in 1936, after her "breathless dash" around the globe. (*Richard K. Smith Collection*)

Her film debut in MGM's *Sinner Take All* (1936). Bruce Cabot starred as fellow reporter. (*Billy Rose Theatre Collection at Lincoln Center*)

At the Trocadero with Tyrone Power during her short stint as Hollywood columnist, 1936. (*Billy Rose Theatre Collection at Lincoln Center*)

The wedding of Dorothy to Richard Tompkins Kollmar. Her people are on the right. (*Wide World*)

In keeping with her growing celebrity came this glamorous portrait by the celebrated Murray Korman.
(*Billy Livingston Collection*)

Vacationing with sister, Eleanor (*left*), in Beverly Hills, 1941.
(*United Press International*)

A close sixsome at the Stork Club in the mid-forties: Dorothy, Clyde Newhouse, Lillian Boscowitz, Richard, Maggie McNellis Newhouse, and Hubie Boscowitz.
(*Courtesy of Huber and Lillian Boscowitz*)

When the couple lived on Park Avenue, the radio show emanated from their mammoth, elegant dining room. (*Black Star*)

With Joan Crawford, 1945.
(*Billy Rose Theatre Collection at Lincoln Center*)

Frank Sinatra rehearsing with Dorothy for a joint radio appearance in 1948. They were good friends until her column offended him.
(*Billy Rose Theatre Collection at Lincoln Center*)

The Bachs and the Kollmars at their favorite haunt, listening to jazz pianist Nicky DeFrances, shoring up against "last call" with back-to-back doubles, in the early fifties. (*Jean Bach Collection*)

The Kollmars in their Americana Black Room. Jill and Dickie in customized minichairs. Dorothy holds Kerry, 1955. (*Gary Wagner Associates*)

The "What's My Line?" cast in 1955: (*left to right*) Fred Allen, Dorothy, John Daly, Arlene Francis, and Bennett Cerf. (*Jean Bach Collection*)

Portrait of the Science Club regulars *et al* was a Christmas gift to Dorothy. Standing (*left to right*): Lou Stoecklin, Jim Downey, Bob Bach, Dan Lavezzo. Seated (*left to right*): Bill Helburn, Howard Rothberg, Paul and mascot, Skippy. (*Bob Bach Collection*)

MISS FRANCIS   MR. CERF

Yves Montand with Marilyn Monroe and Dorothy, 1960. (*Jean Bach Collection*)

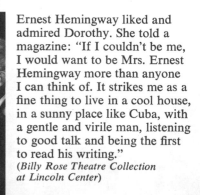

Ernest Hemingway liked and admired Dorothy. She told a magazine: "If I couldn't be me, I would want to be Mrs. Ernest Hemingway more than anyone I can think of. It strikes me as a fine thing to live in a cool house, in a sunny place like Cuba, with a gentle and virile man, listening to good talk and being the first to read his writing."
(*Billy Rose Theatre Collection at Lincoln Center*)

With Johnnie Ray at the Waldorf, 1960.
(*Johnnie Ray Collection*)

With Sophia Loren, 1962. (*Billy Rose Theatre Collection at Lincoln Center*)

Dorothy and ten-year-old Kerry on the Hollywood set of *Pajama Party* in 1964. Kerry made his film debut in the movie opposite Annette Funicello and Tommy Kirk. (*Associated Press Wirephoto*)

Dorothy, in Dallas, returns to the Jack Ruby trial after lunching with his defense attorneys, Melvin Belli (*at right*) and Joe Tonahill. (*Photo by Eamon Kennedy*)

Dorothy, with Richard, in January of 1965.
(*Jean Bach Collection*)

a small cul-de-sac off the Champs Élysées. They entered Le Club Mars, an intimate room next door to the first discothèque in the world, Whiskey-à-Go-Go.

Back in the States, Jean had raved about a young black pianist named Bobby Short, who she said sang and played like no one else. She had somehow lost contact with him. He had left for Paris in late '51. ("I fell into a velvet-lined rut. I had become the young colored boy who was all chic . . . and that was as far as I could go." [21]) Dorothy discovered him on her first night in Paris, introduced herself as a friend of Jean Bach's, and sat studiously captivated as he sang "My Funny Valentine" for her. Jean was thrilled now to see him again.

When she returned home, Dorothy began a concerted campaign to acquaint her readers with this virtually unknown performer. Bobby Short recalled:

I was astonished. Here I was playing at a club in Paris and friends kept sending me clippings from Dorothy's column, raving about me *in absentia*. Once she devoted a whole column to the subject of First Ladies. The Presidential race was on. Dorothy said that any woman would look good entertaining at the White House with Bollinger in the champagne glasses and Bobby Short at the piano. Then a reader wrote, "I know about Bollinger, but who is Bobby Short?" She went into a long ecstatic explanation. When I left Paris to return to New York, everything was easier because people, who had never heard my work, knew my name. I couldn't have been more surprised. She never mentioned to me what she was going to do. There was never any of that "I'm-gonna-make-you-a-star" stuff. The only thing she wanted in return from me was my friendship. And that was hardly a problem. Dorothy Kilgallen was responsible for the beginning of a whole new career for me.[22]

In Paris, the Kollmars stayed at one of the top-flight hotels, the Bachs at a charming but modest five-dollar-a-day suite on the Left Bank. "They'd come in and say, 'Hey, this place isn't *bad!*'" Bob recalled. "To them, it was kind of amusing to have these friends living on the Left Bank." [23]

Jean had not complained, but her limited wardrobe had made her feel like a poor relation on their evenings out in Paris. When they planned their next trip, in 1954, a list arrived at Jean's apartment several weeks before their departure. Hand delivered and in Dorothy's own writing, it included everything the columnist was planning to take. No furs. A couple of sweaters and cotton dresses. There was even a price next to some of the items. "It was just an example of how thoughtful Dorothy could be when she took the time to think," Jean said.[24]

As a public personality, Dorothy appeared to be blithely unaware that everyone was not as well fixed as she. But on a one-to-one basis, she was not so careless. Press agent Michael Sean O'Shea had a party once for Tallulah Bankhead. Guests were instructed not to tip the help. Dorothy, nonetheless, slipped five dollars to a ladies' room attendant.

"I'm not supposed to take any gratuities, Miss Kilgallen."

"I never met anyone who couldn't use five bucks," Dorothy replied. "Please take it." [25]

Now, in 1954, the foursome traveled to Capri, after taking a straw vote on little slips of paper. Three of the ballots indicated a desire to go somewhere with a beach. Dorothy lost. While the Bachs and Richard sunned and swam, Dorothy emerged periodically from her cabana, followed by enough gear-carrying beachboys to people a Tennessee Williams play. She sat at the water's edge, behind huge sunglasses, under a pup tent, a parasol, and an enormous hat. Wrapped like a diseased Bedouin, she waved a gloved hand at her frolicking friends and assured them that she was having a wonderful time. And she was. But the light of the sun remained a poison.

They went on to Pompeii. She and Jean, slim and fashionable in their reasonably priced cotton dresses, were walking and chatting gaily by the ruins one morning. There were whistles and shouts of *Bella! Bella!* from the Italian peasants. It became obvious immediately that it was Jean to whom the attention was being directed. They each tried to pretend nothing was happening. Having passed through the humiliating gauntlet, they were approached by a touring Texas couple.

"Well, if it isn't Dorothy KILL-gallen," said the man. "We watch you every week on television."

Dorothy, feeling safe again, brightened.

"I just want to tell you," he continued, "that you are the smartest person on that EN-tire panel."

Jean and Dorothy walked on in silence. They came to a little brick structure. "Wow," Dorothy said. "I'm suddenly tired. Let's sit down for a minute." She stared plaintively.

"What's the matter, Dorothy?" asked Jean, who knew precisely what the matter was.

"Maybe I'm tired of being the smartest person on that EN-tire panel," she bristled.

"It beats being the dumbest person," Jean said. "What's better than smart?"

"Blonde!" Dorothy answered.[26]

Dealing obliquely, Jean bought a red wig for Dorothy that Christmas, which evoked copious compliments. Dorothy dyed her hair the color of the wig and maintained it. Jean had been relieved, in Pompeii, that Dorothy had been "too cool to say beautiful."

Friendship with Dorothy was a delicate and sensitive affair, given her congeries of repression and avoidance, her sometimes indecipherable private code. Beyond, there was the universal problem of coping with celebrity and power.

Bob, a resilient, amiable man, enjoyed witnessing the phenomenon. At a normal gathering of impressionable New Yorkers, people tended to direct their comments toward Dorothy. Ernest Hemingway closed the Stork with her one night. Bob took special delight in calling, "Waiter, more champagne for Mr. Hemingway," in experiencing the man despite the fact that he was well aware that Hemingway was socializing with Dorothy Kilgallen *and* her escort. He watched, with a mischievous thrill, as Jack Kennedy, a young senator out late with someone other than his wife, "touched base" with her: "Hello, Dorothy. Do you remember the night we played charades at your house? What fun it was!"[27] Kennedy was tacitly soliciting clearance. There would be no mention ever in the column of his extramarital permutations, though she knew through the years that he played.

Jean loved Dorothy a great deal, but she had more problems than Bob with her celebrity. An incident on their Italian trip was emblematic.

"I have a picture in my mind's eye," Jean said, sitting poolside in the tiny, well-sculptured garden on her country home in Bedford, New York,

> of Dorothy boarding the *moto-scoffo* in Venice. Dick and some pages are helping Dorothy on one side. Bob is running around to assist her on the other. And I'm getting on, about a beat later, all by myself. And it was always that way. If there were ten men around, they'd all be helping her through the door. She really was a kind of Mount Rushmore.[28]

Jean, undoubtedly, would have experienced less resentment if she knew how hard and long Dorothy had worked, not to become a kind of Mount Rushmore, but simply Queen of the May.

Whatever demons racked Richard were baited by Dorothy's success. Pridefully, he avoided any connection with "What's My Line?" He would never permit himself to be seen as Johnny at the stage door. The Boscowitzes perceived that he was not only accepting but proud of Dorothy's accomplishments. He was, however, secure with the couple. Hubie was his closest friend, encouraging Richard in every professional step he took. But there is nothing so telling as a round with an upstart. A fledgling press agent, Harvey Daniels, once said, upon being introduced to Richard, "Oh, yes, you're Dorothy's husband." Richard ignored the proffered hand and corrected the young man. "No," he seethed, "Dorothy is my wife: *Mrs. Richard Kollmar!*" [29]

In his own little world, among struggling staff artists, he was domineering and bombastic. But even they knew something was wrong. "I really felt that he needed something to *do* in life," Jack Faragasso surmised.[30] Lee Nordness, a cultured, beautiful young man with a master's degree in Fine Arts whom Richard considered a social equal and who eventually bought the studio from him, had no respect for his taste or his business acumen. Nonetheless, Lee was fond of Richard and discerned about him "a certain *tristesse* that I never saw in Dorothy. He was obviously doing something very wrong for himself, but he just couldn't seem to extricate himself from it." [31]

Richard had always been a heavy drinker. Now, in his

middle years, his face began to bloat, making his teeth appear shrunken. He was never totally sober. The drinking obviously concerned him, because he began to legislate for himself. He would not take his first shot until the evening cocktail hour. But abstaining until 5:30 is no arduous feat when one rises at 4:00.

After fourteen years of marriage, Richard and Dorothy were going in separate directions on several levels. He was experiencing the malaise and torpor associated with advancing alcoholism. Dorothy, on the other hand, was in her prime—healthy, successful, perilously energized.

There was something marginally bolder about her sexuality. She and Jean played a game derived from a phrase that Harriet Van Horne used in an opprobrious essay about country music. Van Horne wrote that she found the form silly because someone was always singing about his or her "little darlin'." Now, when the two women were out together, Jean would spot a particularly attractive man, often a musician, and whisper to Dorothy, "That one over there." Dorothy would pluck her harlequin glasses out of her lucite bag, scan the room, and agree, "That *is* a little darlin', isn't it." [32]

The danger signs were manifold. Richard's philandering was part of the problem. He was a lush who was never going to edit the military papers of his illustrious forebear, nor act in Shakespeare, nor relieve her of the burden of her own sexuality. Dorothy, who craved support, tenderness, and even domination, was losing respect for this man, her husband.

Unable to break and unready to loosen the bonds of matrimony, she did the next best thing by tightening them, using the most traditional modalities—land and child.

Ignoring the admonitions of Edgar Hatfield, they put all their savings into a five-story, elevated town house at 45 East Sixty-eighth Street, right off Park Avenue. The house cost $95,000. They spent $8,000 just to move. Most of the money that they earned would go into the mortgages.

The union that produced their third child was suspiciously identifiable. They were late for a dinner party at the Boscowitzes, offering a flushed and clearly bogus excuse. Hubie and Lillian giggled at their embarrassment and could pinpoint, years later, the evening Dorothy had conceived. On March 19, 1954, Kerry Ardan Kollmar was born at the

LeRoy Hospital. He was named Kerry after a county seat in Ireland and Ardan for an Irish warrior who, Dorothy wrote, "was said to have the most beautiful singing voice in all Erin." [33]

She was ecstatic about the baby, who was seven pounds, fourteen ounces, with flat ears, unlike Dickie's, and a beautifully shaped head. She told Jean, "He's just like a diamond bracelet that somebody gave me."

Dorothy rarely visited the offices of the *Journal-American*.
When she did, perhaps once every two years, she was received with decidedly mixed emotions. Nick Lapole, nightclub editor of the paper and the first copy checker of *The
Voice of Broadway*, recalled her biennial appearances:

> She came in trailing mink. So, of course, there was a
> lot of envy and a lot of smirking contempt. But then
> there were those who would gather round and be
> genuinely glad to see her.[1]

Among the celebrants were the good old boys at the
paper whose respect for Dorothy never flagged. Edward
Mahar was one. He was the reporter who had covered the
Cushman bakery murder with her, ducked into a phone
booth, and transmogrified the victim's address book to a
lurid love diary. He was now assistant city editor of the
Journal. City editor Paul Schoenstein, the Spartan who had
called the CIA from his hospital bed, was another devotee
of both Kilgallens. Sam Day, managing editor, an extreme
right winger, lanky and, since his youth, white-haired, also
greeted her enthusiastically, as did Danny Brooks, to whom
she would always be "The Boss!"

Igor Cassini, reflecting the resentment while describing
their attitudes, observed:

> She had all those old-timers kowtowing to her because
> she was Jim Kilgallen's daughter. Mostly Sam Day.
> He just worshipped her. She was the great sob sister,
> and they gave her all the assignments.[2]

The old-timers' loyalty to Dorothy had many sources.
Respect was primary. They knew that she could handle any

story to which she was assigned, and that she was among the best, if not *the* best, of the *journal* writers.

Not to be dismissed by any means is the sentiment that binds together comrades with shared secrets and common enemies. When the *Journal* finally closed shop in 1967, only the basic back-copy morgue was contributed to a college library. Everything else—memos, personal papers, letters, memorabilia—was shredded by the routed Hearst army.

A fierce fealty lingers among Hearst people.

Olga Curtis of INS was a fledgling reporter at the time she and Dorothy covered the wedding of Princess Grace in Monaco. Curtis was described by Bob Considine as "a beautiful and talented girl who felt eclipsed by the presence on our team of our strikingly efficient and confident Dorothy Kilgallen." [3] She was to Dorothy what Dorothy had been to Adela Rogers St. Johns back in Salem, at the trial of Jessie Costello. During a telephone conversation in 1978, Curtis volunteered that she had been treated shabbily by Dorothy, indicated that there were stories to tell, but refused finally to tell them.

Inez Robb, a top-flight Hearst veteran, complained frequently to the organization that Dorothy's feature assignments were given preferential play. Neither would she elaborate or contribute "gossip"—which is to say that she would not talk about Dorothy's behavior.

Adela Rogers St. Johns declined to answer three letters.

The normally affable, glad-handing Bill Hearst made a hasty retreat from an overpriced French restaurant when the subject of Dororthy was broached.

Sam Day, retired to Queens, answered written interrogatories informatively, if somewhat guardedly. Dorothy, during Nikita Khrushchev's visit to the United States in 1959, vituperatively attacked Mrs. Khrushchev's matronly couture, and then reportedly expressed some contrition. The *Journal-American*'s own Louis Sobol wrote, in a posthumous and reverential series about Dorothy:

> She confessed to some intimates that perhaps she had been a bit overzealous and somewhat cruel in her sarcastic observations. . . . To a friend she explained: "Sometimes you sit at a typewriter and the words come out sharper and maybe a bit more unfair than you

would want to if you took more time and thought it over." [4]

Day commented on the Khrushchev episode: "No recollection of talk with D.K. about K.," he wrote. "Was Sobol correct 'in asserting that she was contrite, that she recognized she overstepped the limits of good taste'? Good Lord, girl, how do you manage to manufacture a bit of unconfirmed hearsay into grease for your hatchet. Why don't you apply for a job on the *Inquirer*? The editors there would welcome your style." [5]

Sam Day eventually emended his philippic in a follow-up letter. He had meant the *Enquirer* and not the *Inquirer*.

During her years as a columnist and a television luminary, Dorothy wrote an occasional news story for the *Journal*, still deriving enormous pleasure from front-page exposure. These dispatches were a function exclusively of her Broadway beat: the Lonergan trial, a brawl among baseball players at the Copacabana, Eartha Kitt visiting Albert Einstein, Pat Ward discovered *in flagrante rumba* at a New York night spot when she should have been home ironing a white collar for the ongoing trial of vice-lord Mickey Jelke.

In the mid-fifties, however, she began accepting assignments from the city desk and turning out running, front-page stories of enormous impact. Flashy, skilled, rapturously or peevishly reflective of her own world view, they are among the best examples of colorful, personal reporting.

No compliment in her professional life gratified her as profoundly as the one she received from Ernest Hemingway. Interviewed in Cuba, where he was following the trial of Sam Sheppard, Hemingway told a representative of the *London Times:*

> They call these girls sob-sisters in the old-fashioned Hearst tradition. But they're not. They write well. And when you consider the speed at which they have to tell their tales, it's good, very good. A trial like this, with its elements of doubt, is the greatest human story of all. . . . This is the real thing. This Dorothy Kilgallen is a good girl. Don't you think so? Not as good as

Rebecca West maybe. Nobody's as good as all that. But those girls are damn good.[6]

She clipped the Hemingway piece and pasted it prominently in one of her voluminous scrapbooks, underlining the master's words vigorously in red—up until the part about Rebecca West. He would kiss her hand deferentially at the Stork Club, and report his encomium personally.

Dorothy's return to "the real thing" as a media superstar was a remarkable phenomenon in the journalism of the time, coming as it did after the era of Adela Rogers St. Johns and before the advent of Barbara Walters. At the end of the Sheppard trial, for instance, it was not the guilty verdict that the *Journal* featured on its front page but *her response* to that verdict. The screaming, streamer headline, run above the masthead, each letter one-and-a-quarter inches high, read:

Dorothy Kilgallen on Sheppard trial:

ASTOUNDED BY VERDICT
SEES REVERSAL POSSIBLE

About her involvement with that trial in 1954, *Time* magazine wrote:

Looking at the headlines, it becomes increasingly difficult to tell the reporter from the principals. We momentarily expected to hear that she had been chosen to deliver the summation or, at least, to be a surprise witness.[7]

She was tagged, by one of her colleagues, "a newspaperman in a $500 dress." When she covered inaugurals or visits from heads of state, she did so with imperial perquisites, which also made it difficult to distinguish her from the principals—and perhaps obliterated fine lines in Dorothy's own psyche.

William Randolph Hearst arranged for her to be provided with a car and chauffeur, and not an ordinary black Cadillac limousine. When Queen Elizabeth returned to the United States and Canada in 1957, Dorothy kept up with her favorite regent in a $24,982 Silver Wraith Rolls-Royce replete with Persian-lamb floor coverings, solid gold fixtures, French walnut bar, and leather interior. In New York, Dorothy's car slipped into the procession that was forming at City Hall.

Press agent Emmett Davis was among the observers. Elizabeth and an official were in the first car, followed by Prince Philip and his party, and then Governor Harriman and company. Sitting alone in the Rolls, fourth in the royal procession and peering out from the backseat—Dorothy. She wore her standard white gloves and waved demurely at the cheering crowd. She used a circular motion, palm turned inward as though applying rouge to her cheek. "It was the old Queen Mary gesture," Emmett Davis recalled, "and I just stood there thinking, 'Now I've seen everything!' " 8

The idea of sending Dorothy to Cleveland to cover the murder trial of Dr. Samuel Sheppard originated with the *Journal* at a time when Dorothy was ripe for change and abounding with energy.

The alterations she had made in her life, not surprisingly, ameliorated her basic problems hardly at all. Six-month-old Kerry was plainly adored. When the Kollmars' new bookkeeper, Anne Hamilton, appeared for her first day of work, Dorothy could barely wait to finish the morning broadcast so that she could rush to the nursery to scoop him up and show him off. Jill Ellen was faring all right, but pubescent, super-bright Dickie was in his runaway stage, bitter and rebellious. Dorothy resolved to try to spend more time with Kerry. For the moment, he was in the hygienic hands of Nu Nu, the strict German housemaid who had raised the other children.

Dorothy loved the house, put most of what she earned into mortgage payments, and ignored Edgar Hatfield's continuing advice to unload it. "What do you need it for!" he railed in his high-pitched voice. "You're never in it. Your husband's certainly never in it. You don't entertain anymore. And you can't afford it." 9

The house was in capable hands, staffed by an upstairs and a downstairs maid and a young black couple, James and Evelyn Clement. James buttled. Evelyn cooked the meals that the family hardly ever took together.

As Dorothy prepared to leave for Cleveland, Richard was involved once again in the theater, producing a play in conjunction with Jimmy Gardiner and Yvette Schumer, *Plain and Fancy*, a musical set in Amish Pennsylvania. It had taken more than thirty auditions to raise the money for the production, most of them held at the grand new house. Richard sang the songs, told the story, worried about the cost of the considerable Scotch and bourbon guzzled by the prospective angels, and made the pitch. But even as he sang one of the lovely ballads from the show, a backer turned to watch James, in his white jacket, ascending the winding staircase with a sandwich for Dorothy on a silver tray. "Is she really up there?' he whispered to Jimmy Gardiner. "I was sort of hoping to meet her." [10]

"Miss Kilgallen," a bailiff said to Dorothy, who was wearing a short-sleeved dress and a little flowered hat as she prepared to take her seat in the press section of the tiny Common Pleas Court in Cleveland, "the judge would like to say hello to you."

When she entered his chambers, Judge Edward Blythin, angular, seventy, and bespectacled, was donning his robe. Once mayor of Cleveland, Blythin had been a judge of the Common Pleas since 1948, was currently running for re-election to a six-year term, and had assigned this case, which had created a sensation in the city and was beginning to be known around the country, to himself.

He extended his hand to Dorothy.

"I'm very glad to see you, Miss Kilgallen," he said. "I watch you on television very frequently and enjoy the program. What brings you to Cleveland? Why come all the way from New York to cover this trial?"

"It has all the ingredients of what in the newspaper business we call a 'good murder,'" she replied. "It has an attractive victim, who was pregnant. And the accused is an important member of the community—a respectable and attractive man. Then, added to that, you have the fact that it is a mystery as to who did it."

"Mystery?" Blythin said. "It's an open-and-shut case."

"What do you mean, Judge Blythin?" she asked.

"He's guilty as hell," the judge replied. "There's no question about it." [11]

Dorothy was startled. She had conferred with many jurists in private, and none had ever made such a clear and flagrant statement of personal prejudice. In this case, the jury had not even been completely impaneled.

Blythin left the chamber with Dorothy. They posed for pictures together. "She's a lovely person," he told the photographers. "I can understand why she's so popular."

"Hey, Dorothy," asked one of the reporters, "how do you feel about all this attention? Can you do your job and be a celebrity, too?"

"It complicates life a bit, but I can't say that it ruins it, or that I don't like what it means. I've been working hard since I was seventeen years old to get where I am now, and although the situation slows me down, I'm grateful." 12

She put Blythin's confidences in her pocket and went about the business of reporting the unfurling drama. This was more than a "good murder," it was among the best.

The crime for which Dr. Samuel Holmes Sheppard now stood trial had been committed in the predawn hours of July 4, 1954, in the lakefront suburb of Bay Village, Ohio. The couple involved were the very model of prosperous, upper-middle-class, decent middle Americans.

Samuel Sheppard and Marilyn Reese were sweethearts in high school. He was handsome, six feet tall, a football hero, and the man voted Most Likely to Succeed. She was blond, yearbook-comely, and was said to have a good sense of humor. They married and settled in Bay Village. Sam had designed to follow his father and his two older brothers into osteopathic surgery. He joined the staff of Bay View Hospital, which had been founded by his father, a neurosurgeon. By 1954, he was earning more than $30,000 a year. He was known and liked in the community. She taught Sunday school at a local Methodist church and was pregnant with their second child. Marilyn was thirty-one. Sam was thirty.

On the day before the crime, the Sheppards were planning a July fourth picnic on their lakefront beach. Marilyn baked a blueberry pie. Sam was called out to treat a local boy who had been run over by a truck and critically injured. Though the boy eventually died, Sam spent hours over him, opening his chest and massaging the boy's heart until it beat on its own.

They had neighbors to their house that evening. The Sheppards were openly affectionate with each other. Even before his guests departed, Sam snoozed on the living-room couch. Marilyn went upstairs to their bedroom and retired.

During the night, she was brutally murdered, battered with a sharp metal instrument twenty-seven times. She was in her bed. Sam Sheppard was the only adult known to be in the house.

Dr. Sheppard was questioned repeatedly in the weeks before his arraignment. He would contend over and over that he was still sleeping on the couch when he was awakened by Marilyn's screams and had rushed upstairs to their bedroom. There he saw and grappled with what he called a "white form." He was knocked unconscious for an indeterminate period of time. After regaining consciousness, he ascertained that his wife was dead, chased a "bushy-haired man" along the beach, struggled again, and was again beaten into unconsciousness. He awakened by the water's edge, returned to the house, and telephoned for help.

The murder and Dr. Sheppard became the biggest story in the area, with the influential Cleveland *Press* daily demanding the arrest of Sam Sheppard for the murder. On July 30, the paper ran an eight-column story with the streamer headline: WHY ISN'T SAM SHEPPARD IN JAIL? Though nothing but circumstance linked him to the crime, he was arrested that evening and jailed. He pleaded not guilty. During ten years of trials, appeals, and imprisonment, neither his plea nor his story would change.

Dorothy, like most of the press corps, came to Cleveland believing that Sheppard was guilty. The story of the "white form" and the "bushy-haired intruder" struck her as quite incredible. She very quickly altered that perception.

She sat in the second row of the courtroom, just outside the bar railing, beside her friend Bob Considine, who was covering the trial for INS, and Inspector Robert Fabian of Scotland Yard, who had been hired by Scripps-Howard. As the jury was impaneled, she was being sketched by Burris Jenkins, whose drawings and doggerel accompanied her stories. She was rendered, by Jenkins, prim and attentive, in a cloche hat and glasses, her legs and her steno pad both folded in front.

Her attention was riveted to Sheppard, who sat next to his counsel indicating subtly which of the prospective jurors he found acceptable. Dorothy called the process by which the defendant made his judgments "Dr. Sheppard's eye test." When she saw a slight disdain in his face as he listened to a voluble, frumpily dressed woman answer questions about her suitability as a juror, she scribbled a note to Considine: "Sam doesn't like her." The woman was dismissed. Dorothy smiled triumphantly and gave the osteopath points for taste and discernment.

Dorothy wrote: "The handsome young doctor, loaded with sex appeal and attractive to women all his life, is at this crucial hour, wary of women and fearful of their judgment." [13] Dorothy would prove that he had nothing to fear from her.

Her approval of Sheppard, her apparent attraction to him as a man, did not prejudice so much as it predisposed. In her stories, which appeared in the Hearst newspapers the Fort Worth *Star-Telegram*, the Cleveland *News*, the Minneapolis *Star-Tribune*, the Houston *Post*, and the St. Louis *Post-Dispatch*, she marshaled cogently all the evidence that militated against Sheppard's credibility:

Sam's brother Richard asserted that, from the beginning, he had absolute faith in the innocence of his younger brother. Why had he then asked him, as some testimony indicated, if he had done the deed?

Given the roughness of the lake on the night of the murder, how did Sam survive his period of unconsciousness by the water's edge? Why was there no sand in his hair?

There was no testimony to the effect that the doctor's sleep was interrupted before he responded to Marilyn's chilling screams. He had been observed to fall asleep wearing a corduroy jacket. How was it then that the jacket was discovered folded neatly at the foot of the couch?

The apparent ransacking of the house, which the defense attributed to a mad intruder, Dorothy called "a mincing kind of burglary . . . out of keeping with the fiendishness of the alleged bushy-haired stranger." [14]

Against Sam Sheppard, also, she weighed the expert

testimony that the X rays of the head injuries, said to have been incurred during his fight with the maniac, had been faked. Then there was the very inculpatory statement by a woman on the stand that she had discussed with the doctor, just a short time before the crime, the ease with which such X rays could be faked.

What happened to Sam Sheppard's T-shirt? Why hadn't his dog barked when the stranger entered the house?

Dorothy's first important lead read: "Dr. Sam Sheppard, who goes on trial here tomorrow, is either a brutal killer or a man in a nightmare." [15] She was more and more inclined to believe that he was a man in a nightmare. A basic trust in him suffused her copy. Nothing at the trial disabused her of her faith.

Sitting at the Express Grill, a local diner two blocks from the courthouse where she and her colleagues repaired for lunch during the noon break, Dorothy constantly returned to the question of motive. Considine reminded her that it was not necessary to establish a motive for murder in Ohio, but merely a case that the murder had been done by the defendant. Considine evidently believed Sheppard guilty. On a local radio show, during the trial, the usually congenial reporter had compared the doctor's veracity with that of Alger Hiss—which, from a Hearstling, was no compliment.

Throughout her stories, Dorothy returned to the question of motive. She knew about Ohio's law, but she also knew jurors. She stressed that they would have to be shown "a series of events so neatly consecutive and so closely knit that the most obtuse juror can see it all in his mind like a smoothly unreeling movie." [16]

The trial was to last for nine weeks. When Dorothy was on the scene, or close enough to it to play on her own fantasies, she gave her editors corking copy, characterized by a romantic vision of the man, his history, and his lifestyle.

Near the beginning, Judge Blythin ordered the jurors bused to the scene of the crime, the white-frame house trimmed in green where the murder had been done. Sheppard, accompanied by a deputy sheriff, arrived in a police car. Dorothy, her forty colleagues, and several hundred spectators stood behind police lines, watching Sheppard return. She watched in the biting cold as the participants slushed through the muddy lawn into the house and out again. A helicopter hired by a competitive newspaper hovered above.

She described Sam Sheppard:

> As he walked with the deputy sheriff across the leaf-covered lawn, their wrists so close the handcuffs barely showed, he was hatless and ramrod straight in a light brown and tan small-checked topcoat, Burberry style, which he wore unbuttoned. Except for the stern set of his jaw and his pallor, he looked almost collegiate; he might have been, standing in the icy wind not seeming to notice it, the local high school's football coach.

Only one pool reporter was permitted to follow Sam Sheppard and his jurors into the house, but Dorothy used the barren data fed to her to confect an idealized tableau, taking sweet liberties in the subjunctive voice on behalf of the Sheppards:

> In an alcove off his room was a picture of the doctor, and a picture of Marilyn, and on a small dresser, a souvenir the young wife had saved from happier days —a card, such as might have been sent with flowers, saying, "To My Girl With All My Love, Sam." [17]

The other reporters all related the fact that he had broken down when he encountered the reminders of his seven-year-old son, Chip, who had slept through Marilyn's murder. But none imbued the osteopath with such tragic stature. She wrote,

> On the dresser sat a furry teddy bear, and the sight of this was too much for Dr. Sheppard to take with his usual immobility. His face crumpled like a child's; he made no sound or movement, but the color of his eyes deepened and glittered, and the tears flowed down his cheeks.[18]

Though Dorothy's skill as a writer had improved considerably since her days as Dolly Mae, Girl Reporter, there was no growth evident in her romantic view of the alternately collegiate and hellenic Dr. Sheppard. On "The Day They Brought Marilyn into Court," however, Dorothy got in touch with something new. For the first time in her writing career, poetically and authentically, she drew upon the iconography of her Catholic background.

In court, over the shouted objections of the defense, the state introduced the evidence of Dr. Samuel Gerber, the coroner who had performed the autopsy on Marilyn's body. Thirty-five color slides were shown, with extreme close-ups of the victim's wounds as she lay at the morgue just hours after she was murdered. Each picture was three feet wide and three feet high. Pointer in hand, Phi Betta Kappa key dangling, Gerber rapped at the opaque screen and described the wounds in crisp, scientific tones.

The exhibit in the darkened and stunned courtroom lasted forty-five minutes. Dr. Sheppard, who had intentionally placed himself in back of the screen, wept at the narrative. Two jurors broke down. Some viewed the startling photographs through splayed fingers; some could not look at all. The spectacle was dismissed resentfully by Dorothy's colleagues as "gruesome," "grisly," "sickening," "an ordeal." Though Dorothy commented on "the horrid lack of privacy about being murdered," she was transfixed. Having inured herself to the sight of violent death, she was now half in love with it. She wrote:

> It was strange. No picture of Marilyn Sheppard, of the many taken when she was smiling and wide-eyed and alive, has shown her to be so lovely as she was in death—discolored and slashed and broken.
>
> Her face was oval, her skin the very fair kind with fine pores. Where there were no wounds, it had a peach-like tint, faintly damp with the dewiness of the newly dead.
>
> Her eyebrows were light brown and delicate, her mouth pale pink, generously curved, perfectly and definitely cut like the mouth of a Roman statue.
>
> Her face was not distorted at all; it was in remarkable repose considering how she died. But the wounds of her forehead and cheeks were too numerous and too gaudy, like the wounds of St. Sebastian in the cheap plaster statues seen in the churches of little

Italian towns. Marilyn's slayer was an extravagant slayer, wasteful of blows. . . .

In the profile pictures of Marilyn, her nose showed clearly broken—flattened rather classically, like the nose of a goddess in an archaic statue.

In the slides of her hands—the right one broken across the knuckles, the left one with a nail all but torn off the fourth finger, just hanging by a bit of tissue—her delicacy was emphasized. . . . She was beautiful. So lovely and so bruised. So gentle with her eyes closed, sleeping under the vermilion gashes.[19]

She recoiled only once. A perplexing mass appeared on the screen, bloody and suetlike, resembling nothing human. "This," Gerber said, "is the skull of Marilyn Sheppard after the scalp has been peeled away."

Dorothy's schedule on location in Cleveland was hectic. She left the Statler Hilton, where everything, including what she termed "the more surprising facilities," was wrapped in cellophane, and where the elevator, much to her dismay, played "Hernando's Hideaway" in muted pizzicati—every morning at seven.[20] She taxied to the local radio station to broadcast "Dorothy and Dick," live in the morning and prerecorded for the evening. Richard, too, was on location with *Plain and Fancy*, which was looking good prior to its New York opening. The *Journal* had agreed to pick up the considerable cable costs. They were reluctant at first, but the incredible success of Dorothy's Sheppard stories more than justified the expense.

"Sweetie," Dick said, from WNHC in New Haven, "snow has fallen on Vesuvius."

"That is the dullest-looking volcano," Dorothy replied, from WHK in Cleveland. "That was the volcano we saw near Naples when we were there, wasn't it, dear?"

He read a doll-carriage commercial and segued into a discussion of a *Life* magazine piece he was reading about old hunting rifles and their various-sized bores.

"Maybe I shouldn't be so forward," Dorothy giggled, "but it is my opinion that most *hunters* are various sized bores." [21]

And there was the column. She relied heavily during this period on guest columns and press agents, but she nonetheless had to oversee and edit *The Voice of Broadway*, check the hotter tips, and stay in constant touch with Myrtle by telephone. How else would her faithful readers learn that friends of Muriel Reynolds, wife of the tobacco millionaire, were concerned because Muriel was in a Paris rest home "recovering from a case of nervous exhaustion"? Or that Betty Hutton, in Las Vegas, was battling with her drummer-beau: "She's beefing about the way he's banging his bongos"? That a trusted aide of Batista was "in Gotham incognito"? That Johnnie Ray's wife had flown to Atlanta "just to be near him"?

On weekends, Dorothy commuted to New York to appear on "What's My Line?" These were particularly rewarding times. Her fellow panelists, who did not approve at all of *VOB* were genuinely impressed with the quality of her trial coverage and always eager to hear Dorothy's thinking on the murder. Even stuffy John Daly must have thought that this was the real thing.

Then there were the *de rigueur* New York social situations, which Dorothy could not miss. On leaving Cleveland once, she told a local reporter that she was going home "for an evening with her three children and her husband." Actually, she was catching a plane for the opening of the Metropolitan Opera, which she attended with Richard. They were a glittering couple, he in white tie and tails, she in ermine and diamonds. She took the time to turn out a piece for the paper, bemoaning the abundance of "television-blue" in the formal attire of the men.

Even in Cleveland, Dorothy was compelled to function as a celebrity in residence rather than as a full-time trial reporter. Nervous as a cat, she stood and fielded questions from fifty aspiring high school journalists, telling them of her beginnings at the *Journal*, the importance of reading to a good writer—mysteries especially, because they trained one to remember details—and her abiding admiration for her father.

"How do you have any time for your family?" one of the youngsters asked.

Dorothy replied in a soft, solemn voice, "My husband and three children are more important to me than anything. I wouldn't miss their school plays or any other school meeting that was important to them."

Typically, she captivated the young crowd with her surprising warmth and her apparent fragility. One of them wrote: "A true picture of this charming individual is never seen." [22]

Dorothy ran into trouble with a colleague at the Sheppard trial because she could not put in the time required for normal court reporting. Ordinarily a writer covering a running trial story must be on hand every moment of the time, have a colleague do backup if he or she has to leave for a short period of time, or split the work with an associate. For an odd and wayward assortment of reasons, Dorothy made no accommodations for the long periods of time during which she was not in court, and then either could not or would not admit that someone else's copy was being used under her by-line.

Jack Lotto, a burly, ambitious, award-winning journalist, was covering Sheppard for the Hearst afternoon syndicate. His stories, in the beginning, were being run side by side with Dorothy's on the front page of the *Journal:* By Jack Lotto, INS. Because New York was Lotto's home, he derived particular satisfaction from such visible play.

As the trial progressed and it was generally perceived at the *Journal* that the Kilgallen by-line was responsible for a soaring circulation, it was apparently decided to incorporate the best of both under Dorothy's by-line—her flashy, frequently extraordinary prose and his journeyman's, nuts-and-bolts reportage. The practice is not uncommon where a paper has access to the work of two reporters.

Lotto grievously resented his relegation to anonymity. He had worked, as a very young reporter, on the rewrite desk of INS and had frequently fashioned Jim Kilgallen's telephone reports into viable news stories. He had not relished it even then. "The star goes out, covers the story, and often the unsung hero is the rewrite man in the office," he observed. "After a while, you say to yourself, 'This guy's famous and I'm writing more stories than he is.' "

After two George Holmes awards and a career of distinction, Lotto was being treated like a cub reporter: "Now I'm up against his *daughter* and the same thing is happening." [23]

He went to see Dorothy. She had, by this time, left the

noisy press room, where more than forty representatives of the nation's leading newspapers were working shoulder to shoulder, and had insinuated herself into a semiprivate office occupied ordinarily by a detective and two officers of the court. She had pulled it off by feigning temporariness: "Do you mind if I put a couple of things down on your desk? You're not using it now? Are you sure?" A beachhead was eventually established. She had her very own desk, and the detective who shared the little room plugged in her electric typewriter every morning.[24]

Lotto told Dorothy: "Your stuff is appearing in the *Journal*, but it's my copy."

Dorothy replied icily, "I would not permit your copy to appear under *my* by-line." [25]

The Lotto-Kilgallen skirmish became a joke among the press corps. They avoided each other at the Express Grill.

Memos flew between Lotto's people and the *Journal* editors, who denied his accusations. On Friday, December 3, a day when Dorothy apparently could not be in court at all, Lotto took two stories and pasted them side by side: the story from the *Journal-American* that appeared under her by-line, the story from the Pittsburgh *Sun-Telegraph* that appeared under his by-line, and his original Western-Union duplicates thrown in for good measure.

With the exception of some minor differences in editing, they were the same story:

> *Para. I, Lotto:* The brother of Dr. Sam Sheppard loaded a gun and rushed upstairs into the murder bedroom without talking to anyone on the morning Marilyn was clubbed to death.

> *Para. I, Kilgallen:* The brother of Dr. Samuel Sheppard today admitted he loaded a gun and rushed upstairs into murdered Marilyn Sheppard's bedroom without talking to anyone on the morning his sister-in-law was clubbed to death.

> *Para. II, Lotto:* This testimony was given today by Dr. Stephen Sheppard under heavy prosecution hammering and a demand to know how he knew where to go and why he took a gun and not a medical bag.

Para. II, Kilgallen: Under heavy prosecution hammering, Dr. Stephen Sheppard was unable to explain how he knew where to find the body and why he took a gun and not a medical bag.

Lotto attached a note as he sent the package off to the *Journal:* "I rest my case."

The only reply he received from Dorothy, who was obviously apprised of the situation by her office, was a copy of a Western Union message:

Memo to Jack Lotto
From Dorothy Kilgallen

Quote from Edward Mahar, assistant city editor of the Journal
"Lotto is 1,000 percent wrong. His lead was not used Friday or any other time under your by-line. If he wants any further information, have him call me." [26]

Dorothy never spoke to Lotto again. Jim ignored him for months. And a considerable time passed before the *Journal* consented to use any of his stories.

Dorothy was, of course, lying. Given the turbulence that Jack Lotto caused, there was no way that she could have remained unaware that his copy was, at times, appearing under her by-line.

But her lies were never simple. It would not be surprising if she saw herself, in this case, as the injured party.

She could not be in court all day long. And the *Journal* had no right to expect it. Astoundingly, she was always a kind of package deal to Hearst. She made less than most of the male columnists—half of what was paid to sports writer Bill Slocum. When she agreed to put her life on remote to cover a trial such as Sheppard's, they gave her only expenses, no extra pay. There would not be a bonus when she returned. The accounting department would even complain about her large tips to ladies' room attendants. She would blush and say, "But it's *expected* of me," and the matter was dropped.[27]

Since she could not be in court for an occasional surprise, her editors had done what they had done for the good of the paper. She could not have been that keen about having Jack Lotto's stuff under her name. But it had been done and to admit it now would have been to betray her editors, who had lied to him first. Further, Lotto had broken one of the unwritten laws of journalism and other professional activities. Stars got top billing, sometimes all of it. Do presidential speech writers blow the whistle? Lotto had put everyone in an embarrassing position.

Dorothy must have realized, too, that any breach in public confidence could be disastrous. Had it leaked out that some of Dorothy's writing was not Dorothy's, it would have eventually been bruited about that none of it was hers, which was a far cry from the truth. Had there been the slightest doubt, her reputation as flimflam girl reporter would have been seriously imperiled. That was to be avoided at any cost.

"She liked to be thought of as a good trial reporter," recalled Theo Wilson, the dean of trial reporters. "I could tell that from the things she said and the way she acted. She *wanted* to be one of us. And she was up to a point; and she wasn't up to a point.

"She could not be. It wasn't anybody's doing. That's just how it was. She was a celebrity and that made a difference." [28]

At the Express Grill, where hamburgers were 40¢ and nobody's check ever came to more than $1.83, Dorothy and the rest of the press corps measured the passing time at Sheppard's trial by what got most play on the jukebox. They discussed the case to "Papa Loves Mambo" in October, "Let Me Go, Lover" in November, and "Adeste Fidelis" in December.

Dorothy was certain that the jury could not convict Sam Sheppard on the evidence, nor on the testimony of Susan Hayes, the witness supplied by the prosecution in an attempt to supply motive. Sheppard, they implied, had done the foul deed out of love for this pretty laboratory technician with whom he had had a brief love affair.

She made it a point to be in court when Susan Hayes testified in December and wrote, under the headline SUSAN TELLS ON DR. SAM:

She was a nervous witness but in a way impressive. Her voice, though quavery, was well-bred, and she gave the appearance of testifying honestly if with reluctance. She remained in control of herself throughout the ordeal.

The attire was perfect courtroom garb for "the other woman": the slim black dress, the restrained black hat, and the one touch of innocence—the white collar. She looked pretty and neat and almost chic. Clean-faced and clear-eyed, errant perhaps, but not flamboyant.[29]

No, Dorothy was not buying the almost-chic Susan Hayes as the motive for the murder, especially because the stylish doctor had not even attempted to telephone her in four months. She printed and became identified with and subscribed to Dr. Richard Sheppard's evaluation of the prosecution's case, which he related to her in an exclusive interview: "It makes as much sense to say Dr. (Sam) Sheppard killed Marilyn because she made him blueberry pie that night and he distinctively told her he wanted apple."[30]

None of the reporters were permitted to meet Sam. But the accused wanted Dorothy to know how much he appreciated her stories. He dispatched his brother, who caught her by the arm as she prepared to leave the courtroom. "Dorothy," Dr. Richard Sheppard said, "Sam asked me to thank you for the article on him and Susan. He says it couldn't have been better if he'd written it himself."[31]

She was pleased, and the *Journal* had a banner edition, based on the secondhand reaction: DOROTHY KILGALLEN EXCLUSIVE: Dr. Sheppard Says: "I Didn't Love Susan."

The jury was out for five days. On Tuesday, December 21, they voted to convict. Blythin sentenced, "It is the judgment of this court that you be taken to the Ohio penitentiary, there to remain for the rest of your natural life."

Dorothy was appalled. Under the screaming streamer that gave primacy to her response, DOROTHY KILGALLEN ASTOUNDED BY VERDICT, she excoriated the jury:

The prosecutors for the State of Ohio did not prove he was guilty any more than they proved there are pin-headed men on Mars. . . . I have covered a score and more of murder trials. This is the first time I have ever seen what I believed to be a miscarriage of justice in a murder case. It is the first time I have ever been scared by the jury system and I mean scared.[32]

Her column was dropped from the Cleveland paper the next day. She would be linked indelibly in the public mind with the fate of Sam Sheppard, though her real impact on the skein of juridical events would not be perceived for a decade: She kept Blythin's confidence.

Dorothy sailed through the early Eisenhower years on the Good Ship *More-of-Same*.

She covered the storybook wedding of Grace Kelly of Philadelphia to Prince Rainier of Monaco, indicating to friends and editors that she had entrée to the serene couple. Actually, she had made a deal with a New York couturiere to personally deliver an evening gown to the bride-to-be. She was devising to use the gift to secure an interview with Grace. When she got to Monaco, neither Rainier nor Grace was talking to her on account of some items she had run about the actress and her past suitors. She was royally snubbed, the package was accepted by a maid, and Dorothy was reduced to relying on her wits for whatever advantages she could secure. Which was all right, too. At the lavish wedding, Dorothy feigned a case of vapors right after she got a look at the beautiful bride, covered her face with a handkerchief, and hied out of the church to the bidet shop she and Bob Considine had rented as an office. Dorothy had her story in before most of the other 1,197 representatives of the world press, with the possible exception of some of the English reporters, who, she contended in one of her dispatches, made everything up.

She sat one day at the Hôtel de Paris with Bob Considine. They drained their teacups and complained about the lack of news. As Dorothy stared plaintively in his direction, Considine clasped his hand over his cup. "Stop reading my notes," he said.[1]

In the summer of 1956, Dickie took off again. This time he was gone for more than twenty-four hours. Questioned by detectives, the boy said he had spent most of that time in Central Park. It fell to Richard to deal with the crisis, because Dorothy conceived of discipline as the husband's role.

"Dickie and Dorothy would get through to each other," Jean Bach observed, "but when he took off, it was Richard's department to deal with it. I'm sure if the kid ever wrote a letter to her and said, 'Hey, Ma, I'm really unhappy. I want you to look after me!' it would have been fine. But there were errors on both sides, and he would pull away and not try to get to her. Richard dealt unimaginatively with the problem." [2]

The fourteen-year-old was sent off, this time, to experiment with ranching in Laramie, where his grandfather had edited the *Boomerang* forty years before.

Dorothy was still making stabs at keeping the marriage sparky. For her husband's forty-sixth birthday, she flew Bobby Short in from California to be the surprise attraction at Richard's party. Richard had not seen Bobby since Paris. "The plan was engineered with all the secrecy of a surprise attack upon an enemy," the pianist recalled. "There were calls to the airport. I was supposed to arrive at just the right hour to be at the piano when Richard came into the room." [3]

For the time, Dorothy's behavior with regard to blacks was laudably liberal. Many of her friends socialized with black people for the first time at Dorothy's house. At one party, Lillian Boscowitz was seated next to singer Al Hibbler, who was not only black but blind. He took Lillian's hand, felt the enormous diamond on one of her fingers, and commented, "Oh, I see you're very beautiful." [4]

Of course, one had to be the right kind of black to be invited to Dorothy's parties, but, also, you had to be the right kind of white.

Dorothy danced with Bobby Short at the Plaza Hotel at a time when mixed dancing simply didn't happen at the Plaza Hotel. She did not intend it to be a revolutionary gesture; such a display would have been anathema to her. She and Bobby were at Eartha Kitt's opening. When the music began, Dorothy said to him, "You're probably a very good dancer." He replied, "Would you like to dance?" And they did. Bobby was thunderstruck. There was neither incident nor comment.[5]

"What's My Line?" remained one of the hardiest television shows in the country. Dorothy, in these years, continued to be perceived as the prosecutorial one around whom a group of loveable, cosmopolitan wits played the game just for the fun of it. The producers introduced a wild-guess segment into the format. "I think he raises goldfish," Dorothy hazarded one Sunday night. "I think he lowers goldfish," Steve Allen countered.

The panel of stalwarts was still subtly divided against Dorothy. The wedge widened between Arlene and Dorothy when the columnist printed an item about Humphrey Bogart, who was a close friend of Arlene's. Dorothy implied that Bogart was dying of cancer at a time when his wife, Lauren Bacall, maintained he was trying to believe he'd recover. Dorothy got the tip from the lesbian lover of a comedienne, who'd gotten it first from one of the nurses attending him. Bacall was furious and Arlene totally sympathetic.

"I thought Dorothy was a *marvelous* journalist," Arlene said, "when she covered something like the Sheppard trial. As opposed to her gossip column. Betty was furious and she was right. Whose business is it? Is it anyone's business to know that?" 6

In the early part of 1956, Johnnie Ray appeared on "What's My Line?" as a guest celebrity. The twenty-nine-year-old singer, sandy-haired and boyishly lanky, was still headlining in clubs, though the hysteria of the early 1950s had cooled. He remained, however, one of Dorothy's pet-pailletted crushes. Endsville!

Dorothy, with her blindfold in place, was mystified. Arlene picked up on him and sallied in for victory. "Are you the young man who made crying a national institution?" she asked.

After that appearance, Dorothy and Johnnie began to see each other socially. In Johnnie's words: "We decided to be nice to each other." That meant, among other things, that she stopped japing at him in the column. She could only be a viper at a distance.

During one of their first evenings out, they went, with a group, to a screening of *An Affair to Remember*. The movie starred Deborah Kerr as Terry McKay, an attractive and witty nightclub singer, and Cary Grant as Nick Ferrante, an attractive and witty playboy. They fall in love aboard a luxury liner while each is on the way to marry another. They decide to break off their respective engagements and meet six months later on top of the Empire State Building. Terry is, alas, struck by an automobile while on her way to the skyscraper and is crippled. She falls out of sight but not out of Nick Ferrante's mind. When he catches up with her finally, she is lolling on a sofa pretending not to love him and not to be crippled. As Vic Damone sings:

> *Our love was born with our first embrace*
> *And a page was torn out of time and space*

the playboy fathoms the situation and vows his eternal adoration.

Johnnie sobbed through the movie. Dorothy wept. She gave it considerable space in the *VOB*, raving that it was a boon to those "who are getting tired of pictures about dope addicts, alcoholics, unattractive butchers, and men who sleep in their underwear." [7]

After the screening, the group, which included the Bachs and Elaine Lorillard, founder of the Newport Jazz Festival, went to an opening of Count Basie's. Dorothy and Johnnie finished a bottle of vodka between them.

Presently, at forty-four, Dorothy began her first affair.

Johnnie did not possess the polish and panache to which Dorothy had gravitated all her life. He was tender, guileless, show-biz smart but essentially neither intellectual nor verbal. One of his first friends in New York had been Wyatt Cooper, who eventually married Gloria Vanderbilt. Johnnie talked to Wyatt about wanting to become an actor.

"In that case," Wyatt Cooper said, "you'll want to see *Peter Pan*. It's playing at the Winter Garden."

"I don't know," Johnnie replied in his soft, smoky voice, "I've never liked Shakespeare a whole lot." [8]

He was born John Alvin Ray in Oregon, the son of a lumberman. The almost total deafness he sustained when he fell at a Boy Scout jamboree went undetected for a time. He was mocked by his schoolmates and passed his days in class staring dreamily out of windows. He had always sung and played the piano; it is thought by some that his furious, rocking style derived from his inability to hear his own music.

Johnnie did the usual knocking about after graduating from high school. His hearing aid and his odd, frenzied style were redoubtable impediments in the beginning. He claims, however, that he always knew he would succeed in show business. And after being rejected in an early attempt to break into movies, he climbed a hill overlooking Hollywood and screamed, "Someday, you'll all know who I am!" [9]

Despite his professed readiness, his sudden and staggering success was a traumatizing experience. There had been nothing comparable to it since the early crooning of Frank Sinatra. Mobs came at Johnnie brandishing razors to snatch a lock of hair or a hank of suit. At the Palladium in London, he was compelled to quell a riot that his presence had provoked by climbing out on the roof and waving at the throngs of hysterical women. He was secreted out of the Paramount in New York—where he broke all existing records—through a hidden tunnel. "The problem with that tunnel is that it led to a part of *The New York Times* where they load papers on the trucks. And once you were there, you weren't anywhere." [10]

He became distrustful of people and occasionally tempestuous, though he could be brought down with humor. During a rehearsal once, he was dissatisfied with the performance of his musicians and railed at his drummer, who was named Cappy, about the fact that he was, after all, a star, a very big star.

Cappy countered quietly: "Twinkle. Twinkle." [11]

Johnnie surrounded himself with managers, accountants, musicians, and chums. His life became a series of frenetic road tours interrupted by excessive drinking, at which point Johnnie was rendered rather helpless. In 1951, he was arrested in Detroit for making an "indecent proposal" to a plainclothes vice-squad policeman who specialized in entrapment. He remembers little about the episode except that the cops convinced him, for the sake of his career, to plead guilty and pay the two dollars.

The following year he married Marilyn Morrison, the daughter of a Los Angeles nightclub owner. The ceremony was performed at a suite in New York's Warwick Hotel. The president of Johnnie's Brooklyn fan club fell upon his chest and sobbed.

The couple settled in an apartment on Sunset Strip, to which the bride's sister and Johnnie's manager moved.

After seven months of dormitory life, she and Johnnie split.

His life consisted of late company, heavy drinking, and an entourage of free-loading boon companions. Dinner was spaghetti out of a can. A night on the town was taking fourteen people, in two limousines, to the Bon Soir in Greenwich Village. He made few accommodations on Dorothy's behalf, which was all right for a time. He claims to have loved her.

Johnnie, Johnnie, Johnnie lit up the life she had. She mentioned him so often and so effusively in the column that he had to tell her to cool it.

She had a group at the time, which met every Monday afternoon at P. J. Clarke's. The group, for no particular reason, called itself the Science Club. Its membership included Bob Bach; Howard Rothberg, the interior designer; Bill Harbach, a television producer; Jim Downey, who was in advertising; and Lou Stoecklin, an executive with a whiskey company.

They gathered at a round table in a little alcove under a pendulumless clock. They ate chili, played the jukebox, invented games, discussed the nature of the wine and the state of the world. Mystery guests were invited. Minutes were kept. And a good deal of laughing was accomplished.

When Johnnie was in town, he sat by her side and attempted, with more heat than light, to join in the games, one of her favorites being the Song Game, in which participants tried to match an isolated snatch of lyric to the song from which it was derived.

"Whose broad," Dorothy offered.

South Pacific was the immediate consensus: "There Is Nothing Like a Dame."

"No," Dorothy chided. "That's who *is* broad where a broad . . ."

Total bewilderment.

Dorothy said triumphantly, " 'The Star Spangled Banner'—*Whose broad* stripes and bright stars."

If Johnnie was not in town or unavailable, Dorothy frequently introduced his name into the conversation while she played his records in the background. When Howard Rothberg was secretary pro tem, he kept the minutes of the meeting in French. One Monday they read in part:

Mr. Stoecklin a dit 'Paul a lassié le vin respirer' . . .
Le nouveau disque de Mr. Johnnie Ray, *"Strollin'*
Girl" a été jouer pendant toute la réunion, il est des-
tiné pour le "Hit Parade." [12]

Dorothy did nothing to hide the relationship from Richard. But it is doubtful that he apprehended the nature of it in the beginning. By 1957, Richard had opened and was presiding at an elegant little restaurant, which he called the Left Bank. It was an attempt to bring something unique, namely style, to the West Side of Manhattan. He called himself a boniface and wrote in his letters to celebrities whom he was attempting to recruit as patrons, "How far West can the East Side get?"

The Left Bank featured fine French food, posh settees, a cocktail pianist who could play every tune Cole Porter ever wrote, and an opportunity for Richard to do whatever swinging he was still capable of doing. He kept a well-appointed third-floor apartment, to which he brought his women. Pianist Lee Evans, who began his professional career at the Left Bank, recalled, "It was conquest after conquest. There was no one face that I saw for any period of time." [13]

In opening a restaurant and accessing himself to a bar, Richard made the heavy drinker's worst possible mistake. He was tanked most of the time. Worse, to alleviate his maddening insomnia, he began to take barbituates recklessly.

His punchiness was a joke among the staff. One night they all hovered over him as he attempted to deposit the receipts in the club safe. He was hunkered down precariously, diddling unsuccessfully with the combination lock. One of the waiters joked, "Boston Blackie's lost his touch!" [14]

Johnnie and Dorothy were at the club quite a bit. He sometimes sat down at the piano and played. There was talk, but Richard was cordial to Johnnie. "He was in no position to be anything else," the singer recalled. "Dorothy and I were both on to him." [15]

There were times when Dorothy joined Johnnie on the road. To avoid any possible problems at home, she confected a traditional cover. Jean Bach went with her to Chi-

cago, where Johnnie was opening, and then took off to visit
her mother. In Chicago, Dorothy indicated to Johnnie that
she wanted to catch a young comic about whom she was
hearing a good deal—Lenny Bruce. Johnnie knew Lenny
and his work, and tried unsuccessfully to dissuade her. He
was well aware of her reputation as top prig and her power
to injure a performer.

They went to a little club called the Cloisters. Johnnie
excused himself and went backstage to warn Lenny to keep
it clean. Lenny said, "Give me a kiss on the cheek and get
out of here."

When Lenny Bruce walked out on the stage, the first
words he spoke had to do with oral copulation. Johnnie
ordered a couple of vodkas and thought, "Well, his career
is over." He looked at Dorothy, who appeared amazed but
interested. She started to giggle and then, in her new and
unconstrained way, to laugh.[16] Dorothy became one of
Lenny Bruce's most ardent followers.

Dorothy was totally and terribly in love with Johnnie.
Jean Bach recalled Chicago: "Anything that he introduced
was interesting to her. She was on cloud nine because it
was all so perfect. She told me that as far as she was concerned it would never be over."[17]

She came to Johnnie with staggering emotional and physical appetites. She had not had any sexual relations with
Richard for years. What they had had together had apparently not been fulfilling to either. She was naive and in-
experienced and had to be taught a great deal. "God, she
was starved for affection," Johnnie said. "Sometimes I
didn't know how to handle it."

She felt no guilt, or none of which he was aware. "We
came to peace with the Catholic problem," he maintained,
"once we decided to have some kind of commitment. It
resolved itself, though it didn't resolve itself in terms of
her mother finding out."[18]

Johnnie was fond of Dorothy, and attracted to her, and
a bit in awe. He did not have the macho peer problem that
turned so many men off. That she was not regarded by the
community as beautiful did not affect his feeling for her
or his pride at being seen with her.

"She was probably the most *feminine* woman I've ever
known," Johnnie said. "And I always thought she was a

pretty lady—the softest thing you ever touched. All the people that made fun of her—that was just plain sick. I've always been a very ordinary-looking man. I'm neither cute nor ugly. It never occurred to me why all those girls were screaming. I thought it was just a fad that would pass. And it did." [19]

This was a period when Dorothy needed desperately to feel beautiful and desirable. Whatever insecurities she had about the way she looked, she at least, in more polite times, passed muster in terms of the feedback she got from the world. Now her enemies were beginning to strike back at her in a most brutally effective manner, right out in public.

Frank Sinatra began the trend. He had provocation. She had been sniping away at him for years. She published his New York address. When he moved, she published his new New York address. She wrote a series about him on the front page of the *Journal*. It began,

> Success hasn't changed Frank Sinatra. When he was unappreciated and obscure, he was hot-tempered, egotistical, extravagant, and moody. Now that he is rich and famous, with the world on a string and sapphires in his cufflinks, he is still hot-tempered, egotistical, extravagant, and moody.[20]

There were references to his obsession with Ava Gardner, whom she called "the most gorgeous creature who ever walked." When Ava left the singer, according to Dorothy's articles, an agent from William Morris was assigned to Sinatra

> just to do his bidding, soothe him as much as possible and try to keep him from slashing his wrists.[21]

Dorothy attacked Frank Sinatra so often and so multifariously that none of her friends was able to determine which straw finally broke his camel's back.

When Sinatra decided to *get* Dorothy, he did it from the floor of the Copa in New York and the Sands in Las Vegas. Old blue eyes broke between "Young at Heart" and "The Second Time Around" to tell the people what an ugly broad he thought Dorothy was. He likened her face to a chipmunk's. And, as far as such a thing is determinable, he had the distinction of coining the term "the chinless wonder."

Nick Lapole of the *Journal*, who had taken several perilously litigable Sinatra items out of *VOB*, caught Sinatra's act at the Copa: "There was a lot of laughing from his entourage and from the people in show business on whom she had been tough." [22] Igor Cassini heard his material in Vegas: "He was really very, very nasty. People laughed." [23]

Word got back to Dorothy, and she was shattered. Friends did not have the heart to broach the subject with her, but there was an awareness that he had accomplished precisely what he had set out to do. She talked to Edgar Hatfield about suing. Hatfield advised her that the tirades were not actionable.

Actually, Dorothy was no more "chinless" than either of the Gish sisters, who were considered to be rather good looking in their time. What Sinatra did was alter the public perception about Dorothy, to cause her to be seen in a new way by people who did not like her. The "What's My Line?" mail, for instance, had never focused on her unattractiveness before Sinatra's remarks. Now the cry was, "Get that chinless wonder off!" Mark Goodson observed: "Any leader who starts that will get a follow-through. He makes it permissible to say what would normally be considered very rude." [24]

The effect upon Dorothy was immediate. She went to an opening on Broadway with a young record producer, Ben Bagley. She was feeling very glamorous and jolly. They had plans for the later part of the evening. They got out of her limo hand in hand, passing in front of the barriers that the police had erected to hold back the crowd. Suddenly an old shopping-bag lady broke through the line and came right up to Dorothy. "Hiya, chinless," she shrieked.

"*I* was stunned," Bagley recalled. "Even as her escort, it was like being hit in the face. Dorothy's hand began to shake. She would never speak about it. Never mention it. After the play, I took her home." [25]

Dorothy needed Johnnie to love her, to make love to her, to see her as a soft and pretty woman. The relationship played out in the present, with Dorothy nurturing a vague idea of future change. They made love in his apartment. She saw him during the afternoon, when she was supposed to be at the hairdresser, and almost always on Sundays,

after "What's My Line?" His unaccommodating life pre-
cluded privacy. His people, many of whom resented her,
were in the living room with complete awareness of what
was happening in either the bedroom or the den.

Stylish Dorothy was not about to stint on an affair of
the heart; consequently, word of the liaison filtered back
to her household. Every month Myrtle Verne's new assistant, Pearl Bauer, received a bill from Carey Cadillac for
five or six hundred dollars. The bill was puzzling, since it
showed waiting time at an apartment house where, coinci-
dentally, both Myrtle and Johnnie resided.

"Would you mind telling me something," Mrs. Bauer
said to Myrtle one day, after receiving the bill for a month's
limousine service. "Does Dorothy visit you at night?"

Myrtle, who deplored Richard and wondered only what
had taken Dorothy so long, said, "Oh, no. She goes to see
Johnnie Ray."

"You must be kidding," Pearl Bauer said.[26]

Dorothy taught Johnnie to eat snails, though she could
never convince him that caviar was palatable. He taught
her that Central Park was for walking. And, on some of
those walks, she even abrogated her lifelong aversion to the
wearing of slacks.

She brought him gifts from Bergdorf's and Cartier, including a pair of cufflinks with diamonds and sapphires,
which he was afraid to wear because of their value. He
sent her lavender roses when he could get them from his
little corner florist: "They were almost steel-blue and gorgeous. I think they were brought in from Holland. I could
never understand why she loved them more than pink or
red." [27]

She was as sentimental as a pop tune. Johnnie was constantly receiving surprise packages. A note might arrive reminding him of an anniversary. One of them, he recalled,
was delivered by messenger and written in Dorothy's lovely
hand. It said: "This is the third Thursday since we had
chili at P.J.'s." There was another package from Steuben,
containing twin decanters engraved, "Just Gin" and "Johnnie's Vodka." [28]

She tried, often without success, to mesh their lives.
Most of her friends objected to Johnnie's drinking, his raw
exuberance, and his rough edges.

She invited Orson and Carrie Munn to a party at Johnnie's apartment. Orson Munn was a socially prominent New York patent lawyer and founder of *Scientific American*. Carrie had been Dorothy's dress designer for many years and was one of the first deb-celebs to be featured in *The Voice of Broadway* in 1938: "At the Colony, Carrie Munn, collared in ropes of pearls and assorted necklaces, puts salt on her butter." The Munns and the Kollmars had dune-buggied together in Southampton. They were understanding of Dorothy's need for affection.

At the party, Johnnie grew restless. He constructed a track of chairs in his mammoth living room to display the agility of his equally mammoth dog, which Carrie Munn remembers as a big, black Doberman. At Johnnie's command, the dog jumped, too close to the Munns for comfort. Carrie Munn recalled:

> It came right at me, and I said to Orson, "Let's get the hell out of here." Which we did. The whole thing was so wild, though the dog didn't seem to disturb Dorothy because she knew him so well by that time.
>
> I never saw him again after that. Orson said that he didn't want him around. When he came into the picture, a lot of her friends didn't want to be with them, didn't want to be seen with him.
>
> But she brought him around to everybody.[29]

The Boscowitzes were the least kindly disposed to Johnnie and everything they thought he represented. Johnnie consented to see them on Dorothy's behalf, but they were not among his favorite people. One night Dorothy invited them to join her and Johnnie on an excursion to a Third Avenue joint called the African Room, which was, for openers, not one of Hubie and Lillian's favorite continents. The foursome passed through the crowded front room, Hubie showing signs of displeasure at the look of the patrons at the bar. Dorothy assured him that it was better in the back. When they arrived, Hubie said, "It smells terrible in here."

Johnnie said stubbornly, "I don't smell anything."

Hubie seethed, "If you'd take that thing out of your ear and put it in your nose, you'd smell it!" [30]

*　*　*

To this day, the wealthy couple are incredulous about the relationship. They sat and chain-smoked in their lavish drawing room.

"They tell the story of their being at Morocco," Hubie said. "He took her shoe off and kissed her foot."

"To keep the vestige of the friendship we had left, we had to keep our noses clean," Lillian said.

"Very frankly," Hubie said, "we didn't get Mr. Ray's message in any way, shape, or form. It had to mean that we weren't going to see as much of her."

Lillian said, "If she had divested herself of him, we could have continued our close relationship. But I'm afraid everything had gotten off-kilter. . . . Why Dorothy—being such a sensitive person—couldn't see through this man, I will never understand. It was so obvious the way people treated him. You would have supposed that would make her think a little bit. But it was completely blind."

"They wound up a twosome!" said Hubie.

"She was *mad* about him," Lillian said. "She didn't want to waste any time away from him when she had the opportunity to be with him. He wasn't even scintillating conversationally. . . . But when she was with Johnnie Ray she was extremely happy. She was exuberant." [31]

The music people on whom Dorothy had, for two decades, focused lavish and respectful attention were more understanding of the changes in her. Singer Thelma Carpenter happened upon them in a show-biz-cum-gay-club called the Grapevine. Thelma had known Dorothy casually for years and was a special friend to Johnnie since the time she had saved him from himself by placing him in a cab when he was hopelessly drunk, decked out in kilts, and in a most vulnerable state. At the Grapevine, Johnnie asked Thelma to dance. When they had finished dancing, Dorothy was no longer speaking to her. Thelma Carpenter had heard some talk about the nature of the relationship, but she hadn't believed it until that night.

That was the first time I felt, "Hey, she does dig him." My response was can you be-lieve it. Johnnie Ray and Dorothy Kilgallen—the odd couple. I couldn't fathom this pillar falling for him. But there was no doubt that she did. And she didn't give a damn when she was with him. She didn't even care.[32]

Musical-comedy actress Carol Bruce had harbored mixed feelings about Dorothy. A vagrant item in *The Voice of Broadway* had almost broken up an early marriage of hers; yet Dorothy had been otherwise very generous to her, from the time she made an overnight success as Julie in *Show-boat* through the many problem periods in her singing career. During a particularly bad time, Carol was on her way to the incinerator to burn all her scrapbooks. She decided to take one last flip through the pages and noticed that the books abounded with plugs from Dorothy. Carol said:

You can't take issue with a lady who's been that good to you on account of one incident, but I always thought she was a *cold* woman, and I wondered, "Who is she? What is she *really* like?"

During the period that Dorothy was seeing Johnnie, I used to run into them at the old Basin Street East. On one or two occasions, I joined their party. And, man, she had come to life with a crash and a bang. All of a sudden, she was looking glamorous and alive. She really seemed more beautiful then. I felt she was like the princess in the story being awakened with a kiss.

They were drinking pretty good. Pretty good. But I thought, "Good for her. She's having fun." She was real, less rigid, more unbending. I told a friend of mine, "I don't know what happened, but I think she's joined us."[33]

On a Saturday morning in October, 1959, Dorothy was making up in her bathroom to leave for the Yale-Columbia football game with the Boscowitzes and Richard. She became suddenly ill, fell back, and hit her head on the marble floor. The Boscowitzes went on to watch Hubie's alma mater, Columbia, trounce Yale. A doctor was summoned for Dorothy, who was taken to LeRoy Hospital, where she remained for more than two weeks.

Faye Emerson substituted for her on "What's My Line?" Julia Meade held up Dorothy's end of the chatter show. And the press agents monitored the Broadway scene on her behalf.

Jean Bach visited her at the hospital, bringing along singer Andy Williams as a bonus. Dorothy had tubes runnng into her hands. "Everything is going fine," she told Jean. "I'm making my own blood again." [1]

This was the first of several episodes the exact nature of which is obfuscated by the unwillingness of the many doctors who treated Dorothy to divulge any information.

The waters remain muddied. Many of her closest friends were told, by Dorothy, that she had a form of anemia. A United Press story described her condition as "exhaustion and anemia." [2] At some point, it was feared that she had Hodgkin's disease. Despite rumors to the contrary, she did not have any form of cancer. Such conditions would have shown up on her autopsy report.

Kerry Kollmar recalled transfusions, a bevy of specialists, and the early knowledge that there was something seriously wrong with Dorothy. Of course, he was told almost nothing, except that she had the best doctors available. [3]

The vague, catchall term *anemia* must, therefore, suffice. Whatever part her increasing drinking played in the decline of her health this early on, she was advised to curb it and be less cavalier about the care and feeding of Dorothy Kilgallen.[4]

Her tart and contumelious views were not noticeably affected by the state of her health or by her feverish sexual affair with Johnnie Ray. Indeed, her most notorious and vigorous imbroglios were yet to come.

In 1959, the *Journal-American* dispatched their favorite girl reporter to cover the visit of Premier Khrushchev, his wife, and children to the United States. Khrushchev's mission was to last nine days, during which time he was scheduled to see President Eisenhower, address the United Nations on the balance of power, and stop over in several major American cities.

With owner-driver Roosevelt Zanders at the wheel of the Rolls, Dorothy followed the Russian leader over the course of several days, beginning with his dawn touchdown at Andrews Air Force Base. She reported that the rotund Russian leader stuck out his tummy and waved at her.[5]

Dorothy, however, was more interested in Mrs. Khrushchev's avoirdupois. Dorothy had always characterized by couture. Her vehement anticommunism was most readily aggravated by the lackluster trappings of Marxism. Grandmotherly Nina Khrushchev became, therefore, a natural target for Dorothy's careless animosity.

And so she wrote, on the second day of the state visit, with regard to Mrs. K:

> The grisliness of her attire amounts almost to a demonstration of piety. . . . It would be difficult to find clothes comparable to hers in the waiting room of a New York employment agency for domestic help; in this decadent capitalistic republic, applicants for jobs as launderesses, chambermaids, and cooks usually are far more a la mode than Russia's first lady.

Mrs. Khrushchev's blue-and-gray suit she called

> dismal . . . wrinkled . . . at least four inches shorter at the hem than is currently correct. . . . It had no point of view, right or wrong. It was just there like a home-made slip cover on a sofa.[6]

Her editors, themselves fierce cold-warriors, were obviously tickled pink, playing her captious copy under the banner headline:

OUR MISS K SAYS MRS. K'S CLOTHES
FIT LIKE SLIP COVER

There were, alas, some unpredicted reactions. Reader mail was heavy, and it ran anti-Dorothy in the extreme. "Shirley," the pseudonymous *Journal* secretary, recalled that four typists were assigned to answer the indignant letters. Albany petitioned the Hearst hierarchy to rein in Dorothy's *ad hominem* attacks while the Russian first family visited New York. For perhaps the first time in Hearst history, Bill Hearst and aide-de-camp Frank Conniff admitted for publication that they had permitted a staff person to overstep the limits of good taste. Conniff commented to an outside reporter, "Nobody raised a flag on that till it was over. We all passed it and then, suddenly, somebody said, 'Holy Gee, maybe we did blow one.' " 7

What was said to Dorothy is not clear. But that she was censured was obvious by the pettish defensiveness of her subsequent copy. After a reception for the Russian leader, she limited herself to: "His wife and daughters whipped out evening dresses." Further along in the story, she whined that Khrushchev's visit had "set usually clear-headed Americans to arguing whether international relations are harmed by describing them [the clothes of the Russian first family] in accurate detail. When Queen Elizabeth visited this country her attire was described stitch-by-stitch, silhouette-by-silhouette, hour-by-hour. And the proper English never got mad at us." 8

Dorothy's troublesome brickbats were hurled in the Wednesday paper. That Saturday, in place of an *apologia*, the *Journal* devoted a good part of the editorial page to a conspicuous display of their angry reader mail.

One Constant Reader opined:

Her column on Mme. Khrushchev was not only in bad taste, but revolting to any American woman who places the big issues involved in the USSR Chairman's visit beyond the patterns of clothes, size, etc. It rebounds on all of us provincial, snobbish people, and reacts most favorably to the maligned lady.

"A new low," said another letter writer. And six *Journal* faithfuls co-signed an acerbic message that ended, "We are ashamed of Miss Kilgallen."

Dorothy was accustomed to absolute fealty from her paper, to retaliation rather than capitulation. She was fully aware of the significance of the publication of the hostile reader mail. And since she had been encouraged by her editors to attack full throttle, she was now probably feeling doubly betrayed. Dorothy tendered her resignation.[9] *The Voice of Broadway* did not appear on the following Monday.

The appeasement steps were standard: telephone calls to Dorothy, a sweet-talking lunch at "21," a recitation of her value to the organization.

By Tuesday, *The Voice of Broadway* was heard again in the land.

Ruth Montgomery, of the Hearst Headline Service, had also done a good job on Mrs. Khrushchev. She called her a "dowdy spouse" who "waddled on puffy feet and swollen ankles." [10] Though she had been even more savage than Dorothy, she took far less heat in the national weeklies. Montgomery was a molehill; Dorothy had become a mountainous cultural phenomenon. Marya Mannes, an articulate and distinguished liberal, was among the few writers who chastened both Kilgallen and Montgomery. She wrote a poem in the *Reporter* that ended: "Pity not her, but ladies of the press / Who rate a people by the way they dress."

Dorothy had never been a popular figure. There exists no evidence, for instance, that she ever had a fan club. Ludicrous as they may be, it is astounding that no little group of pubescent girls organized to know more about Dorothy or to endeavor to emulate her.

From the late fifties until her death, she grew more notorious than she had ever been popular. The *zeitgeist* was pervasive. And now, as if by some premonition of weakness, her enemies were emboldened.

Dorothy was prideful and scrupulous about the probity of "What's My Line?" In almost ten years of playing the game, she took liberties once only. Motion picture mogul

Sam Goldwyn was slated to appear as the mystery guest on the show. He ran into Bennett Cerf and said, "I'll be seeing you on Sunday when I'm guesting on 'What's My Line?' " Cerf moaned and explained to Goldwyn what he had done wrong. Goldwyn then encountered Dorothy and told her the amusing story of how he had inadvertently tipped his hand to Cerf, whereupon Dorothy also moaned, "Oh, Sam!" On Sunday, she and Bennett Cerf played the game as usual, trying blindfolded to tread water and elicit only *no* answers from the legendary flapdoodle. The round turned out to be a travesty and henceforth she determined properly to disqualify herself if such a situation recurred.

When the maitre d' of swank Maxim's signed in as an occupational rather than a mystery guest, she happily disqualified herself. It was as much a source of pride to her to recognize the Parisian notable as to be recognized by him. When a fireman who had put out a blaze in her house the week before appeared on the show, she did not have to disqualify herself for the simple reason that she did *not* recognize him.

Dorothy's fierce vigilance vis-à-vis her good name and the integrity of the show was manifest in Edgar Hatfield's client file. The lawyer had reams of retractions that he had sought on her behalf from writers who impugned its honesty. A 1956 item from a column identified only by its name, "Channel Chatter," typifies the Hatfield collection: "Channel Chatter reported that Dorothy Kilgallen was able to see through her mask. The statement was erroneous. Channel Chatter meant no harm to anyone and apologizes for the incident."

In 1959, at the height of the quiz show and payola scandal, Jack O'Brian, the truculent television columnist and a former friend to Dorothy, began running blind items about the integrity of the Goodson-Todman shows and "What's My Line?" in particular. He charged in his column that material was supplied to panelists "for purposes of heightening the public's acceptance of the panelists as exceptionally funny and smart people." [11]

At the time, such an accusation could be disastrous. A congressional committee was investigating the whole area of rigging and payola. People tainted by scandal were cashiered from the industry.

Dorothy was so infuriated by O'Brian's allegations that

Bob Bach and Mark Goodson rushed over to East Sixty-eighth Street to calm her down. She had already written a strong denial of the O'Brian smear, which appeared in her column, beckoning him to

> mention me by name rather than by innuendo so my lawyer can take it from there. . . . I do not think "What's My Line?" should be classed with the "rigged" shows as it has been by a local television critic. . . . The show is neither fixed nor semi-fixed. I would like to go on record as saying that I have never been "supplied" with any questions, answers, helpful hints, or jokes by the producers, director, or anyone else connected with "What's My Line?" and when I say on record I mean on record. I will repeat that under oath to District Attorney Hogan [of NY], the grand jury, or the congressional investigation committee.

She added that Arlene, Bennett, and John Daly had lived lives of honesty and integrity and were also "above reproach." [12]

Shades of High Noon at Lindy's. The feud was on. O'Brian blinded a nasty item. In retaliation, Dorothy dispatched a private investigator,[13] possibly to confirm a report that O'Brian accepted one thousand dollars from a Philadelphia department-store owner, Max Hess, to publicize Hess's enterprises. The fee was paid to O'Brian ostensibly for an appearance on one of Max Hess's local radio programs; door-to-door limo service was also provided.[14] O'Brian does not deny that he accepted the fee (though he cannot remember whether it was $1,000 or $500), but "I never mentioned the Hess Department Store in my column," O'Brian insisted.[15]

Whatever Dorothy discovered about O'Brian and Hess was written, submitted, and set up in type. It was ready to go at the *Journal* when, at the eleventh hour, a newspaper employee loyal to O'Brian called the television columnist. O'Brian telephoned Hearst executive Richard Berlin and implored him to stop the presses. Berlin agreed on condition that he never mention Dorothy, Goodson-Todman, or "What's My Line?" in his column again.

Dorothy's *VOB* appeared half its normal size that day. Eventually, Dorothy sent intermediaries to attempt to patch up the feud. He was having none of it. O'Brian walked into the Stork Club one night with Walter Winchell. Dorothy said, "Hello, Walter. Hello, Jack."

O'Brian fumed, *"Hello!* Don't talk to me as long as you live because you're a filthy, low, malicious, vengeful, rotten woman. I don't ever want to talk to you again. You're completely out of my life." [16]

A very good hater, Jack O'Brian waited.

During her vinegary salad days, Dorothy controlled two of the only available outlets for the ventilation of personal grievance: the Broadway column, which from Winchell's day had invested frightening power to its purveyor, and the radio chatter show, which she had turned into a forum for the broadcasting of blistering personal opinion.

Now the burgeoning talk format on television became a formidable foe to Dorothy. First, it provided a showcase for publicizing personalities and their properties far more effectively than print. Winchell had had his *Hellzapoppin,* and Dorothy her Bobby Short. But no bouquet from Winchell and certainly no encomium from Dorothy could compare, in effectiveness, to what a Jack Paar or a Mike Wallace could do for the likes of Barbra Streisand, Hans Conreid, Mimi Hines, Alexander King, Dody Goodman, or Peggy Cass, all of whom became stars through the projection of their personalities on the talk-show format.

In addition to making television stars out of personalities the *oeuvre* helped usher in an era of candor that began to make the seriously injurious gossip column obsolescent. When people tell on themselves, the professional tattler is rendered somewhat redundant. Moreover, the talk show encouraged the dicey, the opinionated, and the off-beat angry to ventilate their own grievances. Performers, who were once at the mercy of columnists, were no longer hamstrung by their roles. If they could cut it, they were all commentators. It was no accident, therefore, that Dorothy and other Broadway columnists were the prime target of the hosts and participants affiliated with the talk format, the most successful of which reached more people with more impact and intimacy than the most widely read syndicated column.

Hermione Gingold, the English actress and comedienne, appeared regularly on "The Jack Paar Show," which provided her with immediate celebrity, a soupçon of clout, and all the work she could handle in the theater. She toured one summer in a musical review in which she did an attic-rummaging number called "Souvenirs." The high point in "Souvenirs" was Miss Gingold holding up an old photograph of Dorothy and framing it with a toilet seat.

Dorothy was intrigued when she heard about the routine and asked Ben Bagley to find out what he could about it. He called the producer, who confirmed timorously that Miss Gingold was indeed framing Dolly Mae with a toilet seat Tuesday through Sunday and twice on matinee days. Bagley asked the producer for a reading of the material and repeated it to Dorothy.

"She will smart for this," Dorothy said with mock toughness, "the *nerve* of that woman." [17]

Gingold fared no worse than before in *VOB*. Dorothy had always found her somewhat unattractive as a performer. But the only vengeance exacted was on Bagley, who was required to submit to Dorothy's terrible impression of Hermione Gingold performing "Souvenirs."

Dorothy was becoming fully aware of the degree of hostility she provoked. She could be shattered or amused or incredulous. But she was finally dealing with it.

Johnnie Ray had dealt with it from the beginning of their relationship. He had so often recited his litany about "the real Dorothy" being separate from the column she wrote and the impression she created on "What's My Line?" that he tired of the words and simply abandoned any attempts to defend her.

One weekend she planned to fly to Dallas to see him perform in *Guys and Dolls* at the State Music Fair. A local television station learned about her intended visit and planned a short interview with her. They asked Johnnie to meet her at the airport and help set it up. Milling among the television people, he overheard the usual repertoire of anti-Kilgallen cracks. As she disembarked, he kissed her on the cheek, took her arm, and warned, "They're waiting for you, honey. They're *just* waiting for you."

She sighed with resignation, "I know it." [18]

As a satellite of Dorothy's, Richard was fair game. In his case, word was out and had been for some time among New York's illuminati that he was a homosexual.

Those who proposed the theory as "common knowledge" pointed to the fact that he was surrounded by men who were known to be gay. Jimmy Gardiner, for instance, was particularly flagrant. The little studio drew its share of homosexual artists. And the Left Bank became a gay gathering place especially during the cocktail hour, which is bound to happen in a tasteful place that features a pianist who knows every song that Cole Porter ever wrote.

Stories about Richard's purported homosexuality had begun circulating in the fifties, when a business partner of his appeared at a party with scratch marks on his face, etched, it was subsequently bruited about, by an enraged Dorothy, who discovered him and her husband together. There are those who claim to have been at the party and to have seen the scratches. There are those who claim to have been at the party and to have seen no scratches. The rumor was fanned, no doubt, by Richard's talented impression of a stereotypic male homosexual—a flawless, subtle arching of the spine, amused his friends handily.

The rumors appear to be utterly without foundation. No one who knew him well, gay or straight, can confirm that Richard was anything other than a strictly heterosexual reprobate who adored beautiful women. Lee Nordness, who was close to him at the little studio, commented: "I never saw *any* indication. And I saw Richard all the time. Even their social friends would come by the gallery and make absolutely bitchy remarks about Dick and some man. And I would be flabbergasted." [19]

Richard was not unaware of the resilience of such rumors. They bothered him. When Lee Evans, who was an attractive young man, first started entertaining at the Left Bank, he was rather naive and often went to Richard for advice. Another man who regularly frequented the club asked Lee to dine with him and then go to the theater. Lee knew him to be a homosexual. He also knew him to be influential in the music business. "Maybe I should go," Lee Evans said to Richard. But Richard was adamant: "Don't be seen with him in public. He'll stigmatize you." [20]

Rumors are true or not, but as a cultural phenomenon, they are seldom gratuitous. They gratify or they don't survive.

Richard's gift for imitation notwithstanding, he could not take credit for the robustness of the rumor about his homosexuality. A multitude of Dorothy's detractors was delighted to think that he was. They were saying, in effect, that *she* was so unattractive that only a man who liked other men would tolerate sharing a life with her.

In Johnnie's case, the situation was a bit more complicated. But it was almost as if her enemies would not consent to acknowledge the fact that she was having a lusty sexual affair with him—as though they refused to credit her with conquest, albeit of a complex and ultimately destructive nature.

When the *New York Post* sent out five of their reporters to research "The Dorothy Kilgallen Story," an exhaustive, in-depth, somewhat hatchety series that ran in the spring of 1960, her relationship with Johnnie was pointedly dismissed as platonic:

"In recent months," the *Post* stated

> she has often been in the company of singer Johnnie Ray, a troubled young man whose career suffered serious setbacks in the past few years. Her relationship to Ray has been described—there has never been a hint of anything else—as "maternal and protective," and sometimes her maternal instinct is positively fierce.
>
> "I saw her at the Waldorf with Ray," a friend recalled. "She left the table for a moment and some young, pretty girl usurped her chair and proceeded to tell Ray how good she thought he was. Dorothy came back, flew at the girl telling her to 'Keep your hands off my escort and leave the table.' It was the only time I ever saw her lose her temper in public."
>
> "It's an odd relationship but it's certainly antiseptic," said society photographer Jerome Zerbe. "Ray is rather an insecure person and she gives him security and companionship. And he's an excellent escort for her—her husband is busy so many evenings. It's one of those relationships that is mutually satisfactory." [21]

With all their manpower and all their digging, it is remarkable that the *Post* would take pains to emphasize the platonic nature of the relationship. By the time the series was published, Johnnie and Dorothy had flaunted their manifestly sexual desire for each other far and wide.

During an elegant party at Howard Rothberg's, Betty Lee Hunt, the press agent, caught their act on a double chaise, one of Howard's best pieces. "They were lying on that double chaise of Howard's giggling and fondling and boozing. There must have been ten other people in the room just as *amazed and embarrassed* as I was. But it didn't make any difference." [22]

Nick Lapole, who had been asked back to Johnnie's dressing room when the singer was headlining at Basin Street East, discovered them in a heated embrace and quietly withdrew.[23]

According to Dan Lavezzo, the owner of P. J. Clarke's, they regularly sat at one of the front tables and "necked in the corner with the whole world watching." [24]

Michael Sean O'Shea was moved by what he saw when she and Johnnie danced together at a benefit in Chicago. O'Shea loved Dorothy and had known for a long time about her situation at home. "They were clutched together so tightly there was nothing between them," O'Shea recalled. "It was wonderful to see if you understood what her life had been like. She idolized him. It was almost like a mother holding a teenage son in her arms. It was just so close, so intimate." [25]

Jack O'Brian was less kindly disposed. An avowed enemy of smut, rigged quiz shows, communism, and adultery, he roiled at the sight of them. He recalled disdainfully:

> The *groping* of each other and the *kissing* and the *necking!* Two tables away from me. This is no hearsay. I observed it myself at El Morocco and the Stork. It turned out that while she criticized other people, *Miss* Kilgallen was not too blameless in her own life.[26]

Drinking, of course, had a great deal to do with the radical change in Dorothy, though it was as much a symptom as a cause. Dorothy had been a good drinker all her life; she was one of the few columnists who managed to drink in moderation on her nightly rounds. Now she was keeping up with Johnnie, who drank enormous quantities of straight vodka.

Marlin Swing met Johnnie in 1959, when the singer starred in a short-lived show that Marlin produced for CBS. He befriended Johnnie and eventually became one of

Dorothy's closest confidants. He accompanied them once to Trader Vic's, a posh Polynesian restaurant. Marlin settled for a less exotic brew, but both Johnnie and Dorothy ordered Scorpions, very large, very potent, very rum, with gardenias floating on top. They laughed and drank and handed the flowers to Marlin, who fashioned them together. By the time the threesome left Trader Vic's, Dorothy was trailing a daisy chain of thirteen imported gardenias.[27]

Exhibition, one must suppose, played some part as well. Johnnie had one arrest and a reputation to overcome. Dorothy had no arrests and a desire to prove that somebody wanted her. They knew that people were watching and talking. Johnnie contended: "Maybe we weren't the most discreet people in the world. But we were having the most fun. . . .[28] At certain times people got uptight, but that was their problem. I was never reaching for her boobs. We were just two people having a good time and enjoying each other. Where does it say we're supposed to be saints?"[29]

Primarily, Dorothy was not so much exhibiting herself as taking what she could when she could, coping indiscreetly with a wild and unmanageable lust. In her mid-forties, she had suddenly shed an outer skin that had protected her for her entire life. This late late-blooming passion was permitted no peace. Johnnie would never build for her a safe house, a sanctuary. Having no tough second skin, Dorothy would be badly burned.

There was a radical change in Dorothy, but change within a framework. She altered her sensibilities to accommodate her obsession, but she was still basically a fantasist. Dorothy knew about the men in Johnnie's life. There was no way, this side of dementia, that she could not have known. She simply refused to endow them with any significance. And Johnnie gave her reason to hope. He had always considered himself basically heterosexual. The men in his life were exigent, unimportant, the result of the superstardom that he perceived as somehow unnatural and constricting. He did not tell her anything that he was not telling himself.

Dorothy saw male homosexuality as mincing and flagrant. In the absence of beaded bags and silver lamé, she would not acknowledge a perilous predilection.

She was lunching once with Jean Bach, and the name of

a common acquaintance came up. The man surrounded himself constantly with nubile boys who would have made Tadzio of *Death in Venice* appear positively butch. Since Dorothy liked him a great deal, because he was once married, walked flatly on the balls of his feet, and talked a good game of heterosexuality, she took him to be still marriageable.

"Mark [a pseudonym] is really very nice," Dorothy said tendentiously to Jean.

"He's all right," Jean replied, not meaning it at all. In fact, she thought he was a lean and hungry social climber. He populated his famous parties by bagging one biggie and then announcing to his other guests that the biggie was bagged. "Anyway," Jean said, stressing the positive, "he's gifted."

"You really don't appreciate him," Dorothy continued. "He said to me, just the other day, 'If Jean weren't married, that's just the kind of girl I'd like to marry.'"

Jean sighed and marveled at her dear friend's gee-whiz-worthy naiveté.[30]

Jean remembered, "She loved being surrounded by men. And they were all supposed to be mad for her. She couldn't conceive of the fact that they might prefer some big, hulking guy to her. Johnnie had this resident. And she'd go out with the two of them. It looked like she was twice as popular." [31]

Dorothy's commitment to Johnnie's essential availability was irrecusable. One of his future road managers, Bill Franklin, would comment: "She was a typical proper lady. Dorothy was just jealous of the women in Johnnie's life. And she seemed to have no doubt that some day, somehow —she would end up with Johnnie." [32]

When Dorothy entered Johnnie's sphere, he was involved with a young man who modeled under the name Steve and acted under the name Stan. He was a pleasant chap, and Dorothy liked him well enough, though she could never decide whether to call him Steve or Stan and decided on Steve-Stan, alternating with Stan-Steve. Her little joke angered Johnnie for some reason.

Then there was a gaunt, baby-faced Englishman who will be called Monty (not his real name), staying at Johnnie's apartment. He was on a temporary visa and planned, he maintained, to return to England straightaway. On Johnnie's behalf, she used her considerable influence to have the visa extended, which was a big mistake. He claimed to come from a wealthy, landed family, but he had no profession and no visible means of support. Like so many of the people who surrounded Johnnie, Monty was a leech. And fond of Johnnie. And fonder still of his well-stocked bar.[33]

Johnnie, Monty, and Dorothy became, in the most respectable but nevertheless nettlesome sense of the word, a threesome. If Dorothy invited Johnnie to an opening night, Monty tagged along. When they returned to the apartment after a rare night out alone, Monty, who was already tawny with cirrhosis, sat up in his favorite chair and drank until he passed out. Dorothy and Johnnie did not make love in the apartment while Monty was there. Since Monty was ubiquitous when not comatose, they were forced to confine their displays of affection, in an even greater degree, to posh and public settees in *boites* all over Gotham.

Dorothy was undeterred when Johnnie was arrested— again in Detroit—for allegedly "accosting and soliciting" a policeman for "immoral purposes."[34] The incident occurred in a bar called the Brass Rail where Johnnie had gone late one night, with four men, to wait for a musician who was doing some musical arrangements for him. While Johnnie waited, Eugene Caviston, who represented himself as a salesman, came up and asked Johnnie for an autograph. Caviston handed him a handkerchief on which the singer wrote, "To Gene—Glad to know you. Your buddy always—Johnnie Ray." Caviston mumbled something and disappeared.

As Johnnie left the club, a police car backed toward him with its lights atwitter, and Caviston flashed his badge. "You're under arrest," he told Johnnie, which came as no surprise.

"I have nothing to say," he replied, remembering the last time.[35]

At the trial, Caviston claimed that Johnnie had invited him back to his hotel for a drink, making an indecent suggestion in the process. Johnnie maintained that his proposition included only a nightcap.

A jury of twelve women deliberated. When forewoman

Rose Pracinga stood and read the verdict for acquittal, Johnnie felt his knees buckle with relief. He fell into a faint. Rose Pracinga rushed toward him, cradled his head in her arms, and keened, "Oh, the poor boy!" [36]

Newspapers around the country, including the New York *Daily Mirror* and the *Daily News*, had their front-page story and their centerfold spreads. The *Journal* eventually ran a small and decorous item on the inside pages.

During the week between arrest and trial, Dorothy used her influence to assure Johnnie a fair trial.[37] She volunteered to take the stand as a character witness, but was told by his attorney that it would not be necessary. When he returned to his apartment, a group of friends waited to greet him. He rushed toward Dorothy and embraced her. Johnnie asked Dorothy whether it was advisable to sue. She told him that a suit would constitute a problem, since the burden of proof would fall to him. Within minutes, they were all laughing.[38]

The Boscowitzes were hard put to understand the unshakable faith that Dorothy had in Johnnie. During the time of the arrest, Lillian remembered that Dorothy insisted the charge could not be true: "She said it wasn't that way at all, that she knew him too well." [39]

Whichever way it was, Johnnie could not alter his style of living sufficiently or commit himself to her satisfaction.

Dorothy had a little room on the fifth floor of the house that she called the Cloop. Kerry Kollmar speculated that the name could have been a play on *reclusive;* but the definite origin is indeterminable. The Cloop was Dorothy's sanctuary at home. A telephone was installed there. Only Johnnie knew the number. It pleased her to know that when that phone rang, it could only be he. They would talk for hours.

She telephoned him—too often, apparently, for Johnnie. There were times when he pretended to be unavailable.[40]

When she was out with him, Dorothy endeavored to prolong their evenings. She never seemed to tire. She hated returning to her house. When they argued, it was almost exclusively about his availability.

"I've had it, honey," he would say. "I'm goin' home to bed. This boy's tired."

She asked frequently to go home with him.[41] Sometimes he used Monty as an excuse for the space he neede̶ more often he referred to the line he felt compelled to draw between his house and hers. She would whine in her little-girl's voice, "But why can't I go with you?" He was firm in the distinctions and limitations he imposed.[43]

With any semblance of sobriety, Johnnie, caring less, maintained the upper hand.

Dorothy ventured to California in early 1960, to cover the
trial of society surgeon Bernard Finch, accused of shooting
his wife, Barbara, once in the back while his co-conspirator
and mistress, Carole Tregoff, cowered in a clump of bou-
gainvillea. The two were tried together at the new Los
Angeles County Court House. Dorothy stayed at the Ambassador Hotel, and was back and forth between coasts for
more than a month.

In spite of the wealth and attractiveness of Finch, who,
to Dorothy's dismay, insisted upon being called Bernie, the
trial had none of the classical dimensions of the Sheppard
trial. The crime was a slapdash do-it-yourself job done after
a hoodlum named Cody took payment for the hit twice
from the lovers, lost his nerve, blew the money in Vegas,
and then lied to Finch about having done the murder.

"You must be nuts," the doctor was reported to have
said to Cody. "I called my home this morning and talked
to my wife."

"Well, I killed some woman," Cody improvised, to justify
the expense he had not expended. "I put the body in the
trunk of an automobile standing in the street, near the
Hollywood Hills Hotel." [1]

At this trial, too, Dorothy employed her characteristic
taxonomy to buttress her judgments about credibility and
culpability.

Carole was "a pretty chic number, a brunette with a
come-on smile, a figure that would make a preacher leave
town." Of Finch, she quite approved: "gray . . . getting a
bit bald on top, but his profile is aristocratic and his smile
has great charm." But he was no Sam Sheppard. She imputed to Carole Tregoff a power that she had not permitted
Susan Hayes. After she managed to obtain a personal interview with Finch, Dorothy allowed for the alliance as a

feasible motive for murder. "The doctor does not look like putty," she reported. "He looks more like leather-encased steel, but the legend of the siren who can make strong men weak is old and undying." [2]

Cody she described as "a grifter, a forger, a bum. He looks like a dissipated choirboy, and he calls a photograph a 'pitch-uh.' " [3]

She was baffled, therefore, by the reported meeting between the surgeon and his prospective hit man. She wrote, "How do you account for a country club and fashionable chap like Dr. Finch having cocktails and dinner or anything else with someone as socially remote as the shady, shifty Cody with his ear-splitting grammar and his terrible clothes?

"This trial is more than a whodunnit," she wrote. "It's a who'd believe it!" [4]

She seemed to be having a good time in California. She was photographed at Ciro's with Johnnie, looking lush, loose, and attractive. Her borders had disappeared. Her hair was a bit frizzed and Hispanic; her breasts seemed finally to be self-governing. She leaned in toward Johnnie, who was handsome in his light dinner jacket.

The modernity of the courthouse delighted her. The press room was something to write home about. And in a way, she did:

> It is not only commodious but clean . . . gauzy pink curtains and comfy couches. There is a large round table in the main room that looks as if it would be perfect for a poker game, and a gadgety little hot-plate shelf for perking coffee or fixing snacks. No, Daddy, I am not making this up; it exists.[5]

The place was packed with celebrities. Actor Mark Stevens testified for the state. Actress Terry Moore of *Mighty Joe Young* fame attended, explaining that she was doing research for a forthcoming role in *Girl on Death Row*. There was a producer, a screen writer, and someone affiliated with television's "Perry Mason"—all researching.

Only the celebrity-writers—Pamela Mason and Jayne Meadows—abraded Dolly Mae. She called them "reporters for a day" and claimed they "generally have their stories half written before they get to the scene." [6]

On the day the jury was scheduled to come in, Dorothy invited guests to court: Clifton Webb, Sonja Henie, and society matron Cobina Wright. Cobina called Dorothy early in the morning for reassurance. "Now, darling," she asked, "are you *sure* it's going to be interesting today?" [7] Dorothy wrote:

> Sonja looked adorable in a pale blue cashmere sweater that matched her eyes and her courtroom jewelry, a square star-sapphire and diamond clip the size of a library card.[8]

Though the ambience was *ancien régime*, Dorothy's professional behavior remained strictly old Hearst. She wrote glowingly of the rugged good looks of several of the court's officers, suggested, in print, that one be screen-tested, and even arranged for the test.[9] She did think him "terribly cute" and irritated Johnnie by going on about him. The talk among the press corps was that information was being leaked to her about the sequestered jury's deliberations, which lasted eight days.[10] There was no way that she could have used what she was learning, however, while the jury remained out.

She acquainted herself with Eddie Bright, a Runyonesque savant who ran a newspaper stand outside the courthouse.

She was flying to New York every weekend to appear on "What's My Line?" At the close of one show, in response to John Daly's traditional, "Good night, Miss Dorothy," she replied, "Good night, John. And good night to Eddie Bright and to all the rest of the gang at the new courthouse. See you tomorrow."

Bright was flabbergasted. "I almost fell outta bed," he said. "Imagine such an important dame saying good night to me." [11]

Back in 1954, at the Sheppard trial, she had made newspaper history with the headline in which her name was featured above the verdict. That was a mixed blessing to Dorothy, who resented any assessment of her work that detracted from the presentation that she preferred—Daddy's little girl, the reporter's reporter. Al Davis of the *New York Post* had impressed her and Jim, after the Sheppard verdict, when he came out the next day with the personal recollections of the jury, which he obtained by driving around Cleveland for most of the night knocking on doors.[12] Dorothy couldn't drive and wasn't about to knock on doors, but she decided to replicate the Davis coup.

At the Finch trial, the jurors emerged from the courthouse, having been unable to reach a verdict. A mistrial was declared. Jurors and press were asked by the judge not to communicate. His instructions were roundly ignored by the hoards of press people who descended on the tired jurors, most of whom simply wanted to go home.

Dorothy waited for her chance. She approached one of the two jurors responsible for the deadlock, Dolores "Jim" Jaimez.

"Hello," she said, "I'd like to introduce myself. I'm Dorothy Kilgallen. You want to get home, don't you?"

"You're right," Jaimez said. "All these questions."

Jaimez called to a fellow juror, Eddie Lindsey.

Dorothy walked into a clump of bushes where the flabbergasted Eddie Bright had told her the cab company maintained a hidden telephone. Within minutes, a taxi arrived. The three climbed in. Tired as they were, they were thrilled when Dorothy Kilgallen invited them back to the Ambassador for a drink in her suite.

It was Saturday evening. They drank and talked about the trial. Jaimez produced a book for her with his day-to-day account of the jury deliberations. She excused herself and telephoned her paper.

"I have two of the jurors—the men who wouldn't convict Finch and hung the jury—here in my room," she said. "Do you have somebody who could take quotes from me?"[13]

She was given high marks for the exclusive and for her coverage of the Finch and Tregoff trial—both of them were convicted of murder in 1961 and sentenced to life—even by *Time*, one of the many snide weeklies that loved to hate Dorothy Kilgallen. *Time* wrote:

> In Los Angeles, busy Dorothy sometimes attracted more attention than the trial. She posed for pictures with the defendant, signed scores of autographs for admirers, received an orchid from an unidentified California judge. Yet, for all that, her copy, rattled

off on an electric typewriter in her hotel room, provided the best coverage of the Finch-Tregoff trial.[14]

While covering Finch, she took a two-hour lunch break with her old beau Kit Kuittinen, who was, by then, a successful trial lawyer in Los Angeles. They reminisced. He sensed a fatigue in Dorothy that transcended her redoubtable work load.[15]

Neither one of them had produced a novel or anything between hard covers. *Girl Around the World*, which was a collection of Dorothy's dispatches on her air race, had been put together in book form by Herb Spiro.[16] When she returned from the Finch trial, Bennett Cerf asked her to do a book for Random House. She and Cerf agreed that it should focus on the famous trials she had covered over the years. Not an anthology, but a retrospective—a book about murder, murder trials, Dorothy's experiences reporting them. She thought she could knock it out in a year.[17]

She hired a research assistant to go to the public library and duplicate all of the reams of copy she had filed in the thirties: on Mary Creighton, lacer of chocolate pudding; pitiful Anna Antonio, whose only legacy was a spaghetti recipe; the Murton-Miller-Farber case, during which she had scooped Sheilah Graham; Jessie Costello, "the Smiling Widow"; Eva Coo and Dorothy's roadhouse dance partner, Harry Nabinger; and poor Bruno Hauptmann. (Myrtle now pasted everything written by and about Dorothy in scrapbooks, including her employer's day-to-day trial coverage. Early on, Dorothy had adhered to the cavalier newspaper tradition that scrapbooks were sissy stuff. Consequently, the retrieval process must have been formidable.)

Dorothy was scared and diffident. She telephoned James Horan, who had risen high in the Hearst hierarchy and was also a prolific writer of books. She asked him astonishingly basic questions—like how to begin.

"I guess I'd do a detailed outline first, Dorothy," Horan said. "But you know what it's all about. If you're going to do it, you've got to sit down and do it."

Horan would comment: "It was a very interesting part of her life: the need to do something which she considered more important, more tangible." [18]

Bennett Cerf was amazed that Dorothy, who had written so prolifically for so many years under deadline pressures, should suffer any anxiety at all. Someone very close to the publisher, who does not wish to be named, wrote that Dorothy was "delighted" by the prospect of a book, but "terrified" of not coming up to Bennett Cerf's literary standards.

Dorothy forestalled beginning through the use of one of the more traditional chips off the old writer's block: she redecorated. Not one room in her five-story town house had the proper preexisting ambience for her. She redid the Cloop. Almost a year passed before she considered the room a proper office. In the meantime, she continued to use it as a retreat and a bedroom.

Once, of course, when her life was controlled, restrained, and predictable, she could drop off to sleep at the emplacement of a mask. But she had lost that talent along with the control. From the accounts of those closest to her, she began, like Richard, to rely increasingly on barbiturates to sleep, in addition to her use of alcohol. Pharmaceutical records would indicate that the drug was Seconal.

If she was depressed about something Johnnie had done or said—or *not* done or *not* said—she usually telephoned Marlin Swing. By 1960, he was probably her closest friend. A soft-spoken, intense, highly intelligent man, he began his professional life as a musicologist and was working toward a Ph.D. at Columbia University when he yawed off into broadcasting. He was in awe of Dorothy at first ("She represented the New York I wanted to be a part of. When I was out with her I couldn't believe it, little me and Dorothy Kilgallen. I told her that. Openness was the basis of our relationship."); his feelings turned to love, concern, and deep respect. She would cry if there had been a problem with Johnnie. Under the influence of the barbituates she lost all her natural defenses. She did not always make a lot of sense. When Marlin perceived that she had been drinking as well, he kept her on the telephone, verbally walking her.[19]

Bill Franklin, who would manage Johnnie presently and serve as another of Dorothy's confidants, described similar late-night calls begun by Dorothy's revealing, "I just took a good-bye." He likened her attitude to "a little girl's," beckoning, "Tell me a story, Daddy." [20]

* * *

Below Dorothy's Cloop resided her putative responsibilities. The fourth floor was the children's, though two of them hardly qualified as children anymore. Dark-eyed Jill, at sixteen, came closest to Dorothy's fantasy of blue-book issue. She was poised and attractive. She was an accomplished pianist, Mother Leo apparently having done her job well. Marlin Swing was amazed at the skill with which she played a difficult Katchaturian toccata. Jill had vague theatrical aspirations. At the Knox School, she played the Josephine Hull part in *Arsenic and Old Lace* in 1960 and did very well, indeed. Dorothy journeyed to see her with her parents and was moved to tears by the adeptness of her performance. She left a note for Richard, who planned to see it the next week: "Lambsie—She was Daddy's girl and just wonderful. You would have been so proud—Chop." [21] At school, Jill was popular and funny. Like many children of celebrities, she was wary of exploitation. Jill knew about her mother's relationship with Johnnie and she did not approve.[22]

In one of the traditional profiles about Dorothy, obviously approved word for word by its subject, she described her daughter as:

> A very sensible girl. For the past two years, she has done her own shopping and buys things so simple and chic and has such good taste. She wouldn't think of walking out of the house without gloves—although, honestly, it took me five years to indoctrinate her.

About eighteen-year-old Dickie, she commented,

> It's an excellent example of history repeating itself. He's studying privately because he didn't want to go to college. He was dead set against it, and I've never been one to pressure children. Besides, he could say to me, as I said to my father, "You didn't need a college education." [23]

Privately, Dorothy hardly talked about Dickie, who had turned out to be a disappointment to her. He wasn't studying privately, though he was a great reader. And he was not only dead set against college, he had not finished prep school. When that profile was published in 1960, Dickie was working for the Ocean Beach Sanitation Service on Fire Island. To the *Fire Island News*, he submitted an Emersonian paean to the glories of his recently chosen life-style. The essay read in part:

> It is revealed that after all I was suited to become a civil servant. Garbage collecting is not without advantages. It is a wholesome form of labor which lights the soul with that warmth that is usual after a day of true accomplishment. The early hours which I keep restrict my social activities to a small but highly virtuous and almost moral sphere.[24]

Perhaps he had, after all, written that letter to Dorothy of which Jean Bach spoke, though it was more a declaration than a petition.

Kerry, at six, was cute and captivating and always in trouble. He attended a small, exclusive school on the East Side, St. David's, where he was instructed by Jesuit laymen. Bill Hearst sent his children there. Buster Crabbe had taught him to swim. Kerry was a talented natural athlete.

He was poignantly protective of Dorothy, defensive with regard to the unspoken accusations that she was not the best of all possible mothers. He missed the companionship of a father, adored his older brother, and resented it mightily when Richard foreboded that he was in great danger of turning out like Dickie. "What really worried him, I think, is that he was afraid I'd turn out like *him*," Kerry Kollmar commented.[25]

On Saturday mornings, while the rest of the household slept, six-year-old Kerry repaired to the Black Room, turned on his cartoons, lit up a cigarette, and poured himself a shot of Scotch, laced heavily with Coca-Cola. "I guess," he said, "I wanted to get into adult things like my parents." [26]

Dorothy adored him and was forever repeating his *bons mots*. Once he watched her getting ready for "What's My Line?" She put on a pair of chic and scanty sandals. "Why are you wearing shoes that can hardly be called shoes at all?" he asked her.

She struck him only once, when, as they were passing on the staircase, he made some obnoxious child's comment. Kerry hit her back. Dorothy, who was not built physically or emotionally for contact sport, ran crying for her husband.

He was aware early on of his parents' problems. When there was no school, he was welcome to enter the broadcast room, read the Anbesol commercials, and sit on his mother's lap. "My father was falling asleep in his coffee," Kerry remembered. "They were both, of course, bleary-eyed. It's amazing that they sounded as good as they did." [27]

Dorothy did everything she could to hold up the breakfast show. She charmed sponsors, attended their parties, and primed herself, torpor notwithstanding, to sound light and lively. The broadcast was the lynchpin of their lifestyle, netting them easily sixty to seventy thousand a year in 1960. It paid for St. David's, Knox, the cook, the butler, the upstairs maid, Anne Hamilton, and the shoes that weren't shoes at all.

Though they fooled their audience for a while, the savants at the station were aware that the contrapuntal vigor had gone out of "Dorothy and Dick." There was a period of about a year when the show was prerecorded. Jim McAleer, who eventually functioned as their producer, recalled, "His voice was beginning to start sounding sick, and who needs that." They recorded at noon for play the next day, but WOR was still not happy. "There's nothing like a live show," McAleer said. "You can't beat it for sound and spontaneity. And it's cheaper." [28]

In a typical program of that year, Dorothy sounded as compelling and irritating and mobile as ever. She talked about attending the wedding of Princess Margaret:

> You know the mental block I have about filling out forms, darling. Well, since I'm going to England next month, Myrtle checked my passport and decided I had to renew it. But I did get at least one little kick out of filling *this* one out. It said "Give the number of countries you were in in the past five years." And I thought, "Oh, golly, what countries was I *not* in in the past five years?" But I did get a little pleasure out of the part that said, "Where are you going? Duration of stay?" I put "Duration—one week. Purpose—to attend the wedding of H.R.H. Princess Margaret."

She talked about a new word game she was playing, about buying a deerstalker hat for Kerry just like the one Prince Charles wore, about the Finch trial and a recent opening of Lena Horne's that she had attended with "the gang," with whom her listeners were apparently already on first-name basis. Howard and Don were Rothberg and Linsley. Marlin was Swing. And Dorothy was Gray. At the opening, a representative of Air India had approached her, asked for an autograph, and requested that she come along on an inaugural flight. Howard apparently had gotten a "big kick" out of repeating "Madam's" response to the man, to wit, "I'd certainly love to go. I haven't been to India in ages!"

Dick said, "You were never to the Taj Mahal?"

"That's an I-Have-Never," Dorothy chattered, referring to the game in which one collects a dime if one has *not* done something that one suspects all the others in the group have done—"I wonder what I'd collect on *that* around *our* set."

It was obvious to any astute listener that Dorothy's set was not Dick's set. But more important, it was obvious that the other half of "Dorothy and Dick" was, these days, doing little of anything. His most exciting contribution to the show was a slice-by-slice account of a raid he had made on the household refrigerator the Sunday before, quickly adding and probably dissembling when he said that he was on his way to meet her.

Dorothy responded patiently, as to a putz at a party.

DICK: Sunday night I was raiding the icebox before— er—meeting you and I experimented with something I haven't eaten in a long time. And I am rather annoyed. Someone has taken the excitement out of liverwurst.

DOROTHY: Well, darling, I'll tell Mr. Ferrari. What seems to be the trouble?

DICK: I don't know. It's lost some of its fun somehow.

DOROTHY: Well, if you could sort of pinpoint. What did you have with it or before?

DICK: Oh, I had an assortment of things. I ate a chicken leg. And you know I think I'm the only one in this house that loves the drumsticks. They always seem to be left there. And I thoroughly enjoy them. I like dark meat. And when you're eating in the kitchen you can pick up the drumstick.

DOROTHY: Like on a picnic.

DICK: And that's part of the fun.

DOROTHY: Oh, yes, I love that, too. I think it's *good* that they leave something for you. Heavens!

There was a pause. Dorothy cleared her throat and read a letter from a listener.

Richard slept two floors below her, in one of the two beds in the master bedroom. In spite of all the pills he took, or perhaps because of them, he had a frightful sleep problem. When he lumbered into Anne Hamilton's little fifth-floor office to dictate a letter or two before returning to bed—when the program was live—he often complained, "I didn't sleep at all, Anne. Not one wink." He was, in his way, as guarded as Dorothy. But he did indicate to Anne, just once, that he felt he had been something of a failure in life.

Anne, who had been hired to manage the Kollmars' financial affairs, was amazed that, after years of prodigious earnings, they had saved nothing at all: "They overspent. The house was a white elephant. With all the money Dorothy was making, I was holding back bills until I had it coming in. They were maintaining what they had, and that was it." 29

The elevator needed repairs, the roof leaked, and pay raises were unknown to the staff. When Richard's father, John, suffered a stroke in 1960, Richard's half-sister, Betty, footed the bills for private nursing home care. She had finally to place him in a state home, and she was furious at Richard for not contributing.

Dorothy continued to try to help get Richard back on his feet. The Left Bank was failing. He affiliated himself with yet another nightclub in New Jersey, which he designed, called Paris in the Sky. It comprised a series of rooms, all of which replicated some aspect or mood of Paris. There were strolling musicians, boutiques, crepes, and a singer "of French extraction" named Suzanne Bernard.

Dorothy had flown back from the Finch trial just to preside at the opening. Two buses took a group of celebrity friends to the mammoth club. According to *Variety*, it was "a move to create a bigtime atmosphere in a monied community." The monied community—the Oranges and Montclair—was not ready. Though Richard had partners here and more or less fronted, he managed to drop some money.

His taste in popular music was indisputably good. With Dorothy's encouragement, he tried managing some of the talent that he was so adept at spotting. Lee Evans signed with Richard. And was started off with a bang: the Left Bank, an album for RCA, an appearance on television's "The Gershwin Years," bookings at some of the best showcases in New York.

Dorothy wrote the liner notes for his album, or at least allowed her name to be signed to them. And she even agreed to sit for an in-depth interview with Mike Wallace on his television show—*if* Evans was allowed to appear. She managed to charm Wallace and indicate to him that everything was hunky-dory at home. She did boggle a few million minds when she implied that Sinatra had begun his vituperative attacks on her because she (Dorothy) had resisted his (Sinatra's) sexual advances.[30]

Richard lost Lee Evans at the beginning of a lucrative career by dint, as ever, of his fickle attention span. He turned the management of the young pianist's career over to a new factotum of his, an ex-drummer named Al Rubenstein, who had none of the contacts or even the punchy panache of Kollmar-cum-Kilgallen. Evans got fed up.

Their contract stipulated that Richard, to renew his option, had to send Evans a registered letter within sixty days of its expiration date, expressing a desire to continue the relationship. This Richard did not do, out of sheer negligence. Evans was aware of that when he met with Richard at the Left Bank to ask to be let out of his contract. The meeting was strictly a courtesy.

At first, Richard amiably agreed. Then he decided to consult with Rubenstein. He excused himself and left the table.

"I'm sorry, Lee," he said, upon returning, "but Al thinks not."

"I'm sorry, too, Dick," Lee Evans replied, "but you

neglected to send me that registered letter, and I've already signed with a new manager."

Richard turned red in the face, left the table, and bellied up to his bar.

"Give me a tall one, Tom," he said to the barkeep.[31]

Dorothy's sere and sorrowful marriage offered her nothing, neither fulfillment nor protection. At forty-seven and in her sexual prime, she was more than ever full of need for Johnnie.

Johnnie became ill. For years, he had been abusing his health—popping pills for all persuasions, chain-smoking, subjecting himself to the disorienting rigors of the road. In the spring of 1960, he suffered a worrisome onset of fatigue. He was losing weight and spitting up blood. He was certain that he had cancer. When his doctor diagnosed the condition as a bad lung infection, he said "Thank God," and checked obediently into Mount Sinai Hospital.

She visited him as often as she could. On one occasion, she and a group of his friends were asked to quiet down or leave when they became boisterous. Dorothy returned at another time alone. His high fever and enforced celibacy had begun to take their toll. He beckoned to her. She drew the curtain and climbed into bed with him. They were discovered by a nurse, who ejected Dorothy from the hospital.

If she had not been involved, Dorothy would have turned the story into an ecstatic blind item, winking like neon. Even without the assistance of the *VOB*, word traveled southeast to Richard. The shocking tale of the pillar and the pop singer was just too good to remain within the confines of the medical profession.

The Boscowitzes begged Richard to take a stand. But he was not ready yet to confront Dorothy. Instead, he asked Anne Hamilton for drinks at the Drake. Anne was the most worldly of the Kollmar employees. She had a theatrical background, a rocky marriage of her own, and a certain fondness and regard for Richard. She recalled their meeting:

The invitation was very unusual for him. But it turned out to be nothing more than an occasion to tell me his sad story. He was feeling sorry for himself. I wanted to say, "All your wife needs is a little attention. Stop going off in other directions." I couldn't say it; he didn't really give me an opening. So I finally gave up and just listened to him.

But you must remember that, although Dick didn't correct the problem, it was *important* to him. Dorothy was his strength, his whole life. I don't care what Dick did otherwise, he could not visualize life without her.[32]

There were other turbulent fronts in 1960.

Dorothy was aware that the liberal *New York Post* was preparing an exhaustive piece about her, and that five of their reporters (David Gelman, Beverly Gary, Peter J. McElroy, Sally Hammond, and Richard Montague) were out in the field ferreting out information from whoever would consent to talk to them. Old friend Dorothy Gulman, who had moved back to her home town of Chicago by this time, telephoned Dorothy after she was approached.

Knowing full well that she had nothing to fear from her loving chum, Dorothy told Gulman, "For Heaven's sake, talk to them. At least you know me, which is more than I can say for most of the people they're talking to." [33]

Since the time fifteen years before, when the man from *The New Yorker* had come calling and made her look rather silly with her immobile features and her overdressed life, she'd had a policy of never granting interviews to journalists who might prove adversarial. She staved off unauthorized pieces with her reputed litigiousness—which accounts, probably, for the absence of any reference to the Johnnie Ray affair in the scandal sheets.

There had been some snide little items about her in the columns, an occasional short profile in the magazines, and frequent strafing from television performers. Jack Paar led the pack in 1960, taking up Sinatra's slack. That tempestuous round began when Dorothy swiped at him in the column over his impassioned support of Fidel Castro. She was violently opposed to the new Cuban leader and peppered her column with anti-Castro items, many of which appear to have been fed to her by Miami-based exiles or CIA fronts on an almost daily basis. Paar retaliated on his prime-time, high-rated television show. At one point, after one of his famous you-won't-have-Jack-Paar-to-kick-around walkouts, he returned to the show and opened with a monologue about press abuse. Winchell he called "a silly old man;" Harriet Van Horne was, inexplicably, "Novocain lipstick." He saved his best stuff for Dolly Mae. Referring to the Khrushchev affair and mixing her excess up with that of Ruth Montgomery, he chided Dorothy for her "poor taste" in "calling attention to the thickness of Mrs. Khrushchev's ankles," adding, "I've always kept my guests from making remarks about your appearance—that you have no chin." [34]

Bob Considine, alerted to the impending *Post* profile, deployed a preemptive attack against the prospective series, devoting a whole column of his own to the callowness and essential inferiority of the woman reporter who had come to interview him about Dolly Mae:

> She would very much like to be Miss Kilgallen but, of course, lacks the drive, determination, and ability. She said she had been assigned to share in the hatchery and, well, you know how it is. . . . Well, she said, on a story like the Sheppard trial, didn't Dorothy use a lot of leg-men to run errands for her and write a lot of her stuff. Dorothy, I said, needed leg-men about as much as Dempsey needed another left. The pencil stopped in the middle of a word. [35]

The *New York Post* series appeared in ten full-page installments and told more truth about Dorothy than had ever previously appeared in print. Despite its snide thrust, all of the nice things were there, too: the sweetness, the loyalty, the vulnerability. The series' weakness was its datedness. Had it been written ten years before, when Dorothy was still gagging on repression, "The Dorothy Kilgallen Story" would have been dead on. (The *Post* saw the essential conflict in its subject as one between malice and manners, at a time when those hoary combatants had been supplanted by Eros and Thanatos.)

Reporting her youthful malice, the *Post* cited an anonymous source:

> A classmate, who went on to become a successful press agent, remembers that she thwarted his efforts to join the literary staff at Erasmus and relegated him to selling ads, after which he quit "in disgust." [36]

The Erasmus graduate who had endeavored to join the staff of the school magazine when Dorothy was also attending Erasmus and was now a successful press agent had not accomplished a whole lot by requesting anonymity. Dorothy took him to be Eli Lloyd Hoffman, who worked now creating gags for columnists. Hoffman denied to Dorothy and his associates that he had spoken to the paper. Nonetheless, she stopped returning his calls or using his material.

In *Time* magazine, she rebutted the *Post*'s assertion that she and Richard led a life of less than total togetherness. "How ridiculous!" she snapped. "Why Dick and I were at the Colony and the Copa last night, and we were at El Morocco two nights ago." [37]

Unable to leave it alone, Dorothy wrote her own *VOB* rebuttal, which, characteristically, dealt with none of the substantive issues raised in the *Post* series:

> Newspapermen all over town are laughing over the fact that it took five alleged reporters to set the facts wrong in the first sentence of a series running in New York's most inaccurate gazette. And every paragraph that followed compounded the joke. Here is what the quintet of by-liners wrote: "It was drizzling on the morning of October 21, 1957, as Queen Elizabeth II and Prince Philip rode up Broadway receiving a soggy welcome from the city of New York. Behind them came a procession of limousines jammed full of city officials and diplomats in undignified congestion. Behind these came another limousine in the rear seat of which, in lonely splendor, sat its sole passenger, Dorothy Kilgallen . . ." [38]

Dorothy countered that it had *not* rained at all on said morning:

> Don't take my word for it, though I was there and rode under fair skies similar to the Queen's weather. . . . A check with the weather bureau discloses this official record. October 21 was a Monday. Highest temperature 61 degrees, lowest 45 degrees. A good bit of sunshine. Just a few clouds. [39]

By 1960, Dorothy had signed approximately six thousand columns and had written, or had written on her behalf, three and a half million words, exclusive of her features.

According to her FBI file, the Hearst corporation had been sued at least once because of something she had written. Beginning with Constance Bennett, way way back, there were rumblings. But, quite remarkably, Dorothy had never paid a penny to a litigant.

"She was always being threatened with libel suits," Edgar Hatfield recalled. "There were a lot of claims made against her, a lot of suits started. But, to my knowledge, no one ever got a judgment against her." [40]

She was very clever in averting successful libel action. Whenever she had doubts, she resorted to the "blind item," the nameless nebula that identifies the subject only to employers, spouses, friends, and family, but not to the community as it is understood by law.

Edgar had given her a book called *Say It Safely*. She kept it close to her typewriter and referred to it when she had doubts. To say it safely and avoid libel *per se*, she knew not to call attorneys ambulance chasers, businessmen crooks, politicians scoundrels, doctors abortionists, drinkers boozehounds, hotels brothels, journalists libelous, or anyone a nudist, skunk, horse thief, mistress, or poltroon— unless she was prepared to prove it.

Her clean slate was challenged in November, 1960, when Elaine Shepard commenced suit over an item that appeared in *The Voice of Broadway* on December 22, 1959.

> Washington's political insiders are buzzing over "the lowdown" on a rather curious feature of the press plane that covered President Eisenhower's global tour. The explanation is quite simple, but causing a stir because it involves an important member of the White House staff and the premise that sex is here to stay.

Elaine Shepard was first shown the Kilgallen column soon after she landed at Andrews Air Force Base, having accompanied the President on his goodwill mission to Europe, Asia, and Africa as an accredited representative of the North American Newspaper Alliance. New to the business of reporting after several careers as a top model, actress, television performer, and Washington hostess, she had been proud of the job she had done on the trip, proud of the distinguished company she had been in, proud of being accredited in the first place, and looking forward to turning her experience into a book.[41]

Elaine had no trouble figuring out who it was that Dorothy meant in her arch column copy. There were eighty-three reporters who accompanied President Eisenhower on his global tour. Elaine Shepard was the only woman.

Fearing that the case might be turned into a political football during the coming presidential elections, she waited a full year. Then she hit Dorothy with a $750,000 action, charging that the Kilgallen column had maliciously implied that she was a person of lewd and unchaste character.

Hatfield was worried. He met with Dorothy in his office. He warned her that if she planned to defend herself successfully, he would have to know the truth.

"Don't kid me, Dorothy," he said, "this is serious. Did you *mean* Elaine Shepard in the piece and did you *mean* that she shacked up with someone to get on that plane?" [42]

Dorothy told Hatfield that a year had passed since the appearance of the item, that she kept no records, and that she was unable to remember who it was she did mean when she originally composed the paragraph. She maintained that it could *not* have been Elaine Shepard. She knew the woman slightly because Jill attended school with her niece, Linda. Jill and Linda were best friends. If she had meant Elaine, she said, she would remember. Dorothy assured her lawyer that at the time the piece was published, she did not know Elaine was aboard the plane or even that she was a writer. She was unable, because of the passage of time, to recall whether the item was fed to her or whether she obtained it herself.

"I don't know if I believed her," Edgar Hatfield recalled, "but she was smart enough to take that position so that nobody could say that she had libeled Elaine Shepard." [43]

If Dorothy was lying—and the trial in 1964 would indicate that she was—she had good reason. Dorothy was the sole defendant in the case. She had carried libel insurance for years, but the cost had become prohibitive and she had dropped it in favor of *Say It Safely*. If she lost, Dorothy alone would be responsible for paying whatever damages were awarded to the plaintiff.

Dorothy was carrying a lot of weight on her fragile and delicate frame. She welcomed the coming of Christmas, her favorite season. Soon after her conferences with Hatfield, she planned her yearly tree-trim party, to which guests were invited to help her hang her collection of antique ornaments on the behemoth tree. Once the Kollmars' tree-trim parties had been the most elegant in New York.

Twenty-two-year-old Mary Brannum was among the thirty or so invited guests that year. Her husband knew Dickie, though to the best of her recollection, the boy was not there when she arrived after midnight. As she entered the town house, Johnnie's Doberman came thundering down the stairs, followed by his master. Mary was greeted graciously by her hostess, whom she had not met before. She introduced herself as "Dorothy Kollmar."

Richard did not appear, nor did young Kerry. Jill, shy and well comported, talked to Mary, who was a graduate of the school she was now attending.

They were all ushered into the Black Room for a musical evening. Virginia De Luce, of *New Faces*, sang show tunes. Then Johnnie, clearly the star of the evening, performed. He led off with a parody musical of *Suddenly Last Summer*, the Tennessee Williams play about a lad who is cannibalized by beachboys. One of the numbers was called "Whatever Happened to Sebastian?"

As Dorothy draped herself contentedly over the piano, amused and adoring, he did another original song, the lyrics of which Mary Brannum has not forgotten; they seemed to her so utterly and extraordinarily outrageous. Johnnie sang: "When I take my fanny out to eat/He doesn't want vegetables he just wants meat."

Jill listened politely. Mary shot an amazed look at her husband.[44] It was, all considered, a very far cry from love born with first embrace and pages torn out of time and space.

Dorothy had no clear preference between contenders in the 1960 presidential election. She predicted in her column that John Kennedy would win because (a) "he's adorable on television," (b) "his promises and connections would get him the labor vote and the machine Democrats," (c) Sammy Davis's support "would guarantee him the Negro vote," (d) the majority of Jews would go to the polls for him "on the theory that the election of any representative of a minority group is a civilized step forward," and (e) "no true Frank Sinatra fan would dare to vote for anyone else." [1]

She couldn't see, however, that there was any important difference between Kennedy and Nixon on the issues, and she did not vote in the election. But Dorothy would not have missed the glamour and excitement of Jack Kennedy's investiture on a bet. She left for Washington on January 18, 1961. The *Journal-American* photographed her purportedly boarding a train at Pennsylvania Station. However, she did not take the train to Washington. Dorothy was driven there by Roosevelt Zanders in his Silver Wraith Rolls. It may be assumed that she was simply fed up with the flack she was taking from her journalistic colleagues on account of the royal perquisites accorded her.

Zanders, a husky black man who also chauffeured John Wayne, Nikita Khrushchev, Margot Fonteyn, Winston Guest, King Saud, and Fidel Castro, described his function vis-à-vis Dorothy as "protector, chauffeur, and lookout." [2]

She planned to cover two of the five inaugural balls, the inaugural ceremony, and the so-called Rat Pack gala featuring Frank Sinatra and friends—a hundred-dollar-a-plate affair designed to recover the election debt. The gala was scheduled for the eve of the inaugural ceremony.

Zanders's invincible machine arrived in Washington unhindered by the blizzard whose severity was paralyzing the capital. The Washington area was clogged with stalled automobiles and derailed trolley cars. An Associated Press report attributed forty-seven deaths to the storm.

Dorothy was one of the few celebrities who was able to proceed normally to the Mayfair Hotel, change into evening clothes, and arrive on time for the Friday night Rat Packer at the mammoth armory. Backstage, before the show, she offered her brocade coat to Bette Davis, whom the storm had separated from her luggage. "It's terribly cute of you," Davis said, "but there's no use pretending that I'm anything that I'm not." [3] She performed in street clothes for the incoming President; so did fickle Republican Ethel Merman, who sang "Everything's Coming Up Roses."

At some point in the evening, Dorothy became "ill," though the etiology and precise nature of the illness remains unclear. Jean Bach was there and recalled seeing her friend accept a shot of Jack Daniel's from one of the musicians: "And the next thing I knew she was ragingly ill and on her way back to New York." [4]

Ed and Pegeen Fitzgerald recollected that there was "talk" at the Mayfair of a violent episode, of a slight to Dorothy, of her ripping a telephone out of a hotel wall. [5] Zanders, who was there, denied that the episode was violent in any way.

According to Zanders, Dorothy was well enough to attend the inaugural ceremonies on Saturday. He recalled that she sat in the fifth row, with Bob Considine, Clifton Fadiman, and a representative of *Life* magazine. She would have seen Robert Frost, his white hair buffeted by the winds, impeded by the blinding glare of the snow, read his poem, "The Gift Outright." She saw the coatless President take the oath and call for a new beginning: "Let us never negotiate out of fear. But never let us fear to negotiate."

The sparse and unextraordinary copy that ran under her by-line that day, however, indicates that she was not well enough to file a story about the ceremony.

Back at the hotel afterward, Zanders realized that he had to get her back to New York.

"Let's not use the word 'drunk,'" Roosevelt Zanders insisted as he described the Washington episode.

I don't say drunk. One of the things that brought it about was having one or two drinks and not eating. Her system ran down that way. There were problems back home. It took an awful lot of money to run that house. Dick had lost a lot out in New Jersey. And the Left Bank wasn't going too well. Then there was something not too pleasant going on at the radio station.

I think all of these things must have stepped up something to make her not be the regular Dorothy Kilgallen. And I didn't want anyone to see her in that condition, ill or otherwise.[6]

Zanders made the preparations. He hired a woman to dress and care for Dorothy. He readied the staff at the hotel to help him to smuggle Dorothy out. He brought the woman to Dorothy and said soothingly to her:

I have a lady here whom I have *all* the confidence in. She's gonna prepare you. Get you dressed. I will be back. You remain here. I'll take care of the hotel and the check-out. And we're gonna journey on back to New York. The care that you need is not available here in Washington.

Dorothy replied quietly,

Yes, Roosevelt. I'll do what you say.

When all systems were go, Roosevelt Zanders picked Dorothy up in his arms, carried her to the back elevator, and placed her in the waiting Rolls. She was driven to Le-Roy Hospital, where she remained for more than four weeks.

Whatever the involvement of pressure, anemia, alcohol, or pills—it was her way of saying *enough*.

On recovering from her illness, Dorothy made her first appearance as the "mystery celebrity" on "What's My Line?" John Daly had barely finished his standard introduction when she popped out from behind the studio curtain in a sensational mink-trimmed gown and made herself visible to the studio audience. There were immediate and spontaneous gasps and cheers and bravos, which must have deeply touched her. Once seated beside Daly, she emitted little Boopish *coo-coos* to fool her colleagues, who were under the impression that she was still in the hospital. But they were not fooled for long.

"What a nice surprise!" alternate panelist Tony Perkins said.

"We're so very glad to see you," Arlene concurred.

During the turbulent sixties, such an outpouring of affection toward Dorothy was rare indeed. "She knew she was disliked," Marlin Swing observed, "and she wanted so desperately to be loved." [7]

When it came time finally to choose a jury of her peers to preside at the trial of Elaine Shepard *vs.* Dorothy Kilgallen, Edgar Hatfield experienced considerable difficulty finding twelve good and true who could convince him that they felt no animosity toward his notorious client.[8]

She had her first encounter with the adversary in this matter during March, 1961. Dorothy was required to appear at the law office of Elaine Shepard's attorney, Irwin M. Taylor, for the preliminary examination before trial. Hatfield accompanied her.

Dorothy maintained her basic defense on the troublesome blind item of December, 1959, elaborating on the story that she had told Hatfield: Thousands of tidbits were fed to her every year from hundreds of sources. She kept notes for a couple of weeks and then disposed of them. She had no idea to whom the item referred, though she had discussed it with Myrtle Verne and racked her own brain from the time that she was served with the complaint. She was not even aware that Elaine Shepard had turned to writing until after the item appeared. Richard had met Elaine at the Left Bank and then told Dorothy that "Linda Shepard's aunt" was writing articles. If she did not know she was a writer, how could she possibly have placed her on the press plane? [9]

As she purported to have no memory of her own process of ideation, that blind item was now a hieroglyphic whose meaning was as indeterminable to her as she hoped it might be to the jury that ruled.

Hatfield gave her permission to speculate as to what she "might have meant" in the item. Dorothy suggested that she could have been referring to some homosexual activity between a male reporter and some important member of the Presidential staff.[10] She threw out still another possibility somewhat apologetically.

"What it might be," she said, "this is pure supposition, pure fiction. But, believe me, this type of item has reached me from time to time. It might mean that somebody in the State Department or somebody important on the Presidential staff had arranged for a Maharaja to bring dancing girls to entertain the members of the press. Because, believe me, I have gotten items like that. But it would be entirely in the realm of fantasy, I would have to fictionalize to give you a good supposition at this point."

"I suppose," Taylor told Dorothy Mae, "that if you were to fictionalize we might get some exotic results. But I don't know as they would be accurate." [11]

The possibility exists that Dorothy was telling the truth and that the tangled web she wove derived from the fearful recognition that the truth would not suffice to serve her in this case. It is possible, but unlikely. Elaine Shepard was the very model of the parvenu female rival who was high priority on the agenda of Dorothy's grievance committee. She had never paid her dues in the way that Dorothy had been compelled to pay hers, had never counted swollen corpses in New York harbor, had never gagged at the implications of a disinfected morgue. Elaine was a still-beautiful, overaged starlet in the profession, hyperbolized, after a mere two years of writing, as a "female Ernie Pyle" by Winchell and lauded even by Bob Considine on the front page of the *Journal-American*, in another piece Dorothy swore to Taylor she hadn't seen. Dorothy roiled at such crash intrusion. No sister, she.

There was a host of rivals against whom Dorothy mounted campaigns of varying vitriol. Sheilah Graham was a favorite target. Despite the fact that the Englishwoman had been in the profession for as long as Dorothy, she was still a tootsie posing as a reporter.

"She was full of nasty blind items about me," Graham recalled:

> Once I wrote in my own column, after Judy Holliday split with Gerry Mulligan, that she was "marching to a different drummer." I knew that he didn't play the

drums. But she was nasty about the fact and composed one of her blind items pointing to my ignorance of American jazz.[12]

Toward Elaine Shepard and Sheilah Graham, Dorothy was patronizing rather than malicious. She was less reserved about Cindy Adams, another professional intruder. Mrs. Adams wrote a feature story about "What's My Line?" to which Dorothy, for no discernible reason, took violent exception. When she and her husband, comedian Joey Adams, embarked upon a State Department tour of Asia, Dorothy began to strafe at them regularly in her column. On one occasion, using a format striking similar to the Shepard item, she commented, "Show business insiders are snickering at the U.S. State Department's odd choice of Joey Adams to head a variety junket to S.E. Asia and Europe. The big question: Who knows them over there?" [13] She accused the couple of "playing nothing but palaces, amusing Heads of State and the elite of various lands at the U.S. taxpayers' expense." And then she wrote: "Mrs. Adams is bombing around the globe, sending home whole columns guaranteed to insult the Moslems, the Hindus, and the Buddhists." [14]

With an Old Testament vengeance, Cindy Adams responded. Her "Open Letter" to Dorothy Kilgallen appeared on December 28, 1961, in a New York community weekly called *Town & Village*. Mrs. Adams defended the contribution she and her husband were making and went on to accuse Dorothy of envy and maliciousness. She referred scathingly to her excessive drinking, her relationships with younger men, and the joyless state of her marriage to Richard. She called Dorothy a "vulgar old crone." She ended the reprisal: "I don't have to try to hurt other people to get my satisfaction out of life. But just as David had to stand up to Goliath and hit him between the eyes, I'm warning you not to stick your chin out any more. You can't spare it!"

Dorothy returned her copy of *Say It Safely* to Edgar Hatfield crammed with markers on her pink and personalized note paper. She virtually annotated the book with Cindy Adams's lengthy "letter" in mind.

"See Pages 18 and 19," she scrawled, underlining the list of actionable words and phrases. From the libel *per se* category Drunkenness or Liquor, she reddened "booze-hound" and "toper"; in category Honesty (see also Reputation), "guilty of falsehood" and "liar"; "affinity" was the best she could find under Morality; moving right along to Reputation, she found "vile and slanderous tongue"; from assorted other sub-heads, "unladylike conduct," "libelous journalist," and "publisher of libel."

To further facilitate Hatfield's understanding, she bracketed the definition of libel, "Any expression which tends to bring public hatred, contempt, or ridicule." *Vulgar old crone?* Dorothy recapitulated in the margin.

Edgar Hatfield had his work cut out for him. He tried for a time to placate Dorothy. But, in the summer of 1962, suit was filed against Cindy Adams for the sum of one million dollars.[15]

The *Town & Village* philippic had been timed with devastating precision. The day after the scorcher hit the street, Jill, who was now in her freshman year at Northwestern University, made an informal debut into society at a series of parties lovingly arranged by Dorothy. For the eighteen-year-old, there was a small party at the Pavillion, followed by a supper dance at the St. Regis Roof. The elegant room was decorated for Jill in pink silk and crystal, with a low ceiling of stars and blossoms. Ersatz snowflakes fell softly to the dance floor.

Joan Fontaine attended with Charles Addams. Mary Martin, in a Mainbocher, danced with all of Jill's young men. Jim Kilgallen cornered Anne Hamilton and regaled her with stories about newspapermen who were newspapermen.[16] Linda Shepard, who was trying not to allow her aunt's libel action to interfere with her close friendship with Jill, danced with troubled Dickie, who, she recalled "was still unhappy about himself and his situation." [17]

The party was a huge success, in spite of the fact that Igor Cassini thought it unworthy of space in *Cholly Knickerbocker.*

Just days after Jill's debut, Dorothy took Kerry for a weekend of sightseeing in Washington, D.C., which turned out to be as high as the Cindy Adams letter was low.

A tour of the White House was *de rigueur*, and Dorothy telephoned Pierre Salinger beforehand to arrange for the excursion. The presidential mansion is normally closed to the public on weekends. Salinger told her to bring the boy anyway and that arrangements could be made.[18]

When she arrived with her redheaded eight-year-old in tow, Salinger met them and chose to guide them himself. They stopped in the Cabinet Room, where Kerry was permitted to swivel in the impressive black leather chairs. Kerry then handed the press secretary a batch of letters to the President that his third-grade class had been instructed to write.

A door opened at the far end of the Cabinet Room and a figure appeared. Dorothy, who was not wearing her glasses, asked Salinger excitedly, "Is that the President?" Salinger responded that it was indeed the President and that he was apparently beckoning them into the Oval Office.

The youthful President made an enormous fuss over Kerry, proffering every available souvenir. He gave him a ball-point pen with the presidential seal. He bent down and clipped a gold pin in the shape of *PT-109* on his striped school tie. When he asked Kerry about school, the grinning youngster told him about his class assignment. John Kennedy asked Kerry where the letters were.

"We gave them to Mr. Salinger," Kerry said. "Our teacher told us that statistics show you can only read one out of every fifty letters you get, but she made us all write one, anyway."

The President buzzed Salinger and requested Kerry's letter. When he had finished reading it, he told the beaming boy, "That's very well written. Very well done."

John Kennedy winked at Dorothy and added, "I hope this is all right. I don't know whether Kerry is a Democrat or a Republican."

Dorothy answered, "I don't know either, Mr. President. But I have a feeling that after today he may well be a Democrat." [19]

There were other heady and validating experiences for Dorothy during these precarious times. Many of them she shared with Marlin Swing, who remained close to Dorothy and Johnnie, separately and as a couple. The threesome had fantasy names for each other. Johnnie was "King"; Dorothy, "Princess"; and Marlin, "Prince Consort."

Marlin loved Johnnie for his talent, which he considered as significant as Elvis Presley's for its impact on contemporary music, and for his basic sweetness as a man. "He is *so* kind, so innately generous," Marlin commented, sitting in his sunny terraced Murray Hill apartment. "Someone could come in and move his whole house around. That table was his," he said, pointing to a drop-leaf mahogany dining table, "and those copper and bronze antique lamps. I said I needed a table and he said, 'Take mine.' But Johnnie has to have people around him. And they can turn him any which way, particularly when he's been drinking."

When Marlin was between apartments in the fall of 1962, he moved into Johnnie's spare room while continuing to maintain normal business hours as a CBS producer. "It was insane," he recalled. "They stayed up all night. Monty didn't go to bed until six or seven in the morning. Half the time, when I went to work, he was in his chair passed out."

He loved them both very much, but saw the toll that Johnnie's carelessness took on Dorothy, and was profoundly disturbed by what he saw: "Apparently, Johnnie led her to believe that there could be a future. And once she had that in her mind, it was impossible to get it out. I guess she was naive." [20]

Marlin and Dorothy saw each other several times a week. Their evenings out would frequently begin with a telephone call from the columnist. "Are you up to Restaurant Roulette tonight?" she would ask. "I'm game if you are," he might reply.

In their game-playing parlance, Restaurant Roulette meant going to the best restaurants in the city—Barbetta, Colony, Morocco—ordering the most sumptuous dream meal conceivable, and waiting to see if they would get stuck with a check. They watched the byplay between waiter, maître d', and management with amusement. Marlin was quite prepared to pay, but never once was he required to. It was always a polite and cordial, "There will be no check."

The rules of Restaurant Roulette were suspended only at the Stork Club, which was being kept open by Sherman Billingsley because he had little else in his life that mattered. Labor unions, the dwindling power of the columnists to whom he had catered, the Josephine Baker episode, and the changing sensibilities of New Yorkers all conspired to make the restaurant that had once been the symbol of glamour to Dorothy obsolete. She felt sorry for Billingsley, wanted to pay, but was never permitted. She and Marlin were often the sole diners in the clubby Cub Room.

She and Marlin went to game parties, though with a gamier group than in times past. The newest rage was the Song Game, a crypto-narrative in which one made up a story containing clues that implied a title. Dorothy stumped the stars one night with the following epic: Syngman Rhee has come to the United States, out of work. He meets Henry Luce, who gives him a job at *Life* magazine. Rhee is gainfully employed, but one day disappears. Luce searches everywhere for him. Luce drops into P. J. Clarke's, looks across the crowded room, spots the object of his long search, and exclaims . . . ?

Ah, sweet Mister Rhee of Life, at last I found you.

Marlin delighted in Dorothy's childlike exhilaration at the benefits of her own position. She never quite became accustomed to her celebrity, never took her peerage for granted. She glowed girlishly as Judy Garland sang "Happy Birthday" to her. When Cary Grant came to tea, she telephoned Marlin breathlessly with every last detail of the afternoon, from what he wore to how the servants had manufactured excuses to peek in on him. Warren Beatty telephoned her and played romantic piano music, which is something she quite liked but never entirely fathomed. If she had been out with Sophia Loren, she made a point of mentioning it. She adored her, considered her the quintessence of movie star, and found their friendship remarkable.

"Dorothy had a thing about looking like a famous movie star. And she was very coy about it," Marlin recalled. "A couple of times, she was fishing for something, but I wasn't sure what the right answer was. She'd say, 'People have told me that I remind them of a certain movie star. Can you guess which one?' I never could figure out what she wanted to hear. Do you suppose she meant Sophia?" [21]

She and Marlin had some rather more serious times. They discussed religion, though the talk was unstructured and hardly Jesuitical. She listened and she queried mostly. The substance has become vague in Marlin's mind. He knew that she "did beads" for Johnnie wherever he flew. He knew that the strongest remnant of her Catholicism was Mae. He suspected that if it hadn't been for her mother, she might have divorced Richard.

"I think what bothered her was the fact that she didn't

believe as her mother would have wanted her to believe. That made her feel that she wasn't totally good. She was confused and inconsistent. She was guilty, maybe, about not feeling guilty."

With her friend Ben Bagley, a lapsed Catholic, an anti-Catholic, and an analysand, she could laugh about their common upbringings and how the nuns equated acne with self-abuse. But she told him, "You'll never get over it, no matter how much psychoanalysis you do." And if Bagley got too far out of line in his heretical utterances, she asked him to stop.[22]

Marlin knew, though it was never made explicit between them, that Dorothy was checking periodically into LeRoy Hospital in New York and Silver Hill in Connecticut, to withdraw from alcohol and pills. When she returned, after several days, she would look plumper, healthier.

She would be all right for a time, and then something would set her off again. He never knew what.

In 1962, Marlin arrived to take her to the opening of a musical comedy called *Mr. President*. James fixed him a drink in the Black Room. Dorothy staggered in, her dress unzipped, struggling to get her earrings on. Unable to dissuade her from attending the opening, he was compelled to keep her upright and as isolated as possible once out in public. When she suggested an intermission drink, he agreed, one more drink being preferable to whatever intermission socializing she might do. He supported her as she returned to her seat. She could not walk unaided. Her left forearm was black and blue the day after from the pressure of Marlin's grip.

At the opening of the movie *Cleopatra*, she appeared on live-television noticeably drunk. Marlin chivied her away from the camera as rapidly as possible.

It was this kind of episode that drove many of her friends away. Howard Perry Rothberg was virtually unrepellable, but nonetheless chagrined by her drinking and by her continuing relationship with Johnnie, whom he considered the source of the problem. "You couldn't count on her at all," he complained. "I used to give dinner parties a couple of times a week. Marvelous people, never more than six. I just could not count on her to show up. She'd make an excuse at seven o'clock at night. She'd say she was busy. I knew she was either out with Johnnie or home with Johnnie." [23]

Marlin maintained his close relationship with Dorothy by never manifesting his basic disapproval. Howard was less discreet. When word filtered back to her that he had expressed his negative feelings about the affair, she sent Howard a hand-delivered note to the effect that he had "joined the enemy camp" and refused to see him for a time. [24] Her feelings for the Bachs cooled somewhat when she discerned their disapproval.

Judgmental Dorothy would not be judged. "I know that she accosted people and rode their ass because of what they said about our relationship," Johnnie said. [25]

Having mended her breach with Howard, she prepared, in August, 1962, to leave for a weekend with him at his summer place on the eastern shore of Long Island. She wrote her Friday column. The source of her lead item was Howard. The subject was Marilyn Monroe.

> Marilyn Monroe's health must be improving. She's been attending select Hollywood parties and has become the talk of the town again. In California, they're circulating a photograph of her that certainly isn't as bare as he famous calendar, but is very interesting. . . . And she's cooking in the sex-appeal department, too; she's proved vastly alluring to a handsome gentleman who is a bigger name than Joe DiMaggio in his heyday. So don't write off Marilyn as finished. [26]

She and Richard then prerecorded Monday's "Dorothy and Dick" show, in which they exchanged light and amusing gossip about the film star.

On Saturday night, Howard had an intimate party for fourteen. They were up very late, and Dorothy drank very heavily. The telephone rang early Sunday morning. Howard answered. It was Paul Schoenstein for Dorothy. "You'd better wake her up," the editor said. "It's a big one. Marilyn Monroe died last night and I want Dorothy on it right away." [27]

Howard awakened Dorothy, who was stunned by the news. She had never known Marilyn Monroe well, except in the sense that all celebrities know each other. They'd met once or twice and had their photograph taken together.

But Dorothy, following the star's poignant personal life and learning more than she was ever able to write, had always rooted for Marilyn and been moved by her screen *persona*. From this house in Amagansett, where she was now awakened, she had watched Marilyn and Arthur Miller drive happily along the beach with his dog. Dorothy had wondered, at the time, what the couple had to talk about. She supposed that Miller would have found anything the intriguing beauty revealed about herself interesting, and that Marilyn had learned from the intellectual Jewish playwright a good deal about books and family life.

Dorothy was unable to cover the movie star's death in the manner that Schoenstein would have wished. She suffered another "episode" and had to be taken off a New York–bound train and placed in a hospital overnight. Bob Considine went to California in her stead.

Her column appeared that Monday, but it was obviously a backup piece. On Tuesday, there was no *Voice of Broadway* and no disclaimer. She was well enough to write for the Wednesday paper, and that column was devoted entirely to Marilyn.

Dorothy wrote that she considered the death a suicide, but not in the conventional Hollywood sense. She called it rather:

> The death of a tortured creature running from the black shapes of a nightmare into the path of an on-rushing locomotive. I think she took a few pills to help her get over whatever her last problem was, and sleepily thought, "Oh, THAT feels better," and took a few more to make sure she wouldn't wake up until morning came along to make the day safe for her.[28]

She ran through a possible scenario of what might have happened that fateful Saturday night. She speculated—indeed hoped—that the unhooked telephone meant that Marilyn had received an *incoming* call, adding knowledgeably that she would have had to pick up "the light end" because "that's all she could manage in her torpor. . . . Caught tight by the drug," she might not have been able to talk. The caller, whom Dorothy referred to only as "The Man in Her Life," "got the terrible picture and realized there was nothing he could do without getting mixed up in it." She surmised that if the actress had taken as many pills as the autopsy indicated, there was nothing he could have done:

> So he let Marilyn slip away from him, which is probably what would have happened anyway, with a little more time.
>
> This is a story I have known I was going to be writing in the not too distant future. When I first heard Marilyn was dead I said, "Oh, no—it can't be true" which is what almost everyone else said, but as the voice filled in the details I found myself thinking, of course. Of course. This is the way it would have to be . . . Nude . . . the pill bottle . . . the record player. And alone.
>
> Among the things the friends kept asking is, "I wonder why she didn't leave a note?" . . . Her life was a suicide note, written for everybody to read, but nobody would believe the message.
>
> Sleep well, sweet girl. You have left more of a legacy than most, if all you ever left was a handful of photographs of one of the loveliest women who ever walked the earth.[29]

Dorothy dwelt on Marilyn Monroe's death. She thought the man on the telephone was Robert Kennedy. She had been told of their relationship by a photographer who was close to the movie star. She said several times to Anne Hamilton, "It didn't have to happen." [30] She wasn't blaming anyone, and yet she was blaming everyone. Someone, she thought, should have made it *safe* for Marilyn.

On the Monday after Marilyn Monroe's death, Richard was obliged to go to the studio and inform the "Dorothy and Dick" audience that the Friday show was prerecorded. The necessity for such a revelation did not please the management of WOR, which presently decided that the Kollmars would have to return to the live format. The program would begin at 9:15 A.M.

In their eighteen years of broadcasting, the couple had worked only with an engineer, who came to the house every morning. Now they were assigned an on-the-spot producer, Jim McAleer. He was a shrewd, shirt-sleeved young station executive whose job basically was to determine whether they were in shape for the morning show. He might rev them up if they were borderline or decide to go with an undated, prerecorded broadcast. Dorothy and Richard understood McAleer's function, and they resented it mightily.[31]

Jim McAleer arrived nervously at the house the first morning. Dorothy put the screws on immediately. Sitting at the broadcasting table with Richard before the show, she took out a book and began to discuss it with her husband. McAleer, who is now the station manager of WOR, recalled:

> It was full of squares and puzzles and intellectual-type parlor games. They were indicating to me that this was the kind of exercise they did every morning around the breakfast table. And she said, "Oh, Mr. McAleer, what *do* you think of this one?" I knew what she had in mind. She wanted to be able to telephone our general manager, Bob Leder, to say that I wasn't quite bright enough to function in my assigned capacity. Which is just what she did. But Leder knew better. I can just hear what the conversation must have been like—Oh, Bob, you know that I *love* to have people with me, and I like direction (all totally untrue) but I would appreciate it if you'd send someone just a *little* bit more intelligent.

After the first game was put away, James Clement, jacketed and elegant, entered the broadcast room with two cups of coffee for the Kollmars. They were sitting just a couple of feet away from McAleer, who had positioned himself in a corner with a little table beside him. He faced Dorothy. Their engineer worked in another corner.

Clement put the coffee down in front of Dorothy, who said to her butler, "Please ask Mr. McAleer if he would like some coffee."

"Mr. McAleer," Clement asked, "would you like some coffee?"

"*Thank* Mrs. Kollmar for me," McAleer grinned, "but I usually have mine on a silver tray."

He got a look from Dorothy that would have frightened horses in the street. But on the following morning, and on every morning thereafter, James Clement put down, on

McAleer's little table, a cup of coffee on a sterling silver tray, with a cloth napkin and a candle.

McAleer grew fond of Dorothy, though he couldn't quite warm up to Richard. And Dorothy apparently learned to accept his presence. They developed a mock adversary relationship, which was to his liking. He was there to get them moving in the morning, and any enlivening response availed.

After the first few days, Dorothy no longer bothered to dress up for Jim McAleer. The days of Sulka robes and Carole Lombard lounge wear had long since passed. When Dorothy rolled out of the adjacent Cloop into the broadcast room, she wore just what she had slept in—a nightgown and a tatty robe. She was always cold.

"The next time I get paid," McAleer said to her one morning, "I'm going to do something about that robe, even if it's just a down payment."

"Make sure you get the right color, Jim," she said.

"I'm only paying for the patches. You've got to buy the robe," McAleer replied.[32]

Richard turned around and glowered at the arrogant young man.

Dorothy had good days, but very few good mornings. She would lumber precariously into the broadcasting room, occasionally supporting herself on the wall. When she approached the table, she touched it with her right hand, not so much for support as for orientation. She stood for a moment, just before sitting, closed her eyes, and drew a heavy, sighing breath. Her skin was kabuki-white. To McAleer, she looked as if she weighed no more than a hundred pounds.

There were mornings when only Dorothy appeared. He had to then fetch Richard by knocking thunderously at the door to his third-floor bedroom. There were mornings when only Richard appeared. Since no noise sufficed to awaken her, he was compelled to enter the insufferably warm, airless Cloop and startle her conscious. This he did by pumping the mattress vigorously, as though applying artificial respiration.

On one particular morning, neither of the Kollmars appeared. They were fifteen minutes from air time. McAleer looked impatiently at the clock. Jill Kollmar entered the room.

"Where are your parents?" he asked.

"Oh, they're not here," she said. "I'm doing the show this morning."

"That's interesting," McAleer said suspiciously. "Don't you think it would have been nice if somebody told us?"

"Weren't you telephoned?" she asked.

"Where are they? Are they here now?" McAleer shouted.

Jill admitted that they were. McAleer tore through the house like an irate sergeant, yelling, "Get your coolies out of bed!"

They each staggered into the broadcast room from their separate lairs. Jim McAleer tried his arisal techniques. They looked at him blankly. They were sluggish and had difficulty articulating. "They saw me," he recalled, "but they didn't seem to understand what I was doing there. I called the station and they ran one of the backup shows." 33

McAleer was probably not in attendance one morning when they managed to do an entire broadcast sounding like well-informed junkies in tandem twilight sleep. Penguins as endangered species was among the topics languorously broached. "Who needs them?" Dorothy asked. Dick replied, after a ponderous pause, "We need each other." "What do they do for us?" Dorothy queried. Her bombed partner replied, "We look at them." Dorothy read a commercial, giggling that the print was too small and the copy too long. It was, as she read it, very long indeed. Dick said that the Mona Lisa was coming to town. Dorothy said that she had never liked the Mona Lisa.

Dick segued into genealogy. "My great-great-grandfather, who was vice-president during Monroe's administration, abolished slavery," he said. "He deserves more credit." After a gaping pause, Dorothy puzzled, "I thought Abraham Lincoln abolished slavery."

Before Richard was able to counter that it was Abraham Lincoln who abolished penguins, their time was mercifully over.

After a good day's sleep, Dorothy was able to function with a degree of normal vitality. She continued to see Johnnie as often as possible. There was no appreciable change in their relationship, and no appreciable change in his career. Neither was going anywhere. Fortunately, he had saved his money and was still a big attraction in England

and Australia, where memories are long and fans faithful. But Johnnie was beleaguered by his dwindling success at home and could do nothing to reverse the trend.

Dorothy did what she could to help. When an old friend, Bette Whyte, became associated with a newly opened night club called the International, she invited Dorothy for an evening, hoping for some attention in the *VOB*. Dorothy agreed to stop by if Bette made some attempt to get Johnnie a booking there. Johnnie was booked and there was no keeping Dorothy away.

Bette sat down beside the columnist one night. "Tell me," she asked, "do you really think that Johnnie is such a great talent?"

"You have no idea of the depth and sensitivity of the boy," Dorothy replied.[34]

Dorothy ventured occasionally to make suggestions to the singer. She told him that his album covers were dreadfully designed. "They make you look like something out of Charles Addams," she said. She criticized him for wearing patent leather shoes and loosening his tie after his first number. More significantly, she begged him to rid himself of his manager, Bernie Lang, whom she felt was coasting at her lover's expense. They argued about Lang and about Johnnie's career choices.

"Why are you so blind?" she yelled. "Can't you see what's happening to you!"

"Tough titty," Johnnie shouted back, "I've got a contract. I've got a manager. And *he* tells me what to do." [35]

There was a new member of Johnnie's circle, Allen Stokes, who felt that Dorothy was doing far more damage to Johnnie than his manager. He disliked Dorothy intensely, believed that she was draining Johnnie physically and emotionally, and perceived her role as that of a predator. Dorothy, he asserted, was a balm to Johnny's ego, fuel for his delusions.

He was among the regulars who drank and stayed up with the singer, who had moved to a new apartment in the East Sixties. Howard Rothberg had decorated the spacious floor-through residence in salmon and light olive greens. The living room was dominated by a salmon couch of antique velvet. There were good paintings, no books to speak of, a den, a guest room, a master bedroom.

When Dorothy visited on Sundays, a salon of people congregated. They drank, talked show biz, analyzed Johnnie's career, and gossiped. By this time in her life, Dorothy no longer eschewed telling tales out of school. She galvanized the group with stories about all the Kennedys' extramarital capering. "My God," Allen exclaimed, "why don't you print some of that?"

"I couldn't possibly," Dorothy said. "Nobody would."

According to Allen: "It was just part of the Sunday routine that she drug Johnnie out of the living room into the den, in which there happened to be a long leather couch. We would sit in the living room and listen to all the activity that was going on in the den. You could hear it. We used to go over to the keyhole and look into the room. It became a joke among us."

Johnnie would admit to being intimidated by Dorothy's superior mind and by some atavistic perception of the power of the Broadway column. But Allen possibly wished her predation into existence. The attraction, if not the emotion, was mutual, the activity eminently consensual.

"It was lust without control," Allen recalled with distaste. And in that regard, he was right on target.

One night in early 1963, Dorothy, Johnnie, Allen, and a large group of frolickers did the town in several limousines. They all drank heavily. While the rest of the group returned to Johnnie's, the singer and the columnist went off on their own.

They stopped at the Left Bank and, with Richard present, they necked. Richard attempted to ignore the situation. They were at a table and he was at the bar. His bartender watched the couple until he could tolerate it no longer and whispered to Richard, "Are you just going to stand here and let her humiliate you like that?" [36]

Richard ordered another drink and said nothing.

Johnnie took Dorothy home to her town house. The two of them were fondling in the Black Room when Richard, bold with booze, burst in on them.

He screamed at Johnnie: "I'll kill you if I ever see you with my wife again."

"That is entirely *her* decision," Johnnie said.

"I want you out of here and out of her life," Richard raged.

As Johnnie put on his jacket and prepared to leave,

Dorothy, her entire face trembling, begged: "I want to go with you now. Please take me with you. I don't want to be in this house anymore."

Johnnie recalled the episode and all the reasons he marshaled against her desperate imploration: "I thought very fast. I knew that if she were to walk out—and she was ready—everything would collapse for her. I explained to her that she'd lose the column, the television show, everything she had worked a lifetime to achieve. She said she didn't care about any of it. And I thought about Kerry. I told her, 'I'm gonna have to walk out and leave you here.' " [37]

Thirteen years later, Johnnie was still rationalizing his reluctance to commit himself. "Henry Luce and Marion Davies are one thing," he said. "But Johnnie Ray and Dorothy Kilgallen!" [38]

Dorothy made some kind of promise to Richard that she would not see Johnnie again. Johnnie, who returned to his own apartment on the verge of collapse, was encouraged by his friends, Allen among them, to make a clean and permanent break.

After a few days, Dorothy telephoned Johnnie at his apartment. He would not come to the phone. His friends handled the matter, explaining how destructive the relationship was to both of them. She rang up constantly, out of control, sobbing. "He can't keep avoiding me. I won't live without him. If Johnnie doesn't come back to me I'm going to kill myself." [39]

One of the young men tried to calm her. He told her that she had everything to live for: family, children, husband, an enviable success, parents who doted on her. She sobbed that her father had never loved her, that he had cared only about his career; that she hated her husband and he hated her; that her children didn't care if she lived or died; that her career meant nothing; that she could not live if she didn't have Johnnie back.

Johnnie had a coterie of comforters. Dorothy was virtually alone.

Late one afternoon, Anne Hamilton was about to leave for the day. She found Dorothy wandering aimlessly on the fifth floor of the house. It was a weekday. Dorothy asked Anne to call her car; she was late, she said, for "What's My

Line?" Anne was aware that something was radically wrong with Dorothy. Her entire demeanor was altered. She was like a sweet and helpless little girl, asking for assistance.

"Okay, honey," Anne said, "you sit right down there and wait. I'll call the car and get everything ready."

Fearful that Dorothy might, in her disoriented state, tumble down the five flights of steps, she raced through the house for help. She found one of the maids, Lempy Osterman; Lempy did not know what to do. James Clement said he could not assume any responsibility. Richard was sleeping.

"James," Anne said, "I am not leaving this house until something is done. You go up there and wake Mr. Kollmar and tell him that Mrs. Kollmar is going to hurt herself if he doesn't get a doctor here fast." [40]

Dorothy was put into the hospital again. She remained there for a month. Richard told Anne that the episode was touched off by Dorothy's anemia, that the doctors who treated her were amazed that she had been able to walk around at all. "The blood was pink," Anne Hamilton said, "and the brain had been affected." [41]

She was still in the hospital in the middle of April, 1963. Dick was carrying the morning show, inviting various guests. McAleer was apparently absent. Josh and Nedda Logan were on with him. Edgar Hatfield received a telephone call at his office. "If you represent Richard Kollmar," he was told, "you better do something quickly. He's on the air and he's smashed."

Hatfield telephoned the house, intending to order James to go in and "drag him away from the microphone." [42]

The line he tried was busy. The station was talking with engineer Ralph Schlegle.

"He looks all right. I don't smell anything. But his tongue is thick," Schlegle told management.

"Take the commercials away from him and tell him to shut up," management ordered. "Let Logan handle the show." [43]

"Dorothy and Dick" was still making money for WOR, but the station could no longer afford it.

The New York Times announced two days hence: "The 'Dorothy and Dick' program, which has been on the air since 1945, will not be back until further notice. . . . Mr.

Kollmar has been doing the radio show with guests since his wife's absence began on March 21. Mr. Kollmar decided to discontinue the show temporarily because of the pressures of business and personal concerns."

Dorothy would never be confidently healthy again. During the last two and a half years of her life, there were several confinements, telephone calls to friends from indeterminate points of origin, times when it was tacitly understood that she was unable to lunch.

Nor would she experience any degree of professional or financial security. The Hearst empire in New York tottered. The *Mirror* ceased publication after the long printers' strike in 1963; Winchell was put out to pasture in a fuzzy little patch at the *Journal*, a defeated and sad old man. "What's My Line?" remained indomitable, but even at that bastion, Dorothy's position was imperiled. She did nothing stupid before the show; she had too much respect for it. However, the cumulative effects of prolonged barbituate abuse were becoming noticeable to the mass viewing audience. On occasion, she would appear jittery, her gait ataxic, her speech thick.[1]

Mark Goodson was worried about Dorothy, but chary. "It was a very delicate, difficult situation because she was so sensitive. She was an intensely personal person," [2] the producer recalled. He asked Howard Rothberg to lunch with him at the Four Seasons. "Howard," he said, "we're getting letters about Dorothy." [3] Howard had information, but no solution. Mark had finally to meet with Dorothy and confront the situation.

"Are you having problems?" he asked her.

"No, not really."

"You seem at times to be thick in your speech. Have you been drinking?"

"No, not really."

"Well, you seem to be bothered by something," Goodson said.

Dorothy replied totally without resentment or rancor,

almost advising, "If I'm in any way hurting the show, drop me. Get me off."

"Why don't you go to a psychiatrist," Mark Goodson said.

"I don't need a psychiatrist," Dorothy said. "I'm a Catholic." [4]

Dorothy did begin to deal with the problems at hand, if only by setting into motion the forces that would compel separation between her and Johnnie. After the episode in the Black Room, they skimmed back together again. He was neither strong enough nor sober enough to maintain the separation while they were living in the same city.

In mid-1963, Johnnie collapsed during a performance in Canada. It was his liver. He was brought back to his apartment, after a hospital stay there, looking like a tawny little old man. He refused to enter another hospital or to allow Dorothy to bring in anyone to cook for him. Monty, who stayed on, brought him offerings of well-intentioned but bloody lamb, which Johnnie could not choke down. Malnourished and cirrhotic, Johnnie languished without strength or will.

She telephoned Bill Franklin, a twenty-three-year-old publicist whom the singer had befriended two years before. Bill was now living and working in Los Angeles. Dorothy begged him to come East and take over: "They're killing him here. He needs someone like you around who can make decisions for him." [5]

Bill flew to New York and cringed when he walked into Johnnie's bedroom. "It was like a dead body was speaking to me," he said. "He was skin and bones. His eyes were rolled back."

With Bill's encouragement, Johnnie agreed—and not one drink too soon—to enter Montefiore Hospital. Dorothy visited him when she could. Having returned to a pattern of civilized deception vis-à-vis Richard, it was difficult.

Johnnie made a good recovery. He returned home under enlightened auspices. A cook was hired. Bill moved into the guest room. Dorothy and the new young man sat on either side of his bed and lectured to him about survival.

Johnnie implored Bill, who had requested a transfer to his firm's East Coast office, to join his life.

"And become another Monty!" Bill said.

"I've got enough money for everyone," Johnnie boasted.

Dorothy and Bill discussed the situation. "You could handle his press," she said. "God knows he could use some help in *that* area." Since the Black Room episode, Dorothy was no longer mentioning the singer in her own column.

"I don't know how to break the columns," Bill confessed.

"I'll show you in an afternoon," she said.[6]

Dorothy arrived the next day by limousine, toting a brand-new typewriter and a sheath of exemplary correspondence from her army of press agents. "This is how it's done, Billie," she said, and proceeded to offer him a crash course in the care and feeding of the Broadway columnist. Beyond the ABC's of *quid pro quo*, she provided him with the lowdown on the sensibilities and idiosyncrasies of her colleagues: "And Earl is very important. Don't write to him. Telephone after 11:30."[7]

She looked at her watch, kissed Johnnie good-bye, and apprised Bill that the portable electric typewriter was a gift. He asked her to christen the machine for luck:

Dearest Bill,

Blessings on this typewriter and love from another typist . . .   Dorothy

Dorothy's fiftieth summer was a busy and a productive time. Jill married Larry Grossman, twenty-four, whom she had met while she was at Northwestern. Larry was a lyricist with Broadway ambitions who had worked the Left Bank playing piano and singing parodies of pop standards. He was now an executive with Bob Banner Associates.

Jill was not the first of Dorothy's children to marry. But this was the first marriage she deigned to talk about. When Dickie took a wife at least a year before, Dorothy apparently disapproved. Announcements were sent out by the bride's people. Bennett Cerf received his in the mail, and took it with him to "What's My Line?" While the panelists were being made up, he shouted to Dorothy, "Am I supposed to do something about this?" He was less concerned with gift etiquette than with teasing Dorothy, whom he knew to have an abundance of off-limit areas. She said nothing and looked sheepish.[8]

Jill's marriage ceremony was performed at St. Vincent Ferrer. Escorted by her father, she walked down the aisle veiled in French silk, with a white satin dress, a cathedral train, and a diamond tiara. Kerry was ring-bearer. Dickie ushered. The Reverend Mark Geary officiated.

The marriage got good play. Igor Cassini, after being indicted for failing to register as a foreign agent for the Dominican Republic,[9] left *Cholly Knickerbocker* to his assistants, who were more kindly disposed toward Dorothy. A picture of Jill and a lengthy paragraph about her appeared in "Cholly's" column. *The New York Times* acknowledged her erroneously as a "great-great-granddaughter of Daniel D. Tompkins, who was Governor of New York and Vice-President under President James Monroe." [10] (Actually, Jill was the great-great-great of Daniel D.)

The reception was held at the Plaza. Dorothy wore her favorite shade of pink. Dong Kingman sketched. Marlin Swing recalled that both Jim and Mae Kilgallen attended.[11]

Linda Shepard had been asked repeatedly by Jill to be one of her bridesmaids. She was compelled to refuse. The Shepard-Kilgallen libel trial was scheduled the following January, and her aunt's attorney advised her not to attend lest the gesture be construed as a token of amity. "That was the awful part of it," Linda Shepard recalled, "not knowing what was part of somebody's strategy and what was honest-to-goodness." [12]

Because Larry was Jewish, there was a good deal of smug talk about Dorothy's displeasure. In fact, she liked Larry and approved of the union.[13]

Immediately after the wedding, Dorothy left for England to cover the trial of Dr. Stephen Ward, which was part of the so-called Profumo scandal. It was a natural for Dorothy, since the case involved osteopathy in high places (Ward was a socially prominent osteopath who numbered Winston Churchill among his patients), vice, international intrigue, and England.

She itemized before embarking,

A high echelon espionage organization dominated by an international society of sex deviates, is about to be spotlighted. It's said to have spread its tentacles into virtually every branch of government in Europe and the United States and to have turned over numerous secrets to the Communists.[14]

Ward was charged with living off immoral earnings after he wrote to a newspaper and to a member of the government, informing each that the British Minister of War, John Profumo, lied when he rose in Commons to deny a relationship with Christine Keeler. She was also the mistress of Russian diplomat Eugene Ivanov. The scandal rocked the Conservative government of Harold MacMillan and almost led to its capitulation.

Dorothy wrote in her front-page story:

> It has been elicited at the trial, and the defendant has admitted, that Ivanov was his friend and that he, Ward, was responsible for introducing him to his girl friends and the many important men in his circle. This must have interested him greatly. But it would have been of no value to him or to the Communist party unless he could somehow manage to bring the situation to public attention at which point it would undoubtedly affect the Conservative government adversely. . . . The situation achieved a tremendous propaganda victory whether it was accomplished by Ivanov or not.[15]

Dorothy stayed at the Dorchester, where her rival Sheilah Graham, also covering the trial, resided. The two reporters resumed the cagey competitiveness that had characterized their relationship for three decades. "She was better at getting news but I was still better at getting interviews," Sheilah Graham boasted. "I got an interview with Dr. Stephen Ward. Dorothy and I ran into each other at Western Union occasionally. She'd ask me about what was happening in court. And I'd tell her *almost* everything. What I didn't tell her, I sent through a different Western Union office. One can't be too careful." [16]

Withal, Sheilah Graham could not gainsay Dorothy's remarkable assiduity. They were in adjacent rooms. Dolly Mae's typewriter clattered into the wee hours. She was working hard and taking great care to maintain her vitality, primarily by eating healthfully and regularly.[17]

Dorothy suspected that the English counterpart of the

CIA knew a whole lot more than it was telling about the international ramifications of the case. Since the fifties, however, American liberals had a tendency to regard any recognition of political conspiracy as hysteria, and any acknowledgment of the occasional efficacy of the KGB as heretical.

Backstage before "What's My Line?" she suggested to Tony Randall that the Profumo affair could have been engineered to topple the Conservative government. Randall considered the notion laughable.[18]

Ordinarily, the Kollmars vacationed together during the summer. This year there was no plan to recreate. Jill's wedding had been expensive. With the loss of the radio show and the closing of the Left Bank, Dorothy became the sole breadwinner in the family, and expenses had to be trimmed. She had been furious at Richard for the loss of "Dorothy and Dick," which she considered an almost intentional act of demolition. But her anger was replaced by concern as she saw the toll Richard's forced and mortifying retirement exacted.

He bumped around in their five-story dwelling now, finding odd jobs to do around the house. He began writing a book—an inane and scattered memoir that he dictated to their new bookkeeper, Pearl Bauer. Anne Hamilton had left the Kollmars' employ when she saw "the handwriting on the wall" and assessed her own salary as beyond their means.[19] According to Edgar Hatfield, Richard literally "hid" rather than face Dorothy, so profound was his embarrassment at having to depend upon her even for his pocket money, most of which he spent at a neighborhood bar.[20]

Dorothy's attitude toward the father of her three children and her mate of almost a quarter of a century remains indecipherable. With her friends, she avoided the subject almost entirely. That she continued to acquiesce to his mandate about Johnnie indicates that she had a certain regard for his sensibilities. Primarily, they shared the tacit understanding that confrontation, having been tested and found wanting, would be replaced by the old rules— vaporous perceptions of survival, based on a mutual understanding of what could not be made explicit.

Mrs. Bauer, aggressive, shrewd, and outspoken, would

blunder monumentally when, in a well-intentioned effort to save the Kollmars a couple of thousand dollars in taxes, she drew up a joint memo that contained an accounting of what each of them had earned in 1963. Dorothy's gross income was $106,170; Richard had made $2,500. When she showed the cold-blooded figures to Richard, he cautioned her to file away Dorothy's copy, to leave it alone. Of course, he was embarrassed by his meager earnings. He knew, however, that the matter was not so simple. Even when his contribution had been more sizeable, Dorothy had endeavored to avoid subjecting either of them to anything so gross as a cost accounting of their widely disparate incomes. And now especially, when his earnings were virtually nonexistent, he knew that Dorothy would blame Mrs. Bauer for subjecting *him* to such a bold rendering. When she disregarded his advice and showed the joint communiqué to Dorothy, the latter was predictably angry at Pearl Bauer.

Mrs. Bauer forwarded a third copy of the memo to Edgar Hatfield, who handled their tax matters. She included a perplexed recap of the situation that concluded: "Well, it is obvious that we are not dealing with business-type people.[21]

After the confrontation in the Black Room, Dorothy and Richard appeared to be trying to revitalize their marriage. A date book kept by Marlin Swing indicates that he began to socialize with them as a couple as often as he had once socialized with Dorothy and Johnnie. The Kollmars continued to observe the formalities, and never ceased in their written and spoken exchanges of endearments. On St. Valentine's Day of 1963, perhaps by accident and perhaps not, Richard picked a card for her of almost mystical appropriateness. The frontispiece featured an enormous stratosphere balloon, tiered with flowers and jewels. Its gondola was a tiny capsule of Arpege. He crossed out the message by Hallmark and scrawled in pencil: "Happy Valentine's Day to My Wife . . . I Love You! Even more this Valentine's Day—Love, love, love—Chop." [22]

That autumn, Richard had the first of a series of drunken accidents. Dorothy was awakened by his screams, rushed down to his third-floor bedroom, and found him sparring punchily with a fire that had started when he passed out with a cigarette in his hand. She helped him douse the flame and administered first aid to his hands. The doctor arrived and admitted him to Roosevelt Hospital.

There had been other fires at the house, which Dorothy endeavored to keep out of the newspapers. The Kollmars were the talk of the local engine company because Dorothy insisted that the firemen take off their boots before entering any light-carpeted room. This episode did hit the newsstands, however, when Dorothy panicked and called the nineteenth precinct. It was left to the doctor who treated Richard to minimize the extent of his injuries, which is second-best to having them not reported at all. The poor physician seemed as perplexed as Mrs. Bauer. "He has minor burns," Dr. T. Scudder Winslow told a reporter. Why, then, had he been hospitalized? "I only put him in the hospital because his bed was burnt up," Winslow replied.[23]

Dorothy took Richard to Puerto Rico in the winter. The trip, she told him to appease his wounded male pride, was a birthday present in lieu of a party. They returned, hale and rested, in time to face the other Shepard trial.

The trial was held at the courthouse of the Supreme Court of New York State, before Justice Thomas A. Aurelio, whose friendship with gangster Frank Costello had led, back in 1940, to disbarment proceedings, which Dorothy had covered for the *Journal*. She arrived, now with Richard, in an outstanding mink coat, stripping down to what one of her jurors, a short, bespectacled man named Miller who owned a clothing store in Astoria, Queens, assessed as "a very expensive suit." [24] They got under way on Friday, January 10, 1964, and ruled on Thursday, January 16. The courtroom was crammed with law students, press, nuns, and assorted civilians who undoubtedly attended to see Dorothy Kilgallen in the flesh.

The trial would turn on Edgar Hatfield's discovery of an early-nineteenth-century precedent that constrained Elaine's side from producing witnesses to testify that they had read the words in Dorothy's column and took them to mean Elaine Shepard. Nor could Elaine contend admissibly that she was told by people that they had read the column and filled in the blanks. Elaine could have easily done this. There were mothers at the Knox School who saw the column and knew immediately that Dorothy was referring to

Elaine Shepard; one even beseeched her to take some kind of legal action against the columnist.[25] There were colleagues, men who traveled with Elaine on the tour, who were ready to swear that she was there by reason of her good work and were astounded by the implications of the blind item, which was highly visible to them.[26] Ernie Kovacs, an old foe of Dorothy's from the time that she complained about the stench of his cigar as he sat on the "What's My Line?" panel, volunteered to take the stand and interpret the item. None of it was permitted. Such people were called "experts" by the court, a concept that some of the jurors—fortunately for Dorothy—found terribly confusing.

Richard Kollmar took the stand and perjured himself on Dorothy's behalf, swearing that Elaine had ridden home with him and a friend from the Knox School after the appearance of the item and after the complaint was served— another symbol of inculpatory amity of Shepard toward Kilgallen. Questioned further by Taylor and then faced with an adversary witness, he waffled pitifully.[27]

The star witnesses were Elaine Shepard and Dorothy Kilgallen, one fighting for what she perceived to be her honor and her professional integrity, the other for her solvency. There was no way that Dorothy could have lost the case and kept the house.

Ironically, the exigencies and language of the law had distanced each from her original intent. Dorothy had not really meant "lewd and unchaste"; Elaine had not intended three quarters of a million dollars. She claimed that she would have settled for a vindicating buck.[28] But in courts, as in supermarkets, small packages cost big money.

Elaine took the stand on the third day of the trial. "I passionately and fervently wish that there had been some slip of doubt in my mind as to the meaning of the article," she told the court.

> It was humiliating and shocking, because it had been an exhiliarating and glorious nineteen days. And this was a shameful thing. It was quite a challenge to keep up with the big-league reporters. And they were the cream, the absolute cream. When you are a woman reporter you are supposed to have to work twice as hard.

For several hours, Elaine responded to her own lawyer, who attempted to inflate her journalistic credentials, and to the defendant's lawyer, who endeavored to deflate them, intimating that her assumption that Washington's political insiders would deign to buzz about *her* was the function of a bloated sense of self-importance.

Elaine broke down at one point in the cross-examination. Aurelio offered her his own handkerchief. He assured the plaintiff that it was newly laundered.

Dorothy followed her on the stand. She was an excellent witness in her own defense, which is to say a consistent one. The vagueness of the language Winchell had invented stood her in good stead.

The columnist established once again that the item was as indecipherable to her now as it was when she was first served, that she had tried in every conceivable fashion to determine what she had meant in the first place. To no avail. What did the item mean? "I haven't a clue," she told Mr. Taylor implacably.

This was a woman, Taylor reminded the court, who for fourteen years had distinguished herself as a supersleuth on "What's My Line?" She had astounded the American public with her acumen, her ability to deduce the occupations of hundreds of total strangers and myriad mystery guests. Yet, here and now, she was claiming that she was unable to decipher the meaning of a group of words that she had herself composed.

"As a matter of fact," he said, "this past Sunday night, with a few questions, you identified an individual as being in the banana business."

"But I was helped by questions that had been asked by other panelists," she responded modestly.

"That's right. But in the course of a few questions, you found out this man was associated with the banana business," Taylor hammered.

"Well, Bennett had established that the vegetable was green."

"Miss Kilgallen, just answer the questions."

There followed an exchange of pettifogging that put Dorothy's thirty years of covering trials and playing games to the test. Given her premise that amnesia was here to stay, she staved off every one of Taylor's attempts to force her to parse the paragraph in question or to extrapolate probable meaning from general usage. She disclaimed knowledge of what she meant or could have meant by "buzzing," except to speculate that it was a "colorful" substitute for "saying." She disclaimed knowledge of why she had placed quotation marks around "the lowdown." He tried to draw from Dorothy an admission that she generally used quotation marks as a kind of literary raised eyebrow. He did not succeed.

Dorothy's amnesia was as inviolate as the language she used was invincible. "I am not a grammarian," she said summarily, "maybe my style is eccentric."

Toward the end of her day's testimony, Irwin Taylor introduced into evidence a second Kilgallen blind item and one for which Dorothy was obviously unprepared. It had run in the *VOB* on September 28, 1960, after the appearance of the one now in litigation but before Dorothy was served with her summons. The item read:

> A female writer visiting the set of "Misfits" got more than carried away by Clark Gable in his role opposite Marilyn Monroe. Her purple prose included this commentary: "He plays the kind of Gable audiences hunger for, a powerhouse, irresistible, determined, kindly, overpowering and rockingly passionate. . . ." Kiddo—kiddo—you have been carried away by cinema tradition.

This later item was introduced over the objection of the defense, claiming it was not relevant "unless it is connected with some attitude of Miss Kilgallen's before December 22, 1959, the date on which the item in litigation was published." Taylor countered that it was pertinent regarding "Miss Kilgallen's attitude toward Miss Shepard." Aurelio asked, "The question of malice, would you say?" "Yes, your honor," Taylor answered.

The article on which Dorothy based this rather patronizing peroration was written by Elaine Shepard and appeared in newspapers throughout the country. The unflappable Dolly Mae was perilously flapped on this one. She claimed she had no memory of how she had come to see the *Misfits* piece or any awareness that Elaine was the "kiddo, kiddo" to whom she referred. Taylor asked her how she might have seen the article without also seeing the by-line on it. "It would be my guess," she said, "that some-one connected with the movie studio had sent me the clip-ping or typed out an excerpt and said, 'There was some lady reporter around, and this is what she wrote.'"

The first Shepard *Misfits* piece admitted into evidence and the one Taylor showed now to Dorothy was clipped from the *Avalanche-Journal* of Lubbock, Texas. Dorothy was heartened. "I don't read the Lubbock, Texas—what-ever it is?"

Taylor then asked her whether she ordinarily read the New York *Daily Mirror*. She replied cautiously, "I might have or I might not have." He then admitted into evidence the same syndicated piece as it ran in Hearst's *Mirror*, by-lined Elaine Shepard and very prominently featured.

"This appeared right here in New York City and not in Texas in the Lubbock *Avalanche*," he apprised her.

"Then why did you show me the Lubbock one first?" she asked.

"That," Irwin Taylor replied, "is obvious."

The trial ended with Judge Aurelio's charge to the jury. He explained that Elaine was suing for $500,000 in puni-tive damages, any part of which the jury, using its collec-tive judgment, might award, and that punitive damages were intended to punish a defendant for malice, thereby discouraging other publishers from engaging in similar acts. Malice, he said, had nothing to do with the general under-standing of the word, but could be applicable if the libel was done "recklessly and with a disregard for the plain-tiff's right."

Compensatory damages were the more measurable, ac-cruing from injury done to one's "good name, fame, and credit." There was $250,000 involved here, any part of which the jury might award.

The eleven jurors deliberated from 10:53 until 4:10 P.M. (A twelfth member of the panel had been excused early in the trial because of a death in the family.) Ten was the magic number. More than half the jury, in the be-ginning, voted to award damages.[29] Then the tide began to turn. As the afternoon wore on, two of their members, the foreman and a professional psychologist, hammered away on the issue of Elaine Shepard's failure to produce witnesses. According to Mr. Miller, who had at first voted against Dorothy, "Both of them said if she were damaged how come she didn't produce any evidence that she was damaged in any way. Then they said she *couldn't* produce any witnesses." [30]

Miller himself believed throughout the trial that Dorothy was lying: "There's no question about it. It said one woman and eighty-some odd men." [31] But he was dissuaded from his original position.

Dorothy, who had excoriated the system at the Sam Sheppard trial of 1954, received a very fair shake from the ten who voted to dismiss the charge. Miller admitted, "I didn't like the woman. I didn't like her looks . . . I never liked her because she was a character assassin. But by the same token, I tried to be very fair." [32]

Dorothy sat alone in the courtroom for most of the day, huddled in her mink.[33] Through the years, for Dolly Mae Girl Reporter, jury deliberation had been a time of camaraderie, gin games, and the boisterous boredom of enforced idleness. This nonprofessional watch was decidedly different. When the verdict came in, at a little after four in the afternoon, ten to one in favor of Dorothy, she burst into tears of relief and thanked each of the jurors individually.

"She acted," Miller recalled, "like she was very emotional about it."

Dorothy told Roosevelt Zanders, "I'm glad that's over." What she told her priest is indeterminable.

A trial of somewhat greater importance was taking place in Dallas, where Jack Ruby was charged with the televised murder of accused assassin Lee Harvey Oswald. Dorothy left for Texas in mid-February to look in on the spectacle. She was not assigned the running story; Bob Considine got it. Perhaps she was not feeling well enough to take on the grueling extra work load. It is possible. More likely, however, her editors were becoming somewhat distrustful of Dorothy's ability to endure the long-distance run.

Back in November, she had reacted like most Americans to the assassination of JFK—with horror, incredulity, and ineffable sadness. On the Friday night of the murder, she watched the muted, keening coverage of the tragedy with

Johnnie and Bill Franklin. Before she left for home, she talked about the column she would have to write for the Sunday paper and wondered what she could possibly say.[34]

She instructed her driver to weave around the East Side. Shelley Winters flagged her down on Fifth Avenue and asked if she would pray with her at St. Patrick's. She stopped at the Stork Club, where Billingsley and Winchell sat by themselves in front of the television set; at a darkened Jim Downey's, where the owner was scrutinizing would-be patrons from behind a locked door and admitting only cronies; and finally at Clarke's where a No Music sign had been placed over the jukebox.

Back at the Cloop, she tapped out the story of her trip to Washington with Kerry, ending the column with a description of the President's enthusiastic search for her boy's essay paper:

> The picture that stays in my mind is the one of this tall man bending over a tall small boy, carefully scrutinizing envelopes until he came to the name "Kerry Ardan Kollmar—Grade 3B." This is the man who was assassinated in Dallas.[35]

Kerry was in the Black Room by himself very early the next morning as Dorothy, in her nightgown, eased open the sliding door and sat down beside him. They stared silently at the television screen. Dorothy took him in her arms and began to cry. Kerry cried with her.[36]

In Dallas, fledgling reporter Jim Lehrer of the *Times Herald*, which carried the *VOB*, was assigned to make her welcome and show her around the courthouse. He conducted a short interview with her in which she absolved the city: "I don't see why Dallas should feel guilty for what one man, or éven three or five in a conspiracy have done." [37] She indicated to Lehrer that she would be in town only until the weekend. The young Texan, who would become a prominent and prestigious television journalist, liked Dorothy enormously. "I was just a little dip-shit reporter," he recalled, "and she made me feel important." [38]

When she appeared in court on Thursday, during the selection of jurors, presiding Judge Joe B. Brown effervesced at the sight of her. Judge Brown, who was referred to as "Necessity" by the local lawyers because "Necessity knows no law," invited her into his chambers. He declined to discuss the case, but went on at some length about his history of heart attacks. He preferred them to head colds.

She lunched with Ruby's two attorneys—flashy Melvin Belli of San Francisco, and mountainous Joe Tonahill of Jasper, Texas. When she returned to the courtroom late in the afternoon, Tonahill was thundering at a prospective juror about the prejudicial coverage of the Dallas *Morning News*. Dorothy whispered to Considine, "This is where I left off at the Sam Sheppard trial nine years ago, only then it was the Cleveland *Press* they weren't supposed to read." [39]

What Dorothy thought about the character of the assassination, she had not yet made clear in either her writing or her conversations with friends. During this first trip to Dallas, she began to nurture doubts about the commitment of the federal government to full disclosure.

It began with Joe Tonahill, who, apparently impressed with Dorothy, showed her an exchange of correspondence between the defense and the Department of Justice. On January 9, 1964, the lawyer had written a ten-page letter to J. Edgar Hoover, to each member of the Warren Commission, including Chief Council J. Lee Rankin, and to Attorney General Robert Kennedy. [40] According to the story that Dorothy filed—her first assassination exclusive, which ran under a banner headline in the *Journal-American* of February 21 and was reprinted in the *American Mercury* —the letter requested "all of the reports and minutes and evidence in the possession of the Warren Commission." Hoover refused to cooperate; so did Rankin. [41] The assistant attorney general Herbert Miller, at the behest presumably of Robert Kennedy, directed his staff to turn over to the Ruby defense team reams of material digested from over fifteen hundred witnesses. All the material had been gathered by the FBI and the Warren Commission.

The material was an unexpected boon to the defense lawyers, who had expected no more than a polite rebuff. According to Dorothy's story,

Miller informed Tonahill that (although it was unusual to be sure) the FBI would be instructed to turn over to the defense the names and present addresses of persons who knew Ruby, or had met him at some time in his life, or who had expressed opinions about his personality or recalled incidents which might be important to the case. The "kicker"—the punch-line? Mr. Miller's sentence: "information concerning Oswald's assassination of the President will not be available as it does not appear to be relevant."

Say that again, slowly. Information concerning Oswald's assassination of the President will not be available. Perhaps it is dramatizing to say that there is an Orwellian note in that line.

But it does make you think, doesn't it? . . .

It appears that Washington knows or suspects something about Lee Harvey Oswald that it does not want Dallas and the rest of the world to know or suspect . . . Lee Harvey Oswald has passed on not only to his shuddery reward, but to the mysterious realm of "classified" persons whose whole story is known only to a few government agents. . . .

Why is Oswald being kept in the shadows, as dim a figure as they can make him, while the defense tries to rescue his alleged killer with the help of information from the FBI? Who was Oswald, anyway? [42]

On the day her Oswald story appeared in the *Journal*, Dorothy was summoned to the defense table by Joe Tonahill during a noon recess. He told her that Jack Ruby wanted to talk with her. This may not have been the first meeting between the New York columnist and the accused murderer of Lee Harvey Oswald. Tonahill received the impression that they seemed to know each other, that they related in a way that bespoke previous acquaintanceship. [43]

Dorothy and Jack Ruby shook hands at the defense table. She tried to cheer him by complimenting him on his composure. He said that he would welcome the chance to go to a hospital, get well, and perhaps do something "worthwhile." It occurred to her that anything Ruby might choose to do would be a step up from his former life in Dallas. [44]

Dorothy asked him whether he was prepared to face the questions about his sexuality, which would undoubtedly be raised at the trial. He replied that he was expecting the issue to be broached. He was, after all, a bachelor who referred to his pet dachshund as his wife. After a couple of minutes, Dorothy returned him to his lawyers. She wrote that she left the courtroom and "went out into the almost empty lunchtime corridor wondering what I really believed about this man." [45]

She was in and out of Dallas between that first publicized meeting and the close of the first Ruby trial on March 14, when he was found guilty and sentenced to death. But the columns she filed reflected only her first four-day visit there. "Doc" Quigg, of the Hearst chain, recalled that she was there "sometime in the middle of the trial," and called out to him, "My father says to say hello." [46] She was there during Belli's summation, at which time she attended a press party sponsored by the wife of a local publisher. One of the Texas women present beleaguered Dorothy by telling her how much "prettier" she was in person. At that same gathering, another woman said to Bob Considine, "Isn't it *awful* about the assassination!" Considine muttered, "Yes, such a young man." Dorothy riposted, "Oh, not that. What's awful is that it had to happen in Dallas." Bob whispered to Theo Wilson, "We'd better get Dorothy the hell out of here, she's going absolutely crazy." [47]

During one of her visits—sometime in March, before the verdict—she prevailed upon Joe Tonahill to make arrangements through Judge Brown for a private interview with Jack Ruby. She told Tonahill that she had a message to give to Ruby from "a mutual friend" of hers and Ruby's. Tonahill recalled that the common friend was described to him by Dorothy as a San Franciscan who "may have been some kind of a singer." [48]

There arises some question about the exclusivity of the controversial private meeting. Melvin Belli wrote:

Dorothy Kilgallen did have several interviews with Jack Ruby. If the reporter was resourceful enough to arrange the interview, Jack would talk with anyone and by this time I had resigned myself to this and didn't try to stop him. Most of what he said, anyhow, was gibberish. He did respect Dorothy very much and saw in her a very prestigious person who could get him an "audience" with almost anyone.[49]

Jim Lehrer flatly rebuts:

> When Belli says that Ruby was accessible for interviews, he is *wrong* about that. I never got an interview with Ruby and neither did anyone else. And I tried. Yes, indeed. All the time.[50]

Belli may not even have known about this particular meeting. According to Tonahill, he was "headed back to the hotel. I had remained behind to assist in working out the arrangements with the sheriff's guards and the Court and Dorothy."

In any case, Tonahill, who functioned as go-between and guide for Dorothy, asserted that she

> had probably a closer relationship with Jack Ruby than many of the other writers who attended the trial. . . . To my knowledge, she may have been the first neswpaper person to see Jack Ruby alone. At least, from the moment I got into the case until I left, I think she was.[51]

Joe B. Brown, awestruck by Dorothy, acceded readily to Tonahill's request. The meeting room in the jailhouse was bugged, and Tonahill suspected that Brown's chambers were as well. Brown and Tonahill chose a small office off the courtroom behind the judge's bench. They asked Ruby's ubiquitous flank of four sheriff's guards to consent to remain outside the room.

Dorothy was standing by the room during a noon recess. Ruby appeared with Tonahill. The three entered the room and closed the door. The defendant and Dorothy stood facing each other, spoke of their mutual friend, and indicated that they wanted to be left alone. Tonahill withdrew. They were together privately for about eight minutes,[52] in what may have been the only safe house Ruby had occupied since his arrest.

Dorothy would mention the fact of the interview to close friends, but *never* the substance. Not once, in her prolific published writings, did she so much as refer to the private interview. Whatever notes she took during her time alone with Jack Ruby in the small office off the judge's bench were included in a file she began to assemble on the assassination of John F. Kennedy.

A voluptuous haze hovers around Dorothy's involvement
with the assassination. Fertile imaginations can fathom
myriad shapes.

There is a story, for instance, which reached Texas from
France, to the effect that Dorothy was so terrified by the
import of what she learned from Jack Ruby that she ran,
with tape recorder in hand, straight to a Catholic priest in
Dallas, leaving the tape with the clergyman. No buttressing
data exist that Dorothy used a tape recorder during the interview. More significantly, everything in her character,
her history, and her behavior vis-à-vis the assassination
would have propelled her toward an editor and not a
priest, an airplane and not a sanctuary. The story and
others like it must be dismissed as unfounded and unlikely.

Paradoxically, in the absence of empirical knowledge of
what actually transpired between Dorothy Kilgallen and
Jack Ruby, or what it is she endeavored eventually to un-
cover as a result of what Ruby told her or what she
learned independent of Ruby, we must wait for a second
veil to form—for her relationship with a dissembling Out-
of-Towner, and for the elaborate cover-up surrounding her
own death in November of 1965—to more tenably apprehend substance in shadow.

It was Penn Jones, a newspaperman from Midlothian,
Texas, who first revealed the meeting between Dorothy and
Ruby.[1] Tonahill and Belli, as reported earlier, have confirmed that the meeting did occur, though there is a specific
and spurious demurral in a book by Lawrence Schiller and
Richard Warren Lewis, *The Scavengers and the Critics of
the Warren Report*.[2]

When Dorothy met with the shady, frightened, eager-to-
please killer, he was rapidly disintegrating. He liked and

trusted her; she symbolized class and clout. Assuming she was there to extract information in addition to carrying a message from the San Franciscan, Dorothy might have learned that the sky was falling, that Jews were being massacred in the streets as a result of his crime, that he knew Lee Harvey Oswald, that there was more than one gunman in Dealy Plaza—all of the above or none. Most salient was her failure to print anything about what transpired between them. Had the exchange been wholly crazed or nugatory, Dorothy would have had no motive not to publish. Other reporters were begging to see Ruby alone; only Dorothy was afforded the opportunity. The staggering singularity of the situation would have justified a *Journal-American* banner, if only to report her exclusive on Ruby's rapid deterioration. That she withheld suggests strongly that she was either saving the information for her book, *Murder One,* a chapter of which she had decided to devote to the Ruby trial;[3] that he furnished her with a lead which she was actively pursuing; that he exacted a promise of confidentiality from her; or that she was acting merely as a courier. Each possibility puts her in the thick of things.

Tracks of Dorothy's were laid down in the clear light of day, independent of her investigation of a possible conspiracy. She knew from the time she read the correspondence between Tonahill and the attorney general's office that the government had more on Lee Harvey Oswald than it was prepared to release. She did not rush to judgment, but neither did she refrain from publishing all responsible information that came her way. In her column of March 20, 1964, after Ruby was first sentenced, she recapitulated her earlier exclusive:

> The point to be remembered in this historic case is that the whole truth has not been told. Neither the state of Texas nor the defense put all of its evidence before the jury. Perhaps it was not necessary, but it would have been desirable from the viewpoint of all the American people.

The point to be remembered in any assessment of her evolving skepticism is that Dorothy was open-minded, accessible, and fearless. In this regard, she was almost unique among heavyweight, establishment journalists in the United States. What she was publishing has been made tepid by time, but doubting the official version then verged on apostasy.

The mind-set of her colleague and friend Bob Considine was far more typical. By March 6, only four months after the assassination and a half-year before the release of the Warren Report, he denigrated the European press for "still clutching to the long discredited notion that there was a dark conspiracy involving JFK's death." He had apparently learned at some point that Jack Ruby had had the opportunity to shoot Oswald on the day before he actually did the crime.[4] Using that datum as a kind of sealing wax, he closed himself hermetically to any and all evidence that challenged the lone-assassin theory.

In 1967, Considine wrote the introduction to *The Scavengers*, characterizing the critics of the Warren Report as "opportunists," "crackpots," and "graverobbers." By that time, two years after Dorothy's death, the merged *World-Journal-Tribune* concurred, editorializing, "We think it is time to ask the ghouls, the buckchasers, the sensation-mongers, and the character assassins to desist—to shut up until they can put up."[5]

Many reporters would have doubtless done as Dorothy did, but they imposed censorship upon themselves, believing, often with justification, that their papers would not publish the fractious or maverick story. Fortunately for Dorothy, he *Journal-American* was in too much trouble during the middle sixties to turn down an exclusive assassination story or to risk meddling with her *Voice of Broadway*.

Of the handful of reporters who had the commitment, the clout, the predisposition, and the intrepidity to go after what the government wanted withheld, some were frightened. Thayer Waldo of the Fort Worth *Star-Telegram* originally furnished to Mark Lane information that Officer Tippit, Jack Ruby, and Bernard Weissman (one of the signers of the notorious black-bordered advertisement that ran in a Dallas newspaper on the day of Kennedy's fateful visit, charging that the President had abrogated the Monroe Doctrine and "sold out to Moscow") had met in

Ruby's Carousel Club eight days before the assassination. Waldo would not use the story himself. Waldo also discovered that the Dallas chief of police had been surprised by the course finally chosen for the President's motorcade and was unable to fathom why the procession was instructed to take this more vulnerable route.[6] Nor did he use this story, though once again he made the information available to Mark Lane. Thayer Waldo was not minimizing the significance of his information. On the contrary, he told Lane that if he published what he knew, "there would be real danger to him [Waldo]."[7] Dorothy eventually published what Waldo had uncovered but was afraid to run.

When Mark Lane, subsequent to Dorothy's death, invoked her name during his lectures to college students, there were invariably derisive giggles in the audience. He told one group:

> You're laughing because you think of her as a gossip columnist. Well, I'm gonna tell you something. She was a very, very *serious* journalist. You might say that she was the only serious journalist in America who was concerned with who killed John Kennedy and getting all the facts about the assassination.[8]

Bob Bach recalled that she was just as enthusiastic, just as eager, to discuss a new music group as a hot lead. That may or may not be totally accurate. She was keenly aware of the tolerance threshold of the people around her and probably took special care not to permit her conversation on the subject to become obsessive. She had, however, always led a multilayered life, and the last twenty months were not excepted.

Still she played to win on "What's My Line?" Once, during this period, Bennett Cerf discovered her weeping after the Sunday-night telecast. When he asked her what the problem was, she replied that she hadn't guessed a single occupation in three weeks. He told her it was just a game.[9] Of course, it had never been *just* a game to Dorothy. Now that she was being watched for any sign of flagging ability, it was even more important to maintain her status as the shrewd, narrowing-in occupational sleuth. The three weeks turned out to be only a fallow period. And she came out of the slump. Whatever physical state she was in, there was never any sign that her deductive powers were in any way impaired.[10]

She remained, to an extraordinary degree, capable of exultation and benign envy in the presence of an enormous popular talent, but much more in touch with the well-springs of her emotions. She went with Bill Franklin to see an early performance of *Funny Girl,* Barbra Streisand's first starring vehicle on Broadway. When she and Bill went backstage after the performance to visit the actress, Streisand was cordial to Dorothy, but reserved. They had a drink together, and Dorothy was emboldened.

"I hate to sound like a fan," she said, "but you were wonderful. When you came down that staircase and sang I thought you really were the luckiest person in the world. That's something I've wanted to do all my life. Come down a staircase and sing a song like that."

Streisand naturally loosened up. And just as Bill and Dorothy left the dressing room, the young star called after her: "You know something. You're a nice lady. I thought you were going to be a *terrible* lady. But you're not. You're a very nice lady." [11]

Dorothy had never had too many women friends. And she was distanced now from the two to whom she had been closest. She and Lillian Boscowitz were simply out of kilter. Jean Bach was selectively inattentive to the depths of her feeling for Johnnie Ray. Dorothy began to draw drinking companions to her. Joan Crawford, whom she had taken to task in one of her first Hollywood columns thirty years before for combing her hair ringside at Mocambo, was among them. She tooled around with Crawford, helping the movie star promote one of her newly released films. They boozed abundantly together in the back of Crawford's touring car, which was well stocked with hundred-proof vodka.[12]

And there was Elaine Stritch, the musical-comedy actress who was as well known for her mordant and hilarious performances on stage as off. Dorothy and Stritch shared some of the same insecurities, and they apparently had a heady discussion about whether it was better for a woman to be beautiful or funny. After what must have been a particularly successful living-room performance, Elaine

Stritch telephoned P. J. Clarke's at three in the morning and asked for Dorothy. She had a pithy message to deliver in her nonpareil whiskey voice:

"Dorothy Mae?"
"Yes."
"Funny is better." [18]

Dorothy would occasionally express some boredom with the daily demands of the column.[14] And she looked forward to the time when she could get down to serious and uninterrupted work on *Murder One,* which was years overdue. But the peregrinations and peccadilloes of the very famous could still galvanize her.

One of Dorothy's new favorite press agents was Harvey Daniels, who handled press relations for the Regency Hotel, a relatively new hospice that was trying to replace Delmonico's as the "in" Park Avenue inn. Dorothy's column was, consequently, important to the management and to Harvey Daniels, who discerned nice change in the columnist in the last five years of her life. He found her "warmer, earthier, easier to talk to." Harvey was sluicing news to her about the Regency's celebrity guests. He telephoned her one afternoon to report that Ava Gardner had been embroiled in a messy fight involving spaghetti sauce and a good deal of destruction to Regency property.

"I don't believe it," Dorothy laughed.

"It's true. Moreover, she's going to have to pay for the damages."

Dorothy thanked Harvey and asked him whether he had given the story to anyone else. He said that he had not. "Make sure you don't," she said.[15]

Elizabeth Taylor, another Regency guest, could never fathom how Dorothy knew about the champagne she and Burton drank for breakfast or the fact that she habitually reserved a separate room only to house her wardrobe. "Goddamn it," Taylor said to Harvey, less annoyed than perplexed, "how did she find *that* out!" [16]

Even when Harvey missed occasionally, as he did when he furnished her with an item about a purported *ménage à trois,* the participants of which turned out to be just good friends, and Dorothy had to print a retraction, she was "maternal" rather than peevish. "Next time," she implored the press agent, "please check it out!" [17]

In late March, 1964, Dorothy agreed to participate in a Book Night at the Overseas Press Club. William Kunstler's *The Minister and the Choir Girl,* a study of the famous Hall-Mills murder case of the 1920s, was the subject of the evening. Kunstler, a radical, up-and-coming defense attorney, had focused a good deal of his attention on the press excesses that led to the indictment of an innocent woman, and specifically upon the zealotry of Hearst's New York *Mirror*, which was forced to make a sizeable out-of-court payment to the wronged defendant.

Dinner was served in the ornate dining room of the club. Dorothy sat on the dais with Kunstler; Anita Diamant Berke, the literary agent who arranged and chaired the evening; Gabe Pressman, then of NBC news; and Irene Corbally Kuhn. It had been Irene who had pulled some strings for Dolly Mae in Shanghai and the Philippines at Jim's behest, after he telephoned with the message, "Irene, I think my little girl's trying to emulate you." The veteran newswoman had felt, at the time, that Dorothy had not properly thanked her, and her cursory encounters with the younger woman over the years had reinforced her initial opinion of Dorothy as quirky, rude, and cold. [18] This night Irene was pleasantly surprised. Dorothy was easy to talk to and very affectionate. They chatted amiably on the dais.

There were about two hundred people attending that evening, seated at their separate tables, lingering over coffee. Jim and Mae Kilgallen, directly in front of the dais, were among them. As the discussion period began, good soldier Jim took William Kunstler to task for criticizing the organization—the usual round robin of defendants' rights *vs.* unfettered press. They were at it rather heatedly, Jim nettling the lawyer by his inability to come to grips with his surname. "It's Kunstler, Mr. Kilgallen," he interrupted at one point. "The name is Kunstler, *K-u-n-s-t-l-e-r.* You'll find it in the program." The old man reddened with anger. [19]

Anita Diamant Berke invited Dorothy to contribute. The subject of the Hall-Mills libel action had been broached. "What do you think, Dorothy?" she asked. "You covered the Sheppard case." [20]

In an apparent attempt to rally to her father's defense, Dorothy replied that Hall-Mills was not so singular as Kunstler might imagine. "Sam Sheppard should collect fifty million dollars," she said, "because he had the worst trial I ever saw." [21]

She then galvanized the press-club audience by relating, for the first time in public, her experience ten years before with Judge Edward A. Blythin in chambers when the jurist asserted to Dorothy that Sheppard was "guilty as hell."

Dan Morris, a bright and articulate writer and teacher, was staggered by Dorothy's revelations. He jumped up without waiting to be recognized by the chair. "Miss Kilgallen," he charged, "this strikes me as singularly the most important aspect of this whole business. If you are the journalist that you are supposed to be, why wasn't your headline the next day, 'Judge Says Sheppard Guilty As Hell!'? Is it not the duty of a journalist to tell the public things as they really are? If you had come forth with this information years ago you could have changed the venue and complexion of the entire case. *Why didn't you do this?*" [22]

Dorothy replied, in what Morris remembers to have been an "upper-lip way," and which the bulletin of the OPC called "obviously hurt," "Things said to a reporter in confidence should be kept in confidence."

Fortunately, F. Lee Bailey, Sheppard's new attorney, was also at the Overseas Press Club that night. Passing through town, he had come to hear Kunstler. He had never met Dorothy and had no idea that she would come forth with such an incredible statement.[23] He rose and spoke at length. He then nudged his table mate, Sheppard biographer Jack Pollack. "Introduce me to Dorothy Kilgallen," he said, "this I want on tape." [24]

Bailey and Dorothy repaired to the press-club bar. He was more interested in what she could do now than in what she had failed to do ten years before. Bailey was about to petition an appellate court for a writ of habeas corpus and then request certiorari from the new and liberal Warren Supreme Court. He needed fresh evidence. Dorothy agreed to do everything she could on behalf of Dr. Sheppard—tape, testimony, deposition. Judge Blythin had died in 1957. She was no longer bound to protect her source.

Her deposition and a similar one obtained from Edward T. Murray, a court clerk, were central to the decision of the higher court, whose chief judge wrote,

> A judge must have no interest other than the pursuit of justice and when he expresses in emphatic terms the opinion that the person before him is guilty the judge then has a personal interest in seeing that the defendant is convicted.[25]

Sam Sheppard was freed temporarily after the appellate decision. The Supreme Court granted certiorari one week after Dorothy's death and subsequently reversed the 1954 decision. He was tried again and acquitted. Jack Pollack recalled that Chief Justice Warren "flushed" when he learned of Blythin's remark to Dorothy, and that one of the two hours the court allotted to the case comprised discussion about Blythin and Dorothy. "Clearly, it influenced the court's ruling," Pollack wrote.[26]

After the death of Judge Blythin, Dorothy had talked to friends about his shocking exclamation. She had always *meant* to do something about it.[27] But for years, Dorothy had no world view, no abstract sense of justice, only a private, intensely personal sense of injustice. She howled only for Dorothy. It was only in her last years that she began to experiment with a world view that took the world into account.

She would not abrogate her passion for style, though she learned to accommodate styles that the younger Dorothy would have eschewed. Excess continued to alienate her. She wrote in her column that she would gladly break every copy of Peter, Paul, and Mary's "If I Had a Hammer," if she but had a hammer.[28] She called the Supreme Court decision on school prayer "a victory for Moscow." [29] She took the Black Muslim movement to be racist and unfriendly and would not consent to call Cassius Clay Muhammad Ali.[30] Yet she hit the hustings for Robert Kennedy when he ran for the Senate in 1964 and would have climbed every mountain with the younger Kennedy.

Her right-leaning politics, however, were now totally free from the glanglia of repression usually attached to the conservative point of view. She proved that dramatically when she volunteered to appear as a witness at the trial of

Lenny Bruce, shortly after the episode at the OPC. Bruce was facing jail on an obscenity charge after Manhattan District Attorney Frank Hogan, under pressure from religious groups, arrested him following a performance at the Café Au Go Go in Greenwich Village.

Dorothy was the surprise witness for the defense, as Marya Mannes, an outspoken, eloquent liberal, was the surprise witness for the prosecution. The former was a boon to Bruce's lawyers, Ephraim London and Leonard Garbus, as much for what she said as what she stood for.

Dorothy was still considered the very model of the prim, the proper, and the diocesan. The radical changes in her behavior over the past few years were known only to the New York cognoscenti. Dorothy was still Dorothy to the three judges who presided at the Bruce trial and to Frank Hogan, who was flabbergasted when she appeared one morning, put her arms around Lenny Bruce, and repaired to the corridor with Leonard Garbus to discuss strategy.

She testified for several hours, removing her white gloves in full view of the three justices, who sat impressively robed on a lofty dais. She was posture-perfect and concise. She knew the law and she knew the issues. Her function was to convince the court, as a cultural expert, that the language Lenny Bruce employed and the heretical thrust of his routines did not violate the existing New York State statute on obscenity.

Dorothy explained to the judges that she had first seen the satirist work while visiting Chicago with "some friends." She stated that she considered his work "brilliant." Lenny Bruce, Dorothy insisted,

> is a very moral man trying to improve the world and trying to make audiences think, which is a very good thing and a very moral thing and to be applauded. He seems to be concerned with religion, with civil rights, with the behavior of people in a given situation. He seems to want things to be better.[31]

Under the amicable questioning of Leonard Garbus, she averred that she had read the transcript of the performances in question. Yes, she was fully aware that the words "mother fucker," "fuck," "shit," and "asshole" were contained therein. Yes, she had heard the words before and even used some of them herself. In her opinion, there was "artistic purpose" to his employment of these words.

> I think that Lenny Bruce as a nightclub performer uses these words the way James Baldwin or Tennessee Williams or playwrights employ them on the Broadway stage for emphasis or because that is the way that people, in a given situation, would talk. . . . His unity, I believe, is social commentary. He goes from one subject to another, but there is always a thread of the world around and what is happening today and what might happen tomorrow, whether he's talking about war or peace or religion or Russia or New York. There is always a thread and a unity.[32]

Richard Kuh, of the district attorney's office, cross-examined Dorothy. According to Bruce's biographer, Albert Goldman, he

> appeared to be walking on cracked eggs; he was terribly anxious not to give the impression that he was lacking gallantry to a lady. Nevertheless, he pressed home points with his usual relentless style.[33]

Kuh read to Dorothy some portions of a routine that the comedian had done about Las Vegas, in which the phrase "tits and ass, tits and ass, that's what the attraction is, tits and ass" appeared. He asked her whether she found the words shocking.

> KILGALLEN: No, I don't think it's particularly shocking. It's just a word.
>
> KUH: Just two words in fact. Do you in your column use the words tits and ass?
>
> KILGALLEN: Never.
>
> KUH: Do you know exactly what Lenny Bruce was talking about?
>
> KILGALLEN: Yes.

KUH: And you think, this constant repetition of these words "tits and ass," "tits and ass," "tits and ass" was not to shock?

KILGALLEN: No, I think he's being critical of the monotony of what is on view in Las Vegas.

KUH: And you found his constant repetition of the words are necessary to express the monotony?

KILGALLEN: I think he felt that it was.[34]

She and Kuh jousted exegetically about a chicken and that portion of a Bruce monologue that referred to a woman returning home to find her husband in bed with one. Dorothy found it difficult to comport herself with the solemnity expected of her in her role as social critic. But she nonetheless asked Kuh and the court to clarify the issue for her: Did they know whether it was a crime to have a chicken if there was no sexual act with the chicken? Ephraim London, Bruce's chief counsel, said that it was, in fact, illegal to keep a chicken or chickens in an apartment in New York City. Kuh riposted that they were traditionally kept in the deep freeze and not in bed. Dorothy agreed that it had been established that the chicken was in bed, but that she was uncertain about the implied activities between the man and the chicken. If, indeed, they had gone beyond the stage of heavy petting, Dorothy conceded that they were then dealing with a monologue that had broached the subject of sodomy. "Sir," she said pawkily to Kuh, "sodomy is in the Bible, to be read in churches. I wouldn't rule it out of Mr. Bruce's act if he cares to comment on it." [35]

Near the end of her testimony, Dorothy made one statement that disturbed many of the civil libertarians present in the court and led Albert Goldman, author of *Lenny Bruce!!*, to view all of it with contempt. Kuh fished for what it was that Dorothy did find obscene and offensive. She cited a recently published novel called *Naked Lunch*, which she said she was unable to finish reading. "But it's published," she said, "and I think the author should be in jail."

Kuh remonstrated, with obvious delight, "Unfortunately, Miss Kilgallen, we can't do everything at once." [36]

Dorothy was aware immediately of what she had done. As she stepped down from the witness stand, she touched Lenny Bruce's arm and whispered, "I hope I haven't hurt your case." Bruce, who considered that Dorothy had more to lose than any of the other experts who had come forward and who was moved to tears during her testimony because her approval and understanding was a more significant imprimatur than a seal of approval from *The Village Voice* or the American Civil Liberties Union, assured her that she had been just fine. More importantly, Leonard Garbus, who was aware from the outset that she was not a First Amendment absolutist, was pleased as punch that she had been totally honest. It made the psychological impact of her testimony that much more powerful.[37]

Bruce was convicted by the lower court in spite of a gaggle of First Amendment absolutists, a plethora of allusions to Swift and Rabelais, and the imprimatur of Dorothy. The conviction was overturned by an appellate court, and Garbus believed that Dorothy's appearance was important:

> I have to think that she had a lot to do with the ultimate result of the case. The briefs that were filed placed an enormous reliance on her—again because of who she was and what she stood for.[38]

Johnnie Ray, who had convoyed Dorothy into the enlightenment that permitted her to defend Lenny Bruce, was on his way out of her life by the time she articulated her views on the comedian's behalf. Bill had settled in, taken over, and jettisoned all the excess weight from Johnnie's littered life. Monty was the first to go, taking with him a goodly quantity of valuable hootch and some hi-fidelity equipment. Bill had plans to rebuild the singer's foundering career; Dorothy was not included in those plans. But she was prepared for a separation; indeed, she might have welcomed it. After the hysteria, the suicide threat, the collapse, Dorothy finally accepted the fact that she could not have what she wanted, annealed, and assumed an almost maternal role toward him, in which capacity she was able to see Bill Franklin as the best thing that had happened to Johnnie since tear ducts.

In the spring of 1964, Bill began to implement the plan.

They took a house on the Mediterranean in Torremolinos. Johnnie would rest and revitalize himself. Bill would decide on the best way to extricate the singer from his contract with Bernie Lang. "It was a beautiful time for the both of us," Bill Franklin recalled.

> We studied Spanish in a little hut. Johnnie stopped drinking, took long walks through the woods with a wild dog that he'd picked up. I became more protective than ever. He missed her. There was some question of visiting. She said she would come. We both invited her. But she never did.[39]

Dorothy, who was no longer tethered to a daily radio show and free at last from her obsession with Johnnie, enjoyed a new mobility. She began to accept some of the many seductive invitations offered her as an eminent Broadway columnist. One such was a press junket to Salzburg, Carrara, Rome, and London—all expenses paid by Twentieth Century-Fox, which had three pictures in European production: *The Sound of Music; The Agony and the Ecstasy*, a film biography of Michelangelo; and *Those Magnificent Men in Their Flying Machines*.

In early June, 1964, she joined the junket in progress. She flew to Salzburg to meet more than a hundred of her colleagues, who represented newspapers from all over the United States. She interviewed some of the stars of *The Sound of Music*, walked in the warm Salzburg rains, and dined in a castle where a string quartet played Mozart.[40]

The day after her arrival, she traveled to the site of *The Agony and the Ecstasy*, in Carrara. Here the company planned a filmic extravaganza for the press. They were driven seven thousand feet up a mountain—an all-marble, shiny-plated mountain of white—out of which was quarried, four hundred years before, the material that Michelangelo had used for his titanic sculpture. Three Todd-AO cameras were positioned to film an explosion that would replicate the original quarrying technique.

After the harrowing ride up the mountain, the press milled about, waiting for the big bang in the rarified air of the bald mountain. Dorothy stood next to the press agent who had helped convince her to make the trip. (He was the donnish press agent, "Mitch," who had described the technique of replicating the exact style of the columnists he serviced.) She leaned toward him and whispered, "Who is that attractive young man over there?" The press agent replied that he did not know his name, but understood he was from a small, out-of-town newspaper.[41]

She was standing by the bus, ready to board. "Who are you?" Dorothy asked the Out-of-Towner. He told her his name. "And I know who you are," he said. "I'd know you anywhere. You're Clare Boothe Luce."

Dorothy giggled.[42]

They became friends fast. In London, the last leg of the tour, they broke away from the main group, drank at a posh private club, and walked over the Waterloo Bridge at dawn.[43]

In the course of several interviews, he would deny roundly and often that there was ever *anything* but a deep platonic bond between him and Dorothy. He talked about the Waterloo Bridge:

> We'd taken a very simple walk. We had one of those "Isn't it a beautiful night" conversations. I told her a story on the bridge having nothing to do with her. It was a plot line of something I was writing. Dorothy was a tremendous romanticist.[44]

Five days after Dorothy met him, she was back in New York, sitting in the downstairs bar at Delmonico's with Marlin Swing. Marlin had his arm around her as she told him about the Out-of-Towner. Having been through the Johnnie Ray affair with her, worrying all the time about her intense unhappiness, he was delighted with her revelations:

> She was like a little girl after her first date, going on about how they'd met, how marvelous he was, the moonlight and the clouds and the poetry he had recited to her. It was obvious that he had become very important.[45]

When they met in Carrera, the Out-of-Towner had been in the newspaper field for only a few years and was ambitious to transcend it.

Dorothy was not his first luminary. He was exceedingly attractive to women and had dated several beautiful young actresses, the last of whom broke off their relationship when she realized that he had a problem with liquor. They were in a living room with friends of his when he picked up a table and threw it across the room. Glass was broken; the police were called. "Something in his brain clicked when he drank," the actress, who does not wish to be named, recalled, "and he went bananas. The cops came and took him away. He told me later that it had happened before, that he had rammed his car into five other cars. Once I saw that, I didn't even want a superficial relationship with him." [46]

While maintaining that he had neither poetry nor passion for Dorothy, the Out-of-Towner nonetheless furnished several letters from her that appear to belie his demurrals. They can only be paraphrased here. But they are clearly letters from a woman in love, written with the comfortable intimacy of shared sentiment.

The first is dated July 3, 1964, less than three weeks after their first meeting. It is addressed to him at a post-office box. It is typed on a lovely piece of white stationery with a large raised rose in the left hand corner. She calls him "darling." She describes her environment at the moment of writing. The record on her stereo, she tells him, "is very YOU." She wonders what he is doing. She had spent the night before reading a book that he had recommended to her. Corresponding with him now, she claims, is both difficult and unnecessary; he understands even her silences. Call me, she implores; she longs to hear his voice. [47]

And there is one reference, even in this earliest missive, to the Regency Hotel in New York and *their* little room.

Six days later, she writes another letter and refers again to the Regency. Harvey Daniels had taken a picture of her there for some charity, with two business-type fellows. Dorothy attached a small note to the photo, sent it to the Out-of-Towner, and complained: "Where were you when I wanted you?" [48]

The Out-of-Towner proffered her letters and explained that they were sentimental merely. "Nothing in those letters about my 'bod', nothing about missing my body," he said. The room at the Regency that Dorothy had expressly described as theirs? It was his room, he maintained. Dorothy kept a change of clothes there for the evening if going home was inconvenient. [49]

The Regency is located at Park Avenue and Sixty-first

Street; Dorothy's town house was off Park and Sixty-eighth.

After he met Dorothy, he stayed at the Regency exclusively on his frequent visits to New York. Dorothy had set up a room arrangement with the hotel. The woman who handled the assignment of rooms at the Regency in 1963 recalled that "he used to stay at the Regency all the time ... the keys were given to her." Another staff person maintained: "She used to stay at the Regency maybe one day a month. She said she was working on a book. I thought she was collaborating with him."

Dorothy gave the Out-of-Towner the private number to the phone in the Cloop, on which previously only Johnnie had called.[50]

At a party for the opening of *The Carpetbaggers*, she asked Nick Lapole if the Out-of-Towner could sit at his table. Dorothy and Richard occupied an adjoining table. She and the Out-of-Towner sat back to back. "He never said a word to her that night," Lapole recalled.[51] "She danced with Richard."

Through the late summer and early fall of 1964, Dorothy began producing a series of explosive exclusives related to the assassination. The first was a corker. Howard Rothberg picked her up one night in mid-August, after what he understood, from Dorothy, was "some kind of meeting." She was toting a heavy sheath of papers inside the cover of the *Life* magazine that featured Lee Harvey Oswald on the cover, hefting the Mannlicher-Carcano with which he was alleged to have shot the President. Howard relieved her of the package as they left his car and headed toward a restaurant.

"What are all these papers?" Howard asked.

She answered jauntily: "Oh, it's just the Warren Commission Report." [1]

The report was not due to be released until late September, until which time it was classified Top Secret. Dorothy had somehow obtained a verbatim copy of a portion of the voluminous study, consisting of Jack Ruby's testimony to the commission, which had transpired in Dallas back in June of that year.

It would take Dorothy three days to convince her newspaper to publish the long-awaited document. She had first to swear to her publisher, Joseph Kingsbury Smith, and to the lawyers at the *Journal-American*, that she had done nothing illegal in obtaining the transcript and that the person from whom she obtained it was in rightful possession of the 102-page segment. Smith asked her to name her source. This she would not do.

Dorothy assumed that her paper's reluctance to publish transcended the legal issues involved. She would tell Mark Lane that she perceived a compliant self-censorship at the *Journal*, that the publisher knew that the government would not be pleased and that he might, as a result, become *persona non grata* at White House functions. Lane asked her if she didn't fear the same kind of social ostracism. "Oh, Lyndon's a bore," she replied. "Who wants to go to his parties?" Mark Lane was not buying her flip response. He believed that she was just too modest to proclaim that getting the facts out about the assassination dwarfed any social considerations she might have had.[2]

In her dealings with the paper, she permitted Paul Schoenstein to photostat only one page of the document, which was run to authenticate the coup. The rest she demanded back after its contents were typed. The testimony was published in three parts, with Dorothy's comments, questions, and assessments running alongside. The installments were treated with proper hoopla. She was making available, for the first time, one of the most eagerly awaited documents of the century.

The first installment of the Ruby transcript was published on August 18. Two days later, Lee Rankin of the Warren Commission requested J. Edgar Hoover to conduct an investigation of how Dorothy came into possession of the classified report.[3] The investigation was exhaustive, with agents interviewing everyone who was in the room during the Ruby interview or had access to the transcript thereafter. They questioned sheriffs, a jailer, a court reporter, secretaries, district attorneys, and lawyers. The Warren Commission was allowed to investigate its own people. There is no indication in the FBI dossier that the source was ever uncovered. When Dorothy somehow learned that the federal agents were narrowing in on a female court reporter who had transcribed the proceedings, she made her one concession, insisting that a man and not a woman was the source of her material.

Two federal agents knocked on her door on August 21. She asked them to tea, told them that she "would die rather than reveal her source," and noted, with amusement, that they appeared to be embarrassed, recognizing the futility of their mission. As they were about to leave, she gave them one clue, in jest. "I can tell you that it wasn't John Daly," she said. Daly was married to the daughter of Chief Justice Earl Warren.[4]

Immediately after she caused the Ruby transcript to be published, Dorothy made another trip to Dallas. There she somehow obtained the original police log that chronicled the minute-by-minute activities of the department in the immediate wake of the assassination, as reflected in its radio communications.[5] She ascertained from the exclusive material a surprising datum that would not be incorporated into the massive Warren Commission Report. Chief Curry of the Dallas police department, who was in the first car of the motorcade, had reacted to the shots he heard with an initial command: "Get a man on top of the overpass and see what happened up there." [6]

Dorothy noted, in her banner story based on this latest acquisition:

> Twenty-four hours after the assassination, however, Chief Curry assured reporters that the sound of the shots told him at once they had come from the Texas School Depository and that "right away" he radioed an order to surround and search the building. But actually, as we see from the Police Department's official version of events, Chief Curry's immediate concern was not the Depository, but the triple-tiered overpass towards which the Presidential car was moving at about eight miles an hour when the fatal shots were fired.[7]

J. Edgar Hoover was following the dispatches of the "flighty and irresponsible" Dorothy Kilgallen with extraordinary and painstaking attention. Her dossier is annotated in Hoover's own handwriting, a phenomenon that Mark Lane, who has seen voluminous documents released under the Freedom of Information Act, considers most unusual.[8] Hoover quibbles in the margin with some of her conclusions. "Wrong" he scrawled underneath her surmise that the overpass must have been unguarded. He also corrected the time at which she deduced that police were dispatched to the Depository. He did not and could not correct her startling revelation about Curry's order, which was treated in a somewhat truncated fashion in the still-unpublished Warren Commission Report. It reported only: "The Dallas police log reflects that Chief of Police Curry reported the shooting of the President and issued his first order at 12:30 p.m." [9] The commission did not choose to mention what that order was.

Invigorated by her growing skepticism, Dorothy, with Richard's assistance, reenacted the assassination from her swank five-story town house on East Sixty-eighth Street.

From the information she was assembling, Dorothy learned that the testimony from which the Dallas police first radioed a description of Oswald's height and weight came from the eyewitness observations of Howard Brennan, a steam fitter who was sitting on a concrete wall more than a hundred feet away from the sixth-floor corner window out of which the purported assassin took aim and fired. The Warren Commission Report would state: "Brennan was in an excellent position to observe anyone in the window." [10]

Late one night, with the lights on in the house, Richard positioned himself, broomstick in hand, leaning out of one of their fifth-floor corner windows. Dorothy went outside to East Sixty-eighth Street. Standing at the approximate distance that Brennan had been situated, she craned up at her play-acting husband, hoping, doubtlessly, that they were unobserved by neighbors. Dorothy concluded that there was no way in the world that such a description could have been accurately determined by Brennan. [11]

The report would be masterly in its accommodations to the statements of the witness, who asserted that he discerned no change in Oswald's stature as he saw him walk around inside the Depository and then fire his shots, though it was definitely determined that the assassin would have had to kneel to shoot, given his height and the fact that the window pane was not broken. [12]

Dorothy was never convinced that Brennan could have seen what he was reported to have seen. And the Zapruder film, which was not available to her at the time, eventually revealed, according to Mark Lane, that the steam fitter "was not even looking up at the time the shots were fired." [13]

Dorothy did not publish this particular observation. But she did describe the reenactment to Mark Lane when they came face to face for the first time at her town house.

Lane and Kilgallen were an unlikely match. He and she were miles apart politically. As a New York assemblyman, he was an outspoken critic of Governor Rockefeller's pet bomb-shelter project and uncovered information that some of the sponsors of the proposed program had a financial interest in its implementation. He was a civil rights worker and a defense attorney. He had gone to Dallas at the request of Marguerite Oswald, who asked him to defend her son's interest before the Warren Commission. As a consequence of that brief encounter, he embarked on an independent, scrupulous investigation, which would be published eventually as *Rush to Judgment*. In these years, he was chipping away, gathering information, and battling for access to media, which was usually denied to him.

When he was told, at his New York office of the Citizens' Committee of Inquiry, that Dorothy Kilgallen was on the telephone, he thought, "My God, what does *she* want? Hasn't enough happened to us already!" [14] He had never liked her or what she appeared to represent. He perceived her to be a provincial, insignificant gossip columnist.

When they met, he found himself charmed and moved by her. He had fought a long and lonely fight. And here was a woman of some power and goodly access to the public weal who shared both his passion and his persuasion. Dorothy told Mark that she hoped to "break the case." He reminded her that there would be formidable obstacles placed in her way and possibly danger. "That doesn't concern me," Dorothy replied. "They've killed the President, the government is not prepared to tell us the truth, and I'm going to do everything in my power to find out what really happened." [15]

They established a working relationship, exchanging information and ideas. Dorothy functioned frequently as a conduit to bring to public attention, through her newspaper, the fruits of his investigation.

Dorothy told Mark that she knew her phones were tapped from the time she published the Ruby transcript, and that his probably was, too. "Intelligence agencies will be watching us," she warned. "We'll have to be very careful." [16]

The enlightened modern heretic remains mindful, to some extent, of being dismissed as paranoid. When Marguerite Oswald told Mark Lane that she suspected her son was an agent, he advised her to keep her suspicions to herself lest she diminish her credibility.[17] Neither did he now disclose his own fears of surveillance or repeat Dorothy's admonition about the intelligence community to anyone. Mark Lane did not, however, consider that Dorothy was overcautious when she suggested that they would be watched. He was to say, in 1976, "I would bet you a thousand-to-one that the CIA surrounded her as soon as she started writing those stories." [18]

When he and Dorothy needed to communicate on the telephone, they arranged to go to separate phone booths. At her suggestion, he was code-named "Parker" and she "Robinson." They met several times at her home, once or twice with Richard present. Richard listened quietly and excused himself before the termination of the meetings. Dorothy usually had a drink in her hand; she was never anything close to drunk. Dorothy and Mark also met at P. J. Clarke's and other East Side saloons. Once, late at night, they exchanged information under a lamppost.

She began to produce headline stories based upon statements and affidavits that Mark Lane supplied to her at these clandestine meeings, material gathered from personal interviews he and his small staff gathered in Dallas. He had talked about some of the dissident data on local radio stations. The networks had systematically prohibited him from appearing.[19] Dorothy had a wider audience, access to print —a more suitable medium for the complex stories that wanted telling—and new insights.

Using information furnished to her by Mark, she asked questions, in her front-page stories, that would be conveniently begged when the report was finally issued.

From her first reading of the purloined transcript, Dorothy could not accept the theory that Ruby had shot Lee Harvey Oswald because he "loved the President." Nor did she believe it credible that Jack Ruby, a police buff, had never met Officer J. D. Tippit. She paid a good deal of attention, in one of her stories that accompanied an installment of the Ruby transcript, to the alleged meeting at the Carousel Club between Jack Ruby, Officer Tippit, and Bernard Weissman. She pondered how it was that Ruby, who loved the President, and Weissman, who sponsored the black-bordered advertisement in the Dallas paper that had allegedly "infuriated" the ferret-man, could have met eight days before the Presidential visit. She noted that the commission's questions to Ruby about the alleged meeting were lax, and that "while he never admitted that the reported meeting took place, he never directly denied it either." [20]

With Mark Lane's input, she built upon that dubiety. He gave her a copy of his own secret testimony to the Warren Commission, never before published. It was that testimony of Lane's, based on information provided to him by Thayer Waldo, which introduced to the commission the possibility of the meeting, and it was on the basis, presumably, of that testimony that the commission asked Ruby the pertinent questions.

Under the headline NEW DOROTHY KILGALLEN EXCLUSIVE—TALE OF "RICH OIL MAN" AT RUBY CLUB—Dorothy printed Mark's secret testimony. But his testimony implicated a *trio* at the Carousel: Ruby, Tippit, and Weissman. Reexamining the transcript of Ruby's testimony before the commission, she noticed that the questions posed to him concerned not a trio, but a quartet. Earl Warren, in his questioning, informed Ruby that Lane had said: "In your Carousel Club you and Weisman [*sic*] and Tippit . . . and a rich oil man had an interview or conversation for an hour or two." [21]

Dorothy, who did not have access yet to the complete Warren Report, had to deduce,

> The mention of the "rich oil man" by Chief Justice Warren would indicate then, that the Commission was informed of the meeting by a source other than Mr. Lane, and that this second source provided the name of a fourth party—the oil man. If that is not the case, if the Commission had only Mr. Lane's testimony to go on, it would appear that the oil man was "invented" by the investigators. And it is difficult to imagine the Commission doing any such thing. [22]

The introduction of the rich oil man into the questioning effectively discombobulated the already-confused Jack Ruby.

When the report was released, it was clear that *no* testimony was given by any of the 552 witnesses about a rich oil man. Either there was a significant omission in the report of the Warren Commission, or the oil man was part of the unofficial corpus of information to which Warren was privy, or Dorothy's thesis—however "difficult to imagine"—was correct.

Through August and September, Dorothy hung out all the dirty linen of the official case. She printed story after story of witnesses who had been threatened by the Dallas police or the FBI. She indicated that there was some evidence that the rifle used was a Mauser and not a Carcano.[23] She had in her possession, transcribed, excerpted, and published, a taped interview between Acquila Clemmons, one of the witnesses to the shooting of Officer Tippit, and Shirley Martin, a co-worker of Mark Lane's. The story was run on the first page of the *Journal-American*.[24]

Mrs. Clemmons stated that she saw two men running from the scene, neither of whom fitted Oswald's description. "I'm not supposed to be talking to anybody, might get killed on the way to work."

Q. Is that what the policeman said?

A. Yes. See they'll kill people that know something about that. There's liable to be a whole lot of them.

Q. Who?

A. There might be a whole lot of Oswalds and things. You know, you don't know who to talk to, you just don't know.[25]

Mrs. Clemmons was not called to testify by the Warren Commission.[26]

None of Dorothy's published information was incontrovertible. None of it, perhaps, would have constituted the rosetta stone of the case against the official version. But Dorothy was the first reporter to publish most of it, based responsibly on affidavits, tapes, documents, and interviews with witnesses.

When the Warren Commission Report was finally published, she had an insider's view of the way in which the Commission systematically omitted, minimized, or denigrated what detracted from the case that they had set out to prove: that Oswald was the lone, unaffiliated assassin; that Ruby was a vagrant psychopath.

Dorothy responded to the release of the report in her column:

I would be inclined to believe that the Federal Bureau of Investigation might have been more profitably employed in probing the facts of the case rather than how I got them . . . At any rate the whole thing smells a bit fishy. It's a mite too simple that a chap kills the President of the United States, escapes from that bother, kills a policeman, eventually is apprehended in a movie theater under circumstances that defy every law of police procedure, and subsequently is murdered under extraordinary circumstances.[27]

She was bolder when talking with friends. She told Marlin on several occasions, "This has to be a conspiracy!"[28] She expressed the same thought to Bill Franklin, Johnnie, Bob Bach, and her makeup man, Carmen Gebbia. To Mort Farber, a lawyer and manager of music talent, she said that the Warren Commission Report was "laughable . . . I'm going to break the real story and have the biggest scoop of the century."[29]

And she was in love again.

She arranged a private screening of *The Sound of Music*. Marlin Swing was there and suspected that she did it just to revivify the first blush of Salzburg and her meeting with the dark-haired man on the bald marble mountain. She and the Out-of-Towner junketed together again in late October to Rome, Florence, and London.

In her girlish fiction, Dorothy Mae could not have fantasized a more romantic ambience for a love affair. They stayed, in Florence, at a hotel with their adjoining balconies overlooking the city. Sunlight streaming in, they rattled off their respective stories. The Out-of-Towner climbed onto Dorothy's balcony, pleased with what he had just written.

Impressed, she laughed and covered her typewriter. "Let's go out," she said. "I can't write a column after that."[30]

They walked hand in hand through Florence. She excused herself to duck into a little church. A non-Catholic, he stood back as she walked buoyantly toward the altar. "Pssst," he called to her, "you forgot the Holy Water."

And there was more laughing.

He would claim, during one interview, that he was made aware of her drinking problem for the first time in Rome. Dorothy was returning to the States the next morning, and he was continuing on. They dined and got back to the hotel very late. She suggested a nightcap in her room. They each had one or two drinks out of a full bottle of vodka.

According to his story, she said, "I think I'll go," and she took the bottle with her. When he went to awaken her so that she could make her plane, he discovered that the bottle was empty.

"God, you drank a lot last night," he said.

"I know," Dorothy replied.[31]

After the fall junket, Dorothy began to use her considerable power to advance his career as a writer of popular songs. She was able to convince at least one important recording artist to include a work by the Out-of-Towner in a forthcoming album.

Dorothy telephoned the Out-of-Towner excitedly. By this time, they had their standard opening exchange.

"Hello," Dorothy would say. "This is Susie Ding-Dong, your New York secretary."

"Hmmmm," he would reply, "that name has a *ring* to it."

"She was so thrilled to be able to do something like that," he recalled. "She loved being a part of something." [32]

She arranged to have a company set up to publish all the Out-of-Towner's songs. Someone affiliated with the company recalled: "He wouldn't have gotten in the front door without Dorothy. His stuff just wasn't that good."

Through 1965, Dorothy's health varied considerably. She was still taking Seconal to sleep, and the Out-of-Towner experienced the same petering-out conversations from the Cloop to which Johnnie, Marlin, and Bill had been subjected. Carmen Gebbia recalled that there were some evenings before the television show when she entered the makeup room holding on to the wall, asking "How do I look? Do I look all right?" [33]

In March, she fractured her left shoulder. The condition was attributed publicly to a fall. She was hospitalized twice after that fall. The length of her stays seems too long for treating the injury. The only obtainable data from University Hospital includes one page of unsigned and scrawled handwriting that says "sustained injury to (L) shoulder." None of the three doctors who treated her on admission or readmission will comment. One stated to Kerry Kollmar that he kept her in the hospital for an inordinately long period—there was a short stay, followed by another of three weeks—to withdraw her from alcohol and barbiturates. Included in the medical report is the designation "Allergies," which refers probably to barbiturates. Her general health was described as "excellent," her blood count "within normal limits."

At one point during her confinement, Pearl Bauer recalled, Richard brought her "pills and liquor that damned near killed her." [34]

When Myrtle Verne lunched with Harvey Daniels, she referred to the "goings-on at the house." [35] She was no more specific.

Dorothy began writing *Murder One*, which was four years overdue at Random House. She did some work updating the Sheppard case and finally came face to face with the attractive osteopath in Cleveland, where there was a cocktail party in his honor. They evinced tremendous fondness toward each other. He was grateful and Dorothy faithful.

Afterwards, she discussed Sheppard with the Out-of-Towner. She asked him: "What do you *really* think?" He answered, "I *think* as little as possible. But if he's guilty, he's one of the strongest men who ever lived." [36]

He would comment during one interview, "A good Sam Sheppard, a *very* good Sam Sheppard, could have fooled Dorothy. She was easily taken in." [37]

Dorothy was working as well on the Jack Ruby chapter. Joe Tonahill collaborated on that segment of the book. He wrote, in a letter of January 12, 1978:

> You asked why she never published an account of the episode [her private interview with Ruby]. I think she was in the process of doing a book called *Murder I* [*sic*] when she died. At least, she and I talked many times over the phone about the book and I was doing a piece for it for her which had to do with "Irresponsible Murder" as opposed to "Murder I". . . . She may have the material that I sent her in her notes. [38]

Producer Joe Levine, to whom Dorothy was excessively attentive in her column now, evinced great interest in the property as a possible television series, with Dorothy doing the voice-over. They had at least one meeting, at which they discussed some of the legal problems involved. Levine had seen a general outline and the chapter on Sheppard, but not the Ruby material. In conversation, he told an associate who prefers to remain anonymous, "She's got some good stuff there. It could be a helluva thing." Six figures were mentioned as the purchase price of the property. It was money that would have alleviated her financial problems considerably.

Litigation as avocation ceased. She dropped the Cindy Adams matter after the Adamses countersued Dorothy, Hearst, King Features, Hearst Consolidated, the Chicago *American*, the *Journal-American*, and the Chicago American Publishing Company—each for one million dollars. Dorothy dropped Edgar Hatfield when he presented her with a bill for $20,000 on the Elaine Shepard matter and threatened to involve her "in unfavorable publicity" if she didn't make a healthy payment on the money owed to him, which was long overdue.[39]

She could no longer afford the extravagances of pique, though she did indulge occasionally. There was a latter-day brannigan with Johnny Carson, whom she accused of tastelessness because he told some off-color jokes during the inauguration of Lyndon Johnson. Carson came back at her during a White House photographers' dinner: "Dorothy Kilgallen took issue with some of my material," Carson said. "That's like having your clothes criticized by Emmett Kelly. I don't know why Dorothy should take offense at a joke I made. I didn't when her parents made one."[40]

She rather liked Carson and regretted the exchange of vitriol.[41] Unlike Paar and Sinatra, he stopped short of the grotesque.

Jack O'Brian was not so charitable. After Dorothy blinded a rather tepid item about him in the *VOB*, he appeared on the Fitzgeralds' radio show and vilified her.

He recalled the substance of the broadcast pridefully.

> I said to Ed Fitzgerald that I doubted Miss Kilgallen will appreciate my replying this way, but since you brought it up, I'd like to talk about Johnnie Ray and a few other men in her life. . . . And I talked and Ed fed me questions. . . . It all involved things I had observed myself at parties in her house, at El Morocco, at the Stork—the groping of each other and the kissing and the necking. We finished up with that and Ed said,

"That certainly answers the question." And I said, "I doubt very much that she will answer me because bullies are usually yellow."

Dorothy did not answer him. Jim Kilgallen, a buddy of O'Brian's, telephoned.

"Jack," he said, "what did you do to my little girl?"

"It was impelled by the protection of my own good name. And it's a better name than hers."

"I promise you, Jack, she's been destroyed. I just talked to her at home and she's in tears. I hope you're not going to do it again," Jim Kilgallen said.[42]

Dorothy spent a good part of the summer of 1965 in Europe, alone. "What's My Line?" now stockpiled some shows to permit the panel extended vacation time. She clearly missed the Out-of-Towner. Dorothy wired him that she had stood alone on Waterloo Bridge and thought of him.[43]

She went to Ireland as a guest of the Irish Tourist Board to cover the Bal des Petits Lits Blancs—the ball of the little white beds, which was held in an old Dublin castle. Princess Grace of Monaco was also in attendance. "The ball," Dorothy wrote, "was a bore." [44]

In mid-June, she returned to the States and was scheduled to appear on the American Broadcasting Company's "Nightlife," which was then hosted by Les Crane. Bob Bach, who was booking talent for the show, had invited her. She expected that she would be discussing the assassination and showed up with a thick folder full of material. The order came down. Nick Vanoff, one of the producers, went to see her in the dressing room as she prepared to go on. He asked her not to broach the subject. It was, he said, "too controversial." She replied that she had come specifically to talk about the assassination. He implored. She capitulated. Vanoff passed Bob Bach, who was standing in the doorway. "Send her a dozen long-stemmed roses," he whispered to Bob.[45]

At least once during that same summer, she sojourned to Zurich. She stayed at the Grand Dolder Hotel. Friends gleaned various impressions about the purpose of the trip. Jean Bach thought she was there for rest, retreat, and to make a dent in *Murder One*.[46] Mort Farber, who was now handling her legal affairs, claimed she told him that she underwent cell therapy,[47] a Swiss program of rejuvenation through the injection of animal embryo cells into the body. She sent a wistful little note to the Out-of-Towner, indicating that she missed him.[48]

However it was that she occupied her time in Switzerland, Dorothy returned looking and feeling better than she had in years. Kerry Kollmar recalled that this was the first time in a long time that she seemed really well. Johnnie Ray and Bill Franklin, who were back from Spain, were elated by the apparent state of her health. She was plumper. Her color was higher. Many of the quirky symptoms she had manifested disappeared, including an occasional locking of the jaw, about which Bill had asked her once and about which she would not comment. Gone, too, was the whining voice, the regression to dependent little girl.[49]

She spoke with Mark Lane for the last time in late summer or early fall. She said that she planned a trip to Dallas. "I expect I'm going to learn a lot this time," she said. He was about to leave the country, and promised that he would telephone on his return.[50]

They discussed, at some point, another perception, jointly held. The *Life* magazine that she carried with her, featuring the inculpatory picture of Oswald with a Carcano in one hand and socialist literature in the other, was said to have been taken by Marina Oswald in their backyard in Texas, on March 31, 1963. It was purportedly confiscated by the police when they went foraging for Oswald's belongings. Oswald exclaimed, upon seeing the photo, that the picture had been doctored, that it was not his body and that he would prove it in time.[51]

The authenticity of the picture has since been seriously discredited. Photoanalysis, in 1964, indicated that the real Oswald's head was superimposed on another body—a body that was doing all the wrong things for Oswald and all the right things for the Warren Commission.

Robert Sam Anson would comment in *They've Killed the President*, written ten years after Dorothy's death, that the bushes shown in the background of the snapshot were not in bloom at the time Marina asserted she had photographed her husband, that the photo showed bright sunlight when the day in question was cloudy with touches of rain, and that the stance he assumed was a physical impossibility: "When one attempts to stand at such an angle, one invariably falls over." [52]

Photographic expert Robert Grodon told the House Assassinations Committee in September, 1978, that there was "a paste-line through the chin" of Marina's purported portrait of an assassin.

Dorothy had in her possession the *Life* cover and the photographs taken when Oswald was in custody. The chin of the man in the police station is cleft and pointed, that of the man on the magazine cover broad and jutting. It is at the point just above the chin that the fragments were affixed.

She and Mark agreed that the picture appeared to be doctored. She never specifically pinpointed the most telling facial disparity. "And I never mentioned it to her, either," Lane commented, "for rather obvious reasons." [53]

Dorothy's last published item about the assassination of John Fitzgerald Kennedy ran in her column on September 3, 1965:

Those close to the scene realize that if the widow of Lee Harvey Oswald (now married to another chap) ever gave out the "whole story" of her life with President Kennedy's alleged assassin, it would split open the front pages of newspapers all over the world. Even if Marina explained why her late husband looked so different in an official police photo and the widely-printed full-length picture featured on the cover of *Life* magazine, it would cause a sensation. This story isn't going to die as long as there's a real reporter alive—and there are a lot of them.

On Johnnie Ray's return from Europe, he headlined at New York's Latin Quarter on a bill with Johnny Puleo and his Harmonica Gang. The gig was successful. Johnnie's material was new, his voice improved, and his old energy restored. A critic for *Variety* wrote, "Ray opens strong and continues to pour it on, turning a ballad like 'What Now My Love?' into an emotional striptease. . . . He does for tense what Perry Como does for relaxation." [54] Dorothy broke her promise to Richard and raved about the appearance in her *VOB:* "Johnnie Ray is such a smash in this current Broadway engagement, he's been signed for the Tropicana in Las Vegas starting October 5." [55]

"Dickie may not like it," she told Bill Franklin, "but I'm just reporting the facts. He can't deny that the boy is a smash." [56]

She visited Johnnie almost every night during his three-week engagement, waiting backstage for him as he came off. Even though she was out of harm's way vis-à-vis the singer, there was Richard to think about and the recent O'Brian smear. Neither of them would understand that the relation ship had annealed into an intimate and loving friendship. Indeed, Johnnie himself had no idea of Dorothy's emotional priorities.

Dorothy, who was vain enough to think it might hurt— as it would have—did not tell Johnnie about the Out-of-Towner, nor about the many trips she had made to Europe without visiting, nor about the junkets. She resumed a close and loving relationship with Johnnie and Bill. In October, she flew out to Las Vegas to see Johnnie perform at the Tropicana. His opening coincided with Tony Bennett's at the Riviera. She was flown out by Joe Levine, who was hyping Bennett in connection with a new movie.

Bill Franklin met her at the airport bearing a gift. "For you," he said, handing her a lavender and pink purse of brassy mesh with a silver dollar on one side and the words "Welcome to Las Vegas—Big Spender," on the other. She dangled it by its long metal chain.

"I love it," she said.

"I told you I had rich friends," Bill replied.

At her hotel, Bill waited while she changed for the evening. She emerged looking smashing in a slinky black dress with pearls in her hair. She put some money into Bill's hand for taxi and tips. "Everything I need is right here in this extraordinary purse," she said. And she carried it all night.[57]

They met Johnnie at the Tropicana. The three of them caught Bennett's show and made a mandatory stop at the party Joe Levine was hosting for him. After Johnnie's last show, he took her back to the Riviera and kissed her good night. She had an early plane back to New York.

Johnnie turned to watch her as his cab pulled away.

She was so happy that night. As far as I was concerned, nothing had changed. The only reason she came out was to see me. The Levine party was a pretext. She wasn't much on junkets.[58]

Dorothy wrote to the Out-of-Towner on lavender paper she had purchased in Switzerland. They had obviously planned to meet in New York, sometime in the fall, to discuss their publishing venture. Indicating that her schedule was particularly hectic, she asked him to make the trip in "late October or early November." They would then have time "for conferences and all that jazz." She signed: "Kisses, d." [59]

Sometime in October, while Carmen Gebbia prepared her for the television show, Dorothy blurted out to the makeup man that she was "all excited."

"Is it Kennedy?" he asked.

"Yes," she said, "and it's very cloak and daggerish."

She told Gebbia that she was going to New Orleans, where she was going to meet someone who was going to give her "information on the case." Gebbia remains vague about the details: "It was a designated area. She said she didn't know the man, but she'd recognize him because of something—a walking stick, a straw hat. I don't remember. I do know that she said to me several times, 'If it's the last thing I do, I'm going to break this case.' " [60]

New Orleans, of course, was one of the hub cities of the assassination. Big Jim Garrison, the district attorney who evinced ferocious interest in the possibility of conspiracy and brought Clay Shaw to trial if not to justice, reigned there.[61] The months that Lee Oswald spent there prior to the death of the President, distributing pro-Castro literature and, at the same time, attemping to infiltrate the anti-Castro organization of Carlos Bringuier, were never fully explored by the Warren Commission or the FBI. Bringuier was also the publisher of an anti-Castro newsletter supported by the Central Intelligence Agency. The items published in Bringuier's propaganda sheet were strikingly similar to many with which Dorothy, violently anti-Castro, had been peppering her column since 1959.

On October 18, 1965, in her column, she reported on actor Patrick O'Neal's "ostentatious liberalism" while filming outside of New Orleans, alienating citizens by "flashing his CORE card." That is hardly the kind of item that would have been fed to her by the film's press person. It is possible that she was in New Orleans around this time, or at least that she was communicating with a right-wrong informant there.

But this is highly speculative. She was a clam about sources, never once mentioning to Mark Lane, Johnnie, Bill, Bob Bach, Marlin, or Gebbia whom she saw on any of her sundry trips, or what it was she was hypothesizing to supplant the lone-assassin theory, which was long since discredited in her mind.

On Sunday, November 7, "Mitch," the press agent, phoned her at her home around 6 P.M. to find out whether she had late plans after "What's My Line?" Richard answered and said that she was resting. Dorothy then picked up and told her caller, with whom she often socialized, that she had a previous engagement. He assumed she planned to see the Out-of-Towner.[62]

She went to "What's My Line?" as she had done regularly for fifteen years. Bennett Cerf told her that he had read and liked the segments of *Murder One* that she had given him.

The panel that Sunday night included Dorothy, Arlene, Bennett, and Tony Randall. Dorothy wore a low-cut wing-sleeve dress. The show was dull, but Dorothy was not. Her speech was crisply perfect, her mind razor-sharp, her spirits high.

The panel missed guessing a man who operated the Hollywood Wax Museum. A woman named Jones signed in. Bennett quickly established that her product was dangerous, but he went down to defeat on deducing "firearms."

"However," Dorothy asked, "would it do a lot of damage and make a lot of noise?"

"Yes."

"Would it be in the dynamite family?"

"Yes," John Daly said, coyly, "it would be in the dynamite family."

Dorothy pulled back and straightened up, as she always did when she was right there:

"I don't know anyone else in the dynamite family. Is it dynamite?"

Daly asked her what Miss Jones did with the dynamite. "I think Miss Jones sells dynamite," Dorothy said jauntily.

There was applause, after which John Daly complimented Bennett "for opening the door."

Joey Heatherton was the mystery guest, indicating that she was on her way to Vietnam to entertain "the boys." The commercial instructed the audience to "Come all the way up to Kools." Little time remained for the final guest, a lady sportwriter. Eight down, two to go. Daly called time. The panel wasn't even close to determining the woman's occupation. A stubborn hubbub emerged from Dorothy Mae's space.

"What is it, Dorothy?" the moderator asked, rushed and annoyed.

"Is she a writer?" Dorothy asked speedily.

"Good heavens!" Daly exclaimed, genuinely impressed. Time remained only for quick, standard *adieus*.

"And good night, Dorothy Kilgallen," John Daly said.

After the show ended at 11:00 P.M., Dorothy and Bob Bach repaired to P. J .Clarke's. They pressed through the mob at the bar and were seated immediately by Frankie Ribando, the maître d', at table 36, by the blackboard and the rear exit. Dorothy's favorite waiter, young Patty Blue Baker, brought them drinks. She was having her standard vodka and tonic. Dorothy told Bob, in her tantalizing way, that she had a late date. He had not approved of Johnny and he did not like the Out-of-Towner. He and Dorothy were both cute and evasive about their outside activities. Bob never probed for what was not offered. He walked her to her car after midnight. He was "under the impression" that she was on her way to meet the Out-of-Towner.[63] Johnnie was in California.

She entered the reddish-dark cocktail lounge of the Regency Hotel alone, greeting Harvey Daniels, who was at the bar near the door.[64] It was approximately one o'clock. She was bright, cheery, and a little high.[65] She walked to the right, toward a corner table. When Harvey left at 1:30, he was under the impression that she was still at the table.

She would have had to pass Harvey in order to leave, except if she exited through the kitchen.

She would not have remained in a chic piano lounge seated alone. It was simply not in her nature. But Harvey did not see the party or parties with whom she sat.

Harvey Daniels is the last person who will *admit* to seeing Dorothy Kilgallen alive. When she walked toward her corner table, she yawed into oblivion. Nothing further can be directly determined about these last hours of her life.

Dorothy was discovered dead sometime Monday, sitting up in bed, not in the Cloop, but in the third-floor master bedroom. A copy of Robert Ruark's *The Honey Badgers* lay by her side.

The *Journal* headlined the death, of course, and trumpeted their inclusion in Monday's paper of Dorothy's last column, which, it asserted, she had written "early in the morning" and sent, by messenger, at 2:30 A.M. Jim Kilgallen was at work, they said, and was told of the death by Mae. He asked Eddie Mahar, of the transmogrified love diary and the Kilgallen-Lotto communications, at an indeterminate time, whether he could leave. "Mr. Kilgallen," the story continued, "said his daughter apparently suffered a heart attack, her first." [66]

Dorothy had taped "To Tell the Truth," a Goodson-Todman identity game, on November 2. She, Arlene Francis, and Joan Crawford appeared in masks. The panel had to determine which of the three masked ladies was "the real Joan Crawford." The program was aired on Monday, November 8, from 3:00 to 3:25 P.M. Immediately after the show, Douglas Edwards made the first announcement: "Dorothy Kilgallen, just seen on the preceding prerecorded program—was found dead in her home today." [67]

On Tuesday, November 9, the lights went out up and down the eastern seaboard.

Joan Crawford, under the influence of grief and spirits, stared out her window and was heard to exclaim, "What a wonderful tribute to Dorothy!" [68]

Ten thousand mourners filed passed her closed and covered African mahogany coffin at the Abbey Funeral Directors, directly across the street from St. Vincent Ferrer. Dorothy was gowned in cream and gold satin brocade, a pearl rosary draped in her hands, a pink bouquet of tiny flowers from her children. During the first private night at the Abbey, Mae Kilgallen had taken Lillian Boscowitz by the hand and led her up to the casket. "She's so beautiful. She's so beautiful," the old woman keened. "Why. . . ." [69]

What happened to Dorothy?

The heart-attack verdict was short-lived. Over the staunch objections of Richard Kollmar, Dorothy was removed to the Medical Examiner's Office for autopsy. A death certificate issued on November 15 ascribed the cause to "acute ethanol and barbiturate intoxication—circumstances undetermined." It meant that she died from too much pills and liquor. "Circumstances undetermined" is not a common designation. The ME's office, which was headed at the time by the august forensic pathologist Milton Helpern, was admitting that it did not know whether the death was suicidal or accidental. The question of foul play was never officially entertained.

After three years of investigating the events surrounding Dorothy's death, it is clear to me that she did not die accidentally and that a network of varied activities, impelled by disparate purposes, conspired effectively to obfuscate the truth.

A household of family and servants endeavored to protect Dorothy from scandal—either because they thought she had taken her own life, feared that the public would misconstrue, or had reason to believe that she was not alone in the third-floor master bedroom before she succumbed. Dorothy would have enjoyed the Grand Guignol audition for witnesses that was staged on her behalf.

The pathology department of the New York Medical Examiner's Office did its job competently. But what it knew was more than it told; and pathology was itself apparently told much less than it should have been by the chemists in toxicology, upon whom the former relied for analysis and quantification of the barbiturates and basic drugs that were reposited in Dorothy's body. Dr. James L. Luke, who was dispatched to the house on November 8, explained to me in a telephone interview, "You can't just go charging around in a situation like that causing a lot of grief, much of which may be unnecessary. These kinds of cases are much more complicated than, say, Jame Smith." [1]

The New York City Police Department did virtually nothing to determine the circumstances under which Dorothy Kilgallen died. Its reports, if such they may be called, reveal that a woman was found dead in a tidy room. Witnesses were not interviewed. No attempt was made to reconstruct the events of the previous night. A lone and singular police procedure was utilized that seemed designed to obviate any possibility of determining what happened to Dorothy after she greeted Harvey Daniels and repaired to her intimate corner at the Regency Lounge.

The official version disseminated to the press implied accident. Dr. Luke, who performed the autopsy and certified the death, spoke *ex cathedra* for his office. His statements combined inept waffling with extraordinary arbitrariness. Luke was interviewed by the New York *Herald Tribune* for a story that appeared on November 16:

> Dr. Luke would not speculate about the form in which Miss Kilgallen had taken the barbiturates. "We'd rather leave that up in the air," he said. "We don't want to give that out—well, just because." . . . He said that combining alcohol and sleeping pills was a common form of accidental death. Miss Kilgallen had taken only "moderate amounts" of alcohol and the drug before her death, Dr. Luke said. He wouldn't give any figures.[2]

The New York Times had reported on November 10 that "a Medical Examiner's report said that Miss Kilgallen died of 'the effects of a combination of alcohol and barbiturates, neither of which had been taken in excessive quantity.' " That same *Times* piece stated that a bill had been filed for introduction to the New York City Council by Councilman-at-Large Paul O'Dwyer, which would further delimit the disclosing of Medical Examiner's findings in any death because of "the public speculation over the recent death of Dorothy Kilgallen."

Dorothy might have commented, as she did when she discovered that the Department of Justice deemed information about Lee Harvey Oswald irrelevant to the defense of Jack Ruby—say that again, slowly.

Did the public have a *right* to know? To penetrate what was pretty obviously a benign attempt to withhold facts about the death of a Roman Catholic woman?

Darkness, alas, is not selective.

Pete Hamill wrote an exceedingly Pete Hamill column about Dorothy the day after she died, called "The Celebrity." He said that she had been a superb reporter but that she had stooped to conquer, to become a gossip columnist and a television personality instead, and had grown rueful and lonesome in the end. Hamill did not know Dorothy any better than the sentinels of darkness who watched over the truth at 45 East Sixty-eighth Street. He quoted a friend of hers, who said, "Hell, she even died alone." Hamill concluded his piece: "She died in her five-story townhouse . . . in one of the twenty-two rooms, next to one of her eighteen telephones." [3]

Had Pete Hamill been as knowledgeable as he was effective, there would be no reason now to dig further. What he did not mention, however, was that she had resumed her reporting career at the end of her life, that she was pursuing the most important story of her time, and that she had earned the right to think that at least some of her eighteen telephones were bugged by an agency of the United States government.

What happened to Dorothy?

The extent of at least one of the cover-ups that surrounded her death betrayed a power and modality that transcended good works. Dr. James Luke probably did not think she committed suicide, and he remains chary about quantification. By "moderate," he explained in a telephone conversation in 1978, he meant that "the pills were not what we might expect to find in cases that are suicide." He knew, additionally, back in 1965, that there were 50 cubic centimeters of "pink fluid" found in her stomach." [4] The liquid was sent to toxicology for analysis. If the analysis was done, the results were not made available to him on the formal toxicological report.

During our telephone conversation, he perused the autopsy results. "There is material in her stomach which I'm sure is Seconal," he said. "From a quantitative basis, it would have been important to know what was in the stomach. Clearly, it was something that if it wasn't done should have been done. We had a problem with the laboratory. Capabilities were not what they should have been." [5]

Dr. Michael Baden, chief medical examiner for the City of New York, examined the raw data on Luke's autopsy report during an interview in 1978. He concluded that the percentage of barbiturate found in Dorothy's brain and liver indicated that the body reposited the equivalent of "fifteen to twenty" 100-milligram Seconal capsules. Equivalency is significant, as we shall see, for several reasons. Seconal was assumed because it was the drug prescribed to her. Back in 1965, however, the ME's office did not have the techniques to distinguish among the three groups of fast-acting barbiturates. Baden's estimate could not include the unanalyzed pink fluid. When I asked him why, back in 1965, Luke had termed such an ingestion "moderate," Baden replied, "You should see some of the cases we get in here!" [6]

Dr. Donald Hoffman, senior chemist in toxicology at the New York Medical Examiner's Office, examined the autopsy report and concurred that Baden's estimate was "reasonable." He added, "The formal data indicate that it was acute poisoning due to alcohol and barbiturates and that the barbiturates alone could possibly have killed her." [7]

Two other professionals looked at the medical values of barbiturates and alcohol found in brain and liver. Neither wishes to be named. One, a pathologist associated with an independent laboratory, stated, "She apparently drank a lot and took a lot of pills." The other, also a senior chemist in toxicology at the Medical Examiner's office, agreed with Dr. Hoffman. "The pills alone," he said, "were in the lethal range."

On my behalf, two different doctors were questioned in 1978 regarding *what they were told about the Kilgallen case* in 1965. They were both associated with the ME's office then but not directly involved with the work that was being done to determine the cause of Dorothy's death. What had been *presented* to them as the truth?

Both of them recalled that there was alcohol present and "a little Seconal." One was asked, "Can you look back upon what basis you recall it [the Seconal] being present in a small amount?" He responded, "That was the word that was being spread—that there was alcohol and a very small amount of barbiturate."

After a column by Liz Smith appeared in papers throughout the country, alluding extensively to my investigation of Dorothy's death and its relationship to the Kennedy assassination, I received a letter from a forensic pathologist who practices in Michigan. He volunteered to do what he could to assist me in evaluating the medical data contained in the autopsy report. He claimed to have an interest in Dorothy and in the Kennedy assassination. After a purported consultation with other pathologists in the area, whom he would not name, the man from Michigan concluded: "The overall weight of evidence here leads us toward accidental death, two to five capsules." [8]

The process is called "disinforming." It is a favorite ruse of intelligence agencies to disseminate data that is untrue but whose acceptance is useful to them.

How might it avail anyone to "disinform" some members of the Medical Examiner's office in 1965 and a biographer in 1977? To furnish data that is consistent with accident rather than suicide? Suicides must be investigated to exclude the possibility of foul play. Psychological autopsies are performed to elicit information about the decedent's mood and activities prior to the time of death. Steps are retraced. Events are reconstructed. *Some* effort is made to construct a chain between life and death.

In September, 1978, for instance, the thirty-one-year-old heir to the Woodward fortune plunged to his death from his ninth-floor hotel suite in New York. A thorough police investigation was conducted because it was determined that James T. Woodward "had a pleasant conversation" with a hotel clerk thirty-five minutes before his body was found on the roof of an adjacent building. He had been "in good spirits, even cheerful." Such a revelation is not a definitive indication of foul play. It is, however, the kind of information that issues from a routine investigation of suicide and compels even further probing.

After Dorothy's death was decreed an accident by a most extraordinary upending of good sense and common knowledge, any attempt to construct a life-to-death chain was deemed unwarranted. Thus, the skeletal police reports, represented to me as complete, and that part of the Medical Examiner's autopsy report that details gross findings at the scene, reveal only that "a middle-aged," "well-nourished," "white female" was discovered dead abed in "an orderly elegant apartment." She had on a blue robe, false eyelashes, and extensive makeup "involving the face, neck, and upper chest." She lay on her back, her head tilted left on a pillow, the covers pulled snugly up to her chin. She was bathed in the constricted light of a small, overhead reading lamp. A copy of Robert Ruark's new novel had fallen to one side of her.[9]

The sentinels respected her vanity even in death. She had tried, out in public restaurants, to avoid using or at least being seen in the eyeglasses she required to read anything but the boldest menu print. The book was appropriately noted. And the broadly bruited, obvious surmise was that she was reading before she was overtaken. There is, however, no mention of eyeglasses found on or around the bed.

What happened to Dorothy?

She was discovered dead, of that we can be quite sure, at least twice. The official version sets the time at noon or one on Monday. The police report, signed by Detective John A. Doyle of the local 19th Precinct, states: "DOA found by Maid Marie Eicher S/A between 12 and 1 PM lying on back in bed clad in night clothes. Pronounced DOA by Dr. Saul Heller 11 E. 68th St.: ME Dr. Luke present at scene." [10] The autopsy report states: "According to maid, she went in to awaken deceased at 12 noon and found her unresponsive."

James and Evelyn Clement, the butler and the cook, were interviewed in 1978. They subscribe wholly to the official version. Sunday was their day off. After arriving at the house early Monday morning, James contended that he dispatched Marie to awaken Dorothy around noon. There was, he said, a meeting at Kerry's school for which she had to prepare.[11]

Marie was Dorothy's personal maid. Anne Hamilton recalled that she "came in now and then to sew and prepare Dorothy for important engagements. . . . In her forties, pretty, not tall, charming, happy-go-lucky. She was married and did this as a sideline." The only two particulars that appear in the police records about Marie are wrong. Her surname was "Eichler" and not "Eicher." "S/A," which refers to residence and means "same as," is also erroneous. She did not live with the Kollmars. Marie could not be located for questioning. Pearl Bauer, the last of the Kollmar bookkeepers, is "under the impression that Marie has been dead for quite a few years." [12]

Marie may have been the *first* to discover Dorothy, but the time was not one o'clock or even noon, according to several sources.

All the newspaper accounts of the time related that Dorothy, on the night of her death, went to sleep in a house co-occupied by husband Richard and son Kerry. But, in fact, an exchange student who does not wish to be named, but whose status and residency have been confirmed by Kerry Kollmar, awakened early that morning on the fourth floor of 45 East Sixty-eighth Street. He slept in the room previously occupied by Kerry's Nu Nu, Miss Muller, who had returned to her native Germany. The student had been in the employ of the family for more than a year. For his room and board, he tutored Kerry in mathematics and accompanied him, most mornings, either to St. David's or to the bus that went directly to the school. [13]

The student took Kerry to the bus on Monday, November 8. After returning to the house, the young man, who speaks with a heavy accent, went up to Myrtle's fifth-floor office to ask her to type a letter for him.

> First she ignored me completely, which was unusual, and did not respond to my greeting. She was busy shuffling the wheel with address cards. After waiting for a few minutes, I asked, "Could you type this letter?" And she said she was very busy calling doctor. I thought there was something wrong. But what I would not be knowing. And she continued with that very frantically. Then I was coming down to have my breakfast in the tiny room, and somewhere in the hallway on the same floor, I saw James running. [14]

He did not recall precisely when this all happened. "But it must be before ten," he said.

Evelyn Clement had to identify him as "a member of

the family" before he could pass the policeman who was positioned at the door. He talked to James in the early afternoon. The student remembered their conversation:

> This is what he said when I asked him, after coming from the class: that she herself put an end to her life, that it was a suicide combining pills and alcohol. I think predominantly this was the theory of the man.

The young man did not agree with the theory that Dorothy had taken her own life, though if he is correct in his recollections of James Clement's surmise, then James, at some point, saw something different from the pristine scene described in the official reports of the police and the medical examiner. The exchange student commented:

> Knowing her personally, I would like not to think suicide. She was very cheerful about life. She was working on her book, very enthusiastically finishing. It was a kind of committing, day to day. There is much talk about the CIA silencing her, but it is only speculation. Anything could have happened, however, because the house was so big.[15]

James Clement denied, during our interview, that he perceived, had cause to perceive, or communicated to the exchange student that Dorothy had taken her own life. Evelyn Clement was present while we talked. Her only addition to the perplexing reconstruction of the bizarre scene at the house was her clear memory of Dorothy, "lying there with her earrings on." [16]

Jean Stralem—Mrs. Donald Stralem—a friend to the Kollmars for decades, was en route to her office at "about ten in the morning" that fateful Monday. She sat in the back of her husband's limousine, which bore eminently low-numbered and highly visible commissioner's plates. Her home had apparently been telephoned, at which time it was determined that she was on her way to the office. A policeman stopped the car in traffic. She rolled down her window. The policeman advised her that Richard Kollmar wished to see her. There was no mention of Dorothy's death.[17]

Mrs. Stralem exclaimed, during our interview, "I still

have no idea how that policeman found me. But that's something you don't forget. And it had to have been before noon or I would have been on my way to lunch. When I got to the house, Dick was in his chair crying. So drunk! So upset! So in tears!" [18]

Richard needed a little help from his rich friends. Before the official intervention of the police and the ME, he was probably hoping to circumvent the law and arrange to have Dorothy's body taken directly to the Abbey.

If Mrs. Stralem is right about the time at which she was stopped, the police were blatantly malfeasant. I was given what was purported to be complete New York City police reports by the Public Information Division, headed in the beginning of my investigation by Commander Gertrude Schimmel. One document from the homicide division indicates that it was first informed at 1:00 P.M.[19] That designation is contradicted by the testimony of Detective John Doyle, who claimed that the first official police presence occurred at 3:20 P.M.

There is more to buttress the theory that Dorothy was discovered hours before the official version purports.

Michael Sean O'Shea, the press agent, had several conversations with Myrtle Verne about the death and the discovery. Myrtle herself died in 1975. O'Shea related the thrust of his talks with the secretary:

> Dorothy Kilgallen had already passed on when Myrtle arrived before 10:30 in the morning. The maid and the houseman were aware of it, so was the local precinct. Dick Kollmar was aware of it. Miss Verne arrived in the morning with her usual nonchalance, used her key to the house, went to her office, and then discovered that the maid and the houseman were very upset. And that's when Myrtle Verne realized that Dorothy Kilgallen was dead.[20]

Kerry Kollmar interviewed Saul Heller—the doctor who pronounced and the one for whom James Clement ran—on March 16, 1978. Kerry communicated the substance of their conversation to me.[21] To most of Kerry's questions, Heller replied, "I'm 73 years old. I simply can't recall." The doctor claimed to have kept no records about Dorothy or to have been aware of her several confinements. He did not remember who was at the house when he arrived. He did, however, eventually recollect that he was "eating breakfast when James came to fetch me at about 9:30 in the morning."

What happened to Dorothy?

An elaborate cover-up, somewhere in the stylistic middle of Agatha Christie and *Hellzapoppin*, was staged, it would seem, at 45 East Sixty-eighth by some well-intentioned sentinels. To justify the considerable passage of time between the actual discovery and when it was that they were compelled or felt prepared to go public, they moved up all pertinent times by several hours, recapitulating earlier events.

Dorothy's hairdresser, Marc Sinclaire, arrived at the house at about 12:30, late for an appointment. Sinclaire refused to see or talk to me, but he told his story, with minor variations, to several of Dorothy's friends, two of whom I know to be exceptionally accurate in rendering detail.

Jean Bach repeated the hairdresser's tale:

> Marc Sinclaire, who discovered her, said that she obviously didn't know it was going to overtake her. He was supposed to come over and put her together for a lunch date. They were buddies. He was let in by the servants and told that she hadn't come down to breakfast yet. He had expected that she'd be dressed and down. He went upstairs and walked into her room. She was absolutely upright. Her book was in her hand. He said, "Dorothy, you're late for your lunch date." [22]

Marlin Swing repeated the hairdresser's tale:

> Marc was going to do her hair. I think he said that there was a police car outside the house, but he paid no attention to it at the time. James let him in and went to get Dorothy. And then he called down to say, "I'm having trouble waking Miss Kilgallen." Marc said there was no surprise in James's voice. Like they knew it, and wanted things to look right.
>
> When he found her, Marc said she was wearing a matching outfit—the kind she would never wear to go

to bed—a bolero-type blouse over a nightgown. She had her eyelashes on. He said she never slept with her false eyelashes on. He would often wake her up so that he was accustomed to how she looked in the morning. He claimed they had discussed the book she was holding. He knew she'd read it.[23]

Sinclaire's story is not a self-serving fantasy. Most of the newspaper accounts credit him with the discovery. Albin Krebs, then of the *Herald Tribune*, cited the hairdresser in his story. Krebs subsequently recalled, "I'm certain I got the information from a family source, possibly the husband." [24]

The *Journal-American*, which presumably had an inside line, published two versions on consecutive days. Its first breaking story, on November 8, reported, "She was found by a maid who went to wake her about noon." On November 9, they wrote, "She was found dead when her hairdresser arrived at 12:45 P.M."

Whatever the ramifications, his own accounts and the confirmations within newspaper stories that relied on primary sources place Sinclaire at the house and right in the maelstrom of the death events. He is mentioned nowhere in the official reports. Neither of the investigators from the 19th Precinct whom I interviewed remembered his presence. He was not questioned. James Clement denied all.[25]

Then there appeared to have been more physicians at the scene than circumstances required. Heller, of course, is all over the official records as the physician who pronounced right after Marie's discovery. Dr. David Baldwin, however, told Kerry Kollmar that he pronounced late in the afternoon. Baldwin was exceedingly fond of Dorothy, had been treating her for some time, and remains the Kilgallen family physician. It is unlikely that he could have been mistaken about what must have been an event of such impact. Kerry spoke with Baldwin on January 17, 1978, and wrote to me that same day:

> During my conversation with Baldwin this afternoon, he definitely indicated that he had been called onto the scene, and had, upon arrival, pronounced my mother dead. During a subsequent phone call he told me that

he had no knowledge that Dr. Heller was apparently also there. I am almost certain that he told me that he was called by my father.

The remarkable plan could have produced a series of genuinely misled and soothsaying witnesses. Marc Sinclaire was obviously meant to think that he was the first to discover Dorothy's body. Baldwin was probably being used to authenticate an alternative version of events. For some reason, the cabal was aborted, leaving only bizarre clutter. Marie Eichler, aka *Eicher*, became the discoverer of record. Sinclaire disappeared from the official version without leaving so much as a hairpin. Baldwin is nowhere recorded as having been on the scene.

As we shall see, there exists the possibility that a second medical examiner also entered the picture.

What happened to Dorothy?

If official records tell nothing else—nothing about the event that is investigated—there are certain *pro forma* requirements that result in a mirror reflection of the investigation itself. This is the first defense of any bureaucracy. Narcissus with camera and stopwatch, covering his vitals.

The documents that relate to the investigation of Dorothy's death are unusual in this regard.

Manhattan homicide possibly appeared on the scene. A Supplementary Complaint Report signed by homicide detective Peter McPartland indicates that he was informed at 1 P.M. There is no datum revealing how he came to know or what he did once he knew. Nor will he elucidate. A letter to McPartland was not answered.

A second detective with the New York Homicide Squad, Raymond Seiler, is cited in the records as having witnessed the autopsy. Seiler wrote to me in March, 1977:

> If the family had any doubts as to the cause of death of Dorothy Kilgallen they would have contacted me years ago. . . . Your enclosure by Liz Smith gave me the inference that your possible suspects will be Castro, CIA, or FBI. Ridiculous! . . . As far as intense public interest in the death of Dorothy Kilgallen—this can only be generated by poorly informed people making a mystery out of it.[26]

Detective Seiler was unable to lunch.

If he and his colleagues at homicide were informed at 1 P.M., they must have done something to presume that no foul play had been involved in the death.

There is no indication of how the Medical Examiner's office came to know. The autopsy report states that the ME was informed at 2:45. Records do not indicate by whom. Luke suggested that "it must have been by the police." [27] But which police?

The chains, the traceries, the linkages by which responsibility can be imputed, by which a linear reconstruction of the investigation can be made, are all absent from the official reports. Odd.

We do know, however, that 3:20 P.M. is the time when the 19th Precinct admitted to having been informed. They could hardly have done otherwise. Things were beginning to heat up. Word had already leaked to the media. CBS-TV was poised to go with the story, which they had ripped off the UPI wire. Marlin Swing was working at CBS. He was asked by the network to call the house and confirm the story that his dear friend had died.

"May I speak to Miss Kilgallen?" he asked, praying that it was all a gruesome mistake.

Marlin thought he was talking to Anne Hamilton; Anne Hamilton denied it.

"She's not here at the moment," a voice from 45 East Sixty-eighth Street responded. "May I have her call you back?" [28]

By the time the phone call was made, Dorothy had been multiply discovered, police and ME were alerted, and the first signs of lividity had set in.

CBS went with the unconfirmed report.

Things being as public as they were, Dr. Heller telephoned the ME's office to report his pronouncement—"app. natural in bed"—at 3:12.[29]

The most significant *pro forma* omission, as we shall see, related to the vouchering of physical evidence found at the scene. The "Police Manual" is very specific about this procedure in any suspicious death. And the death at home of a young and healthy person is *ipso facto* suspicious. The manual mandates: "The Medical Examiner shall take possession of any portable object which, in his opinion, may be useful in establishing the cause of death."

* * *

What happened to Dorothy?

It was John Doyle of the 19th who headed the police investigation, or thought he had. He was clearly a man to see.

I interviewed the ex-cop, now the owner of Doyle's Terrace Restaurant in La Grangeville, New York, at his establishment. It is fifteen minutes short of apple-picking country, along Dutchess County's Route 55. His afternoon regulars were gathered around the bar watching "The Gong Show" on a large color set, badly tuned and blaring. Doyle is a trim blue-eyed man. He wore polyester, open at the neck.

John Doyle was not an easy man to locate. The pension section of the New York City Police Department had no forwarding address for him, which enabled their representatives to claim that they hadn't a clue. Doyle's whereabouts were on record, however. It was a matter of retrieving through the department's back door. The pension section had no official record of him because he had no pension. Doyle resigned from the department, after thirteen years of active duty, in March, 1966, four months after Dorothy died. He explained, "I found I was married to the force rather than to my wife and six children." [30]

His memories of November 8 were vivid. There had been a $400,000 heist at the Sherry-Netherland and a burglary at Delmonico's. He was assigned to both cases and then had to testify in court. When he returned to the station house, after three that Monday, his commanding officer, Mike Ward, dispatched him to the house on East Sixty-eighth Street. "Ward found out about Dorothy's death while watching television at the precinct," Doyle recalled.

Ward's memory of the informing process differed: "I heard from the chief of detectives, who might have gotten it from the media," Ward said in a telephone interview. "The chief called and asked, 'Did something happen to Dorothy Kilgallen?' " [31]

Doyle and his partner, Jimmy Greene, now deceased, proceeded to the house. Doyle was annoyed: "Supposedly they found her between twelve and one and nobody was notified as far as the police department was concerned until after three."

When he arrived, Jimmy Kilgallen was there, Myrtle Verne, Joan Crawford, Marie Eichler, James and Evelyn

Clement, and Richard Kollmar: "In no shape or form. He was completely inebriated. I don't even think he knew his own name." Jill and Larry Grossman showed up afterward. Heller had left. Doyle took his only formal statement from Marie. He did not remember seeing either Marc Sinclaire or David Baldwin.

Doyle went up to the third-floor bedroom: "She must have fallen asleep while she was reading, in a half-sitting position. The reading light was still on."

At Doyle's Terrace, the man who headed the investigation of what he termed "a very important DOA" delivered a bombshell, which he rapidly detonated: "We were waiting for the ME to show up. She was in bed. And next to the bed was an empty vial that had been previously filled with Seconal."

He and his partner took down all the salient information from the label and went to the Hunter Pharmacy on Madison Avenue, where, he somehow determined, "she had all her prescriptions filled." The bottle had contained fifty 100-milligram Seconal tablets and it was dated October 8, 1965:

> I remember going through all the Seconal prescriptions that she had for approximately three, four years. And when I added up the Seconals and the amount of years, it came out to two a night. Even when she went abroad. If she was away for thirty days, she'd get sixty Seconal.

Utilizing this one and only police procedure and standard short division, Doyle closed the case in his mind. She had taken, he concluded, no more than *two pills*. He did not apparently consider that she lived in a house of pills ("If we'd asked to search Kollmar's bedroom, he would have had a fit"), that she could easily have had more than one prescription active at various drugstores, that she might have been saving a few for a special occasion, that there might have been nights when she took no pills, that the October 8–November 8 symmetry was perhaps as suspect as the orderliness of the room. Her confinements, he somehow learned, were for "alcoholism" and not barbiturate abuse—slurring, ataxic gait, and the common knowledge of her intimate friends, notwithstanding.

"I have never considered two Seconals an overdose of

barbiturates," he said. "As far as I was concerned, that's all she took."

The presence of the empty vial was confirmed by Mike Ward directly and by Dr. James Luke indirectly. Luke could not recall whether he actually took physical possession of the vial.[32] The drug was prescribed by David Baldwin, however, and the autopsy report states that Luke telephoned Baldwin, who deposed that she was "habituated to Seconal—took 3–4 a day." [33] During our phone conversation, Luke surmised, "I must have seen the vial if I made the call."

The vial should have gone to the morgue with Dorothy. Its discovery should have appeared on both the autopsy report and the police reports as "physical evidence found at the scene." Empty barbiturate bottles naturally have high probative value.

Richard Kollmar took his own life in January, 1971, swallowing everything in reach. He was also found in the "neat, tidy, expensive townhouse" (which he had sold and then bought back); he was also "supine in bedclothes" (probably in the same room in which Dorothy had been discovered). His death, like hers, came some time after a fall at home that resulted in a fractured shoulder. His death, too, was reported amiably at first as an "apparent heart attack." [34]

However, there was an empty vial by his bedside which did not go unreported. In fact, the one and only underscored notation by the medical investigator who came to call was: *"Found with empty pill vial at bedside."* Dorothy's vial should have been similarly noted and vouchered. A scrupulous, hand-to-hand record of the evidence and its disposition should have been maintained so that responsibility could be imputed for its loss.

None of this was done.

Doyle maintained that he reported the discovery of the bottle and the pertinent procedure on his police report: "I'm sure I made a note of it on my DD 5." The DD 5 is a supplementary complaint report that records activities pursuant to a complaint. There was no such DD 5 of Doyle's in the file, which was presented to me as complete by the New York City Police Department. When I queried an administrative assistant to Commander Schimmel about Doyle's assertion that he found the vial, went to the pharmacy, and put it all down on his report, I was told, "I don't think the detective was right in his recollection," [35] as though the absence of a record betokened the absence of a reality. Such a detailed recollection, however, could not be a mistake. If Doyle filed it, the document was conveniently lost; if he did not, he was clearly negligent.

The vial evaporated. A careful review of Dorothy's case records from the medical examiner's office showed no indication that the evidence was ever officially received.[36]

Detective John Doyle was either a man who would not allow himself to be confused by the facts or a man to whom the facts were never accurately presented.

"She wasn't long for this world to begin with," he said, "the liver being the way it was."

The autopsy showed clearly that Dorothy's liver, though fatty, was not cirrhotic. She wasn't drinking hard enough long enough.

Doyle claimed, in conclusion, that he received a document from the medical examiner's office that attributed the death to visceral congestion:

> All I got from the ME's office was a slip of paper saying "death due to visceral congestion." No more detailed report that that. If there was any cover-up on this whatsoever, it would have been down at the ME's office.

Luke responded to Doyle's assertion about receiving such a slip:

> I wouldn't have sent him anything like that. "Visceral congestion" is not a term I would use, and it was not the cause of death.[37]

Doyle insisted that he never saw the complete report:

> They never went into detail. Had it been explained to me that there was an overly amount of barbiturates in the system then I probably would have dug a little

deeper. There was no indication at all that there was anything out of the ordinary.

Luke maintained:

> We would have a great deal of information exchanged between the investigator and the medical examiner's office. I can't believe this case was finally certified without having discussed it with them. It would have been discussed with the police.

The complexity of the thing becomes unseemly. There appears to have been official malfeasance in addition to stupidity. The one document that could have verified or rebutted Doyle's story that he received a slip of paper ascribing the death to visceral congestion—the so-called DD15 or Request of Cause of Death from the ME's office —is also absent from the ostensibly complete file of the New York City Police Department.

Why does Doyle continue to insist on "visceral congestion," insist that the slip was filed by him, when he could as easily have taken the actual data, the "moderate" designation of Luke's, still called it an accident, still justified his failure to investigate? Why does he insist that the liver was cirrhotic according to his information, when I am clearly in possession of a document that contradicts that determination? Is it possible that he is truthful and accurate? Is it possible that the only real communication that transpired between the police and the ME's office was unofficial and that Doyle himself was disinformed? That both Doyle and Luke are covering nothing and that communication was transpiring on another level—between some earlier-arriving police and another representative of the New York medical examiner's office?

Whether Doyle's obtuse surmise that Dorothy had taken only two Seconal was actually buttressed by a communication from the medical examiner's office or not, the effect on the investigation was devastating. No attempt was made to elicit information about Dorothy's activities on the night of her death. There remains only one deposition on record—the testimony of Richard Kollmar to the medical examiner, under "Witnesses or Informants" on the autopsy report:

According to husband, deceased had been well recently. Had not seen physician since Fr. [fractured] shoulder last year. . . . Returned from "What's My Line?" last P.M. 11:30 P.M. "feeling chipper." Went in to write column. Husband said goodnight and went to bed. . . . No past history alcoholism or other medicinal habits.[38]

Doyle knew better. Ward knew different. Richard told Doyle that he did not see her when she came in that night. He told Ward that she came in late and that they had had a drink together.[39]

The perjured testimony was tolerated.

Doyle determined that it was Dorothy's custom to go out after the show for a few drinks, usually to P. J. Clarke's. No one at Clarke's was questioned.

Neighbors were not interviewed about whether they saw or heard anything untoward at the house that night.

Bob Bach was never asked any questions about Dorothy.

Doyle was unaware of her visit to the Regency Lounge.

And I have been expressly forbidden by the management of the hotel to question any of their employees, including the bartender who probably served her that night and who might have identified the person or persons she was with just hours before her death.

What happened to Dorothy?

Anything could have and been swallowed up in the frenetic efforts of the sentinels at the house. In addition to the overproduction of witnesses, a good deal of overexplaining issued from 45 East Sixty-eighth Street. Anne Hamilton spoke to James and Evelyn Clement on the telephone that Monday, she claimed, and to the rest of the family on blackout Tuesday. She never spoke directly to Marie—who was "gone" by then—but she was eagerly proffered a story that explained every detail of the bizarre condition in which the householders found Dorothy.

Dorothy was, they said, expecting "photographers." They were scheduled to appear in the morning to take her picture in connection with a movie deal involving *Murder One*. The interested party was not Joe Levine, but Twentieth Century-Fox.

"Marie thought Dorothy was asleep," Anne recapitulated.

She was leaning back, with her eyes closed, almost with a smile on her face. Finally, it got so late, so close to photography, that Marie went over to her for the first time. Then there was the realization.

But you see why she was already made-up. It was for the photographers. She hadn't gone to bed at all. She was just resting, keyed up, probably couldn't sleep. I suspect she took one of Dick's pills and a sip of drink. That did it. That and the excitement.[40]

When Anne spoke directly to Richard on the day Dorothy reposed at the Abbey, he added yet another detail. She had decided to screen Sunday night's "What's My Line?" right after the show was over. Dorothy was so happy with what she saw, with how smart she had been and how pretty she looked, that she couldn't possibly have done anything destructive to herself.

The stories are, of course, outlandish. A television pro, Dorothy would never have prepared herself for a photography session wearing day-old makeup. Nor would she have appointed to have her hair done *after* an early-morning photography session. And she never looked at "What's My Line?" that night. Bob Bach took her directly to Clarke's, where she was seen by at least two employees at a little after eleven. Poor Richard, whose services were no longer required on Broadway, was still engaging in overproduction.

There were lies for insiders, lies for outsiders, lies for the medical examiner.

But the story of the reposeful accident becomes totally incredible in the light of expert testimony on what was actually found in her body. She had no "little accident" involving fifteen pills, which was the low figure given to me by Baden and assented by Hoffman and which did not include the pink liquid. Luke had estimated that she died between two and four A.M., Monday morning.[41] Even if she somehow slipped past Harvey Daniels and arrived home from the Regency as early as one o'clock, there was no time for the traditional fugal blunder, taking, say, five pills thrice, as a result of stupor or impatience. Assuming there were only *ten* pills, it is very hard even to believe that she would have ingested five pills twice in so short a period of time.

Home at one, dead between two and four, a *minimum*

of fifteen pills? The fugue death is simply not played in this major key.

What happened to Dorothy?
She might have committed suicide.

When Pearl Bauer and Miss Muller, who had returned from Germany to be with the family after she heard about Dorothy's death, were instructed to ferret through Dorothy's effects, Mrs. Bauer came upon some jottings in her late employer's handwriting. "They were all about the reason for living and *if* there was a reason for living," Mrs. Bauer recalled. "I had the feeling that they were connected to a newspaperman she knew somewhere in [she named a midwestern state]. I had more or less suspected that someone out there had caught her fancy. I showed the paper to the nurse, and she suggested that we dispose of it." [42]

If Dorothy was driven to an intentional act of self-destruction, there would seem to have been only one person in her life whose acts could have provoked her. And he is the Out-of-Towner. If, in fact, he was at the Regency that night, he might have done it with a few drunken, rejecting words. If he was not at the Regency, it could have happened over the telephone.

If, indeed, he carries this burden with him, this could explain why he remains so insistent upon the platonic nature of their relationship, why he goes so far as to stress Dorothy's acceptance of her role as fifth wheel—an assertion that anyone who knew her well and understood the depths of her feelings for him would gainsay.

The press agent from Carrara, "Mitch," recalled that she grew sullen and despondent when she saw him out with another woman in a New York restaurant, some months before her death.[43]

When I first interviewed the Out-of-Towner, I was not yet aware of Dorothy's heady and euphoric talk with Marlin Swing at Delmonico's. I had not yet spoken to the person who handled room assignments at the Regency in 1965 and confirmed to me that Dorothy was in the lounge on the night of her death. Though that individual had not seen Dorothy, she recalled vividly that the hotel staff was shocked to hear about Dorothy; that there was a great deal of talk about the fact that she had been there on the night of her death.

The Out-of-Towner had contended, during our initial talks, that he was not in New York on Sunday, November 7; that he and Dorothy chatted unextraordinarily at about 12:30 A.M., just before she died, he in his home and she in hers. It was, he said, "a vanilla conversation."

With new awareness and growing dubiety, I questioned him again about the nature of their relationship. These are excerpts from the conversation:

SUBJECT: There was some indication that it was special on her part. I kept that in line, if you can understand that. And we remained, literally to the night of her death, very, very dear friends . . . It certainly was not a passing fancy, our relationship; on the other hand, it was not a love affair, either, unless you want to make your terms very loose.

LEE ISRAEL: No, I don't want to make my terms very loose. I want to know what she was believing and what she was fantasizing.

SUBJECT: . . . We were very close in that we talked long-distance several times a week at least; and I saw her frequently. And I have every reason to believe that she liked me a great deal and needed something to love. I don't think that she was—quote—in love with me. I think there's a possibility that for a short time *she* thought it. But we did work that out.

LEE ISRAEL: How did you work it out?

SUBJECT: Just by saying, "This is silly." And I told her, "I'm not in love with you. I love you. You're my friend." It would frequently come up. It was not infrequent that she would have been drinking. It would be late at night, by the nature of both our jobs, and some of the conversations were not as coherent as I would have liked them to be. I'm having trouble interpreting the questions.

LEE ISRAEL: She told friends—and their revelations put a new slant on things—that she was having a relationship; and they took that to mean a reciprocal relationship.

SUBJECT: (laughing): After Salzburg, she—very early in our relationship—indicated that there was love there. And I tried to direct that love. Again, I come out smelling like a hero. And that's not the way it was. It was *silly* for her, for me, for us, for anyone to indicate a romance in the truer sense of the word. She did, in fact, go on dates when I had a date with another person.

LEE ISRAEL: That had been my impression. I remember your telling me that there were times when she, sadly, was a fifth wheel, and was aware of your situation.

SUBJECT: There are several nights that stand out. And one was when she really had to go to bed. First, she told me she had to get up in the morning very early. And I was out with a lady. And *we* dropped her off at home. She had a few drinks, but wasn't drunk. And she said, "Why can't I go with you?" Not meaning me, but us. It was a group. And I said, "Now, Dorothy, no. You have to get up." Just like dropping off a little girl. And the rest of us went to P. J. Clarke's.

LEE ISRAEL: It has been said to me that she said you had written love poetry to her and for her. And I thought: "That doesn't sound like ———."

SUBJECT: . . . No, I've never written a poem for Dorothy.

LEE ISRAEL: You haven't been able to come up with any recollection of that last telephone conversation you had with her? Which we discussed at great length and I'm nagging you again about it.

SUBJECT: No. There was nothing outstanding. Nothing outstanding. It was like "I'll talk to you the first of the week."

LEE ISRAEL: There are three people I talked to who thought that after P. J. Clarke's, she was going to meet you.

SUBJECT: After . . .

LEE ISRAEL: That's where she stopped ritualistically.

SUBJECT: That night?

LEE ISRAEL: That night of her death in November of 1965, that she was going to meet you.

SUBJECT: No. I was in no way there. It's simple. I was here. My own mother told me about her death. There was no plan, to my knowledge, unless she was at that point fantasizing. There certainly was no plan for me to be in New York. As a matter of fact, I probably wouldn't have been in New York for two or three weeks after that.

LEE ISRAEL: But the telephone conversation was like 12:30, you said?

SUBJECT: Now I don't remember. It was late.

LEE ISRAEL: She called you?

SUBJECT: Yeah.

LEE ISRAEL: Well, it's strange. She must have been fantasizing at that point.

SUBJECT: It had happened before. And I was unaware of the heaviness of her drinking. And I'm gathering this from hearsay after the fact.

LEE ISRAEL: But you found that bottle of vodka in Rome, didn't you?

SUBJECT: Yes. Well, I'm not sure it was vodka. I found a bottle that she had bought that night that I knew about. . . . That was at the Grand Hotel and the bottle was empty. I was really kind of the first one in her room. What I'm trying to say is that the maid didn't go in and empty it. And that bothered me in a kind of intangible way, because I had never seen her drink. To the day of her death, I had never seen her *really* drink.[44]

I submitted the taped conversation with the Out-of-Towner to an analysis by a psychological stress evaluator (PSE). The machine, invented by three retired army intelligence officers less than ten years ago, measures anxiety by involuntary shifts in the human voice. There exists a good deal of controversy about the PSE, but it is currently used by over a hundred law-enforcement agencies as an aid to detecting deception in a subject. The Out-of-Towner's tape was PSE'd by a former CIA intelligence analyst, author of *The Assassination Tapes*, George O'Toole.

In psychological stress evaluation, stress designations run from *A* through *G*. The lower level designations show an absence of stress and are conclusive evidence of truthfulness. *F* levels shows "good to hard stress," *G* "hard stress." O'Toole emphasizes that "Stress is a necessary, but not sufficient condition of deception." [45]

I received the following comments from O'Toole about what the PSE indicated with regard to the truthfulness of the Out-of-Towner. There was some internal contradiction with regard to the alleged last telephone conversation with Dorothy. The Out-of-Towner showed: "only *B*-level stress" when he denied any recollection of his last telephone conversation with Dorothy. But this "rapidly escalates to *E* and *F* levels when he says there was 'nothing outstanding' about it."

O'Toole wrote,

> "He goes to *F* and *G* levels when he denies he was in New York and claims he was in [subject's home town] at the time of K's death; *F* level on stating "You know how I found out" about K's death. *F* level on saying there was no plan for him to be in New York. . . . PSE analysis of [subject's] statements does not confirm his truthfulness regarding not being in New York on the date in question. The analysis is consistent with the hypothesis that he is lying about this. [Subject's] stress might be caused by his own grief and trauma. However, the high level of stress associated with an apparently uncharged statement—that there were no plans to be in New York—suggests the stress on this question is the result of something else. There is also *F* level stress in his statement that he was "unaware of the heaviness of her drinking." I hope you can figure a way to hold this guy's feet in the fire, because I believe he has a lot more to tell you. [46]

In November, 1976, five months after the stressful conversation with the Out-of-Towner, I tuned into "The Long

John Nebel Show," an all-night radio program broadcast over WMCA in New York. Nebel had been a friend to both Dorothy and Richard. The subject of his radio show this particular night was the JFK assassination.

Obviously nettled by the conspiratorial thrust of the broadcast, Nebel trotted out Dorothy as a way to rebut the so-called domino theory, which ascribes sundry Kennedy-related deaths—Dorothy's among them—to a widespread plot to silence the knowledgeable. He designated all of the speculation about foul play and Dorothy "a crock." She was in love, he said, with a young man at the time of her death. He described the object of her affection, naming no name. The description fit the Out-of-Towner. Nebel then asserted that she had been out with the young man that night and returned home happily, at which point she "did a dummy thing . . . combining liquor with a fair amount of Seconal." [47]

There was a great deal wrong with Nebel's logic. Women in love have been known to take their own lives, usually when they fall into a depression about that love. Some women in love have also been murdered.

The story had been told to him, Nebel claimed on the air, right after Dorothy's death, by a close friend who was functioning, vis-à-vis the couple, as a "beard," a third party whose presence militates against romantic inferences by spectators. Neither did he name the beard. He referred to him as a "rock music promoter."

I wrote to Nebel and asked him to name names. He did not respond to the letter. I wrote a subsequent letter to "Long John Nebel and Candy Jones." Candy was Nebel's wife and co-host. She was in the studio during the November, 1976, broadcast.

Candy Jones telephoned me on June 3, 1977, only a few days after receiving the second letter. She had asked John Nebel, off-mike, who the men were. He told her. She now named both men to me. One was the Out-of-Towner; the "beard" had been part of the publishing company that Dorothy had helped set up.

I could not conceive that Nebel's source, the man functioning as the beard, had made the story up, or that Nebel manufactured it. This was no exotic assemblage of details, but a knowledgeable rendering that substantiated much of what I was coming to believe about Dorothy's activities on the night of her death. It placed her with the Out-of-Towner and their business associate at the meeting-cum-tryst to which she had referred in her letter on lavender paper, when she had suggested that the Out-of-Towner try to make his New York trip in late October or early November so that there would be time "for conferences and all that jazz."

I was no longer on amiable terms with the Out-of-Towner. But I did arrange to interview Nebel's purported informant, who will be called the Music Man. He talked about his close friendship with Dorothy and admitted attending her funeral with John Nebel. He denied completely, however, that he was with the couple that night or that he had ever told Nebel the story. Though he held shares in the publishing company, whose sole purpose was to showcase the music written by the Out-of-Towner, and though the Out-of-Towner, during our less fractious talks, claimed friendship with him, the Music Man contended that he barely remembered the company or the man: "I met him once or twice when he came to New York. I don't remember getting any stock."

The Music Man, too, had been "out of town" that Sunday night. He did not remember where he was, but his present wife would vouch for his absence. Dorothy, he said, had sent to him, by hand delivery, on the Friday before her death, an invitation that read: "You stinker. I haven't seen you in ages. Let's have lunch on Monday." He telephoned her Monday morning to accept. The response at the house was strange and evasive. He was pondering the situation when Long John Nebel called him, around noon, to tell him that their friend was dead.

"I'd like to find out what John did mean," he said.[48] I suggested that he telephone and find out. This he apparently never did. Nebel died of cancer in April, 1978. According to Candy Jones, the Music Man was not sufficiently interested to broach the subject to Nebel, though he had become involved in a rather bizarre situation.[49] I am not aware that he ever found Dorothy's note.

Monday the columnist slept late. It would have been quite a day for her, with the early-morning photography session, the appointment with Marc Sinclaire, a column to write, a deal to negotiate, a meeting at Kerry's school, the airing of "To Tell the Truth," lunch with Joan Crawford, lunch with the movie mogul, lunch with the Music Man. . . .

What happened to Dorothy?

The suicide theory presents one nettlesome problem. If she was stood up by, spurned, or in any way emotionally ravaged by the Out-of-Towner, and thereby driven to suicidal rage, she did not take the kind of massive dose consistent with that rage. Had she returned home resolute and seething, she could have availed herself of a virtual pharmacopoeia. Kerry Kollmar recalled that his father had vats of pills around, containers of Tuinal large enough to pickle mice.

But Dr. Michael Baden estimated she had taken fifteen to twenty pills and had, in a casual conversation prior to our more official interview, wiggled his hand iffily when I asked him whether she had intended to kill herself.[50] Luke contended that the dose was not in the range that one expects in cases that are suicide. The 50 cubic centimeters of pink fluid remained unanalyzed; had it proven to be Seconal, the estimated quantifications would have increased: However, in really massive doses, such as the one Richard Kollmar went out with, the barbiturates leave a message in the stomach, whose mucosa become tellingly irritated. Dorothy's stomach showed only mild irritation.[51]

The statement that I had heard from so many pathologists—"Well, they were enough to kill her"—I had always construed as a maddening tautology. Perhaps not. The pills were in a perplexingly moderate range. Too many of them for accident, too few for suicide. But enough to kill her.

What happened to Dorothy?

She might have been murdered. God knows, it would have been easy enough in that house of lies, and pills, and darkness, where power could buy cover and get more than it paid for, where an overdose was an assumed eventuality.

"I was only there once," the Out-of-Towner said, "but the feeling was one of emptiness. Even the entrance, where I would leave her, was depressing and dark." [52]

The method would have been pills slipped into liquor. Just enough to make the central nervous system flutter and take a tiny quantum jump. The fewer the better, just in case you get an honest cop who opts to investigate and would, perhaps, find out that she was happy. The beauty of it is that it isn't even necessary, given habitual ingestion, to succeed the first time. And Dorothy made it ideal for a killer. There is some question about whether a sufficiently inebriated victim would taste the bitter barbiturate powder. But the beverage most likely to succeed in masking the taste would have been her mixer of choice, which she was using on the night of her death: quinine.

For motive and opportunity, Richard Kollmar must be considered. By the terms of a will drawn up in 1941 and never changed, he stood to inherit virtually everything.[53] The children had not been considered at all. They had a little more than three thousand dollars in one checking account. But he got the jointly owned town house and sold it, in 1966, for $290,000. Dorothy's various insurance policies, of which he was sole beneficiary, totaled almost $90,000. There were several pension funds. Only the Goodson-Todman profit-sharing dividend of $82,000 was shared among the three children, and there was $576 in government savings bonds that Dorothy had squirreled away for Kerry.

Richard eventually shipped Kerry off to a foster home.[54]

The problem with Richard as killer is primarily psychological, and was expressed in identical language by many who knew him for years: He did not appear to have the "balls" to do a crime of such magnitude. In addition, he told Detective Mike Ward in one of his hurly-burly of contradictory stories that he had a drink at home with Dorothy on the night of her death, hardly a thing to tell a police officer if he had, in fact, dissolved several barbiturates in the drink. [55] And finally, an official cover-up of any magnitude at all would not have been effected on behalf of a mere uxoricide.

It must be considered possible that, if she was murdered, the crime was done to silence her, by a kiss and-kill representative of whatever faction it is that does not want the facts about the assassination of JFK to emerge.

She would not have been its only victim. In recent history, four witnesses who testified or were scheduled to do so at various inquiries into the assassination have been killed or committed suicide: George de Mohrenschildt, friend to Oswald; Sam Giancana and John Rosselli, mobsters linked to CIA efforts to eliminate Fidel Castro; and William Sullivan, senior FBI official.

The list of other violent or suspicious deaths closer to the assassination has been widely publicized. There were several news people among them. Eighteen witnesses died within a little over three years of the assassination, thirteen as victims of suicide, accident, or murder. The London Sunday *Times* requested an actuary to compute the likelihood of such a cluster of deaths related to an event; the odds were one hundred thousand trillion to one against.[56]

On March 3, 1978, on a snowbound New York night, I met a man in a congenial pub in the East Twenties. He was accompanied by his wife, and I by a go-between who verified the man's identity, his occupation as a chemist, his past status, and the general accuracy of the political factionalism that he described.

From 1967 until 1972, the chemist was "confidant and right-hand man" to Dr. Charles J. Umberger, director of toxicology at the New York City Medical Examiner's Office. He left because of the pervasive factionalism at the office. The chemist now claimed to me that Umberger believed that Dorothy had been murdered; and that he somehow came into possession of inculpatory forensic evidence whose true nature he withheld from the Department of Pathology. In 1968 Umberger shared his information with his young colleague.

Umberger was known for retaining, in his laboratory, hundreds of toxicological specimens. He practiced a kind of forensic cryonics, keeping the beakers pending development of an advanced technology to better understand the cause of death. He was known, also, for the fierce medical politics he practiced. In Dorothy's case, he hoped to use the conclusion he had reached privately as something to "hold over" Milton Helpern and James Luke, who had certified the death.

Umberger gave the chemist, for confirmative toxicological analysis, a basic beaker with an extract from Dorothy's brain, and another beaker labeled "drink." He told the younger man that two glasses, which had contained alcoholic beverages, had been found at Dorothy's bedside, and that the "drink," from which the alcohol had evaporated, was hers.

When Dorothy died, the medical examiner's office of the City of New York was not yet routinely employing tests that could specify which drug or combination of drugs from the three groups of fast-acting barbiturates—secobarbital (trademark Seconal); amobarbital (whose trademark Tuinal is a combination of amobarbital and secobarbital); and pentobarbital (trademark Nembutal)—had been involved in a death. Therefore the results of the original toxicological studies conducted on Dorothy were consistent with several interpretations. Her body could have reposited only Seconal or various combinations of Seconal-Tuinal-Nembutal. Qualitative extrapolations were impossible using the more primitive technology.

At the time Umberger beckoned the younger chemist, it had become possible, using more sophisticated technology, to learn more, to particularize the drug or drugs involved. He tested the basic beaker. "I found all three," he told me. "Amo, pento, and secobarbitol." And in the specimen taken from the glass, he said, "I found Nembutal."

He reported his findings to Dr. Umberger. According to his account, "Umberger grinned and said, 'Keep it under your hat. It was *big*.'"

Besides the word of the chemist, there is one finding that tends to confirm. The Department of Toxicology routinely reports to Pathology a list of basic drugs found in the body. The chemist who ran the tests originally on Dorothy noted that quinine, which might have covered the bitterness of the secreted barbiturates, was found in "brain, bile, and liver." But the quinine, a basic drug, was *not* reported in the official laboratory findings presented to the Department of Pathology. It should have been, as a matter of procedure.

My present informant had no more knowledge. Nothing about the orchestration of the cabal, nothing about how the semisecret physical evidence made its way from the town house to the Department of Toxicology.

Given the mentality of the sentinels and their access to official favor, it is within reason to postulate the following scenario—one which accounts for the disinformation process at the ME's office and the breakdown in communications between Doyle and Luke:

Dorothy was found dead in a scene that bespoke the presence of a lover. Medical Examiner One was called to the house unofficially, because some influential sentinels either wanted the scene expertly sanitized or entertained the possibility of foul play. The sentinel wanted to eliminate unnecessary scandal if she had simply overdosed following a tryst. Medical Examiner One took the glasses to the laboratory and sent them to toxicology for analysis, also off the record. Toxicology's Dr. Umberger now held sway, aware of the vulnerability of his colleague. He found the Nembutal in her glass and surmised foul play. But to have forthrightly reported this would have simply added another feather to the cap of Medical Examiner One. He disinformed, holding his knowledge in abeyance for a time at which he would need it as leverage. He never used the leverage, because he became aware of the political nature of the murder, an awareness that even further increased his political leverage vis-à-vis certain government agencies. He did everything in his power to minimize the possibility of meaningful police investigation. The sentinel was told that the glass contained no evidence of foul play. He remained as confused about Dorothy's death as the general public. The other householders, depending on the extent of their knowledge, endeavored to cover up either a perceived suicide or a perceived accident under scandalous circumstances.

What happened to Dorothy?
Three days after her death, Bob and Jean Bach invited Richard Kollmar to their home for dinner. Bob asked the widower, "Dick, what was all that stuff in the folder Dorothy carried around with her about the assassination?"

Richard replied, "Robert, I'm afraid that will have to go to the grave with me." [57]

Mark Lane also pursued. Dorothy was dead on his return to New York. They had never had the opportunity to discuss the last Dallas trip, before which she had told him that she expected "to learn something important" on her visit to New Orleans.

Mark waited a respectable month before he queried Kollmar, though she was on his mind every day. When he finally telephoned Richard, he asked if he might see the folder. "I suspect she might have really found out something," he said, "something which could affect all of us in the future." Richard equivocated. Mark insisted that he was talking about "the soul of our country."

Richard said, "I'm going to destroy all that. It's done enough damage already." [58]

Richard's post mortems were so riddled with lies, it is impossible to know whether he ever really possessed the material or what he decided to do with it.

The FBI evinced interest as late as 1975, four years after his death. The G-men sought out Dickie, who told them that he knew nothing about the disposition of his mother's papers. He suggested that his grandfather might have them.[59]

Nothing of what Dorothy gathered, surmised, or wrote during her private interview with Jack Ruby or on her Texas or New Orleans sojourns has ever come to light.

A book called *Murder One* was published in 1967. Her name was affixed to the title. The writer assigned to the book, Allan Ullman, worked from the old newspaper clips that she had assembled, and merely edited her reportage. He was under the impression that Dorothy had not put pen to paper.[60] Her editor would not comment. No one approached at Random House was aware that she intended a chapter about Jack Ruby.

She was silent now.

SOURCE NOTES

PROLOGUE

1. Letter from Eleanor Kilgallen to author, July 31, 1975.
2. Letter from Eleanor Kilgallen to author, September 26, 1975.
3. Letter from James L. Kilgallen to author, January 26, 1976.
4. Letter from Jill Ellen Grossman to author, October 23, 1975.
5. Kerry Kollmar told author, December 7, 1975.
6. James L. Kilgallen, *Sixty-Five Years of Deadlines and Headlines*, September 12, 1971. [See General Notes.]
7. Letter from John J. Kilgallen, S.J., to author, November 25, 1977.
8. James L. Kilgallen, "It's A Great Life," 1956. [Ste General Notes.]
9. Newton H. Fulbright, "Kilgallen," *Editor & Publisher*, June 22, 1968.
10. James L. Kilgallen, "Lucky in Love," New York *Journal-American*, July 10, 1962.
11. Irene Corbally Kuhn told author, July 3, 1976.
12. James L. Kilgallen, "The Cinderella Story of Dorothy Kilgallen," Des Moines *Register*, December 19, 1954.
13. Harry Small taped recollections for author, November, 1977.
14. Lincoln Center Collection. [See General Notes.]
15. Martha McKenna, Indianapolis *News*, January 24, 1953.
16. Joseph McGowin, "Jimmy, the Other Kilgallen," *News Workshop* (published by New York University), February, 1955.
17. *Ibid.*
18. Kuhn interview, *op. cit.*
19. *Sixty-five Years of Deadlines and Headlines, op. cit.*
20. Dorothy Kilgallen, *The Voice of Broadway*, New York *Journal-American*, April 26, 1950. (Subsequent references

to Dorothy Kilgallen's *The Voice of Broadway* will be condensed to *VOB*.)

21. "The Cinderella Story of Dorothy Kilgallen," *op. cit.*
22. Jean Bach told author, July 19, 1975.
23. "The Dorothy Kilgallen Story," *New York Post*, April 23, 1960.
24. *Ibid.*
25. *Ibid.*
26. Jean Bach interview, *op. cit.*
27. Bernard Malamud told author, December 27, 1975.
28. *Ibid.*
29. George Kuittinen told author, April 22, 1976.
30. Sister Berenice-Rice told author, February 26, 1976.
31. *VOB*, April 26, 1950.

CHAPTER 1

1. James L. Ford, *Forty-odd Years in the Literary Shop*, New York, 1921. (Cited by W. A. Swanberg in *Citizen Hearst*.)
2. Herb Spiro told author, May 23, 1976.
3. James D. Horan told author, September 12, 1977.
4. Sydney Boehm told author, May, 1976.
5. Letter from Sydney Boehm to author, April 26, 1976.
6. *Ibid.*
7. George Kuittinen told author, April 22, 1976.
8. *Ibid.*
9. New York *Evening Journal*, September 9, 1932.

CHAPTER 2

1. Damon Runyon, "Both Barrels," New York *American*, October 26, 1936.
2. W. A. Swanberg, *Citizen Hearst*, New York: Bantam Books, 1971.
3. Adela Rogers St. Johns, *The Honeycomb*, New York: Doubleday & Company, 1969.
4. Sheilah Graham told author, May, 1976.
5. *The Honeycomb, op. cit.*
6. *Ibid.*
7. Eve Wynn Johnson told author, January, 1978.
8. James L. Kilgallen, St. Louis *Post Dispatch*, July 4, 1954.
9. Dorothy Kilgallen, New York *Evening Journal*, August 1, 1936. (Subsequent references to Dorothy Kilgallen's writings will be abbreviated D.K.)
10. Sheilah Graham, *op. cit.*

CHAPTER 3

1. Richard K. Smith, *The Around-the-World Air Race of 1936*, (unpublished manuscript).
2. *The New York Times*, October 15, 1936.
3. Herbert Roslyn Ekins, *Around the World in Eighteen Days and How To Do It*, New York-Toronto: Longmans, Green & Co., 1936.
4. *The Around-the-World Air Race of 1936, op. cit.*
5. *Radio Guide*, November 14, 1936.
6. *Around the World in Eighteen Days and How To Do It, op. cit.*
7. Irene Kuhn told author, July 3, 1976.
8. Herb Spiro told author, May 23, 1976.
9. New York *World-Telegram*, October 1, 1936.
10. *Ibid.*, September 30, 1936.
11. "The Dorothy Kilgallen Story," *New York Post*, April 26, 1960.
12. Herb Spiro, *op. cit.*
13. New York *Evening Journal*, October 1, 1936.
14. Lincoln Center Collection.
15. *Ibid.*
16. D.K., *Girl Around the World*, Philadelphia: David McKay, 1936.
17. *Ibid.*

CHAPTER 4

1. Michael M. Mooney, *The Hindenburg*, New York: Bantam Books, 1975.
2. New York *Evening Journal*, October 9, 1936.
3. New York *World-Telegram*, October 1, 1936.
4. New York *Evening Journal*, October 1, 1936.
5. *Cosmopolitan*, February, 1937.
6. *Ibid.*
7. Louis Sobol, New York *Journal-American*, November 11, 1965.
8. New York *Evening Journal*, October 3, 1936.
9. Louis Sobol, *op. cit.*
10. Leonard Mosley, *Lindbergh: A Biography*, New York: Doubleday & Company, 1976.
11. See General Notes.
12. New York *Evening Journal*, October 4, 1936.
13. *Ibid.*

14. New York *Evening Journal*, October 5, 1936.
15. *The New York Times*, October 4, 1936.
16. Herbert Roslyn Ekins, *Around the World in Eighteen Days and How To Do It*, New York-Toronto: Longmans, Green & Co., 1936.
17. Lincoln Center Collection.
18. Frank Gervasi, New York *Evening Journal*, October 5, 1936.

CHAPTER 5

1. Richard K. Smith, *The Around-the-World Air Race of 1936*, (unpublished manuscript).
2. New York *Evening Journal*, October 8, 1936.
3. *Ibid.*, October 6, 1936.
4. New York *World-Telegram*, October 8, 1936.
5. Herbert Roslyn Ekins, *Around the World in Eighteen Days and How To Do It*, New York-Toronto: Longmans, Green & Co., 1936.
6. New York *Evening Journal*, October 7, 1936.
7. New York *Evening Journal*, October 10, 1936.
8. *Ibid.*
9. New York *Evening Journal*, October 12, 1936.
10. *Around the World in Eighteen Days and How To Do It*, *op. cit.*
11. *The Around-the-World Air Race of 1936*, *op. cit.*
12. *Ibid.*
13. *Ibid.*

CHAPTER 6

1. Herbert Roslyn Ekins, *Around the World in Eighteen Days and How To Do It*, New York-Toronto: Longmans, Green & Co., 1936.
2. New York *Evening Journal*, October 26, 1936.
3. Lincoln Center Collection.
4. *Around the World in Eighteen Days and How To Do It*, *op. cit.*
5. New York *Evening Journal*, October 24, 1936.
6. Richard K. Smith, *The Around-the-World Air Race of 1936*, (unpublished manuscript).
7. Sydney Boehm told author, May, 1976.
8. Cable in Lincoln Center Collection.
9. *Ibid.*
10. New York *World-Telegram*, October 26, 1936.

11. Don Ryan and Kenneth Gamet, *Fly Away Baby*. From idea by Dorothy Kilgallen. (Unpublished script available at Lincoln Center, Library of the Performing Arts.)

CHAPTER 7

1. New York *Evening Journal*, November 12, 1936.
2. George Eells, *Hedda and Louella*, New York: G. P. Putnam's Sons, 1972.
3. D.K., New York *Evening Journal*, November 19, 1936.
4. D.K., "Holiday from Hollywood," *Cosmopolitan*, June, 1938.
5. Herb Spiro told author, May 23, 1976.

CHAPTER 8

1. "Café Society," *Fortune*, December, 1937.
2. Jerome Zebre told author, March 11, 1979.
3. Hope Hampton told author, December, 1976.
4. D.K., New York *Evening Journal*, July 18, 1938.
5. D.K., New York *Evening Journal*, May 5, 1937.
6. *Ibid.*
7. *Fortune, op. cit.*
8. Rosemary Cox told author, January 28, 1977.
9. Billy Livingston told author, January 7, 1977.
10. Louis Sobol told author, December 3, 1975.

CHAPTER 9

1. Grace Robinson told author, November 16, 1976.
2. "Shirley" told author, February 8, 1977. [See General Notes.]
3. Charlotte Manson told author, October 10, 1976.
4. Letter from Paul Gallico to author, May 10, 1976.
5. Herb Spiro told author, May 23, 1976.
6. "Troubles of the Papa of Two Glamour Girls," *American Weekly*, December 20, 1942.
7. Mary Anne Travers told author, January 11, 1977.
8. Rosemary Cox told author, January 28, 1977.
9. Billy Livingston told author, January 7, 1977.
10. Mary Anita Loos told author, January 16, 1977.
11. *VOB*, November 14, 1938.
12. *VOB*, January 3, 1939.
13. *VOB,* January 5, 1939.
14. *TV Radio Mirror*, (undated article in Lincoln Center Collection).
15. Betty Leggett told author, January 6, 1977.

CHAPTER 10

1. Betty Leggett told author, January 6, 1977.
2. George Allen told author, January 13, 1977.
3. *Ibid.*
4. Brooklyn *Daily Eagle*, November 6, 1938.
5. Brooklyn *Daily Eagle*, December 11, 1938.
6. Htrb Spiro told author, May 22, 1976.
7. "Bea" told author, May 22, 1976. [See General Notes.]
8. Irving Zussman told author, December 16, 1977.
9. Billy Livingston told author, January 3, 1977.
10. "Bea," *op. cit.*
11. Billy Livingston, *op. cit.*

CHAPTER 11

1. "Shirley" told author, February 8, 1977.
2. Rosemary Cox told author, January 28, 1977.
3. Mary Anne Travers told author, January 11, 1977.
4. "Bea" told author, April 29, 1977.
5. Mary Anita Loos told author, January 16, 1977.
6. Betty Leggett told author, January 6, 1977.
7. "Bea,' *op. cit.*
8. "Park Avenue Merry-Go-Round," *New York Post*, July 27, 1946.
9. Bob Considine, *It's All News to Me*, New York: Meredith Press, 1967.
10. Jimmy Gardiner told author, July 27, 1976.
11. Edgar Hatfield told author, September 30, 1975.
12. "Bea," *op. cit.*
13. *Editor & Publisher*, December, 1944.
14. "Father Duffy's Canteen," New York *Journal-American*, June 23, 1942.
15. Dorothy Gulman told author, November 1, 1976.
16. Document in Dorothy Kilgallen's FBI dossier. [See General Notes.]
17. *Ibid.*
18. *Ibid.*
19. Midge Willer told author, January 10, 1977.
20. *Ibid.*
21. *Ibid.*
22. "Park Avenue Merry-Go-Round," *op. cit.*
23. Huber Boscowitz told author, October 9, 1975.
24. D.K., "Romances of Rich American Beauties," New York *Evening Journal*, June 27, 1933.
25. Midge Willer told author, January 10, 1977.

26. *Ibid.*
27. *Cholly Knickerbocker,* New York *Journal-American,* October, 1943.

CHAPTER 12

1. Miles White told author, April 24, 1977.
2. Jimmy Gardiner told author, July 27, 1976.
3. *Ibid.*
4. Dorothy Gulman told author, November 1, 1976.
5. Hope Hampton told author, December, 1976.
6. Al Rylander told author, December 13, 1976.
7. Leo P. Wobido, S.J., "The Gentle 'Voice of Broadway.'" *The Queen's Work,* November, 1944.
8. Partially identified clipping in Lincoln Center Collection, May 18, 1944.
9. New York *Daily News,* Frebruary 11, 1944.
10. Miles White, *op. cit.*
11. Joy Hodges told author, December 16, 1976.

CHAPTER 13

1. *VOB,* October 23, 1944.
2. Bob Thomas, *Winchell,* New York: Doubleday & Company, 1971.
3. "The Dorothy Kilgallen Story," *New York Post,* April 29, 1960.
4. *VOB,* August 14, 1957.
5. George Eells told author, December 25, 1976.
6. *VOB,* December 27, 1946.
7. Jane Kean told author, January, 1977.
8. Joy Hodges told author, December 16, 1976.
9. Dorothy Gulman told author, November 1, 1976.
10. Midge Willer told author, January 10, 1977.
11. Joy Hodges, *op. cit.*
12. Scott Meredith, *George S. Kaufman and His Friends,* New York: Doubleday & Company, 1974.
13. Quoted in: Hamilton Darby Perry, *A Chair for Wayne Lonergrain,* New York: Macmillan, 1972.
14. *Ibid.*
15. Billy Livingston told author, January 5, 1977.
16. D.K., New York *Journal-American,* March 2, 1944.
17. *Ibid.*
18. George Freedley, New York *Telegraph,* May 20, 1944
19. Wolcott Gibbs, *The New Yorker,* May 27, 1944.

20. Dorothy Gulman told author, *op. cit.*

CHAPTER 14

1. Cited in *VOB*, June 7, 1944.
2. *VOB*, June 7, 1944.
3. James L. Kilgallen, "It's A Great Life" (A pamphlet reprinted from *Editor & Publisher*), 1956.
4. James L. Kilgallen, New York *Journal-American*, June 8, 1954.
5. *Editor & Publisher*, February 21, 1953.
6. Jean Bach told author, July 15, 1975.
7. Bob Bach told author, June 30, 1975.
8. Sydney Boehm told author, May, 1976.

CHAPTER 15

1. Ben Gross, New York *Daily News*, May 9, 1965.
2. Jimmy Gardiner told author, July 27, 1976.
3. Jean Bach told author, August 31, 1977.
4. "Onward and Upward with the Arts; The All-American Breakfast," *The New Yorker*, August 10, 1946.
6. "Dorothy and Dick," March 7, 1947. (Broadcast originated WOR-AM, New York. Tape provided to author by management.)
6. Barry Gray, *My Night People*, New York: Simon & Schuster, 1975.
7. The Fitzgeralds told author, October 27, 1976.
8. Edgar Hatfield told author, October 13, 1976.
9. Seymour Peck, "On Dorothy and Dick," *P.M.*, January 22, 1947. (Offending passage quoted in this retraction.)
10. Midge Willer told author, January 19, 1977.
11. Seymour Peck told author, July, 1975.
12. "On Dorothy and Dick," *op. cit.*
14. *My Night People, op. cit.*
14. Kilgallen scrapbooks. Lincoln Center Collection (publica-not identified).

CHAPTER 16

1. Jean Stralem told author, November 19, 1976.
2. Quoted in: George Grim, "Pardon Me, I'm Hopping Mad," Minneapolis *Sunday Tribune*, January 19, 1947.
3. *Ibid.*
4. D.K., "Dorothy Offers Grim Rebuttal," Minneapolis *Sunday Tribune*, February 9, 1947.

5. Ann Pringle, "Some Like It Victorian," New York *Herald Tribune*, February 1, 1949.
6. Lincoln Center Collection.
7. Quoted in: *We The People*, May, 1947 (House organ of Merrill, Lynch, Pierce, Fenner & Beane).
8. *Ibid.*
9. Huber Boscowitz told author, January 16, 1976.
10. Miles White told author, April 24, 1976.
11. Midge (Willer) White and Paul White told author, January 27, 1977.
12. *Playbill*, April 21, 1947.

CHAPTER 17

1. Dell Chandler clipping in Lincoln Center Collection.
2. Igor Cassini told author, June 6, 1977.
3. Charlotte Manson told author, October 10, 1976.
4. Al Rylander told author, December 13, 1976.
5. Edgar Hatfield told author, January 18, 1976.
7. Martha Rountree told author, June, 1977.
7. "The Dorothy Kilgallen Story," *New York Post*, April 27, 1960.
8. Huber Boscowitz told author, October 9, 1975.
9. Maggi McNellis Newhouse told author, January 7, 1976.
10. Mark Goodson told author, November 17, 1975.
11. Arlene Francis told author, January 19, 1976.

CHAPTER 18

1. Junior Spelvin, *Theatre Arts*, November, 1953.
2. Bob Thomas, *Winchell*, New York: Doubleday & Company, 1971.
3. Jean Bach told author, July 15, 1975.
4. Will Jones, "Thirteen Wonderful Nights," Dover *Daily Reporter*, November 29, 1951.
5. Ernest Lehman, "24 Glittering Hours with Dorothy Kilgallen," *Cosmopolitan*, October, 1950.
6. Maurice Zolotow, *The New York Times*, December 29, 1968.
7. Emmett Davis told author, April 15, 1977.
8. *Ibid.*
9. "Mitch" told author, February 24, 1977.
10. Eddie Jaffe told author, October, 1975.
11. Jimmy Gardiner told author, July 27, 1976.
12. Bob Bach told author, October 10, 1977.
13. *VOB*, January 30, 1952.

14. *VOB*, April 14, 1952.
15. Marlin Swing told author, June 13, 1976.
16. Carmen Gebbia told author, June 17, 1977.
17. *VOB*, July 13, 1952.
18. *VOB*, July 25, 1952.
19. *VOB*, April 13, 1953.
20. *VOB*, April 19, 1953.

CHAPTER 19

1. Mark Goodson told author, November 17, 1975.
2. Stefan Kanfer, *A Journal of the Plague Years*, New York: Atheneum, 1973.
3. Bob Bach told author, October 10, 1977.
4. Letter from Louis Untermeyer to author, October 17, 1977.
5. Bob Bach, *op. cit.*
6. Transcript and memorandum regarding broadcast in Dorothy Kilgallen FBI dossier.
7. *VOB*, June 2, 1952.
8. *VOB*, October 16, 1951.
9. Joseph C. Goulden, *The Best Years*, New York: Atheneum, 1976.
10. E. J. Kahn, "The Wayward Press," *The New Yorker*, April 15, 1950.
11. *A Journal of the Plague Years, op. cit.*
12. Gene Knight, New York *Journal-American*, October 21, 1950.
13. *A Journal of the Plague Years, op. cit.*
14. Victor Riesel told author, August, 1977.
15. Igor Cassini told author, June 6, 1977.
16. *VOB*, September 16, 1950.
17. *Ibid.*
18. Martha Rountree told author, June, 1977.
19. *VOB*, November 1, 1951.
20. *A Journal of the Plague Years, op. cit.*
21. Letter of J. G. Sourwine to author, September 28, 1977.
22. Jean Bach told author, August 31, 1977.

CHAPTER 20

1. Arlene Francis told author, January 19, 1976.
2. Mark Goodson told author, November 17, 1975.
3. D.K., "Dorothy Packs for Coronation," New York *Journal-American*, May 24, 1953.
4. Earl Blackwell told author, June 27, 1977.
5. *VOB*, June 4, 1953.

6. *VOB*, June 2, 1953.
7. D.K., New York *Journal-American*, June 2, 1953.
8. *Ibid.*
9. *VOB*, June 2, 1953.
10. Jack Faragasso told author, June 24, 1977.
11. Miles White told author, April 24, 1977.
12. Stewart Klonis told author, May 17, 1977.
13. Ernest Lehman, "24 Glittering Hours with Dorothy Kilgallen," *Cosmopolitan*, October, 1950.
14. Will Jones, "Thirteen Wonderful Nights," Dover *Daily Reporter*, November 29, 1951.
15. *Ibid.*
16. Bob Bach told author, September 10, 1977.
17. Jean Bach told author, August 31, 1977.
18. John Hammond and Irving Thompson, *John Hammond on Record*, New York: Summitt Books, 1977.
19. Jean Bach told author, July 15, 1975.
20. Bob Bach told author, September 5, 1975.
21. Whitney Balliett, "The Human Sound," *The New Yorker*, December 26, 1970.
22. Bobby Short told author, April 7, 1976.
23. Bob Bach told author, *op. cit.*
24. Jean Bach told author, *op. cit.*
25. Michael Sean O'Shea told author, August 14, 1977.
26. Jean Bach told author, *op. cit.*
27. Bob Bach told author, June 30, 1975.
28. Jean Bach told author, July 19, 1975.
29. Harvey Daniels told author, April 20, 1977.
30. Jack Faragasso told author, June 24, 1977.
31. Lee Nordness told author, August 2, 1975.
32. Jean Bach told author, August 31, 1977.
33. D.K., "New Voice Sounds Off to 'Voice of Broadway,'" New York *Journal-American*, March 21, 1954.

CHAPTER 21

1. Nick Lapole told author, November 24, 1976.
2. Igor Cassini told author, June 6, 1977.
3. Bob Considine, *It's All News To Me*, New York: Meredith, 1967.
4. Louis Sobol, "The Dorothy Kilgallen Story," New York *Journal-American*, November 11, 1965.
5. Letter of Sam Day to author, November 29, 1977.
6. London *Sunday Times*, December 19, 1954.

7. Cited in: Jimmy Breslin, "A Reporter's Reporter," New York *Journal-American*, April 21, 1960.
8. Emmett Davis told author, April 15, 1977.
9. Edgar Hatfield told author, October 27, 1975.
10. Jimmy Gardiner told author, July 27, 1976.
11. F. Lee Bailey and Harvey Aronson, *The Defense Never Rests*, New York: Stein and Day, 1971. (Deposition of D.K. quoted.)
12. *TV Guide*, November 13, 1954.
13. D.K., New York *Journal-American*, October 26, 1954.
14. D.K., New York *Journal-American*, November 11 ,1954.
15. D.K., New York *Journal-American*, October 17, 1954.
16. D.K., New York *Journal-American*, October 27, 1954.
17. D.K., New York *Journal-American*, November 4, 1954.
18. *Ibid*.
19. D.K., New York *Journal-American*, November 5, 1954.
20. *VOB*, October 29, 1954.
21. Quoted in: Stan Anderson, "Here's a Day in the Life of Working Gal Kilgallen," Cleveland *Press*, November 19, 1954.
22. "Hi-Newsers Meet TV 'Guest Star,'" Cleveland *News*, December 6, 1954.
23. Jack Lotto told author, December 14, 1977.
24. *VOB*, October 26, 1954.
25. Jack Lotto, *op. cit.*
26. Memo from D.K. to Jack Lotto. (Supplied to author by Lotto.)
27. Letter from Sam Day to author, undated.
28. Theo Wilson told author, May, 1976.
29. D.K., New York *Journal-American*, December 1, 1954.
30. D.K., New York *Journal-American*, December 7, 1954.
31. *Ibid*.
32. D.K., New York *Journal-American*, December 22, 1954.

CHAPTER 22

1. Bob Considine, *It's All News To Me*, New York: Meredith, 1967.
2. Jean Bach told author, July 19, 1975.
3. Bobby Short told author, April 7, 1976.
4. Jean Bach, *op. cit.*
5. Bobby Short, *op. cit.*
6. Arlene Francis told author, January 19, 1976.
7. *VOB*, June 6, 1957.
8. Johnnie Ray told author, May 21, 1976.

9. *Ibid.*
10. *Ibid.*
11. Marlin Swing told author, June 14, 1976.
12. From Science Club Minutes of January 17, 1958. (Provided to author by Jean and Bob Bach.)
13. Lee Evans told author, March 9, 1978.
14. *Ibid.*
15. Johnnie Ray told author, May 20, 1976.
16. *Ibid.*
17. Jean Bach, *op. cit.*
18. Johnnie Ray, *op. cit.*
19. Johnnie Ray, *op. cit.*
20. D.K., "The Frank Sinatra Story," New York *Journal-American*, February 26, 1956.
21. *Ibid.*
22. Nick Lapole told author, November, 1976.
23. Igor Cassini told author, June 6, 1977.
24. Mark Goodson told author, November 17, 1975.
25. Ben Bagley told author, February, 1976.
26. Pearl Bauer told author, November 5, 1975.
27. Johnnie Ray told author, May 23, 1976.
28. *Ibid.*
29. Carrie Munn told author, October 28, 1976.
30. Dan Lavezzo told author, December 28, 1976.
31. Huber and Lillian Boscowitz told author, October 9, 1975.
32. Thelma Carpenter told author, May 6, 1976.
33. Carol Bruce told author, May 20, 1977.

CHAPTER 23

1. Jean Bach told author, July 19, 1975.
2. UPI dispatch, October 24, 1958.
3. Kerry Kollmar told author, December 7, 1975.
4. Edgar Hatfield told author, April 5, 1976.
5. D.K., New York *Journal-American*, September 15, 1959.
6. D.K., New York *Journal-American*, September 16, 1959.
7. "The Dorothy Kilgallen Story," *New York Post*, May 1, 1960.
8. D.K., New York *Journal-American,* September 19, 1959.
9. "The Dorothy Kilgallen Story," *op. cit.*
10. Ruth Montgomery, New York *Journal-American*, September 16, 1959.
11. Jack O'Brian, "Jack O'Brian Says," New York *Journal-American*, October 23, 1959.
12. *Variety*, October 28, 1959.

13. Jack O'Brian told Bob Grant, "The Bob Grant Show," WOR-A.M., January 3, 1978.
14. Jack O'Brian told author, December 16, 1976.
15. *Ibid.*
16. *Ibid.*
17. Ben Bagley told author, February, 1976.
18. Johnnie Ray told author, May 20, 1976.
19. Lee Nordness told author, August 12, 1975.
20. Lee Evans told author, March 9, 1978.
21. "The Dorothy Kilgallen Story," *New York Post*, April 28, 1960.
22. Betty Lee Hunt told author, March 17, 1977.
23. Nick Lapole told author, November 24, 1976.
24. Dan Lavezzo told author, December 28, 1976.
25. Michael Sean O'Shea told author, August 14, 1977.
26. Jack O'Brian, *op. cit.*
27. Marlin Swing told author, June 14, 1976.
28. Johnnie Ray told author, May 21, 1976.
29. *Ibid.*, May 23, 1976.
30. Jean Bach told author, July 18, 1975.
31. *Ibid.*
32. Bill Franklin told author, May 19, 1976.
33. Marlin Swing told author, June 13, 1976.
34. New York *Daily News*, November 22, 1959.
35. Johnnie Ray told author, May 23, 1976.
36. New York *Mirror*, December 3, 1959.
37. Marlin Swing told author, June 13, 1976.
38. Johnnie Ray told author, May 23, 1976.
39. Lillian Boscowitz told author, October 9, 1975.
40. Jean Bach told author, *op. cit.*
41. Johnnie Ray told author, *op. cit.*
42. Marlin Swing told author, *op. cit.*
43. Johnnie Ray told author, *op. cit.*

CHAPTER 24

1. Dorothy Kilgallen, *Murder One*, New York: Random House, 1967.
2. Quoted in: "The Finch-Trial Circus," *Newsweek*, February 1, 1960.
3. D.K., New York *Journal-American*, January 20, 1960.
4. D.K., New York *Journal-American*, January 11, 1960.
5. D.K., "Dotty Takes a Holiday," New York *Journal-American*, January 13, 1960.
6. D.K., New York *Journal-American*, March 7, 1960.

7. *Ibid.*
8. *Ibid.*
9. "The Dorothy Kilgallen Story," *New York Post*, May 1, 1960.
10. *Ibid.*
11. Eleanor Garner Black, Los Angeles *Examiner*, February 3, 1960.
12. Al Davis told author, February, 1978.
13. Jimmy Breslin, New York *Journal-American*, April 21, 1960.
14. "Working Newswoman," *Time*, February 1, 1960.
15. George (Kit) Kuittinen told author, April 22, 1976.
16. Herb Spiro told author, May 22, 1976.
17. Jean Bach told author, July 15, 1975.
18. James Horan told author, September 12, 1977.
19. Marlin Swing told author, June 13, 1976.
20. Bill Franklin told author, May 19, 1976.
21. Note from D.K. to Richard Kollmar, Kilgallen scrapbooks at Lincoln Center.
22. Johnnie Ray told author, May 23, 1976.
23. Martin Cohen, "Her Line Is Headlines," *TV Radio Mirror*, August, 1960.
24. Richard Kollmar, *Fire Island News*, June, 1960. (Lincoln Center Collection.)
25. Kerry Kollmar told author, December 14, 1975.
26. *Ibid.*
27. Kerry Kollmar told author, March 26, 1976.
28. Jim McAleer told author, January 21, 1976.
29. Anne Hamilton told author, March 10, 1978.
30. *Time*, November 24, 1961.
31. Lee Evans told author, March 8, 1978.
32. Anne Hamilton, *op. cit.*
33. Dorothy Gulman told author, November 1, 1976.
34. Paar quoted in: *Newsweek*, March 21, 1960.
35. Bob Considine, "Our Dorothy Is Swift and Sure," New York *Journal-American*, March 20, 1960.
36. "The Dorothy Kilgallen Story," *New York Post*, April 29, 1960.
37. "What's Whose Line?", *Time*, May 2, 1960.
38. *VOB*, April 22, 1960.
39. *Ibid.*
40. Edgar Hatfield told author, September 30, 1975.
41. Elaine Shepard told author, October 10, 1975.
42. Edgar Hatfield, *op. cit.*
43. *Ibid.*

44. Mary Brannum Bringle told author, summer 1978.

CHAPTER 25

1. *VOB*, September 28, 1960.
2. Roosevelt Zanders told author, November 22, 1976.
3. D.K., New York *Journal-American*, January 20, 1961.
4. Jean Bach told author, July 15, 1975.
5. Pegeen Fitzgerald told author, October 27, 1976.
6. Roosevelt Zanders, *op. cit.*
7. Marlin Swing told author, June 13, 1976.
8. Edgar Hatfield told author, January 18, 1976.
9. *Ibid.*
10. Shepard Case #6936-61; Supreme Court, New York County, Special and Trial Term, Part 24. (Affidavit of Irwin M. Taylor.)
11. Shepard Case, *op. cit.* (Examination of Dorothy Kilgallen taken by plaintiff.)
12. Sheilah Graham told author, May, 1976.
13. *VOB*, May 26, 1961.
14. Quoted in: Joey Adams, *On the Road for Uncle Sam,* New York: B. Geis Associates, 1963.
15. Edgar Hatfield told author, October 27, 1975.
16. Anne Hamilton told author, March 26, 1978.
17. Linda Shepard told author, December 1, 1975.
18. *VOB*, November 24, 1963.
19. *Ibid.*
20. Marlin Swing told author, June 13, 1976.
21. Marlin Swing told author, June 27, 1976.
22. Ben Bagley told author, February, 1976.
23. Howard Rothberg told author, June 3, 1976.
24. *Ibid.*
25. Johnnie Ray told author, May 23, 1976.
26. *VOB*, August 3, 1962.
27. Howard Rothberg told author, October 2, 1975.
28. *VOB*, August 8, 1962.
29. *Ibid.*
30. Anne Hamilton, *op. cit.*
31. Jim McAleer told author, December 16, 1976.
32. Jim McAleer told author, January 21, 1976.
33. *Ibid.*
34. Bette Whyte told author, June 16, 1978.
35. Johnnie Ray told author, May 21, 1976.
36. Allen Stokes told author, April 29, 1978.
37. Johnnie Ray, *op. cit.*
38. *Ibid.*

39. Allen Stokes, *op. cit.*
40. Anne Hamilton told author, *op. cit.*
41. Anne Hamilton told author, September 30, 1975.
42. Edgar Hatfield told author, September 30, 1975.
43. Ralph Schlegle told author, October 29, 1976.

CHAPTER 26

1. Jean Bach told author, August 31, 1977.
2. Mark Goodson told author, November 12, 1975.
3. Howard Rothberg told author, June 3, 1976.
4. Mark Goodson, *op. cit.*
5. Bill Franklin told author, May 19, 1976.
6. *Ibid.*
7. *Ibid.*
8. Bob Bach told author, August, 1978.
9. Igor Cassini, *I'd Do It All Over Again*, New York: G. P. Putnam's Sons, 1977 (p. 209–210).
10. *The New York Times*, July 21, 1963.
11. Marlin Swing told author, August, 1978.
12. Linda Shepard told author, December 1, 1975.
13. Anne Hamilton told author, March 10, 1978.
14. *VOB*, July 19, 1963.
15. D.K., New York *Journal-American*, July 24, 1963.
16. Sheilah Graham told author, May, 1976.
17. D.K., New York *Journal-American*, July 28, 1963.
18. Tony Randall told author, June, 1977.
19. Anne Hamilton told author, March 26, 1978.
20. Edgar Hatfield told author, October 27, 1975.
21. Letter of Pearl Bauer to Edgar Hatfield, September 16, 1964.
22. Lincoln Center Collection.
23. *New York Post*, September 6, 1963.
24. David Miller told author, summer 1976.
25. Elaine Shepard told author, October 10, 1975.
26. *Ibid.*
27. *Elaine Shepard vs. Dorothy Kilgallen*, Supreme Court of the State of New York, January 16, 1964.
28. Elaine Shepard told author, October 10, 1975.
29. Shepard Case #6936-61; Supreme Court, New York County, Special and Trial Term, Part 24. (Affidavit of Irwin M. Taylor.)
30. David Miller, *op. cit.*
31. *Ibid.*
32. *Ibid.*
33. Elaine Shepard, *op. cit.*

4. Bill Franklin told author, May 19, 1976.
5. *VOB*, November 24, 1963.
6. Kerry Kollmar told author, December 7, 1975.
7. "Colmnist Says Dallas Not Guilty," Dallas *Times Herald*, February 19, 1964.
8. Jim Lehrer told author, December 30, 1977.
9. Bob Considine, New York *Journal-American*, February 21, 1964.
0. Letter from Joe H. Tonahill to author, January 12, 1978.
1. *Ibid.*
2. D.K., "Defense Got Secret Data," New York *Journal-American*, February 21, 1964.
3. Letter from Joe H. Tonahill to author, April 18, 1978.
4. D.K., "Nervous Ruby Feels Breaking Point Near," New York *Journal-American*, February 22, 1964.
5. *Ibid.*
6. Letter from H. D. (Doc) Quigg to author, August 31, 1977.
7. Theo Wilson to author, May, 1976.
8. Tonahill, *op. cit.*
9. Letter from Melvin Belli to author, June 11, 1976.
0. Jim Lehrer, *op. cit.*
1. Tonahill, *op cit.*, January 12, 1978.
2. *Ibid.*

CHAPTER 27

1. Penn Jones, *Forgive My Grief II* (privately published).
2. Richard Warren Lewis and Lawrence Schiller, *The Scavengers and Critics of the Warren Report,* New York: Delacorte, 1967.
3. Letter from Joe Tonahill to author, April 18, 1978.
4. Bob Considine, New York *Journal-American*, March 6, 1964.
5. Quoted in: Mark Lane, *A Citizen's Dissent*, Greenwich, Conn.: Fawcett Crest, 1969.
6. Mark Lane told author, July 28, 1976.
7. *Ibid.*
8. Mark Lane told author, September 20, 1976.
9. "The Great Woman Hunt," *TV Guide*, July 23, 1966.
0. Gil Fates told author, July 10, 1975.
1. Bill Franklin told author, May 19, 1976.
2. Johnnie Ray told author, May 22, 1976.
3. Bob Bach told author, September 5, 1975.

14. Bill Franklin, *op. cit.*
15. Harvey Daniels told author, April 20, 1977.
16. *Ibid.*
17. *Ibid.*
18. Irene Kuhn told author, July 3, 1976.
19. M. D. Morris told author, September 7, 1977.
20. *Ibid.*
21. F. Lee Bailey and Harvey Aronson, *The Defense Never Rests*, New York: Stein and Day, 1971.
22. M. D. Morris, *op. cit.*
23. Jack Harrison Pollack told author, September, 1977.
24. *Ibid.*
25. Quoted in: *The Defense Never Rests, op. cit.*
26. Jack Harrison Pollack, *Dr. Sam,* Chicago: Henry Regnery, 1972.
27. Bill Franklin, *op. cit.*
28. *VOB*, February 2, 1964.
29. *VOB*, July 3, 1962.
30. *VOB*, March 27, 1964.
31. *People of the State of New York vs. Ella Solomon, Howard Solomon, Lenny Bruce*, Criminal Court of the State of New York, July 1, 1964.
32. *Ibid.*
33. Albert Goldman, *Lenny Bruce!!*, New York: Ballantine, 1974.
34. Bruce trial transcript.
35. *Ibid.*
36. *Lenny Bruce!!, op. cit.*
37. Leonard Garbus told author, November 14, 1975.
38. *Ibid.*
39. Bill Franklin, *op. cit.*
40. See General Notes.
41. "Mitch" told author, February 24, 1977.
42. Out-of-Towner told author, September 9, 1975.
43. *Ibid.*
44. *Ibid.*
45. Marlin Swing told author, June 14, 1976.
46. Actress told author, December 8, 1977.
47. Letter from D.K. to Out-of-Towner, July 3, 1963.
48. Letter from D.K. to Out-of-Towner, postmarked July 9, 1964.
49. Out-of-Towner told author, *op. cit.*
50. Marlin Swing told author, June 27, 1976.
51. Nick Lapole told author, November 24, 1976.

CHAPTER 28

1. Howard Rothberg told author, October 2, 1975.
2. Mark Lane told author, September 20, 1976.
3. Letter of J. Edgar Hoover to Hon. Lee Rankin, September 14, 1964 (Warren Comm. #1489).
4. Mark Lane, *op. cit.*
5. D.K., "Kilgallen Reports Mix-Up at Dallas," New York *Journal-American*, August 23, 1964.
6. *Ibid.*
7. *Ibid.*
8. Mark Lane told author, July 28, 1978.
9. *Report of the Warren Commission on the Assassination of President Kennedy*, intro. Harrison E. Salisbury (The New York Times Edition): 1964 (pp. 61–62).
10. *Ibid.* p. 133.
11. Mark Lane told author, September 20, 1976.
12. Mark Lane, *Rush to Judgment*, New York: Dell, 1975.
13. Mark Lane told author, September 20, 1976.
14. *Ibid.*
15. *Ibid.*
16. *Ibid.*
17. *Ibid.*
18. *Ibid.*
19. Mark Lane, *A Citizen's Dissent*, Greenwich, Conn.: Fawcett Crest, 1969.
20. D.K., New York *Journal-American*, August 19, 1964.
21. D.K., "Warren Told Strange Trio Got Together," New York *Journal-American*, September 3, 1964.
22. *Ibid.*
23. D.K., New York *Journal-American*, September 25, 1964.
24. *Ibid.*
25. *Ibid.*
26. Robert Sam Anson, *They've Killed the President*, Bantam, 1975.
27. *VOB*, September 30, 1964.
28. Marlin Swing told author, June 13, 1976.
29. Mort Farber told author, January 1, 1978.
30. Out-of-Towner told author, September 10, 1975.
31. *Ibid.*
32. *Ibid.*
33. Carmen Gebbia told author, June 17, 1977.
34. Pearl Bauer told author, November 5, 1975.
35. Harvey Daniels told author, April 20, 1977.

36. Out-of-Towner told author, September 9, 1975.
37. *Ibid.*
38. Letter from Joe Tonahill to author, January 12, 1978.
39. Edgar Hatfield told author, January 8, 1976.
40. *Variety*, May 5, 1965.
41. Out-of-Towner, *op. cit.*
42. Jack O'Brian told author, December 16, 1976.
43. Telegram of D.K. to Out-of-Towner, June 5, 1965.
44. Quoted in: *Newsweek*, July 19, 1965.
45. Bob Bach told author, August, 1978.
46. Jean Bach told author, August 31, 1977.
47. Mort Farber, *op. cit.*
48. Undated communication from D.K. to Out-of-Towner.
49. Bill Franklin told author, May 19, 1976.
50. Mark Lane told author, September 20, 1976.
51. *They've Killed the President,* *op. cit.*
52. *Ibid.*
53. Mark Lane told author, July 28, 1978.
54. *Variety*, September 1, 1965.
55. *VOB*, September 15, 1965.
56. Bill Franklin, *op. cit.*
57. *Ibid.*
58. Johnnie Ray told author, May 20, 1976.
59. Letter of D.K. to Out-of-Towner, September 22, 1965.
60. Carmen Gebbia told author, June 17, 1977.
61. See General Notes.
62. "Mitch" told author, December 15, 1977.
63. Bob Bach told author, June 30, 1975.
64. Harvey Daniels told author, April 20, 1977.
65. *Ibid.*
66. New York *Journal-American*, November 8, 1965.
67. New York *Herald Tribune*, November 9, 1965.
68. Marlin Swing told author, January 10, 1979.
69. Lillian Boscowitz told author, October 9, 1975.

EPILOGUE

1. James L. Luke, M.D., told author, March 23, 1978.
2. New York *Herald Tribune*, November 16, 1965
3. Pete Hamill, "The Celebrity," *New York Post*, November 9, 1965.
4. Report of Death, Office of Chief Medical Examiner of the City of New York, by James L. Luke, Case #9333, 11/8/65. (Deceased Dorothy Kollmar (Killgallen) [sic])
5. James L. Luke, *op. cit.*
6. Michael Baden, M.D., told author, March 9, 1978.

7. Donald Hoffman, Ph.D., told author, March 9, 1978.
8. Letter to author, August 22, 1977.
9. Report of Death, *op. cit.*
10. Complaint Report of the City of New York, Police Department, 11/8/65, investigation DOA, U.F. 61, File No. 48, Signed by Lt. M. J. Ward and Det. John A. Doyle, 19th Squad.
11. James Clement told author, April 9, 1978.
12. Pearl Bauer told author, May, 1978.
13. Student told author, April 4, 1978.
14. *Ibid.*
15. *Ibid.*
16. Evelyn Clement told author, April 9, 1978.
17. Jean Stralem told author, November 3, 1976.
18. *Ibid.*
19. Supplementary Complaint Report of Manhattan Homicide, 11/8/65. Subject: Investigate Relative to Death of Dorothy Kilgallen Kollmar [sic].
20. Michael Sean O'Shea told author, August 14, 1977.
21. Kerry Kollmar told author, March 16, 1978.
22. Jean Bach told author, July 15, 1975.
23. Marlin Swing told author, June 13, 1976.
24. Albin Krebs told author, May, 1978.
25. James Clement, *op. cit.*
26. Letter from Raymond G. Seiler to author, March 18, 1977.
27. James L. Luke, *op. cit.*
28. Marlin Swing told author, August, 1978.
29. Report of Death, *op. cit.* "Notice of Death."
30. John Doyle told author, May 13, 1977.
31. Mike Ward told author, June, 1978.
32. James L. Luke, *op. cit.*
33. Report of Death, *op. cit.*
34. Report of Death, Office of Chief Medical Examiner of the City of New York, Case #244, 1/7/71. (Deceased Richard Kollmar) [Made available to author by Kerry Kollmar.]
35. Lieut. Collin told author, April 26, 1978.
36. Donald Hoffman, *op. cit.*
37. James L. Luke, *op. cit.*
38. Report of Death, *op. cit.* Dorothy Kilgallen.
39. Mike Ward told author, June, 1978.
40. Anne Hamilton told author, March 10, 1978.
41. *New York Post*, November 15, 1965.
42. Pearl Bauer told author, November 5, 1975.
43. "Mitch" told author, February 24, 1977.

44. Out-of-Towner told author, June 15, 1976.
45. Letter from George O'Toole to author, January 5, 1979.
46. Letter from George O'Toole to author, March 16, 1977.
47. "The Long John Nebel Show," WMCA Radio, November 20, 1976.
48. Music Man told author, June, 1978.
49. Candy Jones told author, June, 1978.
50. Michael Baden told author, March 3, 1978.
51. Report of Death, *op. cit.* Dorothy Kilgallen.
52. Out-of-Towner told author, September 10, 1975.
53. Last Will and Testament of Dorothy Kilgallen Kollmar, October 17, 1941.
54. Kerry Kollmar told author, December 14, 1975.
55. Mike Ward, *op. cit.*
56. Robert Sam Anson, *They've Killed the President,* New York: Bantam, 1975.
57. Bob Bach told author, June 30, 1975.
58. Mark Lane told author, September 20, 1976.
59. Bob Bach, *op. cit.*
60. Allan Ullman told author, March 13, 1978.

PROLOGUE

Sixty-Five Years of Deadlines and Headlines was a ten-part memoir written by James L. Kilgallen for the Hearst newspaper chain. The series was dispatched to member papers for release beginning September 12, 1971. I worked from a copy of the original typescript. Much of the biographical material about Jim's career was drawn from the series.

"It's a Great Life" was an earlier memoir by James L. Kilgallen, which *Editor & Publisher* magazine used in 1956. I worked from a privately published reprint distributed by the International News Service, 1956.

The Library of the Performing Arts at Lincoln Center, New York, reposits what is presumably the most complete collection of material by and about Dorothy Kilgallen. After Dorothy's death, Richard Kollmar gave the library more than seventy scrapbooks maintained by his wife from the time she became a celebrity until a year before her death. They comprise all her columns, articles by and about her, some personal memorabilia, and photographs. The scrapbooks are not yet catalogued. The review of *One Thing After Another* is contained in one of the scrapbooks. It is a vagrant, early clipping—one of the very few without identification. The review was probably published in the Laramie *Boomerang*.

CHAPTERS 1 AND 2

To reconstruct and understand Dorothy's early newspaper career, the following sources were exceedingly valuable:

Ishbel Ross, *Ladies of the Press*, New York, 1936; Adela Rogers St. Johns, *The Honeycomb*, New York: Doubleday & Company, 1969; W. A. Swanberg, *Citizen Hearst*, Bantam Books, 1971; George Waller, *Kidnap, The Story of the Lindbergh Case*, New York: Dial, 1961.

Richard O. Boyer, "Where Are They Now?—Maid of Salem," *The New Yorker*, September 4, 1937.

I drew heavily on Dorothy's own journalism written for the *Evening Journal* between 1931 and 1936.

For corroboration, additional color, and background information on the trial of Eva Coo, I used Grace Robinson's skillful stories from the New York *Daily News*. For the same reasons, with regard to the Gladys MacKnight episode, I used Robert Conway's fine writing, also in the New York *Daily News*.

For additional information on Adela Rogers St. Johns as a Hearst phenomenon, I read her coverage of Jessie Costello and Bruno Hauptmann as it appeared in the *Evening Journal*.

There was a dearth of reliable written material about Dorothy and her life in this period. My most importance sources, therefore, were people and their memories. They included George Kuittinen, Sydney Boehm, Herb Spiro, James Horan, and Sheilah Graham.

CHAPTERS 3 THROUGH 6

The designation "Nazi" is precise. The *Evening Journal* of October 3, 1936, describes Dorothy's arrival in Germany: "Ready to expedite the landing of Miss Kilgallen, 250 Nazis were drawn up in military array to jockey the Hindenburg into her huge gray hangar." Richard K. Smith's unpublished manuscript, *Around-the-World Air Race*, describes the same landing: "As Captain Pruss nosed his great aircraft closer to the ground, a lineup of 300 men in brown uniforms broke ranks . . ."

The major source for the chapters about Dorothy's round-the-world dash was the day-to-day journalism of the three participants: Dorothy for the New York *Evening-Journal*, Bud Ekins for the New York *World-Telegram*, and Leo Kieran for *The New York Times*.

In addition, there were books about the race by Dorothy and by Ekins: Dorothy Kilgallen, *Girl Around the World*, Philadelphia: David McKay, 1936; Herbert Roslyn Ekins, *Around the World in Eighteen Days and How To Do It*, New York: Longmans, Green, & Co., 1936.

I drew from both accounts, though Dorothy's book, actually compiled by Herb Spiro, was a mere pastiche of her stories. "McKay wanted it in forty-eight hours," Herb Spiro recalled. "Maybe they were trying to beat Ekins. The book did nothing."

Ekins's book, however, contained new information and an overview, and complemented his dispatches. I drew upon it.

For background information on the *Hindenburg*, I used: Michael M. Mooney, *The Hindenburg*, Bantam Books, 1975.

For a general view of the time and the primacy of speed, I drew upon Frederick Lewis Allen, *Since Yesterday*, New York: Perennial Library, Harper & Row, 1972.

For information on the state of aviation at the time, I used an unpublished manuscript furnished to me by Dr. Richard K. Smith, literary editor of *The Air Enthusiast* and *Airliners International*. His book, *Around-the-World Air Race*, was written "circa 1972." It was about the Kilgallen-Ekins-Kieran dash. With a difference. Dr. Smith wrote to me: "As far as *I'm* concerned, it's an air transportation story, not personalities."

Some information was culled from an article D.K. wrote about the trip, published in *Cosmopolitan*, February, 1937.

Telegrams, personal letters to Dorothy, transcripts of radio broadcasts, are all from the Lincoln Center Collection.

Herb Spiro contributed considerable information on the events that preceded and followed Dorothy's dash. Irene Kuhn and Syd Boehm were also of assistance.

CHAPTERS 8 AND 9

A good deal was written on the origin and mores of Café Society by Maurice Zolotow, Thyra Samter Winslow, and Jerome Zerbe. Their occasional pieces were helpful in enabling me to focus on the "right people" and the "in" sports. *Fortune* magazine's "Café Society,' published in December, 1937, was an exhaustive, insightful classic, and I relied heavily on it for the short introduction to Dorothy's New York.

For Dorothy's poignantly precarious "place" in that society, for the feeling of the Kilgallen household in Manhattan, Rosemary Cox and Billy Livingston contributed hours of enlightening reminiscences.

Charlotte Manson and Mary Anita Loos were close enough to Dorothy then to analyze her attitude about marriage and her lightning crush on Richard Kollmar.

Louis Sobol remembered why and how she became *The Voice of Broadway*.

CHAPTERS 10 AND 11

Edgar Hatfield, who grew up with Richard in Ridgewood, told me about their WASP community, its manners, mores, and connections with the motion picture industry. He was particularly helpful with regard to the finances of the Kollmar family, which were quite different from Richard Kollmar's eventual rendition.

Other sources on the childhood of Richard Kollmar were Betty Leggett, Charles and George Allen.

Richard's prodigious sexual appetites were well known to the young men who came up with him, and to "Bea," who, as his part-time secretary, was in and out of his Manhattan apartment.

The wedding was reconstructed through clippings, of course, and the recollections of Edgar Hatfield and Billy Livingston.

Dorothy Gulman provided inside information on the politics of Father Duffy's Canteen and the fun they had while it lasted.

Midge Willer described the Kollmar household when it was fun.

Other Sources:

Dorothy Kilgallen's records were made available to Kerry Kollmar by the Federal Bureau of Investigation in December of 1976, after a year of petitioning. The bureau acted with alacrity after syndicated columnist Liz Smith wrote a column about Kerry's demand for Dorothy's dossier. The records were 165 pages, all released under Freedom of Information and Privacy acts.

Articles Used but Not Cited

Newsweek, April 14, 1941.
"At Home with Dorothy and Dick," American Home, November, 1947.
Good Housekeeping, June, 1941.

Script of radio Voice of Broadway at Lincoln Center, Kilgallen scrapbooks.

CHAPTER 12

Dorothy's heady rendering of Dream With Music's concept was related to me by Hubie and Lillian Boscowitz.

als, tribulations, of *Dream With Music*, including falls, flubs, d misbegotten moons, told to author by Miles White.

IAPTERS 14 AND 15

il Leff and Nick Lapole, who were both at the *Journal* in the 40s, furnished helpful information on the nuts and bolts of e paper vis-à-vis Dorothy and her column.

sights on Walter Winchell's primacy came from these addi-nal sources: Herman Klurfeld, *Winchell: His Life and Times*, ew York: Praeger, 1976; Ed Weiner, *Let's Go to Press*, New ork: G. P. Putnam's Sons, 1955. And from interviews with ess agents: Paul Benson, Mal Braveman, Emmett Davis, Doro-y Gulman, Betty Lee Hunt, and Eddie Jaffe.

ese uncited articles and publications provided nourishing so-ology and history of the breakfast-show phenomenon: *Variety*, arch 25, 1945; June 22, 1945; July 2, 1945; December 27, 72. "Break with the Fitzgeralds," *Cue*, September 23, 1944. nce Packard, "Life in a Goldfish Bowl," *American Maga-ie*, 1948. *Sponsor* magazine, September, 1948. *New York st*, July 27, 1946. Station publicity for "Dorothy and Dick," ntaining ratings, slogans, characterizations, reposited in Kil-llen scrapbooks at Lincoln Center.

e management of WOR provided me with tapes of early Dorothy and Dick" broadcasts.

HAPTER 16

he Kollmar residence during this period was described help-lly in: New York *Herald Tribune*, February 1, 1949.

orothy's painstaking attitude toward gift-giving was described me by Earl Blackwell and Arlene Francis, among many hers.

urces for re-creation of Kollmar party include: Interviews ith Miles White, Midge Willer and her husband Paul White, ubie and Lillian Boscowitz, Maggi McNellis Newhouse, and irley Eder.

he mural was described in *We The People*, May, 1947.

rticles about party, not previously cited, include: *Look*, ay, 1947; *Cholly Knickerbocker*, New York *Journal-Ameri-an*, April 17, 1947. Maggie McNellis featured a detailed de-cription on her radio show, "Maggi's Private World," on NBC. Kilgallen scrapbooks at Lincoln Center.

CHAPTER 17

Uncited Sources for Leave It to the Girls:

Eleanor Harris, "They Always Get Their Man," *Collier's*, November 25, 1950; "How Eloise McElhone Got into TV," *American Weekly*, June 24, 1951.

Uncited Sources for "What's My Line?" *History and Personalities:*

Interview with Bob Bach on origin of *Line*. Interview with Gil Fates, Executive Producer, *Line*. Interview with John Daly.

Uncited Articles:

"Dorothy Kilgallen: Pro and Con," *TV Guide*, October 9, 1953; "Then, There Was the Blonde Plumbers," *TV Guide*, July 3, 1957; Cleveland Amory, "Review," *TV Guide*, January 25, 1964; "The Great Woman Hunt," *TV Guide*, July 23, 1966; "End of the Line," *TV Guide*, June 17, 1967; "Bigger Than a Breadbox," *TV Guide*, May 24, 1975; "John Daly," *New York Post*, January 26, 1964; "John Daly," *Newsday*, April 10, 1967; *The New Yorker*, June 16, 1951; "What's My Line? Leaving," *The New York Times*, February 14, 1967.

Kinescopes of various "What's My Line?" *broadcasts, including premiere, were provided by Goodson-Todman.*

CHAPTER 18

With all the names given to the peculiar relationship between press agent and columnist—*quid pro quo*, tit for tat, scaling, feeding, servicing—I never fully understood what it was all about until I talked, at length, with the professionals who provided Dorothy and others with material. What I learned finally was that there were no rules, only certain queer responses of Dorothy's to publicists, which is why several of her "spies" were also among her closest friends.

I was able to describe how Dorothy functioned as a columnist because of the patient lucidity of Jean Bach, Dorothy Gulman, Eddie Jaffe, Betty Lee Hunt, Emmett Davis, Harvey Daniels, and "Mitch.'"

The story of how Bill Doll beat the system is told in Bob Thomas's *Winchell*.

Some of the more famous Kilgallen inaccuracies were cited originally by Tim Taylor, who devoted some space in the New York *Star* throughout 1948 and 1949 to "press errors." Dorothy was a favorite of his. Taylor wrote on December 6, 1948, that *VOB* had reported that actress Lya De Putti, "the dark-eyed siren who starred with Emil Jannings in *Variety* years ago. . . . is starring in a real life drama now trying to get her daughter (also an actress) over to this country from Hungary?' Taylor emended: "Real life? Lya de Putti died 17 years ago . . .November 27, 1931 to be exact."

Bob and Jean Bach emphasized to me the importance of music in Dorothy's life.

CHAPTER 21

Description of the "routed Hearst army" provided by "Shirley," who was asked to help with the shredding of documents and letters.

Background of Judge Blythin and basic facts about Sam Sheppard's life before the trial garnered from Jack Harrison Pollack's *Dr. Sam—An American Tragedy*, Chicago: Henry Regnery, 1972.

Al Davis and Theo Wilson were helpful with regard to Dorothy's incidental behavior at the trial and in Cleveland; so was Jack Lotto, whose impressions were understandably negative.

Dorothy's dispatches and the liberties she was permitted I understood better for having read the excellent but more conventional stories of Theo Wilson (New York *Daily News*) and Margaret Parten (New York *Herald Tribune*).

Dorothy followed up on the Sheppard story. She had some communication with Earle Stanley Gardner and his Court of Last Resort in 1955. Gardner's letter to her is available through the University of Texas, though the anonymous letter that he received about Sheppard and forwarded to Dorothy was withheld. Her dispatches made it very clear that she doubted the veracity of much of the testimony at the trial and probably suspected at least one of the witnesses of doing the deed or knowing a great deal more than was proffered on the stand.

CHAPTER 22

The lachrymous *Affair to Remember* screening was recalled to me by Jean Bach. Johnnie confirmed that he indeed "cried his silly eyes out."

Bob Bach was invaluable on Science Club activities, including Dorothy's victorious Song Game parry: Whose broad.

I drew on these pieces for background information about Johnnie Ray: *Life*, March 24, 1952; "Prince of Wails," *Look*, June 3, 1952; Lee Mortimer, New York *Mirror*, June 7, 1955; "Johnnie Ray Weds Without Weeping a Tear," New York *Herald Tribune*, May 26, 1952; Booten Herndon, "Why Johnnie Ray Cries," *Coronet*, December, 1952; George Frazier, "The Atomic Ray," *The American Weekly*, June 15, 1952.

CHAPTER 24

Two of Kerry's teachers at St. David's, Tony De Filips and Tom O'Toole, were aware of the child's rather poignant defensiveness of Dorothy.

The earlier "Breakfast with Dorothy and Dick" tapes were made available to me by WOR radio. The session quoted here, in which Richard reviews his refrigerator raid and Dorothy talks about her night out with "the gang," was transcribed from a tape made by Marlin Swing. Dorothy was thoughtful enough to apprise her friends before she mentioned them on the broadcast so that they could listen, spread it around, or record it, as Marlin did.

CHAPTER 25

Irwin M. Taylor, attorney for Elaine Shepard, contributed his recollections of the Kilgallen-Shepard events, pretrial through determination. "I thought we had a very good crack at the case," he said.

Neither Cindy nor Joey Adams would comment on their dispute with Dorothy Kilgallen. Joey explained to me that he and his wife would as soon forget the incident since they are both "love people."

Games, game parties, and Mr. Rhee of *Life* recalled by Marlin Swing.

CHAPTER 27

Brief biographical sketch of Mark Lane from Robert Sam Anson's *"They've Killed the President."*

During one of Dorothy's sojourns to Switzerland, she rather mysteriously left behind nineteen items of jewelry at the Dolder Grand Hotel in Zurich. She made no attempt that is known recover the valuables, appraised, after her death, at more than ten thousand dollars. Marlin Swing perused the posthumous inventory of the jewels and concluded, from the description on her estate form, that the "platinum-set earrings with diamonds, flower-design" were her standard and favorite pair. He was surprised that she would leave them, and astonished that she made no attempt to recover them.

A group of film documentarians based in Florida is at this writing preparing a feature about the knowledgeable who died in the wake of the Kennedy assassination. Dorothy's death will be sketchy. They have information that Dorothy was communicating with Jim Garrison prior to her death and that he was her New Orleans contact. The information came to them through associates of Garrison. But he has not himself confirmed to them. Two letters of mine to Mr. Garrison, written early on in my research, went unanswered.

The congressional committee investigating assassinations has, at the time of this writing, just implicated a high-ranking New Orleans syndicate chieftain in the murder of John Fitzgerald Kennedy.

INDEX

Dell Bestsellers

- [ ] **COMES THE BLIND FURY** by John Saul $2.75 (11428-4)
- [ ] **CLASS REUNION** by Rona Jaffe $2.75 (11408-X)
- [ ] **THE EXILES** by William Stuart Long $2.75 (12369-0)
- [ ] **THE BRONX ZOO** by Sparky Lyle and
      Peter Golenbock $2.50 (10764-4)
- [ ] **THE PASSING BELLS** by Phillip Rock $2.75 (16837-6)
- [ ] **TO LOVE AGAIN** by Danielle Steel $2.50 (18631-5)
- [ ] **SECOND GENERATION** by Howard Fast $2.75 (17892-4)
- [ ] **EVERGREEN** by Belva Plain $2.75 (13294-0)
- [ ] **CALIFORNIA WOMAN** by Daniel Knapp $2.50 (11035-1)
- [ ] **DAWN WIND** by Christina Savage $2.50 (11792-5)
- [ ] **REGINA'S SONG**
      by Sharleen Cooper Cohen $2.50 (17414-7)
- [ ] **SABRINA** by Madeleine A. Polland $2.50 (17633-6)
- [ ] **THE ADMIRAL'S DAUGHTER**
      by Victoria Fyodorova and Haskel Frankel $2.50 (10366-5)
- [ ] **THE LAST DECATHLON** by John Redgate $2.50 (14643-7)
- [ ] **THE PETROGRAD CONSIGNMENT**
      by Owen Sela $2.50 (16885-6)
- [ ] **EXCALIBUR!** by Gil Kane and John Jakes $2.50 (12291-0)
- [ ] **SHOGUN** by James Clavell $2.95 (17800-2)
- [ ] **MY MOTHER, MY SELF** by Nancy Friday $2.50 (15663-7)
- [ ] **THE IMMIGRANTS** by Howard Fast $2.75 (14175-3)

At your local bookstore or use this handy coupon for ordering:

DELL BOOKS
P.O. BOX 1000, PINEBROOK, N.J. 07058

Please send me the books I have checked above. I am enclosing $_____
(please add 75¢ per copy to cover postage and handling). Send check or money
order—no cash or C.O.D.'s. Please allow up to 8 weeks for shipment.

Mr/Mrs/Miss _____

Address _____

City _____ State/Zip _____

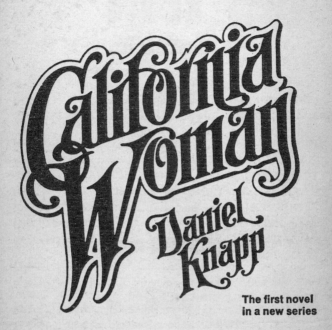

California Woman

Daniel Knapp

**The first novel
in a new series**

A sweeping saga of the American West

Esther left New England a radiant bride, her future as
bright as the majestic frontiers. But before she could reach
California, she had lost everything but her indomitable
courage and will to survive. Against the rich tapestry of
California history, she lived for love—and vengeance!

A Dell Book $2.50 (11035-1)